Copenhagen

www.timeout.com

Time Out Guides Ltd
Universal House
251 Tottenham Court Road
London W1T 7AB
United Kingdom
Tel: +44 (0)20 7813 3000
Fax: +44 (0)20 7813 6001
Email: guides@timeout.com
www.timeout.com

Published by Time Out Guides Ltd, a wholly owned subsidiary of Time Out Group Ltd.
Time Out and the Time Out logo are trademarks of Time Out Group Ltd.

© Time Out Group Ltd 2011
Previous editions 2001, 2003, 2005, 2007.

10 9 8 7 6 5 4 3 2 1

This edition first published in Great Britain in 2011 by Ebury Publishing.
A Random House Group Company
20 Vauxhall Bridge Road, London SW1V 2SA

Random House Australia Pty Ltd 20 Alfred Street, Milsons Point, Sydney, New South Wales 2061, Australia

Random House New Zealand Ltd 18 Poland Road, Glenfield, Auckland 10, New Zealand

Random House South Africa (Pty) Ltd Isle of Houghton, Corner Boundary Road & Carse O'Gowrie, Houghton 2198, South Africa

Random House UK Limited Reg. No. 954009

Distributed in the US and Latin America by Publishers Group West (1-510-809-3700)
Distributed in Canada by Publishers Group Canada (1-800-747-8147)

For further distribution details, see www.timeout.com.

ISBN: 978-1-84670-117-7

A CIP catalogue record for this book is available from the British Library.

Printed and bound by Firmengruppe APPL, aprinta druck, Wemding, Germany.

The Random House Group Limited supports The Forest Stewardship Council (FSC), the leading international orest certification organisation. All our titles that are printed on Greenpeace approved FSC certified paper carry the FSC logo. Our paper procurement policy can be found at http://www.rbooks.co.uk/environment.

Time Out carbon-offsets its flights with Trees for Cities (www.treesforcities.org).

Contents

In Context 15

History 16
Copenhagen Today 26
Danish Design 32
Bike Copenhagen 40

Sights 43

Tivoli & Rådhuspladsen 44
Strøget & Around 54
Nyhavn & Kongens Nytorv 61
Slotsholmen 65
Frederiksstaden 71
Rosenborg & Around 76
Christianshavn 80
Vesterbro & Frederiksberg 85
Nørrebro & Østerbro 90
Further Afield 94

Consume 97

Hotels 98
Restaurants 111
Cafés & Bars 128
Shops & Services 143

Arts & Entertainment 163

Calendar 164
Children 168

Film 174
Galleries 178
Gay & Lesbian 182
Nightlife 185
Performing Arts 191
Sport & Fitness 200

Escapes & Excursions 207

Malmö 209
The Danish Riviera 216
North Sjælland 220

Directory 223

Getting Around 224
Resources A-Z 227
Vocabulary 234
Further Reference 235
Content Index 236
Venue Index 238

Maps 243

Copenhagen Overview 244
Street Maps 245
Street Index 254
Local Trains & Metro 256

WHENEVER, WHEREVER YOU NEED MONEY...

WE GET IT THERE IN 10 MINUTES*

CHOICE IS IN YOUR HANDS

1. Arrange for the person sending the money to visit a MoneyGram agent near them. After sending the money, they will give you a reference number.

2. Find your nearest MoneyGram agent at **www.moneygram.com** or anywhere you see the MoneyGram sign.

3. Give the reference number and your ID** to the MoneyGram agent.

4. Fill out one simple form to receive your money.

www.moneygram.com

Introduction

Copenhagen always does well in surveys of the world's most 'liveable' cities, and arriving in the city provides ample evidence as to why. From the moment you step off the plane at Kastrup Airport and hop on the metro for the 14-minute journey direct to the centre, where you'll find the irrepressibly cute Tivoli pleasure park, you realise this is how cities should work. And once you've dropped your bags off at one of the burgeoning range of design-led hotels that now dot the city, you can enjoy life in one of Europe's most easy-going, hassle-free capitals. The shopping is superb; the restaurants are the best in Scandinavia – with one, Noma, now hailed as the best in the world; the cycling culture is admirable (whether or not you choose to partake); the city harbour is clean-enough to swim in (and many people do); and the atmosphere is supremely cosy – or *hygge* as the Danes call it.

There are limitations, of course: traditional 'sights' are suited more to a leisurely long weekend than a week's intensive visit; and Copenhagen currently ranks as one of the most expensive cities in Europe. But somehow sipping a £5 pint in the sunshine on the waterfront at Nyhavn seems an entirely worthwhile proposition – and if you can afford to stay in Scandinavia a bit longer, then Malmö, one of Sweden's most vibrant cities, is just half an hour away across the Øresund Bridge that links Denmark with neighbouring Sweden.

Copenhagen is a compact place and all the sights are within half an hour's walk of the main pedestrian artery, Strøget. One of the things you'll notice as you wander around the charming centre, apart from the fact that everyone is extraordinarily stylish, is that design is everywhere, from the mid-century modern Arne Jacobsen chairs in bars and restaurants, to the raft of stylish new buildings that now grace the waterfront.

Visit on a dark, freezing cold day in January and the city's charms aren't as obvious; they're still there, but they're harder to reach, with more hot chocolate stops required in cosy cafés along the way. But visit on a sunny June weekend and the combination of café culture, gorgeous palaces, striking modern buildings, waterfront living and designer boutiques gives the whole place a feeling of contentedness to rival any city on the Med.

Anna Norman, Editor

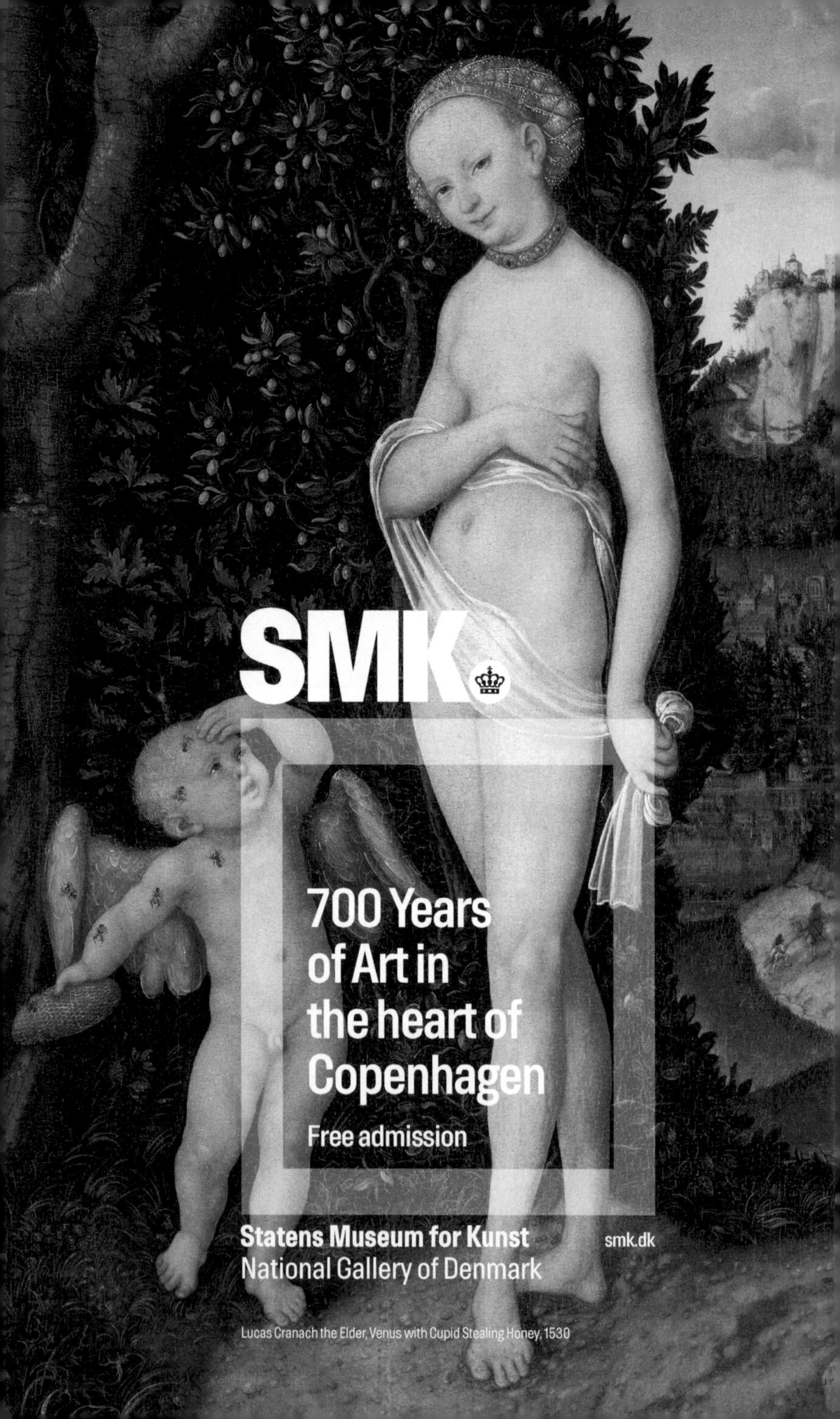

SMK ♛

700 Years
of Art in
the heart of
Copenhagen

Free admission

Statens Museum for Kunst   smk.dk
National Gallery of Denmark

Lucas Cranach the Elder, Venus with Cupid Stealing Honey, 1530

Copenhagen in Brief

IN CONTEXT
Following its historical journey from humble fishing village to top culinary destination, this section of the guide gives an overview of Copenhagen's social, cultural and architectural background, focusing in particular on two elements that help to give the city its distinctive character: its design heritage and bicycling culture. It also looks at why Copenhageners are apparently so happy.
▶ *For more, see pp15-42.*

SIGHTS
Being a small capital, Copenhagen is easily explored. Near the central squares of Rådhuspladsen and Kongens Nytorv are key sights such as colourful Nyhavn, royal palaces and excellent art museums. Head to Østerbro, Nørrebro, Frederiksberg and Vesterbro to see where locals rest and play. And for an insight into alternative Copenhagen, there's the self-declared state of Christiania.
▶ *For more, see pp43-96.*

CONSUME
Copenhagen is at the centre of the New Nordic culinary movement, with Noma gaining column inches around the world. But there are real gems among the city's everyday restaurants, cafés and bars too, which range from trendy Kødbyen venues to establishments that have been frequented for decades. Those with an interest in design can indulge in retro-modern hotels and stylish threads.
▶ *For more, see pp97-162.*

ARTS & ENTERTAINMENT
Copenhagen's cultural scene has been boosted in recent times by two new waterfront performing arts venues: the Opera House and the Royal Danish Playhouse. There are also superb sporting opportunities, including a new skate park and harbour swimming baths. Nightlife venues and galleries are stylish affairs, while for children, there's Tivoli amusement park, the city's beating heart.
▶ *For more, see pp163-206.*

ESCAPES & EXCURSIONS
No trip to Copenhagen would be complete without a visit to the Louisiana Museum of Modern Art, a short train ride away. With a world-class art collection and a beautiful natural setting, the museum is an absolute don't-miss. Seaside fun and sparkling water characterise the Danish Riviera, while Malmö, one of Sweden's most vibrant cities, is reached via the impressive Øresund Bridge.
▶ *For more, see pp207-222.*

Copenhagen in 48 Hrs

Day 1 Christiania to Capitalism

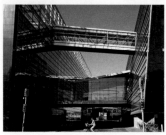

10AM Start the day with a traditional pastry at one of the city's most popular bakeries: **Lagkagehuset** (*see p155*). There are now several branches, but this was the first, overlooking the Christianshavn Canal.

11AM Head round the corner to **Vor Freisers Kirke** (*see p81*). You can walk up around the gold spire for fantastic views – including of nearby Christiania – but hold on tight, as it gets windy at the top.

NOON A visit to **Christiania** (*see p82*) is essential for anyone wanting a greater understanding of the city. The alternative residential area was founded in 1971, and is home to some 1,000 people. Photography is forbidden on Pusher Street, where soft drugs are openly sold. The more interesting zone is on the eastern side.

1PM **Café Wilder** (*see p136*), on Wildersgade in Christianshavn, is a good nearby bet for lunch. Unless, of course, you've been lucky enough to secure a booking at restaurant-of-the-moment **Noma** (*see p122*) on Strandgade, near the canal.

3PM After lunch, head across Knippelsbro bridge to Slotsholmen, the island on which the city was founded. The area has several draws, including **Christiansborg Slot** (*see p65*), housing parliament; the **Thorvaldsens Museum** (*see p69*); and one of Copenhagen's most-striking modern buildings, the extension to the national library, the **Black Diamond** (*see p68*).

4.30PM From Slotsholmen, head west to **Rådhuspladsen**, the city's focal point. From here turn right and along Strøget, the main shopping street. The better shops are at the western end, near **Kongens Nytorv**. Cross over the square for a wander down **Nyhavn**. The canalside path is full of camera-wielding tourists, but we defy you not to take a photo of the colourful buildings.

7.30PM **Salt** (*see p117*) is a good bet for dinner. Aside from the decent modern Scandinavian food, the restaurant has wonderful views of the **Opera House** (*see p194*) across the water.

NAVIGATING THE CITY
It's easy to get your bearings in Copenhagen. Most of the sights are in a compact area to the east of the city, with much new development along the waterfront. The neighbourhoods are on the other side of the lakes, to the west.

EXPLORING THE SIGHTS
The city's medieval centre probably has everything the casual visitor could want. It has the great museums and royal palaces,

it offers ample shopping and fine dining, and you can get anywhere within its beautiful streets in minutes, on foot.

However, Copenhagen's real city living goes on outside the centre's cobbled streets, whether it's in bohemian Vesterbro; confidently graceful Frederiksberg; on in the melting pot that is Nørrebro (for a neighbourhood itinerary, *see above*). This is where you'll see the locals shop, drink and eat out at like it's going out of style.

Day 2 Neighbourhood Living

10AM Start the day in **Østerbro** (*see p92*), one of Copenhagen's most well-do-do neighbourhoods, and home to some excellent cafés. Take a coffee at **Café Bopa** (*see p142*), located in a lovely square.

11AM Østerbro is lovely to wander around. Head up **Østerbrogade** and you'll come to **Brumbleby** on your left, an enclave of cute terraced houses. Now a desirable address, the 'village' is one of the earliest examples of social housing in Denmark.

NOON Take a wander down Sortedam Dossering beside the lakes, a popular path for jogging, cycling and leisurely strolls. Some of the Copenhagen's most beautiful houses line the route.

1PM Turn right up Læssøesgade to reach Ryesgade, running parallel, home to some of the city's hippest shops and eateries, including **Underwood Ink** (*see p142*) and the pioneering **Nørrebro Bryghus** (*see p138*). The latter is a nice spot for a traditional smørrebrød lunch (with a modern twist) and a local beer from its own microbrewery.

3PM After lunch, wander down Ryesgade and turn right at Sankt Hans Gade. Stroll up to **Sankt Hans Torv**, one of Nørrebro's best-known squares; full of cafés and bars, the place buzzes in summer. Then make your way to Elmegade, one of the city's best independent shopping streets. From here, it's a short walk to Nørrebrogade, and on to the **Assistens Kirkegård** (*see p92*) the final resting place of Hans Christian Andersen and Søren Kierkegaard.

5PM Head back along Nørrebrogade to witness one of Copenhagen's most spectacular phenomena: the bicycle rush hour. Some 35,000 cyclists travel along this street every day.

8PM The neighbourhood of Vesterbro, further south-west, is at its best in the evening. Head to **Kødbyen**, the now-trendy Meatpacking District, where you'll find a handful of cool restaurants and bars. You can't go far wrong at **Mother** pizza parlour (*see p125*) or **Fiskebaren** (*see p124*).

PACKAGE DEALS

If you're planning on doing some intensive sightseeing, then you may save money by investing in a **Copenhagen Card**. The card (valid for 24 or 72 hours) offers free travel by public transport (though most attractions are within easy walking distance of the centre) and free entry to more than 60 museums and sights in the greater Copenhagen area, plus discounts to many others. Prices for 2011 were: 24hrs – 229kr, 115kr children (10-15yrs); 72hrs – 459kr, 225kr children. The cards are available from travel agents, hotels, main railway stations and the **Copenhagen Visitor Centre** (70 22 24 42, www.visitcopenhagen.com).

It's worth noting that many of Copenhagen's museums are closed on Mondays, and free on Wednesdays.

For details of guided tours of Copenhagen, *see p226*. Another good way to explore the city is by bike. For a list of bike-hire places, *see p226*.

Copenhagen in Profile

TIVOLI & RÅDHUSPLADSEN

Home to the town hall, Rådhuspladsen, one of Copenhagen's focal points, buzzes with shoppers, sightseers, hot-dog sellers and street performers. Directly to its west is Tivoli, the amusement park that holds a place in every Dane's heart. Top-notch museums and the Arne Jacoben's Radisson SAS hotel are nearby.
► For more, see pp44-53.

STRØGET & AROUND

The eastern, Amagertorv end of Copenhagen's central street is home to the Royal Copenhagen stores. Gråbrødretorv, one of the city's loveliest squares, lies to its north, while east of here is a warren of stylish shopping streets, as well as the Round Tower. The Rådhuspladsen end of Strøget is more downmarket.
► For more, see pp54-60.

NYHAVN & KONGENS NYTORV

Copenhagen's famous canalside street is saturated with tourist-oriented stalls and expensive cafés, but its colourful buildings are still irresistibly pretty. Charming upmarket shopping streets lies behind it, while to its west is Kongens Nytorv, the city's grandest square.
► For more, see pp61-64.

SLOTSHOLMEN

Parliament's 'backyard' is home to Christiansborg Slot itself, as well as the Black Diamond, the impressive new Royal Library building. The library's gardens, Bibliotekshaven, are delightfully peaceful. Top museums here include Daniel Libeskind's Jewish Museum and Thorvaldsens Museum, a must for sculpture-lovers.
► For more, see pp65-70.

FREDERIKSSTADEN

Elegant Frederikskstaden has a regal atmosphere; home to Amalienborg Slot (the royal palace), it also has a host of upmarket restaurants, and two lovely churches. Head to the waterfront for the area's most atmospheric spots and fantastic views of the Opera House. The Little Mermaid sits at its northern tip.
► For more, see pp71-75.

ROSENBORG & AROUND

Site of the Rosenborg Slot – the city's Renaissance palace – as well as the National Gallery (Statens Museum For Kunst), displaying Danish masters as well as works by Picasso and Matisse. Another cultural institution, the Filmhuset, sits on Gothersgade. The lovely Botanical Gardens are also here.
► For more, see pp76-79.

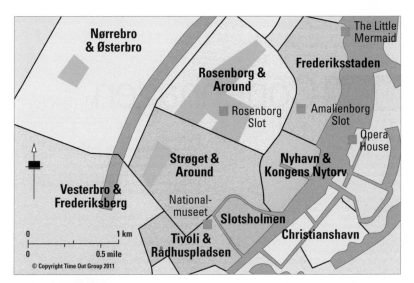

The Little Mermaid

Frederiksstaden

Nørrebro & Østerbro

Rosenborg & Around

Rosenborg Slot

Amalienborg Slot

Opera House

Vesterbro & Frederiksberg

Strøget & Around

National-museet

Nyhavn & Kongens Nytorv

Slotsholmen

Tivoli & Rådhuspladsen

Christianshavn

0   1 km
0   0.5 mile
© Copyright Time Out Group 2011

CHRISTIANSHAVN

Laid-back Christianshavn, across the water, is where you'll find some of Copenhagen's loveliest attractions: boat-filled canals; Vor Freisers Kirke, with its distinctive spire (head to the top for superb views); the alternative Freetown of Christiania; the bathing spot of Islands Brygge; and Noma, the 'world's best restaurant'.
► *For more, see pp80-84.*

VESTERBRO & FREDERIKSBERG

Two very different neighbourhoods sit side-by-side on the city's western side. Vesterbro's Meatpacking District (Kødbyen) is full of cool bars, restaurants and galleries, while Istedgade, its main street, is lined with hipster cafés and boutiques (as well as seedy sex shops on its eastern end). Frederiksberg is a wholesome affair, with tree-lined avenues, elegant buildings and green spaces.
► *For more, see pp85-89.*

NØRREBRO & ØSTERBRO

Hip Nørrebro is Copenhagen's most multicultural neighbourhood. Its trendy shops, cafés and bars are interspersed with some of the city's best ethnic eateries. Famous Copenhageners rest eternally in its Assistens Kirkegård. Genteel Østerbro, meanwhile, is home to young, well-to-do families and top-quality cafés and delis. Its large Fælledparken is the city's most popular park for sports and recreation.
► *For more, see pp90-93.*

FURTHER AFIELD

Explore beyond the centre, around Copenhagen's affluent suburbs, to reach the excellent Experimentarium science museum, the national aquarium, Arken Museum of Modern Art, known for its architecture as well as its contemporary art, and the island of Amager, home to the city's new concert hall, DR Koncerthuset.
► *For more, see pp94-96.*

Time Out Copenhagen

Editorial
Editor Anna Norman
Listings Editor Frank Tamburin
Copy Editor Patrick Welch
Proofreader Johnny Pym
Indexer Holly Pick

Managing Director Peter Fiennes
Editorial Director Ruth Jarvis
Business Manager Dan Allen
Editorial Manager Holly Pick

Design
Art Director Scott Moore
Art Editor Pinelope Kourmouzoglou
Senior Designer Kei Ishimaru
Group Commercial Designer Jodi Sher

Picture Desk
Picture Editor Jael Marschner
Acting Deputy Picture Editor Liz Leahy
Picture Desk Assistant/Researcher Ben Rowe

Advertising
New Business & Commercial Director Mark Phillips
International Advertising Manager Kasimir Berger
International Sales Executive Charlie Sokol
Advertising Sales (Copenhagen) Hans Hermansen,
   The Copenhagen Post (www.cphpost.dk)

Marketing
**Sales & Marketing Director, North America
   & Latin America** Lisa Levinson
Senior Publishing Brand Manager Luthfa Begum
Guides Marketing Manager Colette Whitehouse
Group Commercial Art Director Anthony Huggins
Marketing Co-ordinator Alana Benton

Production
Group Production Manager Brendan McKeown
Production Controller Katie Mulhern

Time Out Group
Director & Founder Tony Elliott
Chief Executive Officer David King
Chief Operating Officer Aksel Van der Wal
Group Financial Director Paul Rakkar
Group General Manager/Director Nichola Coulthard
Time Out Communications Ltd MD David Pepper
Time Out International Ltd MD Cathy Runciman
Time Out Magazine Ltd Publisher/MD Mark Elliott
Group Commercial Director Graeme Tottle
Group IT Director Simon Chappell
Group Marketing Director Andrew Booth

Contributors
History Michael Booth. **Copenhagen Today** Michael Booth, Anna Norman. **Danish Design** Michael Booth, Anna Norman. **Bike Copenhagen** Anna Norman. **Sightseeing** Nikolaj Steen-Møller. **Hotels** Thomas Dalvang-Fleurquin, Jane Graham, Anna Norman. **Restaurants** Tara Stevens. **Cafés & Bars** Michael Booth, Anna Norman. **Shops & Services** Anna Norman, Julia Tierney. **Galleries** Anna Norman, Sebastian Schiorring. **Gay & Lesbian** Daniel Ayala, Patrick Welch. **Nightlife** Trudy Follwell, Thomas Dalvang-Fleurquin. **Performing Arts** Trudy Follwel, Jane Graham, Anna Norman. **Sport & Fitness** Anna Norman, Nikolaj Steen-Møller. **Escapes & Excursions** Michael Booth. **Directory** Cecilie Hahn- Patersen.

The Editor would like to thank Sanne Esseveld, Lene Hald, Martin Holm, Vivienne Lyus, Holly Pick and Frank Tamburin.

Maps john@jsgraphics.co.uk

Cover Photography: Eric Nathan/Pictures Colour Library

Back Cover Photography: Heloise Bergman and Wonderful Copenhagen

Photography by Heloise Bergman, except page 7 (top left) Tivoli; page 16 Bettman/Corbis; page 19 akg-images; page 20 Swissmacky; pages 22, 32, 33, 42, 55 (top), 57, 59, 92, 99, 126, 133 (top), 139, 149, 161, 191, 219 (bottom) Anna Norman; pages 40, 80 Alan Kraft; pages 43, 63 Yarygin; page 62 Jose Antonio Sanchez; page 69 Ole Woldbye; page 69 (middle) Helle Nanny Brendstrup; page 84 Tyler Olsen; page 88 (left), 166, 183 Christian Alsing/www.copenhagenmediacenter.com; page 89 (right) Christopher P. Grant; page 96 Morten Bjarnhof/Wonderful Copenhagen; page 116 Ming Tang Evans;page 163 Ricardo Esplana Babor; page 164 Wonderful Copenhagen; page 192 (top) Jens Markus Lindhe; page 193 Erik Hansen; page 197 Bjarne Bergius Hermansen; page 203 Copenhagen Skatepark; page 209 Antonio Jorge Nunes; page 210 Michael Durinik; page 211 July Store; page 212 Sophie Bengtsson; page 213 Liam Kearney; page 215 Multiart; pages 216, 218, 219 (top) Louisiana Museum of Modern Art; page 220 Niels Thye/VisitDenmark; page 221 Fulcanelli.

The following images were provided by the featured establishments/artists: pages 45, 86, 105, 181.

About the Guide

GETTING AROUND

The back of the book contains street maps of Copenhagen, as well as overview maps of the city and its surroundings. The maps start on page 243; on them are marked the locations of hotels (❶), restaurants and cafés (❶), and pubs and bars (❶). The majority of businesses listed in this guide are located in the areas we've mapped; the grid-square references in the listings refer to these maps.

THE ESSENTIALS

For practical information, including visas, disabled access, emergency numbers, lost property, useful websites and local transport, please see the Directory. It begins on page 223.

THE LISTINGS

Addresses, phone numbers, websites, transport information, hours and prices are all included in our listings, as are selected other facilities. All were checked and correct at press time. However, business owners can alter their arrangements at any time, and fluctuating economic conditions can cause prices to change rapidly.

The very best venues in the city, the must-sees and must-dos in every category, have been marked with a red star (★). In the Sights chapters, we've also marked venues with free admission with a FREE symbol.

PHONE NUMBERS

All telephone numbers in Copenhagen have eight digits. There are no area codes in the country.

From outside Denmark, dial your country's international access code (00 from the UK, 011 for the US) or a plus symbol, followed by the Danish country code (45), dropping the initial zero, and the eight-digit number as listed in the guide. So, to reach the Nationalmuseet, dial +45 33 13 44 11. For more on phones, including information on calling abroad from the UK and details of local mobile-phone access, see p232.

FEEDBACK

We welcome feedback on this guide, both on the venues we've included and on any other locations that you'd like to see featured in future editions. Please email us at guides@timeout.com.

Time Out Guides

Founded in 1968, Time Out has grown from humble beginnings into the leading resource for anyone wanting to know what's happening in the world's greatest cities. Alongside our influential weeklies in London, New York and Chicago, we publish more than 20 magazines in cities as varied as Beijing and Beirut; a range of travel books, with the City Guides now joined by the newer Shortlist series; and an information-packed website. The company remains proudly independent, still owned by Tony Elliott four decades after he launched *Time Out London*.

Written by local experts and illustrated with original photography, our books also retain their independence. No business has been featured because it has advertised, and all restaurants and bars are visited and reviewed anonymously.

ABOUT THE EDITOR

Based in London, **Anna Norman** has edited a variety of books for Time Out, including guides to Buenos Aires, Florence, Mallorca & Menorca, Madrid and London's Best Shops. She has also contributed to the *Time Out London* magazine.

A full list of the book's contributors can be found opposite.

In Context

Operaen. *See p194.*

History   **16**
One Nation Under
the Dannebrog   20

Copenhagen Today   **26**
On the Waterfront   29
Happy Town   30

Danish Design   **32**
Blast from the Past   38

Bike Copenhagen   **40**

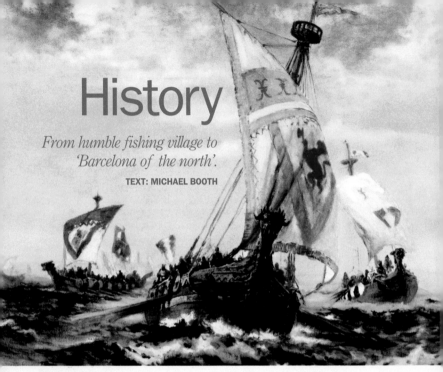

History

From humble fishing village to 'Barcelona of the north'.

TEXT: MICHAEL BOOTH

Copenhagen has not always been the capital of Denmark. In fact, it didn't take over as the royal seat until the early 15th century and, up until that point, was a comparatively humble fishing village and defensive post from which the country tried to protect itself against marauding pirates and Swedes. However, it grew in strength throughout the Middle Ages to become one of the wealthiest cities in northern Europe, a political powerhouse and cultural centre of great importance. At the peak of its glory, Copenhagen was ruled by one of the most fascinating and reckless of Renaissance kings whose ambition and follies would eventually bring the country to its knees.

Evidence of human life in Denmark exists from 80,000 years ago in the form of discarded animal bones. But while the rest of Denmark busied itself with reindeer hunting, flint mining, the Bronze Age, the Viking Age, and the repelling of Charlemagne's advance on the southern border of Jylland (cAD 800), Havn (Harbour), as Copenhagen was known, was little more than an insignificant trading centre for the copious quantities of herring that inhabited the Øresund. It was said that this pungent, oily fish (still a staple of the Danish diet) was so common in these waters, which connect the Baltic with the North Sea, that fishermen could scoop them into their boats with their bare hands.

THE FIRST DANISH STATE

The Vikings, who swept across northern Europe from southern Sweden around 800, established the first Danish state and rapidly augmented it with three of the four Anglo-Saxon kingdoms, as well as Norway. The Vikings (meaning 'sea robbers') even took Seville in 844 and stormed Paris in the 880s. The subsequent retaking by the nascent Danes of Skåne (or Scania, now southern Sweden, directly opposite Copenhagen) was to be the catalyst for the voracious expansion of Copenhagen 300 years hence, but at the time the villagers probably remained oblivious to their strategic potential. It is likely too that they remained unruffled by the conversion of the unifying Viking king Harald I Bluetooth (and eventually the entire country) to Christianity by a German missionary named Poppo around 965. Harald was mysteriously killed while relieving himself in the woods in 987, and many of his successors over the next 170 years met with a similarly murky fate, so that by 1157 Valdemar I the Great was the only royal left standing.

GROWING PAINS

Over the next century, numerous churches blossomed on what was still an unappealing, boggy stretch of coast, among them Vor Frue Kirke (later the site of Copenhagen's current cathedral), and Sankt Petri Kirke (also still a site of worship). In 1238, an abbey of Franciscan Grey Friars was founded; its church (Helligåndskirken) still sits on Strøget, modern-day Copenhagen's main shopping street.

In the late 12th and early 13th centuries, King Valdemar and his sons Knud (Canute) VI and Valdemar II the Victorious reigned over a triumphant and expansionist Denmark, which not only conquered the Baltic Wends, but devoured Estonia and Holstein, and lorded it over Lübeck. This ended ignominiously with the loss of these Baltic territories in 1227.

The second spurt of Copenhagen's growth occurred when Erik VII seized control of the town from the Church in 1417. Not only was the king now in charge, but he had become so fond of Copenhagen that he made it his home. This historic move ended the peripatetic tradition of Denmark's monarchy – wherever it laid its crown was its home.

In 1448, Christian I was crowned King of Denmark, Sweden and Norway in the first royal coronation to be held in Copenhagen. Inevitably, the city now became the economic, political and cultural focus for the nation. By 1500, the town revelled in riches as its guilds dominated those of the Hanseatic League, while the king too grew wealthy from the new tolls demanded of all who sailed from the North Sea through the narrow strait between Helsingør and southern Sweden on their way to the Baltic. There was no doubt that this was now Denmark's capital, and its leading citizens ruled via the Rigsråd (National Assembly), made up of clergy, prominent estate owners and the king. A more apt seat of power the Machiavellian Christian II could not have hoped to inherit. Though politically astute enough to marry a sister of Holy Roman Emperor Charles V, Christian had a tendency to recklessness. He was replaced, in 1522, by his uncle, who reigned as Frederik I.

CIVIL WAR AND REFORMATION

During Frederik's rule, several popular uprisings – with Copenhagen as a particular hotbed – had unsuccessfully tried to unseat the monarch and replace him with the exiled, pro-Lutheran Christian II. But when in 1532 Christian finally returned as a prisoner to a Denmark, now ruled entirely by Frederik I, it was to spend the rest of his life imprisoned in Sønderborg Castle. Upon Frederik's death in 1533, the Catholic prelates intervened to postpone the accession of his son Christian III, whose Lutheran tendencies they were having none of. Unforeseen by the prelates, the Danish people were as keen on reformation (and the consequent redistribution of clerical property) as the rest of northern Europe, and they wanted Christian II back. His supporters in Copenhagen, both peasants and more prosperous townspeople, continued their belligerent stance by seizing control of the town. The involvement of the Lübeckers was to provoke one of the most damaging tiffs in Copenhagen's history: the Grevens Fejde (Counts' Feud) of 1534-6, Denmark's last civil war. The Germans' meddling and the accompanying peasants' revolt so

IN CONTEXT

'Into this brave new world of wealth, expansion and optimism was born one of the great figures of Danish history, Christian IV.'

concerned the bishops that they finally relented and allowed Christian III to take the throne and suppress Copenhagen. His coronation charter did, however, include the handing over of power to the aristocracy of the Rigsråd from the Crown.

As things turned out, the bishops were to lose power anyway as, in order to pay his own German mercenaries (without whom he would never have retaken Copenhagen), Christian III was forced to liquidate many of the Church's assets. As the final stroke of a coup that heralded the Danish Reformation of 1536, Christian III imprisoned the bishops.

In a display of the consensual diplomacy that still typifies Denmark's political machinations, Christian III offered the bishops the 'get-out' of conversion to Lutheranism, with the added sweetener that under the new doctrine they could marry and have children. Nearly all accepted. Lutheranism was now the official state religion of Denmark; Copenhagen celebrated with extravagant festivities. The nobility benefited hugely from the transfer of money from the Church to their all-too-eager hands, not to mention exemption from taxes. Across Denmark, and especially in Copenhagen, this wealth was made manifest in grand Renaissance mansions.

THE SUN KING

Into this brave new world of wealth, expansion and optimism was born one of the great figures of Danish history. Denmark's 'Sun King', Christian IV was a man possessed of heroic appetites. He ruled for 60 years, and is probably the nation's best-remembered monarch. It is hard to know where to begin in detailing the transformation that Copenhagen underwent during Christian IV's reign.

The city grew in all directions in the grandest of styles, with new buildings; a remodelling of its coastal access; improved defences and housing; the construction of entire new districts, bridges, churches, palaces, towers, observatories and theatres; and all the glittering hallmarks of the Renaissance. Upon his death, however, Copenhagen and Denmark would be a spent force, bankrupt, defeated, humiliated and seemingly doomed to an existence of debt and suppression by its enemies.

Christian IV was a complex, highly educated man with interests in music, architecture and foreign affairs. He married Anna Catherine of Brandenburg; after she died in 1612, he went on to father 24 children, half of them out of wedlock by a variety of mistresses.

The problem was that the many ambitious construction projects undertaken during his rule were becoming a burden on the country's finances. When Christian came to the throne Copenhagen had little industry to speak of. But, though he tried his best to establish industry in the capital, its wheeler-dealer trading heritage always seemed to undermine the fruitful work ethic that had developed. Copenhagen's products could never match the quality of those made by the best European craftsmen, which was a source of constant frustration and embarrassment to the king.

Christian's first priority was to cement Copenhagen's position as the major harbour of the region and, with this in mind, the channel between Sjælland and the small nearby island of Slotsholmen was straightened, narrowed and reinforced with wharfs. Slotsholmen was extended and, as the century closed, a new armoury (Tøjhuset) and a new supply depot (Provianthuset) were constructed to maintain the fighting readiness of the navy.

Further symbols of Christian's reign are found in the expanded palaces, prime among them the Rosenborg Slot (Rosenborg Castle). But the most extraordinary of his creations is the Rundetårn (Round Tower), an observatory graced by a stepless spiral ramp.

IN CONTEXT

Christian IV, the 'Sun King'.

Copenhagen-based international trading companies attempted to establish colonies in Africa and Asia, but they were as fleas on the shoulders of comparable Dutch and British enterprises. Instead, to raise money, Christian attempted to turn Copenhagen into the financial capital of Europe by ordering the construction of Børsen (Stock Exchange), but despite the building's unquestionable architectural and decorative splendour that too was a damp squib.

In 1523, Gustavus I of Sweden finally dissolved the Kalmar Union (though the union of Denmark and Norway lasted until 1814). During Christian's reign the increasing strength and confidence of Denmark's northerly neighbour were to threaten the very existence of the Danish state. At stake was control of access to the Baltic, which usually meant control of the region itself. In 1611, in a bid to protect his vital income from the Sound tolls (extorted at Helsingør Castle, the model for Shakespeare's Elsinore, north of Copenhagen), and to restore the Kalmar Union, Christian declared war on Sweden. The Kalmar War raged, with Denmark generally dominant, until 1613, when a peace accord brokered by the British concluded with a large ransom being paid by the Swedes to Denmark.

Danish triumphalism was short-lived, however, as Christian and his forces soon became embroiled in the Thirty Years War, in an effort to protect Danish interests on the north coast of Germany from Swedish expansion. The Danes' involvement in the war ended with a devastating defeat by the Swedes at the Battle of Lutter-am-Barenburg in 1626. The Danes got off more lightly than they deserved in the final peace settlement at Lübeck in 1629, in which Christian had to promise to take no further part in the war.

Christian's reign was to be marked by a third fateful conflict, Torstensson's War (1643-5). It was during this war that the 67-year-old Christian lost his right eye and received 23 shrapnel wounds (his blood-stained clothes are displayed in Rosenborg Slot). A much heftier defeat by united Dutch and Swedish forces in October ended the war and a peace treaty, signed in 1645, saw Denmark cede large areas of territory (chiefly, central parts of Norway, Halland and the islands of Gotland and Osel) to Sweden, and waive future Sound tolls. This was a dramatic and humiliating moment in Danish history. Thirty years followed in which Denmark barely survived as an independent state.

Christian didn't live to see his nation's darkest moment, however. He'd already been dead ten years when his successor Frederik III, Prince Bishop of Bremen (who'd taken the throne after his elder brother drank himself to death), started another Swedish-Danish war in 1658. The Swedes then forced the Danes to accept the humiliating Treaty of Roskilde by which Denmark ceded Scania. Not content, Karl Gustav decided he wanted to take the whole of Denmark and besieged Copenhagen in the winter of 1658-9.

One Nation Under the Dannebrog

The Danes love to fly the national flag.

Though the Danes are always quick to pour scorn on what they see as America's schmaltzy love of the Stars and Stripes, they actually have a very similar relationship to their own national flag, the Dannebrog. Few nations respect and use their flag as much as Denmark. Dannebrogs are hauled up to mark everything from coronations to the cat's birthday. Virtually every garden, be it a Strandvejen mansion or suburban semi, has a flagpole for this very purpose – they even have them in the gardens of their summer houses just in case – and will run up the Dannebrog on al birthdays and anniversaries. Flags fly from public buildings and even buses in Copenhagen on every royal birthday. And during corporate buffets or kindergarten parties no piece of cheese or cake will remain unadorned by a small paper version.

The Danes' love of myth is put to good use in explaining the origin of the Dannebrog. The red banner with a white cross is said to have fallen from the sky on 15 June 1219, as a holy inspiration to the Danish troops, led by King Valdemar II the Victorious against the pagan Estonians at Lyndanise, with an accompanying celestial voice to explain its importance. In fact the flag is more likely to have been given to the nation by the Pope to mark the crusade. It was first used on the seal of the Kalmar Union in 1397, but appeared long before that in the coat of arms of the Estonian city of Tallinn.

Ask any Dane and he or she will tell you that the Dannebrog is the oldest national flag in the world, and most will be well versed in its protocol: flags must be taken down at dusk and raised only during daylight (although a pennant version can be left up overnight by the lazy); a Dannebrog must never be allowed to touch the ground, and so on. Once you realise how dearly they treasure their flag, you can understand how deeply the Danes were affected by seeing it burned in the streets of the Muslim world during the Mohammed cartoon crisis of late 2005.

He led his German troops across the frozen sea surrounding Slotsholmen but, in a last gasp of defiance, Frederik himself is said to have led the fight against Karl Gustav's army. This spirited defence with cannon shot, bullets, pistols, logs and boiling tar and water to melt the ice, gave time for a Dutch army to arrive and save the capital.

The fortuitous sudden death of Karl Gustav at the start of 1660 ended Sweden's ambition to conquer Denmark, but the price of Denmark's salvation was steep, and Frederik was forced to capitulate control of the Sound (and its tolls), as well as all of Denmark's provinces to the east. Europe would never again allow Denmark, now a third of its former size, to hold power in the region.

Once again Copenhagen picked itself up to rebuild and refortify, with the construction of a new rampart to protect Slotsholmen. Out of this came the new quarter of Frederiksholm. The impressive Kongens Nytorv square was laid out in 1670 and was soon surrounded with imposing baroque houses and abutted by Nyhavn Canal – today one of the city's major tourist draws. An improved water supply, a company of watchmen and new street lighting complemented a fast-growing, modern capital whose population had doubled within 100 years to 60,000 by the early 18th century.

FIRE AND RENEWAL

In 1711, during the reign of Christian's successor, Frederik IV, Copenhagen was ravaged by plague in which 23,000 people died. It was also razed by fire twice during the century (in 1728 and 1795). The first fire broke out in a candle-maker's in Nørreport, and strong winds, negligible water supplies and general chaos ensured it travelled swiftly across town, destroying 1,700 houses, the town hall and the university, and leaving 12,000 people homeless. Happily, the building of the new five- and six-storey townhouses, taller than any before them, and the grand public buildings that replaced the combustible wooden, low-rise constructions of the 17th century, were strictly monitored by the building codes of the time, with the result that the capital was reborn more splendidly than ever before. The castle too was completely demolished and vast amounts of money were spent replacing it with the baroque Christiansborg Slot, only for the second fire to return it to the ground.

To celebrate the 300th anniversary of the House of Oldenburg, headed since 1746 by Frederik V, work began in 1749 on a grand new quarter, Frederiksstaden. It was designed by the architect Nicolai Eigtved with wide, straight streets fronted by elegant, light rococo palaces. At the heart of the new area was Amalienborg Plads, circled by four palaces that were financed by the noblemen of the town. When another fire at Christiansborg levelled a large part of the palace, the royal family found themselves homeless. They commandeered the four Amalienborg palaces, employing CF Harsdorff to connect them with an elegant colonnade, and have lived there ever since.

The second, larger fire of the century broke out on Gammelholm in 1795 and was even more destructive than the first, but again this only gave the city's architects and builders the chance to keep up with the fashion for the neo-classical. In 1771, Kongens Have (King's Gardens) opened. This new attraction was a huge success with the flourishing bourgeoisie. One of those less likely to participate fully in the educational revolution was the new king, Christian VII (1766-1808), who managed to rule for 42 years despite frequent and prolonged bouts of insanity.

In 1784, the 16-year-old crown prince Frederik (later Frederik VI) took power and acted as regent until his father's death in 1808. By 1801 he probably wished he hadn't, as the first of two bombardments by the British navy took place; Denmark, against its better nature, soon became drawn into the Napoleonic Wars with losses of territory and power.

During the 18th century Denmark's neutrality proved increasingly irksome to the British. To protect itself from increased interference by the Royal Navy, the Danes entered into an armed neutrality pact with Russia and the old foe Sweden. As a result, in April 1801, a British fleet under Admirals Nelson and Parker sailed into the Øresund and began bombardment of the Danish navy. However, Denmark continued to profit from the

IN CONTEXT

trade that had so angered the British, and anti-British fervour swept Copenhagen. That anger would be fuelled six years later when the British, under the Duke of Wellington, returned with a show of force that made the 1801 battle seem a mere fireworks display.

Napoleon was on the move across Europe and, with his fleet already destroyed by Nelson at Trafalgar, there were strong rumours in 1807 that the French were about to commandeer the Danish navy as a replacement. In fact, Frederik was preparing to defend his country from attack by the French in the south when he was visited by a British envoy who offered him this ultimatum: surrender the Danish fleet to Britain, or the Royal Navy will come and take it. The Danes refused and so the British sailed again on still neutral Copenhagen and bombarded it for three days.

Understandably, the Danes now baulked at an alliance with the British, siding instead with Napoleon. This was a decision they were to rue in the painful years ahead when the British blockaded Denmark and Norway. Much of Norway starved, while Denmark fared little better, enduring great hardship until the defeat of Napoleon. The Treaty of Kiel (1814) saw Sweden (now in alliance with Britain) take control of Norway, which had been for 450 years as much a part of Denmark as Sjælland. A period of introspection, from which many say Denmark has never really emerged, followed, typified by the slogan: 'We will gain internally what was lost externally.' In fact, despite a nationwide drive to grow new oak trees with which to rebuild the navy (many of which still flourish in the countryside), Denmark would not officially go to war again until its troops took part in a UN peacekeeping exercise in Bosnia in April 1994.

DANISH IDENTITY TO THE FORE

Fortunately, this was to be a period of cultural growth for a country struggling to come to terms with a new identity based on little more than a shared language and religion. With all hope of playing a role on the international stage gone, and with little financial power to wield either (Denmark as a state was declared bankrupt in 1813 and sold its colonies in Africa and India), the country instead began to extend itself in the arts and sciences. The storyteller Hans Christian Andersen (born in Odense, but a longtime Copenhagener), existentialist Søren Kierkegaard (the archetypal Copenhagener) and the theologian Nikolai Frederik Severin Grundtvig each contributed to the emergence of a defined Danish identity during the 19th century. This was also to be a golden age for Danish art. Many painters learned their craft elsewhere in Europe before returning to Denmark to depict the unique ethereal light and colours of the Danish landscape. Among the most notable were Christen Købke, his mentor and founder of the Danish School of Art Christoffer Wilhelm Eckersberg, JT Lundbye and Wilhelm Marstrand. Denmark's greatest sculptor, the neo-classicist Bertel Thorvaldsen, also returned to a hero's welcome after 40 years in Rome, while August Bournonville revitalised the Danish ballet at Det Kongelige Teater (Royal Theatre). Denmark also looked to its past to restore its sense of national pride, with the romantic poet

Museum of Copenhagen. *See p86.*

'In 1913 Copenhagen gained its international emblem, HC Andersen's Den Lille Havfrue (The Little Mermaid).'

Adam Oehlenschläger's mythologising of the country's history in his epic poems, and the historical novels of BS Ingemann. As a counterbalance, the Dagmar Theatre (1883) and Det Ny Teater (1908) became known for their adventurous, modern programming.

In contrast to the aftermath of past wars, Copenhagen rebuilt only modestly following the British attack. The town hall was eventually reconstructed on the eastern side of Nytorv, while Christiansborg and Vor Frue Kirke were also repaired (Thorvaldsen's sculptures gracing the latter's interior). The 'corn boom' of the 1830s revitalised growth and the industrial revolution consolidated the city's revival, with a prosperous shipyard, Burmeister & Wain, starting up on Christianshavn in 1843. Tivoli Gardens opened in the same year. Frederiksberg also became an entertainment mecca with its numerous skittle alleys, variety halls and dance venues. To help keep the revellers well oiled, the Carlsberg brewery expanded, moving to the suburb of Valby. Carlsberg's owner, Carl Jacobsen, would later use his profits to create a marvellous art collection, which he opened to the public at what is now the Ny Carlsberg Glyptotek in 1897.

DEMOCRACY AND GROWTH

With such potent augurs of the approaching modern age, Frederik VII knew that the days of absolute power were waning, and when in March 1848 a demonstration culminated with a loud (but relatively peaceful) protest outside his palace, the king capitulated immediately. Denmark's first written constitution followed in 1849.

Copenhagen's political and artistic life may have been moving with the times during the mid 1800s, but the standard of living for most of its 130,000 inhabitants, crowded tightly in cellars and ever higher tenements, had not kept pace with the higher echelons of society. Housing remained a dire problem, despite the progressive new terraces in Østerbro, and in 1852 the ban on construction outside the city's defences was lifted. In the latter part of the century a huge building boom saw swathes of land filled with inhospitable blocks of small so-called 'corridor' flats (one-room properties arranged like the rooms of a hotel along one long corridor). Blågårdsgade, Nørrebro and Vesterbro became notorious for the prevalence of such slum housing. Yet as soon as new housing popped up, the population expanded to fill it. By 1900, more than 400,000 people had moved to Copenhagen to escape the grinding poverty of rural areas. The council granted permission for the creation of a new open space, Ørsteds Parken, where the city's levelled ramparts once stood, together with the building of the Botanisk Have (Botanical Gardens), Statens Museum For Kunst (National Gallery) and a brand new observatory. Strøget, the city's main shopping street, flourished with the arrival of the major department stores Illum and Magasin du Nord. Electricity came to the capital in 1892 (electric trams followed in 1897), as did flushing toilets and a vastly improved sewerage system.

In 1913 Copenhagen gained its international emblem, HC Andersen's *Den Lille Havfrue* (The Little Mermaid), a dstatue planted on some rocks in Langelinie, south of Frihavn. Ever since, visitors who have flocked to see it have been united in their sense of anticlimax.

OCCUPATION AND FREEDOM

Despite its neutrality, Denmark was in Germany's pocket during World War I. It still, however, made provision for an outright attack by Germany, calling up 60,000 men to form a defence force, most of whom were stationed on the fortifications of Copenhagen. Fortunately, they weren't needed, and Denmark survived the Great War intact.

IN CONTEXT

Between the wars the pre-eminent figure to emerge in Danish politics was the Social Democrat Thorvald Stauning, who achieved the feat of transforming his party from near revolutionaries to true social democrats. A champion of inclusive politics and a tactical magician, Stauning appointed the first woman government minister and helped revive the shaky Danish economy with the famous Kanslergarde Agreement in 1933, which allowed for the devaluing of the krone against the British pound and the subsequent resuscitation of Danish agriculture.

When World War II broke out in September 1939, Denmark braced itself to hold tight and sit out the conflict in peaceable neutrality, just as it had 25 years earlier. It was soon disabused of that notion, when at 4am on 9 April 1940 Hitler's troops landed at Kastellet, fired a few shots on Amalienborg Slot (killing 16 Danes) and issued an ultimatum: allow Germany to take control of Denmark's defences or watch Copenhagen be bombed from the sky. After an hour-and-a-half of deliberation the Danish government and king agreed, and entered into a unique deal whereby the country remained a sovereign state, but Germany gained access to Norway, the Atlantic and Sweden. Denmark's Aryan genes ensured it was welcomed into the bosom of the Third Reich and, as a rich agricultural provider, it was spared much of the brutality and suppression endured by neighbouring occupied states.

By the end of the war, the Danish Resistance numbered around 60,000. They were never called upon to fight, however, and documents unearthed after the war revealed that the German army had expected them to be far more troublesome than they were.

POST-WAR DENMARK

After the war Denmark, governed by an endless series of coalitions dominated by the Social Democrats, faced several immediate domestic problems, which the founding of its welfare state would address. Culminating in the Social Security Act of 1976, the provision by the government of a safety blanket for the sick, the unemployed and the elderly has been one of Denmark's most widely admired achievements. Critics, however, point out that it was initially funded by foreign loans and has seen modern Denmark burdened by a vast public sector workforce and the crippling income tax levied to pay for it.

With its capital more densely crowded than ever, the government sought to decentralise industry and intensify urban planning. A somewhat idealistic 'Finger Plan', in which the city's expansion would incorporate open spaces, was drawn up in 1947, but this was soon discarded to make way for more sprawling suburbs. Copenhagen's first tower blocks were built in 1950 at Bellahøj, but a public outcry curbed the extent to which they could be used to solve the perennial housing shortage. Instead, an urban renewal programme saw Adelgade and Borgergade, among other areas, refurbished. Much of Nørrebro and Vesterbro were also developed during the 1960s, and the latter would benefit from a second renewal programme at the end of the 20th century.

The use of cars increased exponentially in Copenhagen during this time and, as a result, Strøget, for centuries the city's main shopping street, was pedestrianised in 1962. During the 1960s, Denmark (along with the rest of the West) was forced to confront the sexual revolution. In June 1967, it became notorious as the first state in the world to legalise pornography.

Meanwhile, in 1968, Copenhagen's students, like those across the rest of the continent, grew restless. This being Copenhagen, though, their protest was hardly cataclysmic. Aside from storming the office of Copenhagen University's vice-chancellor and smoking all his cigars, the students caused little trouble. Nevertheless, the spineless university still went ahead and abolished professorial powers.

Copenhagen's youth unrest lasted well into the 1970s, and its ultimate trophy still draws tourists from around the world. In 1971 a group of squatters occupied Bådsmandsstræde Barracks, 41 hectares (101 acres) of former military accommodation, on the eastern side of Christianshavn. In protest against what they saw as oppressive social norms, the squatters announced the founding of the Free State of Christiania.

Black Diamond

The police moved in, but underestimated the commune, whose numbers had been swollen by many like-minded hippies from across the country. Eventually the government gave in and allowed Christiania to continue as a 'social experiment' and its 1,000 or so inhabitants quickly began creating their own schools, housing, businesses and recycling programmes. The commune became well known across Europe for its tolerance of drugs, but the current government has cracked down heavily on Christiania.

Though Copenhagen's pre-eminence as a port came to an end with the advent of the superships (too big for the Øresund, they made instead for Gothenburg and Hamburg), in the 1970s the city nevertheless enjoyed full employment. That, in turn, led to a shortage of workers and efforts were made to attract foreigners from southern Europe, Turkey and Pakistan, who tended to settle in Nørrebro and Vesterbro. Like London's docks, Copenhagen's waterside was to be redeveloped with expensive housing, exclusive restaurants and impressive new buildings for the city's cultural institutions (*see p29* **On the Waterfront**), such as the Black Diamond national library extension, the Operaen (opera house) and the Royal Danish Playhouse (for all, *see venue index*).

In 1973, Denmark joined the European Common Market (as it was then), mainly to secure its lucrative bacon and butter exports to the UK, but even after 20 years its membership was still the subject of a heated national debate. In June 1992, Europe would twice more turn its attention to Denmark, which emerged from the margins of the European Union to stick a spanner in the works of the progression towards federalism. Denmark has never been a wholehearted member of the EU, and 51 per cent of Danish voters went a step further in June 1992, rejecting the pivotal Maastricht Treaty and causing a mighty kerfuffle in the process. There were protests, some violent, on the streets of Copenhagen. In the end, after a re-vote in 1993, the Danes finally ratified the Treaty (by a majority in favour of just 51.05 per cent), but only after they had been promised the right to abstain from common defence and currency commitments.

Copenhagen celebrated its tenure as Cultural Capital of Europe in 1996 with several new arts projects, including Arken Museum for Moderne Kunst (see venue index) and saw major celebrations in 1997 for the 25th anniversary of the reign of Queen Margrethe. In July 2000, the eyes of the world were on Copenhagen for the opening of the historic and very expensive Øresund Bridge to Sweden and again in 2004 for the royal wedding of Crown Prince Frederik to the Australian commoner Mary Donaldson.

Early 2005 saw the re-election of Prime Minister Anders Fogh Rasmussen at the head of a Liberal-Conservative coalition in which the rather unsavoury power brokers remain the right-wing Danske Folkepartie (Danish People's Party). Two years later, in 2007, Lars Løkke Rasmussen took over as Prime Minister, after Anders Fogh Rasmussen stepped down (he's now Secretary-General of NATO).

In the last few years, Denmark, and Copenhagen in particular, has gained worldwide press more for matters outside of the political realm: its New Nordic cuisine – and in particular the restaurant Noma (*see p121*), named the best in the world by several publications – is drawing more and more visitors to the capital, while the country's strong organic movement, urban design schemes and bike culture is a now a model for forward-thinking governments around the globe.

Copenhagen Today

Bikes, beer and civic pride.

TEXT: MICHAEL BOOTH

Copenhagen is at the very heart of Denmark. Not literally, you understand. In fact it couldn't be further from the centre of the country, lying as it does on the far eastern coast of Sjælland, closer to Sweden than most of Denmark – of course, once upon a time this was the centre of the Danish empire, which then included southern Sweden, Norway and Iceland. But with over a quarter of the country's population living in the city, and many of the rest dreaming of moving there (if they are under 20), or having retired from there (if they are over 60), Copenhagen can justly lay claim to being, if not the soul, then at least the political, cultural and economic nerve centre of the country.

Only 600,000 live in the city centre proper, but Copenhagen has a total population of 1.7 million, including the surrounding 26 communes (the country as a whole has 5.3m inhabitants). But its compact size is a large part of the city's appeal for visitors. You can amble across the centre in an afternoon; take in most of its main sights in a long weekend; and really get to know your way around in under a week. This is an accessible city, in all senses: English is spoken to a high level wherever you go; the transport system is unsurpassed; the tourist board is efficient and slick; there are world-renowned restaurants; and these days, following a massive hotel boom, there is plenty of accommodation of all descriptions.

THE DANES

About the only thing that isn't so easy to get to know about Copenhagen is its people. The Danes are a close-knit tribe. You may be familiar with the concept of 'six degrees of separation'; with the Danes it is generally three degrees or even two – if strangers meet, within a minute they will be able to find a common acquaintance. The Danes have enough in themselves. Although notably good-natured, they are neither welcoming nor unwelcoming towards strangers; they might be slightly bemused as to why you have come to Copenhagen instead of, say, Berlin or Stockholm, but they are basically glad you bothered and will help you, within reason, if you ask for it.

The Danes are a trusting and trustworthy bunch (except when it comes to bicycle theft). Though their obsessive obedience to rules can make them seem sheep-like from time to time (you will notice that they never, ever cross the road unless the green man tells them to – cross on a red and you will be 'tutted' at), they are far more relaxed than the Swedes or Norwegians when it comes to the sale of alcohol and the use of soft drugs. And though the Danes are extremely wealthy in global terms, they consider it deeply vulgar to make any kind of display of the fact. Denmark has the smallest gap between rich and poor of any country in the world. Essentially, the Danes are one giant middle class, with all that implies for the national character and, exchequer both good and bad.

BUILDING BOOM

Perhaps the only exception to this pervasive modesty are the many major construction projects that have been completed in and around Copenhagen in recent years, like the Øresund Bridge from Amager to Malmö in southern Sweden; the ever-expanding Metro; and the various snazzy concrete and glass buildings overlooking the harbour (*see p29* **On the Waterfront**). The building is continuing apace, particularly on the island of Amager where the new town of Ørestad, home to the new Koncerthuset (*see p197* **Profile**), continues to expand close to the airport. While weekend visitors rarely get to see the exclusive apartment buildings that have shot up beside the harbour to the north and south of the city, they can't miss the mammoth opera house (which opened in 2005), or the new National Theatre just across the water from it.

In recent years several former slum areas and red light districts have emerged as 'hot' new shopping and nightlife areas. Vesterbro, behind Central Station, is one. Its red light district (around Halmtorvet) is now a cool café area, and the once infamous 'sex street', Istedgade, is packed with boho cafés and trendy clothing boutiques (the sex shops, hookers and junkies remain, however). It is also a great place to find exotic foodstuffs.

IN CONTEXT

'Many enter a kind of hibernation during the winter, emerging for the Christmas festivities.'

Nørrebro is another buzzing part of town. Its café scene is centred on Sankt Hans Torv and Elmegade, with one of the city's best nightclubs, Rust, and cosiest cinemas, Empire Bio, both just around the corner. Meanwhile the latest street to draw the artsy crowd is Nansensgade, just north of HC Ørsteds Park, where there are now several cool boutiques, cafés, restaurants and bars.

DEATH AND TAXES

There are downsides to life in Copenhagen, of course. The weather is the most obvious one. Bluntly put, it sucks for most of the year. You would expect this not to bother the stoic locals but it does, and many enter a kind of hibernation during the winter, emerging for the brief Christmas festivities (which Copenhagen does very well, incidentally). The weather must be held at least partly responsible for the country's disproportionately high suicide rate, and the fact that the Danes drink, smoke and eat to a more unhealthy degree (despite their large intake of organic food) than virtually anyone else in Europe.

Consequently, they have a shorter life expectancy than most of their European neighbours, attributable at least in part to their stubborn denial of the consequences of smoking (one in five deaths are smoking related). A ban on smoking in public places has been instigated, but isn't is as all-encompassing as laws in many other countries.

They are drinkers, too. Alcohol-related deaths are doubling every five years and 350,000 Danes are said to be technically obese due to an addiction to sweets and chocolates that rivals even that of the Scots.

Metro

On the Waterfront

New architecture, Michelin-starred restaurants and cultural gems.

Until around a decade ago Copenhagen was in denial of its seaside location. You would hardly have known the Øresund Sea and harbour bordered half the city. But in recent years the city has embraced the surrounding seas with radical new buildings overlooking the water, the ambitious lagoon development on Amager Strand (Amager Beach), and the construction of open-air swimming pools in the harbour itself (*see p83* **Come On In, the Water's Lovely**), the best known of which is Islands Brygge near Langebro.

In terms of public buildings, you can date the city's harbour renaissance to the 1999 opening of the **Black Diamond** (pictured; *see p194*) extension to the National Library, by architects Schmidt Hammer & Lassen. This dramatic parallelogram, just north of Langebro, is made from Zimbabwean granite and paved the way for several large-scale leviathans overlooking the water, including the Nordea Bank building beside Langebro, the windswept apartment blocks in Tuborg Havn and the gigantic £232m **Opera House** by Henning Larsen. The Michelin-starred **Søren K** Scandinavian restaurant (*see p118*) is located in the Black Diamond, with waterside views.

On the other side of the water, in Christianshavn, sits another Michelin-starred restaurant, the world-renowned **Noma** (*see p122*), which now has a waiting list of several months. Its housed in the Nordatlantens Brygge (North Atlantic House) that it shares with a popular cultural centre and the Embassy of Iceland. Newer arrivals include the new Norway ferry terminal in Nordhavn by architects 3 x Nielsen, which resembles a giant lightbox, and the dazzling **Royal Danish Playhouse** (aka Skuespilhuset) – opposite the Opera House (for both, *see p192* **Profile**) – at Kvæsthusbroen, on the site of the old ferry terminal, which opened in 2008. Even Sir Terence Conran has got in on the act with the restaurant complex in the former **Customs House**.

In fact, these days virtually every stretch of Copenhagen's waterfront is being developed; Holmen, Amager Strand and Sydhaven (the South Harbour) are all erupting cool, modern apartment blocks. Of particular note is the extraordinary Gemini Residence: two massive, converted grain silos by Dutch architects MVRDV, each boasting that all-important sea view – essential to any self-respecting 21st-century Danish yuppie.

IN CONTEXT

Happy Town

Smile, you're in Denmark.

The people of Denmark have grown used to making headlines around the world in the last few years, what with the fairytale marriage of their Crown Prince to an Australian woman in 2004, the outrage provoked throughout the Muslim world by the publication of cartoons of the prophet Mohammed by the Danish newspaper *Jyllands-Posten* in 2005, and the explosion of New Nordic cuisine, pioneered by Copenhagen chefs Claus Meyer and Rene Redzepi. Nevertheless, many Danes reacted with some bewilderment to the 2006 proclamation that they are the happiest people in the world. ('Why did no one tell us?' pondered one columnist.)

The world's media clamoured to discover their secret, following the publication of a study (and follow-up studies in 2008) by social psychologists at the University of Leicester, which placed Danes just ahead of the Swiss, the Austrians and Icelanders in terms of all-round contentment.

Visitors might be foxed by all this, as the Danes are not the most obviously joyous of people – self-satisfied, perhaps, but gay in the old-fashioned sense of the word? No. True, they have a carnival once a year, and they certainly like a drink but, at heart, they remain a rather serious, often depressive Nordic race in the true Viking tradition. Yes, this is the country that gave us Aqua's 'Barbie Girl', but don't forget it is also the birthplace of Existentialism, as well as Danish film director Lars von Trier (responsible for surely two of the most depressing films ever made: *Breaking the Waves* and *Dancer in the Dark*). Swedes and Danes will argue the night away about which of them lays claim to having the world's highest suicide rate.

So why are they, supposedly, so happy? It doesn't hurt that this is a small country with a small capital, and small countries, particularly small European countries, always do well in life satisfaction surveys due to their inherent sense of collectivism, which breeds a greater sense of civic pride and social support. Money has a great deal to do with it as well, of course. In the early noughties, the Danish economy boomed thanks to an unexpected North Sea oil bonanza, and world-class technology and pharmaceutical sectors. Though not quite as wealthy as their neighbours the Norwegians (which is a constant source of irritation to the Danes), Denmark has one of the lowest rates of unemployment in Europe and some of the highest wages. Social and economic stability ensures the Danes are well looked after by the state in terms of healthcare, education, childcare and social benefits. The streets of Copenhagen are clean, safe and buzzing with confidence and creativity. Public transport is efficient and reasonably priced, and the popularity of the bike as transport creates a strong sense of community on the city's streets.

But aside from the comfort of hard cash, the Danes seem to have mastered several other fundamental prerequisites of contentment. They work a little less than the rest of us, spend more time with their families, read more, don't complain nearly as much as you might expect about their taxes, embrace their horrid climate and spend as much of their lives as possible outdoors. Above all, they try to keep things *hygglige* – which is the name for their unique brand of amiable cosiness and, we believe, the true secret of their happiness.

'Even liberal, well-educated Copenhageners still talk of "second generation Danes".'

Other factors which contribute to the Danes' existential angst (invented, of course, by Copenhagener Søren Kierkegaard) are the punitive tax rates and generally high cost of everything. The *Economist* recently ranked Denmark as the third most expensive country in the world in which to live. Most Danes can expect to say goodbye to as much as 60 per cent of their income at source; cars cost around three times the price they do in the UK; while visitors will wince at 25 per cent VAT and the often exorbitant cost of dining out. House prices are not far off London's, and there is a shortage in Copenhagen, which looks set to stoke them further still.

As for temperament and political outlook, to the outside world the Danes are liberal, open-minded and tolerant. They were pornography pioneers in the 1960s; this was one of the first nations to permit gay marriage; and they give more per capita in overseas aid than any other nation on earth.

CARTOON CRISIS

The Danes are less sceptical about Europe than they were when they rejected the euro in 2000, though they have still not ratified the EU Treaty, and the world economic crisis has postponed the proposed 2008 referendum. In fact, Europe as an issue is one hot potato that seems to have been put on the political back burner in recent years. During the last general election in 2007, race and social welfare were deemed far more pressing by the political leaders, the latter issue continuing to play to the advantage of the odious far-right Dansk Folkepartie (Danish People's Party) with its sinister 'mother' figure, Pia Kiersgaard, at its head. The DF increased its share of the vote, though the Liberal-Conservative coalition, now led by Lars Løkke Rasmussen (after Anders Fogh Rasmussen, now Secretary-General of NATO, resigned in 2009), remains strong. The left, meanwhile, continues its inexorable decline. There last two elections were the Social Democrats' worst since 1973 and, in general, Denmark's left wing has struggled to keep up with the times.

And then, of course, there was the 'Mohammed Cartoon Scandal' that erupted some months after the Danish newspaper *Jyllands-Posten* (the Jutland Post) published a series of 12 cartoons featuring the Prophet in September 2005. The cartoons were considered blasphemous by Muslims, and embarrassingly unfunny by the rest of the world. Several Muslim countries imposed boycotts on Danish products; the Danes' beloved Dannebrog flag (*see p20* **One Nation Under the Dannebrog**) was burned from Tehran to Cairo; and there were riots as far away as Afghanistan. Fogh Rasmussen baulked at offering an official apology, but claimed this was a global crisis. It did more to taint the image of Denmark abroad than anything in its history.

While visitors to Copenhagen are highly unlikely to experience overt racism, even liberal, well-educated Copenhagener still, for example, talk of 'second generation Danes', referring to peope who, though they have been born in Denmark, have lived in Denmark, speak Danish and pay Danish taxes, are still not, well, you know, white. If one Dane tells of a crime he has heard about, the first question asked will be the colour of the perpetrator's skin.

It is a familiar story throughout Europe, of course, and smaller nations like Denmark and Holland are hypersensitive to issues of race and immigration. Copenhageners will tend to accuse their compatriots in Jutland of being the racist right-wingers, and there is some truth in that, but the continuing growth of racial ghettos in the capital suggests this is an issue that even this cosmopolitan capital can't ignore forever.

Danish Design

Are you sitting functionally?
Then let's begin…

TEXT: MICHAEL BOOTH & ANNA NORMAN

Danish design is renowned around the world, beyond all proportion to the size of the nation that fostered it. Collectors and designers flock to Copenhagen to find that original Jacobsen Egg chair or Henningsen lamp in the shops and showrooms of Bredgade and Ravnsborggade, to seek inspiration in the capital's excellent museums, or to clothe themselves in cool Danish threads. But why is Danish design so revered? Why is this the place *Wallpaper** magazine comes to first to furnish its fashion shoots and dip its litmus paper in the test tube of style?

In the first half of the 20th century, a wave of Danish designers and architects emerged on the world stage, influenced in part by the radicalism of Bauhaus, to change contemporary interiors and buildings for ever. They looked anew at the style and function of everyday objects, as well as the materials used to make them, and created icons. Danish design has had a reputation to live up to ever since, and by and large it continues to surpass expectations, not just in furniture, product design and architecture, but also in the fields of industrial design and fashion.

For Danish fashion designers, see p149 Danish Designers.

FUNCTIONALISM/INTERNATIONAL MODERNISM 1928-60

Functionalism was first conceptualised by the Swedish architect Gunnar Asplund in an exhibition in Stockholm in 1930, inspiring architects across Scandinavia to adopt the tenets of international modernism. Architect **Kaare Klint** gave a succinct expression of the new Danish design philosophy when he said, 'The form of an object follows its function'. Denmark was a country late to industrialisation, and this combined with its long heritage of quality craftsmanship meant that it was in a perfect position to develop an exciting new design industry. The first project to create a major impact in the field of architecture was **Arne Jacobsen**'s **Bellavista** housing development (1934; *photo p36*) and **Bellevue Teatret** (1937). Taking inspiration from the German modernists, Denmark's master builder created in Bellavista an uncompromisingly modern development, with white surfaces and large windows (all apartments have sea views), in a posh coastal suburb north of Copenhagen. (Jacobsen's lesser-known **Skovshoved Petrol Station**, situated on the route from Copenhagen to Bellevue, was also built in this era, in 1936.)

Throughout the 1930s, Klint (influenced by his father PV Jensen Klint) wrote again and again in his notes that architecture and interior design should be unified in what he called 'the living life'. Design should be intrinsic to function, and styling should exist only to enhance practicality. Allying this idea with the traditional hallmarks of the best Danish work – industrial quality, outstanding craftsmanship and artistic flair – Klint produced a series of ground-breaking designs, and passed on his theories as a teacher at Copenhagen's Royal Academy of Architecture. Klint's students were advised that if, for example, they were making a chair, then its function (i.e. comfort) should be the starting point – studying human proportions and posture then applying this scientific rationale to the construction of the furniture should always be the primary objective. **Børge Mogensen**, **Mogens Koch** and **Hans J Wegner** were among his students and their production of simple, practical furniture swept across the country in the 1950s and their designs can be seen in homes all across Denmark – and increasingly all around the world – to this day.

Danish architect **Arne Jacobsen** took this notion of functional and stylistic unity to its extreme when he designed one of Copenhagen's most famous buildings: the **Radisson SAS Royal Hotel** (*see p101*), completed in 1960. With this still controversial building (which turned out to be the first and last proper skyscraper to be constructed in the centre of the city), Jacobsen embraced the principle of 'total design' with characteristically obsessive attention to detail, designing not only the building but its

IN CONTEXT

Skovshoved Petrol Station.

lighting, furnishings and interior, right down to the cutlery in the restaurant (which is awkward to use but looked futuristic enough for Stanley Kubrick to have all of his characters use it in *2001: A Space Odyssey*). Today everything in the hotel's room 606 (*p99* **Profile)** – the lamps, fabrics, cutlery, glasses, furniture and door handles – is Jacobsen-designed and has been left untouched as a tribute to his genius. Jacobsen's last architectural project was the transatlantic-style 'slab on a podium' **Nationalbanken** (1965-78); it was finished after his death in 1971 by Dissing+Weitling.

Denmark is still reaping the benefits of this design explosion. The furniture of that era has been (and still is) hugely influential and remains in great demand, but there were a number of Danish pioneers who influenced concepts of modern functionalism before this.

The silverware created by **Georg Jensen**, for example, was revolutionary in its field. Jensen trained as a sculptor and silversmith who opened his first silverworks in Copenhagen in 1904. From then until his death in 1935 he constantly challenged the conventions of silver design with creations that were both aesthetically pleasing and user-friendly. The cutlery, bowls and jewellery he created with the painter **Johan Rohde** were at the vanguard of modern design back then and today the Georg Jensen brand remains as desirable as ever.

LIGHTING THE WAY

At the same time that Jensen was challenging cutlery conventions, fellow Copenhagener **Poul Henningsen** was innovating in the field of home lighting. 'From the top of a tram car, you look into all the homes and you shudder at how dismal they are,' he wrote. 'It doesn't cost money to light a room correctly, but it does require culture. My aim is to beautify the home and those who live there. I am searching for harmony.' So, in 1924, Henningsen designed a multi-shade lamp based on scientific analysis of its function. The size, shape and position of the shade determine the distribution of the light and the amount of glare. The 'PH' lamp, which featured several shades to help correct the colour and shadow effect of the light, won a competition at the Paris World Fair, and Henningsen became a star. His lamps continue to light many Danish households, particularly the classic PH-Contrast (1962).

Other design trailblazers included silversmith **Kay Bojesen**, whose 'Grand Prix' silver service (1938) was the template for aspiring cutlery designers, and the artist **Ebbe Sadolin**, with his plain white tableware, which was considered quite radical at the time.

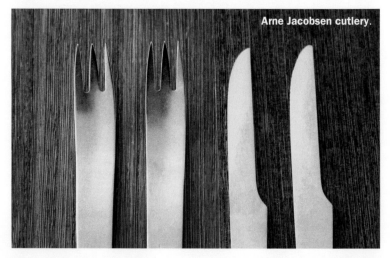

Arne Jacobsen cutlery.

'Bang & Olufsen made a global name for themselves through their radical yet simple designs and superior quality.'

Two major talents to emerge in the field of furniture design in the 1950s were **Nanna Ditzel** (who is still working and winning prizes for her revolutionary designs today) and Jacobsen's contemporary **Poul Kjærholm** (whose PK22 chair was influenced by Mies van der Rohe's designs). In the 1960s, **Verner Panton**, another of Jacobsen's former colleagues, addressed the frequent criticism levelled at designers – that their work was far too expensive and exclusive – and took on the challenge of pushing the boundaries of design aesthetics even further. Panton trained at the Royal Danish Academy of Fine Arts in Copenhagen, and initially worked in Arne Jacobsen's architectural practice. International attention soon centred on Panton's designs, based on geometric forms, and constructed from cheap, tough plastics that had previously only been used for industrial purposes. Combined with a use of vivid colours and outlandish shapes, Panton's inspirational style helped define the 'pop' aesthetic of the 1960s, with design icons like the 'Flowerpot' lamp, the 'Cone' chair and the Panton chair. Although some contemporary critics dismissed Panton's work as a fad, before his death in 1998 it was reassessed and a new generation of designers saw it as being way ahead of its time.

SOUND ENGINEERS

While their neighbours to the south in Germany aspire to owning a Mercedes and the Swedes keep up with the Jensens by buying a yacht, the Danes are a more modest bunch, preferring cheap French cars and perhaps a kayak. But there is one luxury status symbol they all yearn for, one treasure every Dane must own before they reach 30: a **Bang & Olufsen** stereo.

Visit any Danish home and the odds are there will be a BeoSound Beolink system or a Beosound Ouverture with slick flush surfaces, automatic sliding glass doors and still futuristic design, in pride of place in the living room. Older B&O products were built like battleships, so the unit could easily be 25 years old and still working like a dream.

The company was founded in Western Jutland in 1925 by two engineers, Peter Bang and Svend Olufsen, in the attic of Olufsen's family manor house. They were the first to produce a radio that plugged directly into the mains instead of using batteries, and by the 1930s they had made a name for themselves with other firsts, like a push-button radio and a radiogram. The Germans destroyed the factory in 1945, but the pair rebuilt the business after the war.

Between launching their first TV in the 1950s and their first fully transistorised radio, the Beomaster 900, in the late 1960s, they made a global name for themselves through their radical yet simple designs – initially heavily influenced by Mies van der Rohe – and superior quality. In the 1970s and '80s, Denmark's furnitures took a back seat while Bang & Olufsen and other industrial design brands, such as **Bernadotte & Bjørn** and **Jacob Jensen**, excelled.

'Bang & Olufsen is for those who discuss design and quality before price,' went the company's advertising campaigns and, accordingly, several B&O products made their way into the Museum of Modern Art in New York. The company has also managed to attract some of the world's top designers, including Vesterbro-born Jacob Jensen, and usually features in the top five of any 'coolest brands' list.

The Bang & Olufsen families continue to be involved in the running of the company which, though it now has manufacturing plants all over the world, is still based in their home town of Struer. Bang & Olufsen's flagship shop (*see p157*) is worth a visit.

Bellavista. *See p33.*

PRODUCT PLACEMENT

Starting with Verner Panton, the best place to see his work is the funky Panton Lounge in the **Langelinie Pavillion**. These rooms are upstairs and only open for functions, but if you ask at the bar someone might well show you them. Another café dedicated to the work of a single designer is music café **PH Caféen**, on Halmtorvet in Vesterbro, which is a shrine to the work of Poul Henningsen (hence the 'PH'). As well as the SAS Royal Hotel, the **Jacobsen Restaurant** (*see p127*) is another shrine worth visiting for design fans of Arne Jacobsen, as it is furnished exclusively with his designs, including his cutlery. It is housed in one of Jacobsen's pioneering housing complexes, **Bellavista**, close to Klampenborg Station.

You find classic Danish furniture everywhere in Copenhagen, from the chair you sit on in the library, to cool bars and restaurants. For accommodation, the Radisson Blu (SAS) Royal is an obvious choice, but best of all for design fans is the **Hotel Alexandra** (*see venue index*) on HC Andersens Boulevard. Several of the rooms are furnished with design classics by Jacobsen, Wegner, Ole Wanscher and Finn Juhl.

If you are looking to buy, head for the cool second-hand and antiques shops on Ravnsborggade in Nørrebro or the more exclusive dealers on Bredgade. A good one-stop shop for both contemporary and classic Danish design is the design temple **Illums Bolighus** on Amagertorv and the neighbouring **Royal Copenhagen** stores, selling contemporary and classic porcelain, glassware and silverware. Even if you can't afford a major purchase, it's well worth wandering through the gallery/museum-style halls to be tempted by a Jensen stainless steel watch, the perfect porcelain of Bing & Grøndhal, or the crystal creations of contemporary Danish craftsmen like Michael Bang, Torben Jørgensen and Allan Scharf. Even the area outside the store has designer pedigree; the geometric patterns of the marble-paved fountain square were designed by Bjørn Nørgaard in 1996.

Head to the end of Strøget to Kongens Nytorv square for **Bang & Olufsen**'s flagship store. Heading in the opposite direction towards Rådhuspladsen you will pass two **Rosendahl** glass and kitchenware stores – the first on the corner of Bernikowsgade, the second flagship store closer to Rådhuspladsen.

For those interested in learning more about Danish design, **Kunstindustrimuseet** (Museum of Decorative and Applied Art; *see venue index*) houses an expansive collection of items. And since early 2000, Danish design has had the purpose-built showcase it has always been crying out for: Henning Larsen's five-storey **Dansk Design Centre** (*see p50*). Behind the smoked-glass exterior there are interactive installations, interesting exhibitions, a shop that sells design-related artefacts and a café. The centre's aim is to act as a 'window to the world' for Danish design, as well as being a meeting place for designers, industry figures and innovators from across the planet.

CONTEMPORARY ARCHITECTURE & DESIGN

The designation of Copenhagen as the European City of Culture in 1996 prompted a period of intense development, which continued until the international economic crisis a decade or so later. Two major architectural works to come out of the event were **Henning Larsen**'s Impressionists gallery in the Ny Carlsberg Glyptotek (1996) and **Søren Robert Lund**'s ship-like **Arken Museum for Moderne Kunst** (1994-6. Neither was as spectacular as the **Øresund Fixed Link** tunnel and bridge, however, which joins Copenhagen and Malmö in Sweden, and opened in 2000.

But indigenous architects have been under threat in recent times from an invasion of global superstars. **Daniel Libeskind**, architect of the new building for the Twin Towers site in New York, drew the **Jewish Museum** (2004) – housed in a converted 17th century royal boathouse beside the National Library; **Jean Nouvel** has drawn the astonishing, long-delayed blue cube **Copenhagen Concert Hall** for Danmarks Radio, in central Amager, which opened in 2009 (*see p197* **Profile**); even **Lord Norman Foster** has made his mark on the city, working on, of all things, a new elephant house for **Copenhagen Zoo** (2007).

Today, Danish designers and architects seem to be wrestling with two opposing approaches. On one side is the desire to continue with the development of Nordic tradition (simple lines, functional designs); on the other is the influence of international fashions that tend towards the more flamboyant. If a distinctive Danish style is to emerge in the future, it will spring from a compromise between these two tendencies. Projects such as Henning Larsen's **Operaen** (2005) and Lundgaard & Tranberg's 2008 **Skuespilhuset** (Playhouse) demonstrate that Danish architects still have much to offer.

There continues to be a strong focus on design in Denmark, with the focus now on sustainability and integration, in architecture, furniture and industrial design. In 2007, the Danish government launched the DesignDenmark initiative, which aims to elicit a new design-focused dialogue and restore Denmark to the international design elite.

IN CONTEXT

Henning Larsen's Unibank Headquarters.

Blast from the Past

Buildings that survived Copenhagen's 18th- and 19th-century fires.

BIRTH OF THE CITY 1167-1588

Slotsholmen is where Copenhagen was born. There was said to be a fishing village on the site for hundreds of years before King Valdemar I the Great gave the district to his blood brother **Bishop Absalon**. The ruins of Absalon's 12th-century castle were uncovered underneath the Christiansborg Slot and can be visited in the Ruinerne Under Christiansborg.

During the Middle Ages the town spread out from Slotsholmen towards present-day Rådhuspladsen. The oldest standing building in Copenhagen is **Helligåndskirken** (Church of the Holy Spirit) on Strøget. The city's only surviving medieval building, the church complex includes the remains of a late 13th-century convent and the late Gothic Helligåndhus (House of the Holy Spirit), dating from the 15th century.

CHRISTIAN IV 1588-1648

Christian IV was the first king to play a major role in the planning of the city. His grand scheme was to double the size of the city. **Rosenborg Slot**, at the northern corner of the old city, and **Kastellet** (the Castle; 1662-4), along the coast, would be the two main edifices of this new area. The earliest substantial work of Christian's reign was the transformation (1599-1605) of Slotsholmen; he built a naval yard, supply depot (Provianthuset), and arsenal (Tøjhus; now Tøjhusmuseet). The latter still stands. To house the new naval yard workers, the king embarked on another major project (starting in 1617): Christianshavn. A number of residences in this Amsterdam-like district survive, notably on **Sankt Annæ Gade** (Nos. 28, 30 and 32, dating from 1640).

This most ambitious of Denmark's kings was also responsible for a number of Copenhagen's most distinctive individual buildings. The long, low **Børsen** (Old Stock Exchange; 1619-24) is one of Copenhagen's most beautiful buildings.

The king indulged himself most fully in the building of the **Rosenborg Slot** (Rosenborg Palace; 1606-34). With the help of the Dutch architect Hans van Steenwinckel the Younger, Christian transformed Rosenborg from a small summer house into a lavish palace worthy of Denmark's 'Sun King'.

Christian's last project was the extraordinary **Rundetårn** (Round Tower; 1637-42), Europe's oldest functioning observatory, distinguished by its cool inner spiral ramp, wide enough for a coach and horses to climb.

The disastrous fires of the 18th century meant that little domestic architecture survives from Christian's reign, apart from the modest houses at **Magstræde 17-19**.

BAROQUE & ROCOCO 1648-1759

Christian IV's successor, Christian V, completed the fortifications at **Kastellet** in 1660. The most striking of the buildings within its five-pronged bastions is the yellow-stuccoed church.

Christian V also laid out Kongens Nytorv in the 1680s. **Charlottenborg palace** (1672-83) faces this most grand square on the corner of Nyhavn. The huge, sober baroque building marks a decisive break with the previously popular decorated-gable style.

An even better example of Danish baroque architecture is **Vor Frelsers Kirke** (Church of Our Saviour; 1682-96) in Christianshavn. It was built by Lambert van Haven, an expert in European baroque, and boasts a playful spire (1749), with external staircase.

French rococo ornamentation became popular in the mid 18th century. The aesthetic was used in the most ambitious project of the time: **Christiansborg Slot** (Christiansborg Palace; 1733-45; burned to the ground in 1794). A combination of pompous Italian baroque buildings with French rococo touches, it came to define Danish rococo style.

Børsen

Named after King Frederik V (reigned 1746-66), Frederiksstaden was the first major urban building project undertaken since Christian IV. Court architect Nicolai Eigtved masterminded an ambitious grid-plan quarter, the centrepiece of which were the palaces that today make up **Amalienborg Slot** (Amalienborg Palace; 1750-60), home of the royal family.

CLASSICISM 1759-1848

Christian Frederik Hansen was the central figure in Danish architecture during Denmark's so-called Golden Age (1800-50) and during his lifetime became an architect of international renown. The destruction caused by the fire of 1795 and the 1807 bombardment by the English provided a blank canvas for Hansen's disciplined romantic classicism. Fine examples include **Domhuset** (1805-15) on Nytorv and the minimalist **Christiansborg Slotskirke** (Christiansborg Palace Church; 1811-28). In contrast, MGB Bindesbøll's design for **Thorvaldsens Museum** (1839-48) is a late example of neo-classicism.

CIVIC PRIDE & ART NOUVEAU 1848-1914

Following 1848, the year of continent-wide revolutions, the new king Frederik VII accepted the end of absolute monarchy, ushering in a period of major civic building. Among the largest projects were Vilhelm Dahlerup and Ove Petersen's magnificent Italian Renaissance-style **Det Kongelige Theater** (Royal Theatre; 1872-4). Dahlerup was also responsible (along with Georg EV Møller) for the stodgy **Statens Museum For Kunst** (National Gallery; 1889-96) and the richly decorated **Ny Carlsberg Glyptotek** (New Carlsberg Sculpture Museum; 1892-7). Other significant public works built in the red-brick National Romantic style included Martin Nyrop's **Rådhuset** (Town Hall; 1892-1905) and Heinrich Wenck's **Hovedbanegården** (Central Station; 1904-11).

When CF Hansen's Christiansborg Slot burned to the ground in 1884, Thorvald Jørgensen designed its replacement, with its neo-rococo façade clad with 750 different types of granite.

NORDIC CLASSICISM 1914-28

Neutral Denmark had emerged from World War I in relative prosperity and turned its back on the romantic, nationalistic themes of the previous decades to develop a brutally ascetic version of classicism entirely its own.

Public housing projects, such as the massive **Hornebækhus** block by Kay Fisker, show Nordic classicism at its most uncompromising. Belonging to the same period is the sinister-looking **Politigården** (Police Headquarters; 1918-24). Why a social democratic state like Denmark would choose to build such a severe edifice – a chilling precursor of fascist architecture – remains something of a paradox.

Bike Copenhagen

Probably the most bike-friendly city in the world.

TEXT: ANNA NORMAN

Scandinavians are famous for using bicycles as everyday transport. And Danes cycle, on average, 600 kilometres (375 miles) per year. But Copenhageners take things a step further. Almost everyone – regardless of income or social status – cycles in this (famously flat) city. Some 37 per cent of all commuter trips in Copenhagen are made by bike on the city's famous blue bike lanes – a figure that rises to a whopping 55 per cent in the centre. What's more, Copenhageners take their cycling very seriously: woe betide anyone who, during rush hour, ventures out on the city's many kilometres of cycle paths with a faint heart. Copenhagen's two-wheeled commuters take no prisoners.

Propelled by the green movement, Copenhagen's bike culture has become a model for forward-thinking cities around the globe, to the point where a new verb, 'Copenhagenize', is now used to describe urban planning that emulates the city. Danish architect and urban designer Jan Gehl, whose consultancy is based in Copenhagen, is one of the key figures behind the growth in the city's bike lanes and cycling culture; throughout his 50-year career, Gehl has focused on improving the quality of urban life by reorienting city design towards the cyclist and pedestrian, and he's been hired as consultant by urban planning departments in cities worldwide, including London and New York.

And despite, or because of, the international attention, Copenhagen isn't resting on its (two-wheeled) laurels: the first city-to-suburb 'bicycle highways' are due to open at the end of 2011, and new 'green routes' are being built throughout the city.

'The bicycle rush hour is a sight to behold; join the throngs, and you'll feel a sense of community and belonging.'

THE URBAN CYCLING INFRASTRUCTURE

Although Copenhagen has had a strong cycling community since the start of the 20th century (its first bike lanes were created around the lakes in 1910, and cycling became an important means of transport during World War II), it wasn't until the 1980s that the city's present-day bike lanes, with their kerbs segregating cyclists from other road-users, came into effect. As elsewhere, the 1960s witnessed a decline in cycling culture in Copenhagen, with the increasing affordability of cars. But by the 1970s, cycling experienced a revival in the city, in line with the increasing green movement in Denmark. In the mid 1980s, local planners such as Jan Gehl began to develop the urban infrastructure for a bike- (and pedestrian-) friendly city, which now boasts some 390 kilometres (242 miles) of bike lanes. And from the early 1990s, cycling as a form of transportation has steadily risen year by year. Of course, the comparatively small size of the capital, and its flat terrain, are particularly conducive to a strong cycling community. But the extensive and well-designed system of bike lanes and cycle paths, along with other measures to encourage cycling – such as being able to easily take your bicycle on the Metro and local trains – are what has really earned the city the tag of 'most bike-friendly city in the world'.

The busiest cycling street is Copenhagen is Nørrebrogade, where, on the Dronning Louises Bridge, there's an electronic 'bike counter', showing the number of cyclists that have passed the spot since the start of the year. The bicycle paths have been widened along this stretch as part of the Nørrebrogade traffic pilot that began in October 2008, and today some 35,000 cyclists use the street every day. The bicycle rush hour is a sight to behold; join the throngs, and you'll feel a sense of community and belonging that just isn't possible in the confines of a car, where you're more tangibly separated from your fellow road-users.

The city's 100 kilometres (62 miles) of new 'green routes' aim to provide especially safe and green routes in the city, away from automobile traffic, and include the creation of new green spaces. Some 41 kilometres (25 miles) have already been completed, including the Nørrebro green route, which runs from Emdrup in the north to Valby in the south. Further green routes will continue to be rolled out over the next few years. And Copenhagen's first city-to-suburb 'bicycle highways', which will see the city's cycling infrastructure extend to the suburbs and beyond, are due to open at the end of 2011, with more planned for completion in 2012. The highways are connected with Copenhagen being selected as the International Cycling Union's (Union Cycliste Internationale; UCI) first 'Bike City'. The goal is for 50 per cent of Copenhagen's inhabitants to be cycling to work or school by 2015. Bike City Copenhagen also featured a series of big cycling events and races in and around the city as part of Bike City Copenhagen between 2008 and 2011, including various track and BMX championships.

ETIQUETTE AND PRACTICALITIES

There are certain cast-iron rules which foreigners should take note of when cycling around the city. For instance, passengers at bus stops (either embarking or disembarking) have right of way: all cyclists must stop and wait until the bus doors have closed. Left-hand turns on main roads are not permitted for cyclists: you must dismount and cross the road (with the green man, of course) as a pedestrian would. As a rule, you should ride on the right-hand side of the cycle path; if someone rings a bell behind you (never more than once, that

IN CONTEXT

is considered rude), it is to indicate that you should move over and let them pass on the left. When you want to stop, raise your right hand (in a fey salute) to signal this to other cyclists. None of these rules apply to cycle couriers, however. They do as they please.

Copenhageners may seem like a trustworthy bunch, yet bicycle theft is surprisingly common here. So remember to lock your bike, even if you're just popping into a shop. Most bikes in Copenhagen have locks built in to the back wheel, meaning that locking up is quick and simple. You should also make sure that you use lights at night, lest you get pulled over by local police.

It's possible to take bikes on the Metro and on S-trains, local, regional and InterCity trains outside rush hour. All trains require a special bike ticket, which can be purchased at the station. Most S-trains have a special area for bikes.

Copenhageners are a hardy bunch, and many cycle all year round – even in January snow blizzards. Local authorities efficiently keep the bike lanes gritted throughout the winter, ensuring that the bike is a viable form of transport even in the coldest months.

BIKE HIRE AND CYCLE TOURS

Between April and October, the city operates a public bike rental scheme called **Bycykler** (City Bikes); put a 20kr piece in the slot to borrow a bike from one of the 125 bike deposits around town. The sponsored, colourful gearless bikes are only good for short journeys, however, and by midsummer many of the 2,500 have disappeared or lie in ruins. A new, more modern City Bike model will be released in 2013.

A better bet is to rent a bike from a bike shop (*see Directory: Getting Around*). This usually costs from 100kr per day (it becomes cheaper the longer you rent) for a simple three-speeder. Bikes can often be hired directly from hotels, but it's often cheaper to go direct to the rental places, such as **København Cykler** (Reventlowgade 11, 33 33 86 13, www.copenhagen-bikes.dk) and **Baisikeli** (Turesensgade 10, 26 70 02 29, www.baisikeli.dk). The latter is a well-priced and ethical bike-hire organisation and the starting point for the **Bike with Mike** cycle tours (45 26 39 56 88, www.bikecopenhagenwith mike.dk). These aim to get off the tourist trails to experience Copenhagen from a different perspective. Tours focus on the city's history, architecture and modern design, heading through the centre, around the Royal palace, along the canals, and over to the northern tip of Frederiksstaden. The tours cost 260kr, payable in cash.

For further information on Copenhagen's cycling culture and community, visit Mikael Colville-Andersen's **Cycle Chic** blog (www.copenhagencyclechic.com). Known for his eschewing of Lycra, bike helmets and carbon-fibre frames, Colville-Andersen is something of an ambassador for Copenhagen's cycling community, and a keen proponent of cycling in everyday (which means very fashionable in Copenhagen) clothes. Colville-Andersen is also one of the figures behind the organisation **Copenhagenize** (www.copenhagenize. com), a key player in the move to improve cycling urban infrastructure worldwide.

For details of bike shops in Copenhagen, *see p160*. For information on the city's iconic Christiania cargo bikes, *see p170* **Profile**.

IN CONTEXT

Sights

Nyhavn. *See p61.*

Tivoli & Rådhuspladsen	**44**
The Best Places To Go	51
Strøget & Around	**54**
Profile Pølsevogne	59
Nyhavn & Kongens Nytorv	**61**
Profile Hans Christian Andersen	63
Slotsholmen	**65**
Profile Bertel Thorvaldsen	69
Frederiksstaden	**71**
Walk Parks & Palaces	72
Rosenborg & Around	**76**
Christianshavn	**80**
Come On In, the Water's Lovely	83
Vesterbro & Frederiksberg	**85**
Brewing Up a Cultural Storm	86

Nørrebro & Østerbro	**90**
Dead Famous	91
Further Afield	**94**

Tivoli & Rådhuspladsen

Copenhagen's wonderland, and the city's central square.

In many ways, a visit to **Tivoli** is the definitive Danish experience. It is the ultimate expression of *'hygge'*, the unique type of cosiness that the Danes strive to create in all aspects of their lives: there are thrill rides, but none is too extreme (apart from the Demon rollercoaster, perhaps); there are hot dogs and candy floss and beer; and a host of family entertainments, from jugglers to parades.

Not far from Tivoli's gates are some of Copenhagen's major landmarks, including Arne Jacobsen's world-famous, 22-storey Radisson SAS Royal Hotel (*see p99*) – a must for design enthusiasts; the Ny Carlsberg Glyptotek, with its breathtaking line-up of ancient sculptures, and Denmark's National Museum (Nationalmuseet). Also nearby is the city's focal point and central meeting place, **Rådhuspladsen** (Town Hall Square), dominated by the magnificient Town Hall.

| **Map** p250 | **Restaurants** p111 |
| **Hotels** p98 | **Cafes & Bars** p128 |

TIVOLI

Whenever plans are introduced to change Tivoli's appearance, usually to include a fierce new ride, protests erupt. And not just from touchy neighbours who have come to dread half a year of all-day shrieking. The old ladies with season tickets, the visitors from abroad, all the Danes who remember their first visit like it was yesterday – everyone wants the 'Old Garden' to stay more or less the same.

The fact that year after year Tivoli attracts major international artists, albeit those with severe MOR tendencies – people like Tony Bennett, the Beach Boys and Phil Collins – to its open-air stage is testament to its pulling power. Michael Jackson tried to buy the whole place after he played there in the early 1990s, as did Disney a few years back. But the very idea of their beloved Tivoli falling into the hands of Americans, especially Disney, horrified the nation and there was an outcry. The park's long-time owners, Carlsberg, had no qualms, however,

about selling a 43.4 per cent stake to Scandinavian Tobacco in 2000 (the rest is owned by Danish banks and small investors).

Tivoli's glitzy blend of escapist, fairytale gaiety and defiant traditionalism may not be to all tastes, but even the most cynical visitor usually finds themselves won over by its relentless, wide-eyed schmaltz. This is Denmark's No.1 tourist attraction (beating even Legoland on Jylland) and an incredible 4.5 million visitors (a figure close to the national population) pass through the gates each summer. In all, over 300 million people have visited in over a century.

So what is so special about this relatively small, 80,000-square-metre (20-acre) plot of land, sandwiched between Central Station and Rådhuspladsen? By day Tivoli is undoubtedly charming, with its picturesque lake, wide range of rides, over-priced but cosy restaurants and magnificent flowerbeds. It has a particular atmosphere – part traditional beer garden, part Victorian pleasure park, part (whisper it)

Tivoli.

Disneyland. But it isn't really until night falls, when the 100,000 specially made soft-glow light bulbs and over a million standard bulbs are switched on, and the scenery becomes a kaleidoscope of diffused colour (there is no neon here, and the place is a mecca for lighting technicians from all over the world) that the magical transformation from amusement park to dreamland takes place. Passers-by can only glimpse through the trees the beguiling world within and hear distant squeals from the rollercoasters, as Tivoli enters its nightly childhood Twilight Zone. The place becomes genuinely special when night falls, seeming to expand and transform into something really rather, dare we say, magical.

But you might like to OK a visit with your bank manager beforehand. Tivoli is expensive, with a steep entrance fee (75kr-125kr) that verges on the ridiculous once you get in and discover that you have to pay extra (typically 25kr) for the rides. And brace yourself for the bill if you dine: Tivoli's many restaurants are among the dearest in the city.

History

Like most Copenhagen landmarks, Tivoli has royal roots. In 1841 King Christian VIII was vexed by the burgeoning civil unrest in his country and his increasingly untenable position as absolute monarch, and, so the story goes, he allowed the Danish architect Georg Carstensen to build the park as a distraction. 'When people amuse themselves they forget politics,' the king is reputed to have said. Carstensen, a self-made publishing magnate and son of a diplomat, was born in Algiers in 1812. Tivoli grew out of a carnival he arranged for his readers in Kongens Nytorv. Its success is thought to have swayed

the king in favour of a permanent site for public pleasure. His new park would blend three main ingredients: light, fairytales and music, the king's only condition being that the park would not contain 'anything ignoble and degrading'. The original Tivoli, little changed today, was based on similar gardens then extant in Paris and London and named after the little Italian town near Rome known for its fountains.

The park opened on 15 August 1843 and welcomed 16,000 visitors on its first day, Hans Christian Andersen among them. However, for Carstensen, the park's success was bittersweet. Buoyed by its popularity, he attempted to repeat the formula abroad, but failed abjectly. The board of directors at Tivoli became increasingly concerned about his outlandish and expensive projects until, finally, after one argument too many, Carstensen left in dudgeon for America. Legend has it that upon his return years later, the guard at the turnstiles failed to recognise him and he had to pay to get in. Carstensen died a bankrupt, aged 45.

Unlike many other amusement parks, Tivoli is now right in the centre of the city. But it wasn't always so. When it was built, the park stood in the countryside among fields dotted with cattle and crops, on land that was once part of Copenhagen's old fortifications, donated by the government. Today, Tivoli Lake is the model of picturesque charm, boasting flower borders, weeping willows and, at night, illuminated dragonflies, but it used to be part of the city's defensive moat (the remains of which can be seen in the lakes of Botanisk Have Ørstedsparken and Østre Anlæg park).

In 1944, Tivoli's peace was shattered by the occupying forces of Nazi Germany who were quick to recognise the significance of the park to the Danish people. They used it as a target for retaliatory attacks following the increased activity of the Danish Resistance. The main victim was the original Concert Hall. Within a week the resilient Danes had erected a tent in the grounds to replace it. A permanent, new hall (still standing) was built in 1956.

Many of the buildings constructed in Tivoli in the post-war era were seen by Denmark's architects as an opportunity to let their creative hair down and so the park is packed with boisterous structures. Elsewhere many might have been outlawed on grounds of taste, but in Tivoli they somehow seem appropriate.

A tour of Tivoli

There are three entrances to Tivoli: one is located opposite the main entrance to Hovedbanegården (Central Station), another lies across the road from the Ny Carlsberg Glyptotek, but by far the grandest is the

SIGHTS

INSIDE TRACK
TIVOLI AT CHRISTMAS

In late 1994 a new Tivoli tradition started: the Christmas Market, which has since become a fixture on Copenhagen's calendar (*see p167*). Though many of the rides don't run at this time of year, there's lots to do, and many of Tivoli's food outlets serve seasonal fare, such as traditional roast pork, rice pudding and *æbleskiver* (a kind of mini doughnut), all washed down with *glögg* (mulled red wine). The gardens also play host to a large market, selling decorations and gifts, and Father and Mother Christmas administer yuletide cheer. If you think Tivoli is saccharin in summer, wait till you get a load of this.

SIGHTS

main gate (on Vesterbrogade), a Renaissance-inspired confection decorated with Corinthian columns and a dome, dating from 1889. On the right as you enter is a statue to the garden's architect, Georg Carstensen. In front of you, beside the extraordinary Moorish façade of Restaurant Nimb (breathtaking at night), is a Perspex fountain, with bubbling tubes, like a gigantic lava lamp. It was designed by the Nobel Prize-winning Danish physicist Niels Bohr. On your left is the Peacock Theatre, while before you is Plænen (the Lawn), the open-air concert venue. Beyond that is the 1956 Tivolis Koncertsal, a camp orgy of pastel colours.

There are over 30 rides to choose from in Tivoli, from tame roundabouts decorated with winsome HC Andersen characters, to the newer Star Flyer carousel and the mad exhilaration of Det Gyldne Tårn (the Golden Tower) vertical drop. The tower was likened by one sniffy critic to a high tension pylon, but few rides unleash the butterflies with quite the force of this terrifying 63-metre (207-foot) vertical drop. At night, from the top, you can see Sweden twinkling in the distance from the top. Predictably, the tower, which, like much of Tivoli, is designed in a faux-Arabian style, has prompted accusations of blatant Disneyfication from the older generation of Tivoleans. They would prefer that time had stood still with the tepid wooden rollercoaster, constructed in 1914 and still running.

All the traditional fun of the fair is here too, including shooting alleys, electronic arcade games, a hall of mirrors, bumper cars, a test-your-strength machine, an execrable chamber of horrors, the unintentionally creepy HC Andersen fairytale ride, and Det Muntre Køkken (the Crazy Kitchen), where you can vent pent-up frustration by hurling tennis balls at crockery targets. The hot air balloon Ferris wheel, dating from 1943, is a traditional focus for courting couples.

Many visitors, particularly the elderly, who flock here in their thousands, come simply to enjoy the flora. Tivoli boasts hundreds of trees (lime, chestnut, weeping willow and elm) and many more flowers within its perimeter fence. The flowers help to keep the park visually fresh throughout the season – if you visit during spring the tulips will be out, followed by the rhododendrons, then roses, lilacs and laburnum with the summer and, by when the park closes for winter, the chrysanthemums are in bloom.

Slightly contrary to its fairytale image, Tivoli has its own nightclub, open Thursday to Saturday. Although it can hardly be said to push the envelope of contemporary club culture, Mantra Nightclub is still fun for teens, and for many Danes it's their first taste of clubbing.

Performance venues

Tivoli is a riotous collage of architectural styles, from Moorish palaces to Chinese towers, with everything in between. The oldest building in the park is the remarkable outdoor Chinese-style **Peacock Theatre**, designed by Vilhelm Dahlerup (also responsible for Det Kongelige Teater) in 1874. It stages classical pantomime in the tradition of commedia dell'arte. The performances are complex, hard-to-follow shows, starring Pierrot, Harlequin and Columbine, but are worth a look if only to see this extraordinary theatre, operated only by cords and pulleys. The theatre's 'curtain' is a peacock's tail feathers, which fold back to reveal the stage. The oriental theme is echoed elsewhere in the park – a legacy of Georg Carstensen's peripatetic childhood, which fuelled a love of exotic cultures – in the **Chinese Pagoda**.

Plænen (*see p199*) is Tivoli's largest venue. Most of its (capacity) 50,000-strong audience stands in the open air before the circus-like stage. This is where returning Danish heroes (rare, but it does happen occasionally), such as the 2000 Eurovision Song Contest winners the Olsen Brothers, are feted by the crowds, and where big events are celebrated. Performances – musical and otherwise – are twice nightly (international acrobats are a speciality). A recent, popular innovation has been the Friday Rock Concerts. Danish bands usually headline, but each year an international star or two is booked as a treat, free of charge. Naturally, these acts draw huge crowds, so arrive early.

Every Saturday evening visitors are treated to a fireworks display. After over a hundred years with the Barfod family, the new fireworks choreographer is Michael Wullf Pedersen, only

---

INSIDE TRACK
GAUGUIN'S DANISH PERIOD

Paul Gauguin lived in Copenhagen for one winter, at Gammel Kongevej 105 (long since demolished) in Frederiksberg. The broke artist had married a Danish woman, Mette Sofie Gad, whom he met in Paris in 1873, and moved to his wife's home. Gauguin never got to grips with the weather, the coldness of the Danes or the suffocating ways of the bourgeoisie, though he did stay long enough to hold his first ever exhibition at the Kunstforeningen (Arts Society). Gauguin fathered five children with Mette during their nine-year marriage (the rest of which they spent in France), and has over 50 descendants living in Denmark. Several of his works are displayed in the Ny Carlsberg Glyptotek (*see p51*)

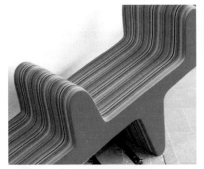

Dansk Design Center. *See p50.*

the eighth powder supremo in Tivoli's history. The bombshells are no longer handmade in Denmark, mostly for financial reasons, but still look (and sound) spectacular in or around the gardens.

Throughout the summer you can also catch parades and performances by the Tivoli Garden Guard, a children's marching band, founded in 1844, and made up of a 100 or so local boys aged nine to 16. The Guard is on holiday for two weeks in mid July.

The renowned **Tivolis Koncertsal** (*see p194*), which seats 1,900, is home to the Sjælland Symphony Orchestra and visiting orchestras, ballet companies, ensembles and soloists of world repute also play here. You'll recognise the hall by the row of Danish flags along the front of its roof.

★ Tivoli

Vesterbrogade 3 (33 15 10 01, ticket centre 33 15 10 12, www.tivoli.dk). Train København H. **Open** *Mid Apr-mid June, mid Aug-mid Sept* 11am-11pm Mon-Wed, Sun; 11am-midnight Thur, Sat; 11am-1am Fri. *Mid June-mid Aug* 11am-midnight Mon-Thur, Sun; 11am-1am Fri, Sat. *Halloween* Dates & times vary. *Christmas Market* (late Nov-30

Dec 11am-10pm Sun-Thur; 11am-midnight Fri, Sat. Closed 24 & 25 Dec. *Ticket Centre* 11am-8pm daily. **Admission** 75kr-125kr; 48kr concessions. **Credit** AmEx, MC, V. **Map** p250 P12.

AROUND TIVOLI

From Tivoli's main gates (and, in fact, from just about anywhere in Copenhagen) you can see Arne Jacobsen's world-famous, 22-storey **Radisson SAS Royal Hotel** (*see p99*). It dates from 1960, though that's hard to believe given its uncompromisingly functional lines. With his customary all-encompassing attention to detail, Jacobsen designed not only the exterior, but the interior too, right down to the cutlery still used in the restaurant.

Across the road from the hotel, you'll find the **Wonderful Copenhagen Tourist Information Bureau, Copenhagen Right Now** (which offers plenty of material in English). A little further down the street stands **Hovedbanegården** (Central Station), from where you can catch trains to the airport, the rest of the country and beyond. The station, which dates from 1911, has a well-equipped centre for Interrailers, complete with showers

SIGHTS

Nationalmuseet.

and lockers, not to mention several food outlets, a bank, a police station and a bookshop.

Close by is the **Copenhagen Plaza** (*see p98*) with its wood-panelled **Library Bar** (*see p126*), redolent of an English gentlemen's club (this being Denmark, women are admitted).

Immediately north of the main entrance to Tivoli is Copenhagen's cinema district. Here you'll find several cinemas, all within a few minutes' walk (*see p174*). To the south-east of Tivoli is the **Ny Carlsberg Glyptotek**. As a member of Sjælland's quartet of world-class art collections (the others are Arken, Louisiana and Statens Museum for Kunst), the Ny Carlsberg Glyptotek has much to live up to. But with a breathtaking line-up of ancient sculptures, the largest collection of Etruscan art outside Italy, as well as an exceptional array of more recent Danish and French paintings and sculpture, it more than holds its own in such vaunted company. And with the opening in 1996 of a well-received extension by the Danish architect Henning Larsen, the Glyptotek boasts a thoroughly modern, yet intimate, space for its impressive collection of French Impressionist paintings. A little further up HC Andersens Boulevard is the **Dansk Design Center** (Danish Design Centre). This beautiful five-storey, 86-million-kroner complex is a centre for education, research and exhibitions.

Head east from HC Andersens Boulevard and you come to **Nationalmuseet** (National Museum). Housed in a sumptuous former royal palace, boasting some of the finest rooms in the city, and extensively modernised in recent years, Denmark's National Museum is the country's oldest historical collection, with its origins as Frederik II's Royal Cabinet of Curiosities (c1650). It focuses, naturally, on Danish culture and history, but there are also world-class Egyptian, Greek, Roman and ethnographic departments. All exhibits have excellent English captions.

★ **Dansk Design Center**
HC Andersens Boulevard 27 (33 69 33 69, www.ddc.dk). Train København H. **Open** 10am-5pm Mon, Tue, Thur, Fri; 10am-9pm Wed; 11am-4pm Sat, Sun. **Admission** 55kr; 30kr concessions; free under-12s. **Credit** AmEx, MC, V. **Map** p251 P13.
Like the nearby Glyptotek extension, the Danish Design Centre was designed by Henning Larsen and opened in January 2000. The basement of the Design Centre is given over to classics from the past, as well as international design icons, while the ground and first floor house temporary exhibitions, both of Danish and international designs. These might focus on one particular designer, a huge corporate manufacturer or a theme such as recycling. The centre has a café and a small shop that sells books and Danish design items. *Photos p49.*

Nationalmuseet

*Frederiksholms Kanal 12 (33 13 44 11,
www.natmus.dk). Bus 1, 2, 8, 10, 11A.*
Open 10am-5pm Tue-Sun. **Admission**
25kr; free under-16s. Free to all Wed.
Credit AmEx, MC, V. **Map** p251 O13.

The National Museum's main home is in Prinsens
Palæ (Prince's Palace). Visitors enter via a large, airy
main hall, once a courtyard, but now enclosed with
a glass roof, which also acts occasionally as a venue
for concerts. To the right, on the ground floor, you
enter the Prehistoric Wing, showing Danish history
from the reindeer hunters of the Ice Age to the
Vikings. Here you can marvel at archaeological finds
from the Early Bronze Age unearthed in Denmark's
bogs – the most impressive of which is the collection
of large bronze horns, or lurs (some still playable),
played to appease the sun god.

Upstairs, the glorious Medieval and Renaissance
department covers the pre- and post-Reformation
periods, and majors on ecclesiastical and decorative
art. Pieces here come from the era of the great
Renaissance kings: Christian III, Frederik II and
Christian IV. The surviving example of Frederik's
tapestries of kings, made for the Great Hall of
Kronborg Slot, is a marvel.

The Royal Collection of Coins and Medals, though
one of the more specialist sections in the museum, is
intriguing. It is said to be one of the most beautiful
in the city, and has views over Marmorbroen
(Marble Bridge) and Christiansborg Slot. On the top
floor is the museum's Collection of Antiquities, a
mini take on the British Museum, with pieces from
Egypt, Greece and Italy. On the same floor is a
charming toy museum, which begins with a mention
of a rattle in Saxo Grammaticus's *Gesta Danorum*
and continues through early 16th-century German
toys, a spectacular array of doll's houses, Lego (of
course) and toy soldiers. Though the main museum
is excellent for kids, in the basement is a Children's
Museum, which attempts to condense all the rest of
the museum into an exhibition suitable for four- to
12-year-olds.

★ Ny Carlsberg Glyptotek

*Dantes Plads 7 (33 41 81 41, www.glyptoteket.dk).
Train København H.* **Open** 11am-5pm Tue-Sun.
Admission 75kr; 50kr concessions; free under-
18s. Free to all Sun. **Credit** MC, V.
Map p251 P13.

The original *glyptotek* (sculpture collection) was
donated to the city in 1888 by the brewer/philan-
thropist Carl Jacobsen (son of the founder of the
Carlsberg brewery, IC Jacobsen) and his wife Ottilia.
He intended the museum to have 'a beauty all its
own, to which the people of the city would feel themselves irresistibly drawn'. His vision has been
financed, run and expanded by the Ny Carlsberg
Foundation for more than a century and is housed
in a building rich in architectural delights that was
specially designed for the original collection by

Vilhelm Dahlerup and Hack Kampmann. During the
summer of 2006, three years of renovation and
expansion was completed. There is now better
access for disabled visitors; the entire cellar level has
been revamped, and the whole collection is displayed
in brighter surroundings. The highlight of the old
building is the glass-domed Winter Garden – a
steamy palm house bursting with monster subtrop-
ical plants and graced by Kai Nielsen's beautiful
fountain piece *Water Mother with Children*. The
Winter Garden's café is a popular meeting place for
art-loving Copenhageners.

The Glyptotek's thousands of pieces can be
roughly divided into two groups: ancient
Mediterranean, and 18th- and 19th-century French
and Danish. The first four rooms are dedicated to
the oldest pieces, some dating back 5,000 years (the
Egyptian hippopotamus is a crowd favourite). The
exhibits proceed to trace the history of sculpture
from the Sumerians, Assyrians, Persians and
Phoenicians, through to a collection of ancient Greek
pieces (one of the best in Europe) and some highly
entertaining, privately commissioned Roman busts.
Jacobsen's Etruscan collection – including bronzes,
vases, and stone and terracotta sculptures – is
another highlight.

The French painting collection is housed in
Larsen's intriguing extension. It includes 35 works
by the post-Impressionist Paul Gauguin (*see p48*
Inside Track) and is home to one of only three
complete sets of Degas bronzes in the world (includ-
ing a ballerina in an original, evocative tulle cos-
tume). There is also an array of paintings by the
Impressionist movement's leading lights, including
Manet, Renoir, Monet, Pissarro and a remarkable
self-portrait by Cézanne. The rest of the post-
Impressionist movement is represented by Van
Gogh, Toulouse-Lautrec and Bonnard.

THE BEST PLACES TO GO

Botanisk Have
For a walk in the park. *See p77.*

Von Freisers Kirke
To get closer to heaven, with a wonderful
city view. *See p81.*

Tivoli
For a day out with the kids. *See p49.*

Nationalmuseet
For a history lesson. *See above.*

Amalienborg Slot
For a glimpse of the royals. *See p71.*

Islands Brygge
For a summertime dip. *See p83.*

SIGHTS

Over 30 works by Auguste Rodin dominate the French sculpture rooms. Another surprise awaits in the collection of Danish sculpture: for those who think that Danish sculpture began and ended with Bertel Thorvaldsen, other leading lights (Dahl, Købke and Eckersberg) are also represented, though the collection of the Danish Golden Age (1815-50) is surpassed by those of Statens Museum For Kunst and Den Hirschsprungske Samling (*see p78*).

RÅDHUSPLADSEN

Tivoli's neighbour to the east is the usually frenetic **Rådhuspladsen** (Town Hall Square). Though the square is less architecturally appealing than Kongens Nytorv at the other end of Strøget, Denmark's answer to Times Square and Piccadilly Circus is more friendly to pedestrians and, at night, when the neon adverts on the surrounding offices are lit up, quite spectacular. This square, stretching out from **Rådhuset** (Town Hall), bustles constantly with a mixture of commuters (the city's bus terminus is here), shoppers, sightseers, *pølse* (Danish hot dog) sellers and, on weekends and holidays, street performers, gatherings and protests. The square is an important focal point for Copenhageners and Danes as a whole (Denmark's matches are shown here on a big screen during The World Cups, for instance). It is also the prime gathering point for New Year's Eve celebrations. And, in the holiday season, a gigantic Christmas tree is lit up in the square on the first Sunday of Advent.

Rådhuspladsen is part of the original site of Havn, the small fishing village that stretched to Gammeltorv and down to the sea before Bishop Absalon set it on its course to regional domination. By the 13th century the city rampart, protected by a moat, stretched from Vester Voldgade on the eastern side of the

square, along Nørre Voldgade and down Gothersgade to what is now Kongens Nytorv, in a defensive arc that marks the boundaries of medieval Copenhagen. All that remains of those medieval fortifications today is Jarmers Tårn, a small ruin located on a roundabout in Jarmers Plads (at the north end of Vester Voldgade). The square itself lay outside the ramparts as it was used (up until 1850) as a haymarket and there was a risk of fire. The layout of the streets within the medieval ramparts also remains virtually intact from that period – a blind Copenhagener from the 14th century could probably still find his way from Rådhuspladsen to Købmagergade (if he didn't become disoriented by the smell from kebab vendors).

Rådhuspladsen is also where the last western city gate stood until the middle of the 19th century. In 1888 the square hosted a million visitors at a huge exhibition of industry, agriculture and art. At that time the square was designed in a shell shape, like the famous main piazza in Siena, but the pressures of the internal combustion engine soon saw its corners squared off.

There's lots to see in and around this area. On HC Andersens Boulevard is a large statue of guess who? In front of that stands the striking Dragon Fountain, by Joachim Skovgaard. Nearby is a small carved stone pillar that marks the centre or 'zero point' of Copenhagen. And high on the corner of the Unibank building on HC Andersens Boulevard and Vesterbrogade is one of the city's quirkiest talking points: a barometer erected in 1936 and designed by Danish artist E Utzon-Frank, featuring a girl on a bicycle (if it's fair) or under an umbrella (if it's not).

Towering over the opposite side of Rådhuset is a pillar crowned by a bronze statue of two Vikings blowing lurs (S-shaped bronze horns). These are similar to the ones you can see in Nationalmuseet. The statue, by Siegfried Wagner, was erected in 1914. Next to the pillar is the elegant façade of the Anton Rosen-designed **Palace Hotel** (*see p101*).

Next door is **Ripley's Believe It or Not Museum**, part of a worldwide chain of freak shows based on an idea by the American showman Robert Ripley. Housed (or rather crammed) within the same complex is a new and, sadly, pitiful **Hans Christian Andersen** exhibition, cobbled together to coincide with the 200th anniversary of his birth in 2005, and featuring fibreglass reconstructions of 'olde world' Odense streets and a few factoids about the great man's life. And little else. Bearing in mind that Copenhagen was Andersen's home from the age of 14 onwards, it is sad bordering on outrageous that it is the only permanent exhibition about the writer in the city.

INSIDE TRACK
JENS OLSEN'S WORLD CLOCK

Rådhuset (*see right*) is home to an horological masterpiece, **Jens Olsens Verdensur**. The clock cost one million kroner to build (and 27 years to make; it was first set in 1955) and is very accurate, losing only milliseconds each century. It displays the local time, sidereal time (gauged by the motion of the earth relative to the fixed background of distant stars, rather than the sun), firmament and celestial pole movement, the movement of the planets, and sunrises and sunsets. The clock is in a room on the right by Rådhuset's main door.

Rådhuset.

Rådhuset, situated on the southern side of Rådhuspladsen, is the city's administrative and political heart, as well as a venue for exhibitions and concerts. Denmark's second tallest tower (105.6 metres/346 feet; the tallest, is part of Christiansborg Slot), located on its east side, is almost incidental to the decorative splendour of this, the sixth town hall in Copenhagen's history.

Rådhuset
Rådhuspladsen (33 66 25 82/83, www.kk.dk). Train København H. **Open** *7.45am-5pm Mon-Fri; 9.30am-1pm Sat; closed Sun. Guided tour June-Sept 1pm (3pm in English) Mon-Fri; 10am, 11am Sat. Oct-May 10am, 1pm, 2pm (3pm in English). Rådhuset Tower tour 11am, 2pm Mon-Fri; noon Sat. Jens Olsens Verdensur 8.30am-4.30pm Mon-Fri; 9.30am-1pm Sat.* **Admission** *Rådhuset guided tour 30kr. Rådhuset Tower tour 20kr. Jens Olsens Verdensur 10kr; 5kr concessions.* **Credit** AmEx, MC. V.
Map p250 O12.
Completed in 1905, Rådhuset has been the site of numerous elections; home to as many city administrations; endured occupation by the Nazis during World War II; and welcomed the returning football heroes from the 1992 European Championships, when Schmeichel, Laudrup and company famously brought the city to a standstill during their appearance on the balcony overlooking Rådhuspladsen.

At first glance Rådhuset, inspired, like the square, by its Sienese counterpart, looks imposing, monolithic and a little bit dull, but at close quarters this national romantic masterpiece by architect Martin Nyrop reveals its witty, sometimes grue-some, but invariably exuberant architectural detail. The balcony is above the front door and above that is a golden statue by HW Bissen of Bishop Absalon. Higher up, lining the front of the roof, stand six watchmen, separated by the city flagpole (watch for a swallow-tailed flag on special occasions, such as the Queen's birthday). This rises from the city's coat of arms, presented in 1661 by King Frederik III in thanks for the people's support during a city siege. Across the façade are countless gargoyles, reliefs and individually crafted stone and iron figures (check out the hilarious walruses guarding the back door), while by the right-hand side of the entrance are three grotesque bronze dragon-gargoyles, hunched as if ready to spring into action.

Inside, Rådhuset's endless corridors, halls, council chambers and meeting rooms offer a decorative feast. Highlights include busts of HC Andersen, the physicist Niels Bohr, Professor Nyrop and sculptor Bertel Thorvaldsen, the library and the banqueting hall. An information office, where you can also buy tickets to Jens Olsen's World Clock (*see left* **Jens Olsen's World clock**) and the tower, is to the left of the main door.

Ripley's Believe It Or Not Museum
Rådhuspladsen 57 (33 91 89 91, www.ripleys.dk). Train København H. **Open** *Sept-Mid June 10am-6pm Mon-Thur, Sun; 10am-8pm Fri, Sat. Mid June-Aug 10am-10pm daily.* **Admission** *85kr; 43kr-68kr concessions.* **Credit** MC, V.
Map p250 O12.
The grotesque bric-a-brac on display here includes two-headed animals, voodoo dolls and Papua New Guinean penis sheaths.

Strøget & Around

Welcome to the shopping quarter.

Strøget might be the best-known street in Copenhagen, but you won't always find its name on maps of the city. That's because Strøget (meaning 'stripe' and often referred to as 'the walking street') is actually made up of five streets – Østergade, Amagertorv, Nygade, Vimmelskaftet and Frederiksberggade – running from Kongens Nytorv at its eastern end, more than a kilometre (0.6 of a mile) to Rådhuspladsen in the west. Formerly called Routen, the streets became so congested with traffic by the early 1960s that extreme measures were necessary: the whole thing was temporarily turned into a pedestrian zone in 1962. It was so successful, two years later the arrangement was made permanent. These days it's hard to imagine it filled with cars.

Behind the eastern end of Strøget, around Købmagergade and Kronprinsensgade, lie some of the city's best shopping streets, lined with fashion boutiques specialising in stylish Scandinavian labels.

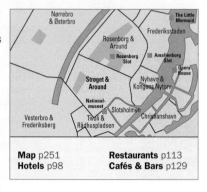

| Map p251 | Restaurants p113 |
| Hotels p98 | Cafés & Bars p129 |

SIGHTS

GETTING YOUR BEARINGS

Broadly speaking, Strøget becomes more downmarket as you approach Rådhuspladsen at the western end, with the posh shops, like Gucci and Prada, as well as global chains such as Urban Outfitters and Topshop, clustered at the eastern end towards Kongens Nytorv. The 'posh watershed' is Amagertorv, where you'll find the Royal Copenhagen stores. The middle of Strøget from Amagertorv to Gammeltorv and Nytorv is middlebrow, dotted with the likes of H&M and Zara, while beyond there is a touristy mix of kebab shops and souvenir shops. Keep in mind, though, that 'downmarket' in Copenhagen is still very presentable.

Despite its cosmopolitan feel and stylish shopfronts, Strøget's medieval origins have ensured that it has retained an intimate charm. In fact, it makes Oxford Street or the Champs-Elysées look like motorways by comparison. And it helps make Copenhagen one of the most user-friendly shopping cities in the world.

EASTERN STRØGET & KØBMAGERGADE

As well as shops and cafés, Strøget has several museums. From Kongens Nytorv the first you arrive at is the **Guinness World Records Museum** (*see right*). Part of a chain, the Guinness museum lures in the passing crowds. Kids like it, though, and the fact that the **Mystic Exploratorie** (a mix of science and the supernatural; *see right*) moved here is a bonus.

Further down Strøget, you come to Sankt Nikolaj Kirke in historic Nikolaj Plads. The church is no longer used for services, but is home to the **Nikolaj – Copenhagen Contemporary Art Center** (*see p179*),

---

INSIDE TRACK
ROYAL COPENHAGEN

Quality porcelein brand Royal Copenhagen is a national treasure and one of the city's landmarks. In business for over two centuries, its signature dinnerware is internationally renowned and, since the opening of its flagship store's Royal Café (*see p132*) in 2007, the brand has been re-appropriated by the local fashion pack.

Rundetårn.

iron lattice; the letters RFP stand for the famously lecherous king's unlikely motto: *Regna Firmat Pietas* – 'Piety Strengthens the Realm'.

Just beside the tower, at its southern side, is one of the city's most popular *pølsevogne* (hotdog stands): the **DØP** pølsevogn, known for its healthier, organic hotdogs, served in sourdough bread (*see p59* **Pølsevogne**). Behind the tower stands **Trinitatiskirke** (Trinity Church; *see p57*), which was erected in 1637, and boasts a baroque altar by Friedrich Ehbisch, as well as a three-faced rococo clock from 1757. Opposite the Rundetårn you'll find **Regensen**, built in 1616 as a student hall of residence for the nearby university, and still in use as such today. Around the corner, on Krystalgade, is the city's **Synagoge** (synagogue), dating from 1833.

Towards the northern end of Købmagergade is **Kultorvet**, a large square that becomes gridlocked in summer with café tables, fruit and veg stalls and beer stands. Continue on over Nørre Voldgade (the northern boundary of the old city ramparts) and you arrive at **Israels Plads**. The square was named in honour of the the Danes who helped 7,000 Jews escape during World War II. Israels Plads hosts a large fruit and veg market daily and, on Saturdays in the summer, a small antiques and flea market.

which holds six shows a year. The church dates from the 13th century, but the fire of 1795 destroyed all but the tower; it was rebuilt in 1917. The square is a venue for the Copenhagen Jazz Festival.

Back on Strøget, among the designer stores, is **Illum**, the city's premier department store (*see venue index*), which stretches to the corner of **Købmagergade**, Strøget's pedestrian tributary. Kronprinsensgade, the area's fashion centre, is off Købmagergade, with numerous stores, plus two cafés and a great chocolate shop. Most of the streets north of Østergade (the first leg of Strøget) – Pilestræde, Grønnegade, Ny Adelgade and Ny Østergade – are eminently wanderable.

Back on Købmagergade is the **Post & Tele Museum** (*see p55*), a surprisingly well-presented museum dedicated to the 400-year history of Denmark's communications services. Visit the rooftop café with views of the old town to rival the Rundetårn's (here there's a lift). It's open afternoons, and late on Wednesdays, when it has a Danish and international menu.

A little further up is Købmagergade's other main draw: the **Rundetårn** (Round Tower; *see p57*). Completed in 1642 at the behest of Christian IV (it was his last major building project), the red-brick Rundetårn was originally intended as an observatory for the nearby university, and is still the oldest functioning observatory in Europe. Christian is commemorated on the front in a wrought

Guinness World Records Museum & Mystic Exploratorie

Østergade 16 (33 32 31 31, www.guinness.dk). Metro Kongens Nytorv. **Open** *Mid June-Aug* 10am-10pm (last entry 9.30pm) daily. *Sept-mid June* 10am-6pm Mon-Thur, Sun; 10am-8pm Fri, Sat. **Admission** *Museum* 85kr; 43kr-68kr concessions; free under-4s. *Mystic Exploratorie* 67kr; 34kr-54kr concessions; free under-4s. **Credit** MC, V. **Map** p251 M15.

Amagertorv, Strøget.

FREE Post & Tele Museum
Købmagergade 37 (33 41 09 00, www.ptt-museum.dk). Metro/train Nørreport. **Open** 10am-4pm daily. **Admission** free. **Credit** MC, V. **Map** p251 M14.

★ Rundetårn
Købmagergade 52A (33 73 03 73, www.rundetaarn.dk). Metro/train Nørreport. **Open** *Tower* Late May-Late Sept 10am-8pm daily. Late Sept-Late May 10am-5pm daily. *Observatory* Mid Oct-Mid Mar 7-10pm Tue, Wed. **Admission** 25kr; 5kr concessions; free under-5s. **Credit** AmEx, MC, V. **Map** p251 M13.

The Rundetårn is unique in European architecture for its cobbled spiral walkway that winds seven-and-a-half times round its core for 209 metres (686 feet) almost to the top of the tower, 34.8 metres (114 feet) above the city. There are only a few stairs at the very top, from where the view, as you'd expect, is superb. Peter the Great rode all the way to the top in 1716 (the Tsarina followed in a carriage); while a car is said to have driven up in 1902. Halfway up is an exhibition space (formerly the university library hall) that hosts a changing programme of artistic, scientific and historical displays. The observatory at the top is sometimes open, with an astronomer on hand to explain what you can see through the telescope. The Rundetårn was deemed such a significant building that during the 18th century the Royal Danish Academy of Sciences used it as the main reference point for a survey of Denmark.

FREE Trinitatiskirke
Landemærket 2 (33 32 09 04, www.trinitatiskirke.dk). Metro/train Nørreport. **Open** 9.30am-4.30pm Mon-Sat; 10.30am Sun for high mass. **Admission** free. **Map** p251 M13.

THE 'LATIN QUARTER'

North of the middle part of Strøget lies what's ambitiously termed Copenhagen's 'Latin Quarter' (on account of its narrow alleyways, cobbled café squares and bustling student life). At its heart is **Gråbrødretorv**, a delightful restaurant square, like Nyhavn without a canal. It comes alive in summer as tables from its (good but costly) restaurants spill out on to the cobbles. The square was created in 1664 after Corfitz Ulfeldt, the secretary of war, had his mansion torn down as punishment for high treason. After a fire in 1728 many houses here were rebuilt with triangular gable-ends, typical of the period.

West, on Nørregade, is Copenhagen's modest cathedral, **Vor Frue Kirke** (Church of Our Lady), where Crown Prince Frederik married his Australian wife Mary Donaldson.

Next to Vor Frue Kirke is a large cobbled square, **Frue Plads**. The rather grimy building opposite the church is part of Universitet, founded by Christian I in 1479. The building stands on the same site as the original (itself built over the Bishop's Palace), and was designed by Peter Malling and inaugurated by Frederik VI in 1836. The ornate great hall is worth a look and, if you have time, pop into the University Library round the corner in Fiolstræde. Halfway up the stairs is a small glass cabinet containing some fragments of a cannon ball and the book in which they were found embedded after the British bombardment. The title of the book, by Marsilius of Padua, is *Defender of Peace*.

FREE Vor Frue Kirke
Nørregade 8 (33 15 10 78, www.koebenhavnsdom kirke.dk). Metro/train Nørreport. **Open** 8am-5pm

Gråbrødretorv.

SIGHTS

Bishop Absalon.

Mon-Wed, Sat; 8am-5pm, 8-11pm Thur, Fri, Sun. **Admission** free. **Map** p251 N13.

Six churches have stood on this site since 1191, the first five suffering from a variety of misfortunes. The destruction of Vor Frue Kirke's art treasures by the Lutherans during the Reformation in the 16th century stands as one of their more barbaric acts. The current structure by CF Hansen was consecrated in 1829 and replaced the church destroyed by the British bombardment of 1807 (they used its 100-metre/328-foot spire as a target). The interior's spartan whitewash is relieved by several figures by Thorvaldsen (*see p69* **Profile**), including his famous depiction of Christ. The church often hosts musical events.

CENTRAL STRØGET & GAMMEL STRAND

In 1985 three venerable Strøget institutions on Amagertorv amalgamated to form **Royal Copenhagen**, the pride of the city's retail portfolio and an absolute must for visitors even if you find the prices a touch steep. Its **Royal Café** (*see p130*), known for its bite-size 'smushi'

INSIDE TRACK
CENTRAL STROLLING

South of Strøget is a network of narrow medieval streets (including Farvergade, Magstræde, Snaregade, Kompagnistræde and Læderstræde), packed with excellent independent shops, as well as some of the best cafés in the city. It's yet another place that the medieval city planners appear to have designed with 21st-century window shoppers in mind.

(a mix amalgation of 'smørrebrod' and 'sushi') is stylish spot for some light sustenence.

Amagertorv dates from the 14th century. In the 17th century a law was passed that meant all the produce grown on Amager island (where the airport is now located) had to be sold at the market here and soon shops grew up around the stalls. This has always been one of Copenhagen's main markets and meeting places and, though the stalls have long gone, the fountain is still much used as a rendezvous. Adjoining Amagertorv, towards Slotsholmen, is another busy square, **Højbro Plads**. Its main feature is a 1902 equestrian statue of **Bishop Absalon**, the founder of Copenhagen, by HW Bissen, with an inscription that reads: 'He was courageous, wise and far-sighted, a friend of scholarship, in the intensity of his striving a true son of Denmark.'

South of Strøget is **Gammel Strand** (Old Beach), home to some pricey restaurants, as well as the popular new **Cocks and Cows** gourmet burger bar (*see p114* **Where's the Beef?**). In the time of Bishop Absalon, and for centuries afterwards, Gammel Strand was where fish was sold (and therefore the city's commercial centre). It was here that the Øresund herring were landed before being transported throughout Catholic Europe – fish being vital for a population that often abstained from meat. Gammel Strand remained part of Copenhagen's seafront, which stretched from what is today Fortunstræde, along Gammel Strand to Snaregade, Magstræde and Løngangstræde until well into the Middle Ages. By the bridge from Højbro Plads to Slotsholmen is a stout stone statue (dating from 1940) of a foul-mouthed and quarrelsome fishwife grasping a huge flounder by the gills, in memory of a trade that continued into the 20th century. There is still a fishmonger's nearby on Højbro Plads (it does a swift trade in sushi). Cross to the other side of the bridge and look into the water and you'll see the sculpture of the Merman with his Sons (it's illuminated at night). All of Gammel Strand, except for No.48, burned to the ground in 1795. During the summer, take a canal tour or harbour trip to the Little Mermaid from Gammel Strand. Or try the excellent kayak tour (visit www.kakakole.dk for details).

The next major sight as you continue west along Strøget is **Helligåndskirken** (Church of the Holy Spirit), dating from 1400.

FREE Helligåndskirken

Nils Hemmingsensgade 5, Amagertorv (33 15 41 44, www.helligaandskirken.dk). Metro Kongens Nytorv. **Open** noon-4pm Mon-Fri; times of services Sun. **Admission** free. **Map** p251 N14.
It was originally part of the Grey Friars monastery, the oldest religious site in the city, founded in 1238. The early monks were hardy, ascetic souls and their

Profile Pølsevogne

Copenhagen's ubiquitous 'sausage wagons' are a Danish institution.

These cute caravan-like mobile or stationary stalls, with their fold-out windows and counters, have dotted Copenhagen since the 1920s, and their bright red *pølser* (sausages) are still a popular snack for locals, served in a fluffy white bun. The long thin hotdogs are available in a variety of guises, but are most often eaten poking out of a hollowed-out roll, laid on a long roll sliced lengthways in half, or from a paper plate with bread on the side – and always with plenty of condiments such as the Danish version of remoulade, plus well as mustard, ketchup, pickles and onions.

There are some 70 *pølsevogne* dotted around the city's streets and squares, and you'll come across them without difficulty in the centre. Yet the wagons have actually undergone a sharp decline in the past decade (they numbered around 500 from the 1950s to the 1990s) due to increased competition from international chains and more 'exotic' takeaway options, as well as increasing health concerns on the part of the Danish public;

made up of processed and dyed meat, and with a sky-high fat and salt content, the humble *pølse* can hardly be held up as a health food. Yet many Danes still flock to the remaining hotdog wagons.

One of the most famous and traditional *pølsevogne* in Copenhagen is **Harry's Place** (Nordre Fasanvej 269, 35 81 26 69), in the outskirts of Nørrebro – in business for over half a century. With two Danish prime ministers on its customer roll call of honour, this is as good a place as any to sample the national snack, washed down with cold chocolate milk – the traditional accompaniment. The seriously hungry, meanwhile, should opt for Harry's famously huge 'Børge' sausage.

If you'd like to try the local fast food without the excess cholesterol, however, there is an alternative: the popular **DØP** (Den Økologiske Pølsemand – 'organic sausage man') *pølsevogn* that has sat beside the Rundetårn (*see p55*) for the past couple of years, selling a new, higher-quality breed of *pølse* in line with more health-conscious times. DØP's hotdogs are 100 per cent organic, its buns made of sourdough bread with rye and linseeds, no less – bringing the traditional *pølsevogn* into a brave new era.

SIGHTS

devoted piety earned them much respect, but when they relaxed their standards during the 16th century they were expelled from the city by the Protestant reformers. The current neo-Renaissance structure dates from 1880. In the churchyard is a memorial to the Danish victims of Nazi concentration camps.

WESTERN STRØGET

West from Helligåndskirken, Strøget starts downmarket, with various cheap eateries serving pizzas and waffles. The watershed comes at Gammeltorv and Nytorv, two picturesque cobbled squares, beyond which things start to get very touristy. During the 14th century Gammeltorv, the oldest square in the city, was the hub of Copenhagen, a busy market, meeting place and (occasional) jousting site for the 5,000 residents of what was the largest settlement in northern Europe. The two squares became one (though they are bisected by Strøget) after the fire of 1795 destroyed the town hall that separated them.

When visitors arrive in Gammeltorv, one of the first things they notice is the extraordinary **Caritas Springvandet** (the Charity Fountain). Dating from 1608, this Renaissance masterpiece is made from copper and depicts a pregnant woman and two children with fishy gargoyles at their feet. On royal birthdays golden apples dance on the water jets.

Of interest chiefly because of its grand neo-classical façade, featuring six Ionic columns, Copenhagen's imposing and elegant **Domhuset** (Court House) on Nytorv was built in 1805-15

(work was suspended for a while in 1807 due to the bombardment by the British). The dusky pink building was designed by CF Hansen, who was also responsible for Vor Frue Kirke (*see p57*), just a short walk away up Nørregade. Domhuset was built on the site of the former town hall and, up until 1905, it served as both courthouse and town hall. Today it houses court rooms, conference rooms and chambers. The nearby Slutterigade (Prison Street) annexe was built as a jail in 1816 and converted to court rooms and chambers in 1944. It is attached to Domhuset via two recently restored arches, one of which joins the many crossings around the world known as the Bridge of Sighs (prisoners, bemoaning their fate, are led across it when going to and from the court rooms).

In 1848 Nytorv was the starting point for the relatively peaceful march by 10,000 Copenhageners on Christiansborg Slot, demanding the end of absolute monarchy. Frederik VII had conceded defeat before they even arrived. Søren Kierkegaard (*see p91* **Dead Famous**) lived for a while in Nytorv in a house on a site now occupied by Den Danske Bank. Look out too for the outline of Copenhagen's first town hall (before it moved to Rådhuspladsen) traced in the paving of Nytorv beneath the fruit and veg sellers who usually pitch here. Incidentally, Mozart's widow Constanze lived with her second husband (Georg Nikolaus Nissen, a Danish diplomat) at Lavendelstræde 1. The street runs from Nytorv's southern corner towards Rådhuspladsen.

The final stretch of Strøget is along Frederiksberggade, which opened up between Nytorv and Rådhuspladsen when the fire of 1728 razed the buildings here. On the right as you approach Rådhuspladsen is the rough and ready Club Absalon, built on the site of the city's first church, Sankt Clemens Kirke. The church was probably built by Absalon in the 1160s, but was demolished in the early 16th century. Rather ignominiously, some of its foundations can be seen in the bar's toilets. In a city that usually cares for its heritage this seems something of a dereliction of duty.

To the north of Frederiksberggade, in an area bookended by Nørregade and Vester Voldgade, lies the liveliest area around Strøget, known as Pisserenden. 'Piss' means the same in Danish as it does in English, and this district was thus named due to its notoriety as an malodorous dwelling for prostitutes and criminals, until it was purged by the first great fire of 1728. Today Pisserenden is one of the youngest and most vibrant shopping and café areas of Copenhagen, full of the coolest (but relatively cheap) clothes, skate, book and record shops. Most of the streets (which include Kattesundet, Vestergade, Larsbjørnsstræde and Teglgårdstræde) are also blessed with great restaurants, cafés and bars.

Caritas Springvandet.

Nyhavn & Kongens Nytorv

Canalside cafés and some of the city's grandest buildings.

King Christian V opened the canal of **Nyhavn** in 1670 to allow ships access to central Copenhagen, but these days water traffic consists mostly of canal tour boats and a couple of floating cafés. The real traffic now is found on the sunny canalside pavements, outside the emblematically colourful buildings – whenever a hint of spring appears, the place is teeming with locals and tourists out for a stroll, a drink or both, sitting at an expensive café or perching on the cobblestones with a shopping bag full of *høkerbajere* (beers from the off-licence).

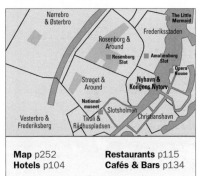

| Map p252 | Restaurants p115 |
| Hotels p104 | Cafés & Bars p134 |

Round the corner from Nyhavn, on Kvæsthusgade, is the Royal Danish Playhouse (*see p196*), one of the city's new architectural landmarks.

Windswept and stately, **Kongens Nytorv** (literally 'King's New Square') always had the potential to become Copenhagen's grandest square and the planting of beech trees (the national tree) and a face-lift have improved things, though the traffic still encircles it 24/7. But the square is graced by some of the city's finest buildings, including the Royal Theatre (Old Stage) and the Thotts Palais. It's also something of a centre for the city, with Bredgade, Nyhavn and Strøget all radiating from it.

SIGHTS

NYHAVN

After the British bombardment of 1807, Nyhavn's so-called 'Palmy Days' of prosperity were brought to a rude end and the wealthy merchants moved out. By coincidence, **Hans Christian Andersen** moved in shortly after, and subsequently lived at three different addresses on the canal. During this time Nyhavn's quayside saw service as one of the city's red light districts, and as recently as the 1950s, this was a disreputable place, lined with drinkers' bars, knocking shops and tattoo parlours; now, one strip club and the famous Ole's tattoo parlour remain. Together with the historic ships moored here as part of Nationalmuseet's collection, they are an evocative reminder of the past.

These days Denmark's greatest writer would hardly recognise the place. If the sun so much as peeps from behind the clouds, hundreds of tables from Nyhavn's ever-popular restaurants and cafés (plus, in the autumn months, the all-important umbrella heaters) pour out on to the quayside. It has to be said that the restaurants along Nyhavn vary from decent to dreadful and few represent good value (Cap Horn at 21 and Salt, around the corner on the harbour front, are exceptions – *see p117*), but the quayside is always a great place for a beer or two before going on elsewhere.

Two charming shopping streets, **Store Strandstræde** and **Lille Strandstræde**, are good for antiques, women's clothes, art and ceramics, and lead off Nyhavn on the north side. On the quieter south side, the main draw

Nyhavn. *See p61.*

is the 17th-century Dutch baroque palace
of Charlottenborg, home to Det Kongelige
Kunstakademi (the Royal Academy of Fine
Arts) since 1754. The former palace offers a
constantly changing programme of exhibitions
of contemporary art in the **Charlottenborg
Udstillingsbygning** (Charlottenborg
Exhibition; *see p178*).

KONGENS NYTORV

Kongens Nytorv was built in 1680 on the site
of former ramparts that ringed the city in an
arc all the way from Rådhuspladsen. It is an
excellent starting point for a tour of the city,

as **Bredgade**, **Nyhavn** and **Strøget** all
start from it and most of the other main
sights are within a few minutes' walk. Around
Christmas its artificial ice rink is a major draw.

The square is dominated to the south-east by
Det Kongelige Teater, Gamle Scene (the
Royal Theatre, Old Stage; *see p199 and p192*
Royal Danish Theatre). Before the opening
of the new opera house, Denmark's national
theatre was unique in that it produced opera,
ballet and theatre together in two auditoria
– Gamle (old) Scene, and Nye (new) Scene –
seating 2,550 people. Since the **Royal Danish
Playhouse** (*see p196*) was completed at
Kvæsthusbroen, however, the Gamle Scene
has been used almost exclusively for ballet
(and is home to the Royal Danish Ballet).

The main neo-Renaissance building (the
fourth on this site), by Vilhelm Dahlerup and
Ove Petersen, dates from 1872, but the theatre
was founded in 1748. The Nye Scene was added
in 1931, connected via an archway to the other
side of Tordenskjoldsgade. The inscription '*Ei
blot til lyst*' outside is taken from the original
building designed by Nicolai Eigtved and
translates as 'Not just for pleasure'. This

INSIDE TRACK **THE CITY RING**

Buildings works for the 'City Ring' metro
line have been dominating Kongens Nytorv
for the past couple of years. The new line
is expected to be completed in 2018, but
the digging in Kongens Nytorv should be
completely finished by summer 2011.

Profile Hans Christian Andersen

Copenhagen's most famous resident was beguiled by the city.

He may have been born in the Fyn town of Odense, but Denmark's greatest writer, Hans Christian Andersen, couldn't wait to leave and seek his fortune in Copenhagen. Andersen arrived on Monday, 6 September 1819 (he had to walk the last few miles into town because he couldn't afford the full fare), a day so momentous that he marked it as his 'second birthday' every year thereafter.

He arrived virtually penniless and alone – but for a few names he thought worth contacting. Yet he possessed an almost supernatural self-confidence. Andersen believed he was something special from an early age and immediately set about making something of his talents at the Royal Theatre. On his first visit, the night he arrived in the city, he was so naïve that he accepted a ticket from a tout as if it were a gift.

Andersen's confidence was shaken by the rejection of his ballet dancing, singing and acting skills, but slowly he built up contacts among Copenhagen's cultured bourgeoisie who would sponsor his education and finance his early attempts at writing. These were not instantly successful, but his first published piece of any significance, a fantasy based on a walk on New Year's Eve across the city to Amager, was a moderate hit. It was all the encouragement his pathological need for recognition required. Poetry, plays and novels followed, few of which hold up to scrutiny today. But in 1835, almost as an afterthought, he published a small book of stories that would be the works for which he would be remembered. Over 150 stories followed, many becoming world famous. Tales like *The Little Mermaid*, *The Emperor's New Clothes*, *The Snow Queen*, *Thumbelina*,

The Princess and the Pea, *The Red Shoes* and *The Little Match Girl* remain widely read and translated, their messages and morals as universal today as when they were written. Copenhagen features often in these stories, both its places and people. When the Tivoli Gardens opened in 1843, Andersen was among the first through the gates; and in fact, it was after one of his frequent later visits that he was inclined to compose his celebrated story, *The Nightingale*.

Andersen travelled more widely in Europe than any other Dane of his time. He also never owned his own home, instead living at various addresses in Copenhagen and, in his later infirmity, at the homes of aristocratic friends. He died, aged 70, in 1875 and is buried in Assistens Kirkegård (*see venue index*).

STATUES & PLAQUES

There are statues of Andersen in Rådhuspladsen and Kongens Have, and plaques on his old residences in Nyhavn (Nos.18, 20 and 67) and Vingårdstræde (No.6). And of course, the city's symbol, the Little Mermaid, is inspired by one of his darkest fairy tales.

SIGHTS

INSIDE TRACK
SQUARE STATUE

In the centre of Kongens Nytorv is a faintly absurd statue (by Abraham-César Lamoureux; 1687) of its patron, Christian V, depicting him as a Roman general astride his horse. The weight of the gilded lead statue eventually proved too much for the horse's legs and it had to be recast in bronze in 1946.

may suggest that productions can be worthy affairs, but that doesn't stop most selling out way in advance, hence the theatre's need for other venues, such as the Turbinehallerne at Adelgade 10 and Baron Bolten in Boltens Gård.

The theatre's most famous former boss was Auguste Bournonville, director of the Danish Ballet from 1830 to 1877. Outside stand statues of two other significant figures from the theatre's history, the playwright Ludvig Holberg (the father of modern Danish theatre) and Adam Oehlenschläger, the poet. Its most famous former employee was Hans Christian

Andersen, who made it his first stop when he arrived from Odense as a 14-year-old in 1819 with hopes of being a ballet dancer.

Working clockwise round the square from the theatre you come to Denmark's first department store, the grand **Magasin**, which replaced the Hotel du Nord in 1894 and now has a stylish Metro station outside its main entrance; Hviids Vinstue, a venerable drinking den dating from 1723; the eastern end of Strøget; and **Hotel d'Angleterre** (*see p104*).

On a corner of the square opposite the hotel is an ornate kiosk decorated by a gold relief depicting Denmark's early aviators. At No.4 is another of the square's finest buildings, the Dutch Palladian-style **Thotts Palais** (1685), named after a previous owner, Count Otto Thott. Today the pink stucco palace houses the French Embassy. On the other side of Bredgade is the **Amber Museum** (*see below*).

Amber Museum

Ravhuset, Kongens Nytorv 2 (33 11 67 00, www.houseofamber.com). Metro Kongens Nytorv. **Open** *May-Sept* 10am-6.30pm daily; *Oct-Apr* 10am-5.30pm daily. **Admission** 25kr; 10kr under-15s. **Credit** AmEx, MC, V. **Map** p252 M16.

SIGHTS

Kongens Nytorv. See p62.

Slotsholmen

The heart of Copenhagen's power for more than 800 years.

This is where it all began. Bishop Absalon, the founding father of Copenhagen, built his fortress here in the 12th century, and a city was born. The island, surrounded by harbours and canals, is a more accessible place these days, with its museums, the great Børsen stock exchange and the futuristic Black Diamond royal library. Hang around long enough, and you might even spot a government minister swanning about.

The largest building on Slotsholmen is **Christiansborg Slot** (Christiansborg Castle, *see p67*), the modern-day parliament building. For many centuries the previous castles that stood on this site effectively were Copenhagen, so central were they to the lives and prosperity of the townsfolk and so important were they as a power base for the region.

Map p251   **Restaurants** p118

CHRISTIANSBORG SLOT

Christiansborg's development can be divided into three stages: Absalon's fortress dating from 1167; the 17th century; and the current palace.

The original building is long gone, but you can still see remnants of its foundations in the enjoyable **Ruinerne under Christiansborg** (Ruins under Christiansborg, *see p70*), a museum dedicated to the 800-year history of the current castle site. The current palace is built directly above and houses the Danish parliament, **Folketinget** (*see p67*), where 179 members sit in a semi-circle in their party groups (of which Denmark has many), facing the Speaker. Government ministers sit on the right-hand side of the chamber with the Prime Minister closest to the platform.

Close by the Ruinerne museum is the equestrian arena with entrances to two particularly enchanting royal attractions: the **Kongelige Stalde og Kareter** (Royal Stables and Coaches) and **Teatermuseet** (Theatre Museum; for both, *see p67*). If you can endure the equine odours, the stables, with their vaulted ceilings and marble columns, offer a glimpse into an extravagant royal past. Teatermuseet, which opened in 1922, is housed in the old Royal Court Theatre, designed by the French architect

Nicolas Henri Jardin. It dates from 1766 and was modernised in 1842 – HC Andersen once performed in a ballet here in his youth.

Continue across the equestrian arena to the archway beyond and you come to Frederiksholms Kanal, which is forded by **Marmorbroen** (the Marble Bridge). Quite a fuss is made over this bridge, which was designed by Nicolai Eigtved for Christian IV and completed in 1745, but, frankly, aside from some decorative sandstone portraits, it isn't all that special (and it isn't even all marble).

INSIDE TRACK
BUILT FOR A... PRINCE

Over the years the various castles/palaces on Slotsholmen have come in for a bit of stick. In 1588 a French traveller commented, 'It is remarkable more for its age than its magnificence'. A German visitor of 1600 said that 'It resembles the dwelling of a little prince rather than a great king'. Englishman William Bromley, writing in 1699, agreed: 'The King's palace is one of the meanest that I ever saw, with a foul stinking ditch about it'

SIGHTS

SIGHTS

Christiansborg Slot.

Christiansborg Slot

Slotsholmen (33 92 63 00, www.ses.dk/ christiansborg). Metro Kongens Nytorv. **Tours** (in English) 11am, 1pm, 3pm daily. **Tickets** 70kr; 35kr-60kr concessions. **No credit cards. Map** p251 O14.

The warrior-bishop Absalon built the original fortress in 1167, on what was then the small islet of Strandholmen. It was ringed by a thick wall of limestone blocks, with its internal buildings made from brick and timber. Bishop Absalon's fortress was badly damaged in 1259 by the avenging Wends and then burned to the ground in 1369 by an alliance of forces led by the Lübeckers against King Valdemar Atterdag. It was replaced by the first Copenhagen Castle. From 1416, when Erik of Pomerania moved in, the castle became the permanent home of the royal family (until they moved to Amalienborg Slot in 1794).

Christian IV had the place demolished in the early 17th century, replacing it with a typically over the top baroque building, with its own chapel and very grand stables. During Frederik II's reign, the castle nearly fell to the Swedes who, following a two-year siege, in February 1659 advanced towards it across the frozen sea, dressed in white cloaks to camouflage themselves. But the boiling oil, tar and water that the Danes rained down drove them back. Soon after, Frederik III build a new rampart where the Swedes had advanced. This became known as Vestervold (Western Rampart) and between it and Slotsholmen a new quarter, Frederiksholm, grew up.

Frederik IV extensively modernised the castle between 1710 and 1729, but, in 1732, Christian VI tore it all down on aesthetic grounds, and because its foundations were weak. The baroque replacement was one of the biggest palaces in Europe; its foundations alone cost three million *rigsdalers*, then equivalent to the entire value of Sjælland's arable land.

On the night of 26 February 1794, the whole lot burned down (bar the stables, which are still in use). The royal family finally gave up on Slotsholmen and bought Amalienborg Slot. Work on the next Christiansborg Slot started in 1803 and the building, a neo-classical masterpiece, was completed in 1828. That too was badly damaged by a fire in October 1884.

You would hardly term the present-day Christiansborg a castle. Nor is it especially graceful. But it is big. Its neo-baroque granite and concrete façade was designed by Thorvald Jørgensen and was the first Christiansborg to have been built by the people's representatives. They were apparently still touchy about the monarchy as, during its design, they demanded to have at least the same number of windows overlooking the palace square as the king. Its central tower is the tallest (by 40 centimetres) in Denmark at 106 metres (358 feet). Frederik VIII laid the foundation stone for the current castle in 1907, and the Ruinerne museum displays several amazing photographs from that time.

Ruinerne under Christiansborg

Christiansborg Slot (33 92 64 94, www.oplevslot sholmen.dk). Metro Kongens Nytorv. **Open** *May-Sept* 10am-5pm daily. *Oct-Apr* 10am-4pm Tue-Sun. **Admission** 40kr; 20kr-30kr concessions. **No credit cards. Map** p251 O14.

Housed in three large underground rooms are excavations of the older castles' foundations, including stonework from Absalon's fortress, remnants of Denmark's most famous prison, the Blåtårn (Blue Tower), and what is called Absalon's Well (though it probably dates from the 19th century). The Blåtårn was used for several centuries to house prisoners of note – most famously Leonora Christina, the daughter of Christian IV. She wrote what was probably the most important piece of 17th-century Danish prose, *Jammersminde*, while held here on suspicion of involvement in her husband's treason plot. Viewing this jumble of ancient masonry is like trying to put together the discarded pieces from several jigsaw puzzles, but the exhibition works hard to help you decipher the rubble (with English captions).

FREE Folketinget

Rigsdagsgården (33 37 55 00, www.folketinget.dk). Metro Kongens Nytorv. **Open** *Gallery sittings* 1st Tue Oct-5 June Tue-Fri (except holidays). *Guided tours* noon, 2pm Mon-Fri; 1pm Sun, during parliamentary recess (July-mid Aug). **Admission** free. **Map** p251 O14.

Folketinget is opened annually in a ceremony attended by members of the royal family on the first Tuesday in October. A public gallery is open when parliament is in session, and there are English-language tours during the parliamentary recess from July to mid August. Christiansborg also houses the High Court, several ministries, the prime minister's department, the Royal Reception Chambers (De Kongelige Repræsentationslokaler) and the Queen's Reference Library.

Kongelige Stalde og Kareter

Christiansborg Ridebane 12 (33 40 26 77, www.ses.dk). Train København H. **Open** *Jan-Apr* 2-4pm Sat, Sun. *May-Sept* 2-4pm Fri-Sun. *Oct-Dec* closed. **Admission** 20kr; 10kr concessions. **No credit cards**. **Map** p251 O14.

The Queen's horses and coaches are still kept in grand style at the royal stables, and are often used for state occasions (as is a rather dusty Bentley convertible from 1969).

Teatermuseet

Christiansborg Ridebane 18, southern wing of Christiansborg Slot (33 11 51 76, www.teater museet.dk). Metro Kongens Nytorv. **Open** 11am-3pm Tue, Thur; 11am-5pm Wed; 1-4pm Sat, Sun. **Admission** 50kr; 30kr concessions; free under-18s. **No credit cards**. **Map** p251 O14.

The exhibits at the Theatre Museum include costumes, set designs and artworks. There is also a special cabinet of objects connected with the Royal Ballet choreographer Auguste Bournonville.

AROUND SLOTSHOLMEN

There is no missing the classical stuccoed mausoleum (by Gottlieb Bindesbøll) that houses the definitive collection of works by Denmark's master sculptor, Bertel Thorvaldsen. **Thorvaldsens Museum** (*see p69* **Profile**) is a must, not only for sculpture fans, but for all art lovers. Immediately behind Thorvaldsens Museum is **Christiansborg Slotskirke** (Christiansborg Palace Church; *see p68*), one of CF Hansen's neo-classical masterpieces, with a columned façade and a beautiful white stucco interior and dome.

Børsen (the Old Stock Exchange), on the other side of Christiansborg Slotsplads, is the oldest stock exchange in Europe, built between 1619 and 1640. It still serves as a business centre and Copenhagen's Chamber of Commerce and, as such, is not open to the public. However, the exterior of this Renaissance wedding cake is a riot of stonework, embellished gables and green copper. Above it towers one of Copenhagen's most recognisable landmarks – a fantastical 54-metre (177-foot) copper spire made of four

Biblioteekshaven, *See p68.*

intertwined dragon tails, built in 1625 to a design by Ludvig Heidtrider. The three gold crowns topping the spire represent the three Nordic nations: Denmark, Sweden and Norway. Børsen (which translates as 'the covered market') was built at the behest of Christian IV, who desperately wanted Copenhagen to become the financial capital of Europe (it didn't).

An unusually ostentatious altarpiece (for a Lutheran church) is the main draw of **Holmens Kirke** (*see p70*), a church dedicated to sailors. Across the street is a forbidding concrete building housing **Nationalbanken** (the National Bank), the work of Arne Jacobsen. Regrettably, its wonderful interior and inner courtyard are not open to the public.

Another treat is **Tøjhusmuseet** (the Royal Arsenal Museum; *see p70*). Comprising an endless vaulted Renaissance cannon hall (the longest in Europe, modelled on the one in Venice), and a mind-boggling number of arms and armour in an upstairs display, this is probably the finest museum of its kind in the world.

Copenhagen's most beautiful 'hidden' garden, **Bibliotekshaven** (the Library Garden; *see right*), lies behind the old ivy-covered **Det Kongelige Bibliotek** (the Royal Library; *see right*), through a gateway on Rigdagsgården, opposite the entrance to Folketinget.

The Danes love nothing more than to juxtapose old and new, but when the designs for the new extension to the Royal Library, by architects Schmidt, Hammer and Lassen, were unveiled, few were prepared for something this radical (despite it

having already earned the nickname the **Black Diamond** before it opened in autumn 1999). Perhaps the best appraoch is to walk through the old library's garden so that you are suddenly confronted with the vastness of the new structure close up. The Kongelige Bibliotek is also home to the **Danish Jewish Museum** (*see below*).

FREE Bibliotekshaven
Rigsdagsgården (33 92 63 00, www.ses.dk). *Metro Kongens Nytorv.* **Open** 6am-10pm daily. **Admission** free. **Map** p251 O14.
Arranged in a square around a fountain and duck pond, the 'Library Garden' blooms beautifully in summer – even the bronze of Søren Kierkegaard looks cheerful. You can see some of the old mooring hoops from Christian IV's time on the walls surrounding it.

FREE Christiansborg Slotskirke
Christiansborg Slotsplads (33 92 63 00, *www.ses.dk).* *Metro Kongens Nytorv.* **Open** *Aug-June* noon-4pm Sun. *Easter, July, 1wk mid Aug, 1wk mid Oct* noon-4pm daily. **Admission** free. **Map** p251 N14.
This church was completed in 1829 and survived a fire in 1884, but the roof was destroyed by another fire that started during the Whitsun carnival in 1992. Restoration was completed just in time for the 25th anniversary of Queen Margrethe's coronation in 1997.

★ FREE Det Kongelige Bibliotek
Søren Kierkegaards Plads 1 (33 47 47 47, *www.kb.dk).* *Metro Kongens Nytorv.* **Open** *Main building* 8am-10pm Mon-Sat. *Study rooms* 9am-9pm Mon-Fri; 9am-5pm Sat. *Exhibitions* 10am-7pm Mon-Sat. All depts close at 7pm in July and Aug. **Admission** *Main building & library* free. *Exhibitions* free-40kr; free under-16s. *Concerts* prices vary. **Credit** MC, V. **Map** p251 P15.
This malevolent parallelogram, made from glass, black Zimbabwean granite (cut in Portugal and polished in Italy), Portuguese sandstone, silk concrete and Canadian maple, abuts the old building with little consideration for the clash of styles that ensues. Its reflective surfaces interact constantly with the sky and water, altering the building's colour by the second. The 500-million-kroner library houses 200,000 books, an exhibition space, a shop, a concert hall, the **National Photography Museum** (with regular temporary exhibitions), a Michelin-starred restaurant (**Søren K**; *see p118*) and a café. The basement also hosts occasional exhibitions from the Book Museum. The old library, the largest in Scandinavia, with its glorious reading room is accessed through a glass walkway from the first floor. Since it opened, the Black Diamond has been a huge success.

★ Danish Jewish Museum
Kongelige Bibliotek, entrance via garden (33 11 22 18, www.jewmus.dk). *Metro Kongens Nytorv.* **Open** *Sept-May* 1-4pm Tue-Fri; noon-5pm Sat,

Christiansborg Slotskirke.

Profile Bertel Thorvaldsen

Denmark's wandering artistic hero.

Denmark's greatest sculptor was born in Copenhagen on 19 November 1768. He studied at the Academy of Art, where he won the Gold Medal, and then, in 1797, a scholarship sent him to Rome, where he lived for nearly 40 years developing a style that was heavily influenced by Greco-Roman mythology and creating works of a majestic, classical beauty, frequently on an epic scale.

His breakthrough, which catapulted him into the highest echelons of the neo-classical sculpture fraternity, came with the piece *Jason*, completed in 1803, and now housed in the museum. His figure of Christ, which can be seen in Vor Frue Kirke (*see p57*), became the model for statues of Christ the world over and remains a religious icon to this day.

Thorvaldsen returned to Copenhagen towards the end of his life and his return helped boost morale and a general artistic revival and contributed to the emergence of a cultural and social essence that is still recognisably Danish today. In 1833 he was appointed director

of the Danish Academy of Fine Arts. Before his death in March 1844, Thorvaldsen bequeathed his works (plaster moulds, sketches and finished works in marble) and a collection of ancient Mediterranean art to the city, and the royal family built Thorvaldsens Museum. The sculptor is buried at its centre.

The **Thorvaldsens Museum** (*see p70*), the oldest art gallery in Denmark, is a charming blend of celestial blue ceilings, elegant colonnades and mosaic floors. Although the monumental scale of Thorvaldsen's work and his prolific output are often hard to take in, it is worth persevering. His subjects include not only figures from mythology, epic studies of Christ and numerous self-portraits, but also busts of contemporaries such as Byron, Walter Scott and the Danish poet Adam Oehlenschläger. Also featured are Thorvaldsen's collections of Egyptian and Roman artefacts, contemporary Danish art and personal belongings. Outside, a fresco depicts the return of the sculptor and his works from Rome. Some English information is available.

WHEN IN ROME...
Thorvalsens' monument to Pope Pius VII is the only work by a non-Italian in St Peter's Basilica in Rome.

SIGHTS

INSIDE TRACK
HIDDEN TREASURES

Slotsholmen museums and sights are generally tucked away behind doors or in unlikely corners, which somehow makes them all the more rewarding when you do manage to track them down – that's a polite way of saying that it's a bit of a labyrinth and its main attractions are, in typical Danish fashion, poorly signposted. (It's a good idea to come on a Sunday afternoon when all the attractions are open at the same time.)

Sun; *June-Aug* 10am-5pm Tue-Sun. **Admission** 50kr; 40kr concessions; free under-16s. **Credit** AmEx, DC, MC, V. **Map** p251 P15.

This striking adaptation of the Royal Boat House was designed by Daniel Libeskind, responsible also for the new development on Ground Zero in New York. The museum is inspired by the Hebrew word 'Mitzvah', which loosely means 'compassion' and refers in part to the good deeds done by the Danes towards the Jewish community during World War II. Danish-Jewish art, history and culture are well represented.

▓▓▓▓ Holmens Kirke

Holmens Kanal (33 13 61 78, www.holmens kirke.dk). Bus 1A, 16. **Open** 10am-3pm Mon-Fri. *May-Oct* 9am-4pm Mon-Fri. **Admission** free. **Map** p251 O15.

This church dedicated to sailors is worth visiting to see Denmark's tallest pulpit (it extends right to the roof, and has recently been restored). Converted, aptly,

from an anchor smithy in 1619 under the orders of Christian IV, the church's rather bland exterior was augmented by the main portal (on the east side), originally from Roskilde Cathedral. Holmens Kirke is often used for royal occasions – in 1967 Queen Margrethe and Prince Henrik married here. Walk through the side door on the left of the altar and you enter a room dedicated to Denmark's naval heroes and graced by numerous ornate sarcophagi.

★ Thorvaldsens Museum

Bertel Thorvaldsens Plads 2 (33 32 15 32 www.thorvaldsensmuseum.dk). Bus 1A, 2A, 15. **Open** 10am-5pm Tue-Sun. **Admission** 40kr; 30kr concessions; free under-18s; free to all Wed. **Credit** MC, V. **Map** p251 O14. *See p69* **Profile**.

Tøjhusmuseet

Tøjhusgade 3 (33 11 60 37, www.thm.dk). Bus 1A, 2A, 15. **Open** noon-4pm daily; 10am-4pm daily during autumn and winter holidays. **Admission** 30kr; 15kr concessions; free under-17s; free to all Wed. **Credit** AmEx, MC, V. **Map** p251 P14.

The Royal Arsenal Museum is based in what was Christian IV's original arsenal building (dating from 1589 to 1604). On the ground floor, within walls four metres (13 feet) thick, are a vast number of gun carriages, cannons, a V-1 flying bomb from World War II and the tiniest tank you ever saw (from 1933). Upstairs, the glass cases, containing everything from 15th-century swords and pikes to modern machine guns, seem to go on forever. Many items, such as the beautiful ivory inlaid pistols and muskets, are works of art, and the royal suits of armour are equally stunning. The small arms section of the museum is housed in Kongens Bryghus (the King's Brewery).

Danish Jewish Museum.

Frederiksstaden

Royal residences, historical museums, and a little bronze mermaid.

Rich on elegance, if not on atmosphere, Frederiksstaden has a regal ambience. There's old money here, and the restaurants around Bredgade and Store Kongensgade are a favourite lunch spot for lawyers and stockbrokers. Along the water, museums, galleries, cruise ships and yachts dominate. Oh, and the area is also home to Copenhagen's reluctant city symbol, the *Little Mermaid*, sitting slumped on a rock. Frederiksstaden's other famous residents, the Queen and her family, live at the low-key Amalienborg palaces right in the centre.

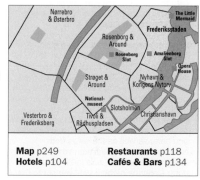

Map p249	**Restaurants** p118
Hotels p104	**Cafés & Bars** p134

You come to Frederiksstaden by heading north from the tourist hubbub of Nyhavn into Bredgade (meaning 'wide street'). Here the architecture changes dramatically, from quaint, multicoloured gabled houses, to the straight, wide, French-influenced streets laid out in the 18th century for Copenhagen's nobility and nouveaux riches.

ROYAL BEGINNINGS

Frederiksstaden was the vision of Frederik V, who wished to celebrate the 300th anniversary of the House of Oldenburg in 1749 with a grand new building project. The king didn't, however, fancy paying for it so, instead, he donated the land on the condition that selected members of Copenhagen's nobility commission the rococo architect Nicolai Eigtved to build a stylistically uniform quarter. Today Bredgade is itself packed with treasures, some more obvious than others.

The main auction houses are based here, as are numerous art and antiques dealers from the higher end of the market, which make for good window-shopping. A short way down Bredgade on the right is Sankt Annæ Plads, a quiet tree-lined square, with a statue of King Christian X at its head and a dull, red-brick church, **Garnisonskirken**, to the right. Another, far more impressive, church, **Frederikskirken**, better known as **Marmorkirken** (the Marble Church; *see p75*), awaits a short walk away.

Down Frederiksgade are the four rococo palaces surrounding a grand cobbled square that together make up **Amalienborg Slot** (Amalienborg Palace). Home to the royal family since 1794, the palaces were originally built by four wealthy

traders as part of Frederik V's scheme for the area. The royal family commandeered the buildings after a fire destroyed their previous home, Christiansborg. As you enter the square along Frederiksgade from Marmorkirken, the palaces are (clockwise from the left) Levetzau Palace, Brockdorff Palace, Moltke Palace and Schack Palace (originally Løvenskjold Palace).

The current, much-loved Dronning (Queen) **Margrethe II** lives in Schack Palace (formerly Christian IX's palace). The Danes' unstinting love for their Dronning is one of the great paradoxes of the national psyche. Bearing in mind their determined egalitarianism in other areas of life, including democratic equality, this royalism can seem downright peculiar to foreigners. Literally every Dane you meet, while perhaps not loving the abstract notion of a monarchy, won't have a bad thing to say about their Queen. And the explanation is simple: Margrethe is a charming, modern, talented, conscientious and hard-working royal. And she smokes, which is always likely to endear her to the Danes.

Margrethe Alexandrine Thorhildur Ingrid was born during the dark days of Denmark's occupation by Germany in 1940, the daughter of King Frederik IX and Queen Ingrid. During the 1960s Margrethe went to universities in Copenhagen,

SIGHTS

Walk Parks & Palaces

A stroll around regal, religious and nautical Copenhagen.

Start Kongens Nytorv.
Finish Nørreport station.
Length 6km (4 miles) approximately.
Time 2.5 hours (not including sightseeing and refreshment stops).

Begin at Kongens Nytorv. With the Hotel d'Angleterre behind you, cross over the square to the historic canal of **Nyhavn** (*see p61*), where Hans Christian Andersen lived at three different addresses. Walk down the north side of the canal (which will be on your right), past **Charlottenborg** (*see p62*), a former royal palace, now an art space. You'll pass Nyhavn's bustling cafés, restaurants and bars, as well as the ships from Nationalmuseet's collection. When you come to the harbour, turn left and walk north along the harbour until you get to the waterside **Amaliehaven** gardens (*see p73*).

If you head inland from here, you come to the residence of Denmark's much-loved Queen Margrethe II, **Amalienborg Slot** (*see p71*), which also offers a great view of the **Opera House** (*see p194*).

Back on the waterfront you come to a replica of Michelangelo's *David* outside **Den Kongelige Afstøbningssamlingen** (the Royal Cast Collection; *see p75*). A few minutes further on is the **Gefionspringvandet** (the Gefion Fountain; *see p73*). Walk inland, past **Frihedsmuseet** (the Museum of the Danish Resistance; *see p74*), and enter **Kastellet** (*see p75*), former home of the Danish army. Climb the ramparts to the east and walk north. At the north-east corner of the fortress you can see **Den Lille Havfrue** (the Little Mermaid; *see p73*).

Head back across Kastellet and walk south along Bredgade. On your left you pass the elegant **Kunstindustrimuseet** (Museum of Decorative and Applied Art; *see p75*) and **Sanknt Ansgar Kirke** (*see p75*), the Roman Catholic cathedral. A little further up Bredgade are the golden minarets of the Russian Orthodox **Alexander Nevsky Kirke** (*see p75*). Turn right at Frederiksgade and you arrive at Copenhagen's most impressive church, **Marmorkirken**, the Marble Church; *see p75*).

Continue west and you come to the junction with Store Kongensgade; turn left. Take the first right on to Dronningens Tværgade, then at the end, cross over Kronprinsessegade and enter Kongens Have (the King's Gardens), home to **Rosenborg Slot** (*see p78*). Walk across the gardens and exit at the northern gate. Opposite is the peaceful **Botanisk Have** (Botanical Garden; *see p77*). After tea in the café, exit by the south-eastern gate and hop on the Metro at Nørreport to Kongens Nytorv.

Cambridge, Århus, London and the Sorbonne, her main subject being political science. She also spent time in the Women's Flying Corp and the WAAF in England. In 1967 she married a French diplomat, Henri, Comte de Laborde de Monpezat (now Prince Henrik, fondly if irreverently regarded by Danes). They have two sons, Frederik (the crown prince, born 1968, and wildly popular, who has a son with his equally adored Australian wife Mary) and Joachim (born 1969, aloof and a little feudal, whose public stock sank in 2004 following separation from his wife Alexandra). Margrethe became queen in 1972 – the Danes had voted in a referendum in 1953 to overturn the laws of succession to allow a female to take the throne.

A major photo op for tourists visiting Amalienborg is the changing of the guards featuring the ever-present Royal Life Guards, whose duty it is to protect Queen Margrethe in the highly unlikely event of an attack. The guards stand in their blue, red and white uniforms beside their pretty red boxes day and night. The daily ritual actually begins at the barracks beside **Rosenborg Slot** (*see p78*) at 11.30am, from where the soldiers process through the streets, with the military band playing a few tunes. The route takes them south-west to Kultorvet, down Købmagergade, left on to Østergade (part of Strøget), around Kongens Nytorv and up Bredgade, before taking a right into Frederiksgade and Amalienborg Slotsplads at noon. The Queen's birthday, on 16 April, is the cause for more impressive pageantry and crowds.

The **Amalienborg Museum** (within Levetzau Palace; *see p74*) features several private rooms and studies belonging to the Royal Glücksborg family in the late 19th/early 20th centuries. In the middle of the square stands French sculptor Jacques Saly's 12-metre (39-foot) statue of Frederik V, modelled on the equestrian statue of Marcus Aurelius on the Capitol in Rome. It took 20 years to complete due to a financial wrangle over payment from the backers, the East Asiatic Company, but remains an important piece of European sculpture.

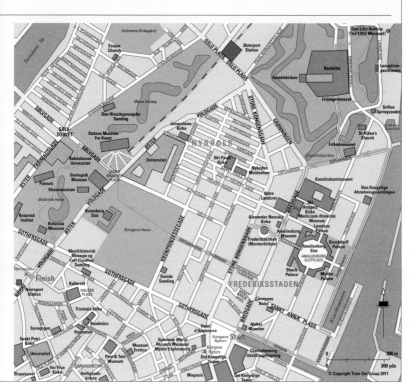

SIGHTS

Behind the mighty statue of Frederik V is **Amaliehaven**, a small harbour-side park donated by the industrialist AP Møller in 1983. In the summer the walk from the vast cruise ships that dock here, past the Royal Cast Collection, the spectacular, newly restored Gefion Fountain and on to the Little Mermaid, is extremely popular among Copenhagen's perambulators, dog walkers and joggers. You may even bump into Queen Margrethe or Prince Henrik, who walk their dachshunds here.

South of Amaliehaven, down along the harbourfront, lies a row of classic warehouses facing the Kvæsthusbroen dock. Behind Kvæsthusbroen, by the corner of Nyhavn, is where the new **Royal Danish Playhouse** (*see p195*) has been built halfway into the actual harbour, with walkways above the water that surround the venue.

A short distance north along the waterside from Amaliehaven is **Den Kongelige Afstøbningssamling** (the Royal Cast Collection; *see p75*), the exterior of which is marked by a bronze replica of Michelangelo's David. Inside, 2,000 plaster casts of the world's most famous sculptures cover a period of 4,000 years.

A walk along the old harbour brings you to Copenhagen's most eye-catching piece of public statuary, **Gefionspringvandet** (the Gefion Fountain). Built in 1908 by sculptor Anders Bundgaard, the statue of the goddess Gefion commanding four ploughing bulls is inspired by the Norse saga of the birth of Sjælland. Gefion was told by the King of Sweden that she could keep as much land as she could plough in a night, and that hard night's labour, with the help of her sons who were transformed into bulls for the purpose, earned her Sjælland.

Finally, after passing the ramparts of **Kastellet** along Langelinie, you arrive at **Den Lille Havfrue** (The Little Mermaid), back in her rightful place after a trip to China in 2010. Sculptor Edvard Eriksen's statue, inspired by the Andersen story, was erected in 1913 and funded by the brewer Carlsberg. Since 1964 it has been the victim of vandalism on eight occasions. She has been painted red twice, had her head hacked off three times, an arm lopped off once and been blown from her rocky perch on the windswept Langelinie harbour front by a bomb. The winsome work was based on the prima ballerina Ellen Price, and, together with the urinating toddler in Brussels, it must rank as one of the most overexposed and overrated pieces of sculpture in the world.

Opposite the Mermaid is the island of **Holmen**, home to the Danish navy for several hundred years. A good walk further along the harbour takes you to Copenhagen's main cruise liner port, busy from spring to late summer.

Back on Bredgade a few of those hidden treasures await. Just around the corner from Marmorkirken is another smaller, but equally fascinating church, **Alexander Nevsky Kirke**, the only Russian Orthodox church in Denmark. Copenhagen's small but beautiful neo-Romanesque Catholic cathedral, **Sankt Ansgar Kirke**, built in 1841, is next door. Immediately north of the church is **Kunstindustrimuseet** (the Museum of Decorative and Applied Art).

Bredgade ends at a small park, **Churchillparken**, located in front of Kastellet, and named after Britain's wartime leader (there's a small, curmudgeonly bust of him here). Maintaining the British theme, you'll also find **St Alban's Church**, a perfect English Gothic flint church (bizarrely, part of the Anglican Diocese of Gibraltar), which looks like it's been lifted straight from the Sussex Downs. Also here is **Frihedsmuseet** (the Museum of Danish Resistance), its entrance marked by a battered armoured car once used by the Danish Resistance during World War II.

Frihedsmuseet is overlooked by **Kastellet** (the Citadel). Built by Frederik III in 1662 after the Swedish siege of 1658, this vast star-shaped fortress with its five bastions was the base for the Danish army for many years. Ironically, it was

right in front of Kastellet that the Germans landed many centuries later in 1940. These days, the path around the ramparts makes a good jogging track. From the north-east you get a good view of the Little Mermaid and the Swedish coast.

FREE Alexander Nevsky Kirke

Bredgade 53 (33 13 60 46, tours 20 76 16 47, www.ruskirke.dk). **Open** 11.30am-1.30pm Tue-Thur; times of services Sat, Sun. **Admission** free. Tours by arrangement only, 25kr; 20kr concessions. **No credit cards. Map** p249 K16.

Denmark's only Russian Orthodox church is easily identified by its three incongruous gold onion domes; to step inside is to travel back into pre-Revolutionary Russia. The church was built in 1881-84 at the behest of Princess Dagmar, daughter of Christian IX, who married Grand Duke Alexander, later Emperor Alexander III, and converted to Orthodoxy. She apparently needed somewhere to worship when she visited Copenhagen (and the fact that Nevsky, Prince of Novgorod, once famously defeated a Swedish army in the 13th century can only have helped get the project through). On the right-hand side of the church an icon of the Holy Virgin, painted in a monastery on Mount Athos in Greece in 1912, and mounted on its own stand, is said, occasionally during spring, to weep real tears. If you doubt it, you can see for yourself where water has run from her eyes and tarnished the paint. The nearby icon of St Nicholas is said to have been the only item to have survived the wreck of a Russian warship.

Amalienborg Museum

Christian VIII's Palace, Amalienborg Plads (33 12 21 86, www.dkks.dk). **Bus** 1A. **Open** *May-Oct* 10am-4pm daily. *Nov-Apr* 11am-4pm Tue-Sun. Also open on some Mondays in Feb and Apr; call for details. **Admission** 60kr; 40kr-50kr concessions; free under-17s. *Guided tours* 770kr-880kr plus admission fee. **Credit** MC, V. **Map** p249 L16.

The museum consists of private rooms and studies belonging to the Royal Glücksborg family from 1863 to 1947, starting with Christian IX. Note Frederik IX's pipe collection, Queen Louise's rococo drawing room and a number of quite abysmal pieces of art created by members of the family over the years (in contrast to the works by the current, more gifted queen).

FREE Frihedsmuseet

Churchillparken (33 47 39 21, www.frihedsmuseet. dk). **Bus** 1A. **Open** *May-Sept* 10am-5pm Tue-Sun. *Oct-Apr* 10am-3pm Tue-Sun. *Air raid shelter* May-Sept 11am-1pm Sun. Guided tours are run June-Aug 2pm Tue, Thur, Sun. **Admission** free. **Map** p249 J17.

Inside this purpose-built wooden hall, arranged around an open courtyard, are numerous moving testimonies to the endeavours of the Danish Resistance and the suffering of their country under

Den Lille Havfrue. See p73.

Marmorkirken.

occupation. The museum is divided into four areas: 1940-1 Adaptation; 1942-3 Resistance; 1943-4 Terror; and 1944-5 Liberation. The letters (translated into English), from Resistance fighters to their mothers before their execution, and indeed the very execution stakes they stood against to face the firing squads, are here, as are the various home-made weapons and sabotage equipment used by the Resistance. There are biographies of the movement's leaders and displays about the boys' groups who were the first to rebel. Nearby in the park is an underground air raid shelter, open on Sundays during the summer.

Denmark was something of a military backwater during World War II, of use chiefly as Germany's larder and, as such, it was in the occupier's interest to allow life to continue as normally as possible. However, when in 1942 Hitler took offence at King Christian X's terse response to his birthday greeting, the German leader sent Werner Best, one of the architects of the Gestapo, to run the country. That year saw numerous uprisings, the largest of which came in August. In the same year around 7,000 Danish Jews were spirited away to neutral Sweden before they could be deported.

FREE Kastellet
Langelinie (www.vejpark.kk.dk). Bus 1A. **Open** 6am-10pm daily. **Admission** free. **Map** p249 H17.
Built by Frederik III in 1662 after the Swedish siege of 1658, Citadel was the base for the Danish army for many years and still houses troops in pretty red terraces inside the ramparts. Note that only the grounds are open to the public, not the actual buildings.

FREE Den Kongelige Afstøbningssamling
Vestindisk Pakhus, Toldbodgade 40 (33 74 84 94, www.smk.dk). Bus 1A. **Open** 10am-4pm Thur; 2-5pm Sun. **Admission** free. **Map** p249 K18.

Kunstindustrimuseet
Bredgade 68 (33 18 56 56, www.kunstindustri museet.dk), Bus 1A, 15. **Open** 11am-5pm Tue-Sun. **Admission** 60kr; 40kr concessions; free under-18s. **Credit** MC, V. **Map** p249 K17.
Housed around a grand courtyard in the old Frederiks Hospital designed by Nicolai Eigtved (where Søren Kierkegaard died in 1855), the 300,000 items here are focused around living rooms from the Middle Ages to the present day, with the emphasis on Danish design and craft. As you'd expect, chairs dominate, but there are also textiles, carpets, clothing, ceramics, cutlery, silverware, glassware, art and other furniture on display. The exhibits from Asia are particularly good. The strength of the museum is its blending of the old with the contemporary in a pleasant, soothing rococo setting. This is yet another of Copenhagen's museums funded by the Ny Carlsberg Foundation. There are English captions throughout.

★ FREE Marmorkirken
Frederiksgade 4 (33 15 01 44, www. marmorkirken.dk). Bus 1A. **Open** 10am-5pm Mon, Tue, Thur, Sat; 10am-6.30pm Wed, noon-5pm Fri, Sun. *Dome* Sept-14 June 1pm, 3pm Sat, Sun. 15 June-Aug 1pm, 3pm daily. **Admission** free. *Dome* 25kr; 10kr under-12s. **No credit cards**. **Map** p249 L16.
Although today it is one of Copenhagen's most breathtaking sights, the circular, domed Marmorkirken very nearly didn't get built. Work on the church, designed by Nicolai Eigtved as the focal point of the new quarter, began in 1749 with the laying of the foundation stone by the king, but was halted in 1770 due to its exorbitant cost, with the walls only ten to 15 metres (33-49 feet) high. It wasn't until the deep-pocketed industrialist CF Tietgen intervened in the late 1800s that the church (by then a grass-covered ruin) was completed in cheaper Danish Faxe marble, instead of the original Norwegian marble. It was topped with a 46-metre (151-foot) dome by the architect Ferdinand Meldahl – inspired by St Peter's in Rome, it remains one of the largest of its kind in Europe (from the top you can see Sweden). Note that the Dome was closed for repairs when this guide went to press, expected to reopen later in 2011; call or visit website for details.

FREE St Alban's Church
Churchillparken (tours 39 62 77 36, www.st-albans.dk). Bus 1A, 15. **Open** *May-Sept* 10am-4pm daily. *Oct-Apr* for services only, 10.30am Wed; 9am, 10.30am Sun. **Admission** free; tour prices vary (ring a week in advance to book). **Map** p249 J18.

FREE Sankt Ansgar Kirke
Bredgade 64 (33 13 37 62, www.sankt ansgarkirke.dk). Bus 1A, 15. **Open** 8am-6pm Mon-Sat; times of services Sun. Mass 8am, 5pm Mon-Fri; 5pm Sat; 8am, 11am Sun. **Admission** free. **Map** p249 K17.

SIGHTS

Rosenborg & Around

Grand parks, fairytale palaces and Denmark's national gallery.

King Christian IV, the architecturally minded 17th-century monarch, may have helped to bankrupt Denmark with his inept meddling in Nordic politics, but he's still one of the country's most admired rulers, not least for the great buildings that were constructed in Copenhagen during his reign. **Rosenborg Slot** (Rosenborg Palace) is arguably his greatest achievement; an excellent Renaissance palace built over the best part of 30 years and a royal residence for over a century.

Nørrebro & Østerbro · The Little Mermaid · Frederiksstaden · Rosenborg & Around · Rosenborg Slot · Amalienborg Slot · Strøget & Around · Nyhavn & Kongens Nytorv · Opera House · Nationalmuseet · Slotsholmen · Christianshavn · Vesterbro & Frederiksberg · Tivoli & Rådhuspladsen

Map pp246-247   **Cafés & Bars** p134
Restaurants p120

Around the palace is a swath of green space made up of the Østre Anlæg park, home to the Hirschsprungske Samling art collection and the **National Gallery** (Statens Museum For Kunst), and the **Botanisk Have** (Botanical Gardens). Also nearby is the jewel of the city's cinema scene, the Filmhuset national film theatre.

ROSENBORG SLOT & AROUND

The lakes of the **Østre Anlæg** park follow the line of the city's old defensive moat. Within the park are two fine museums: **Statens Museum For Kunst** (*see p79*) is Denmark's national gallery and largest art museum, a position that it consolidated in 1998 with the opening of an extension by architect Anna Maria Indrio; nearby is **Den Hirschsprungske Samling** (Hirschsprung Collection; *see p78*), a collection of art from the 19th and early 20th centuries that is particularly strong on the Danish Golden Age.

South from here, across Sølvgade, is the **Geologisk Museum** (Geological Museum; *see p78*), and below this is **Botanisk Have & Museum** (Botanical Garden & Museum; *see right*), providing Elysian relief from the city's streets in summer, while its balmy Palmehus (Palm House), modelled after the one at Kew, can provide refuge from the arctic frost of winter.

Just south of Botanisk Have is **Arbejdermuseet** (Workers' Museum; *see right*). The museum's entrance was once guarded by a statue of Lenin that looks like it's come straight from a provincial Soviet town square, but the current right-wing government turned this into a political issue and the statue has been moved round the back of the museum. In fact, the statue

is here because the Danish co-operative, the Workers' Fuel Suppliers, helped pay for Lenin's passage from exile in Switzerland home to Russia. Arbejdermuseet recently reopened following a nine-month refurbishment, but it remains a rather dry, worthy place and is an unlikely choice for the average tourist.

Diagonally across from Statens Museum, is the entrance to the oldest park in Copenhagen, **Kongens Have** (King's Garden), and **Rosenborg Slot** (*see p78*). A glimpse of this fairytale, Dutch Renaissance castle in the heart of Copenhagen never fails to surprise and more pleasures await, not least the crown jewels.

Just south of Rosenborg is the former venue for the **Musikhistorisk Museum og Carl Claudius' Samling** (Musical History Museum and Carl Claudius' Collection; 33 11 27 26, www.natmus.dk), another of Copenhagen's specialist curio museums, founded in 1898, which is, however, currently closed. The museum is due to reopen in new, not yet disclosed premises in late 2012, when it will once again be able to display its vast collection of musical instruments.

On Gothersgade is **Filmhuset** (Film House; *see p176*), a world-class complex devoted to Danish and international cinema, while on Kronprinsessegade is yet another hidden

SIGHTS

treasure house of a museum, **Davids Samling** (*see below*), a gorgeous collection of Danish, Islamic and European art.

At the north end of Store Kongensgade is **Nyboder**. While Kastellet was for centuries home to the army, the Royal Navy lived in the Lilliputian, ochre terraces of Nyboder, built during Christian IV's time, to house over 2,200 naval staff (a purpose it still serves). There's a small museum, **Nyboders Mindestuer** (Nyboder Memorial Rooms; *see p78*).

Arbejdermuseet
Rømersgade 22 (33 93 25 75, www. arbejdermuseet.dk). Metro Nørreport. **Open** 10am-4pm daily. **Admission** 65kr; 55kr concessions; free under-18s. **Credit** MC, V. **Map** p246 L12.
Arbejdermuseet is housed in an atmospheric building, formerly the headquarters of the Social Democratic Party with a wonderful period basement café and *ølhal* (beer hall). While the museum's aim – to show how Danish workers' lives have changed over the century – is admirable, its political bias gets a little oppressive, though it does offer glimpses into how Danes used to live. The most interesting exhibit is an entire apartment that remained unaltered through the course of the last century, and was donated to the museum in 1990. The various rooms tell the moving story of the real-life Sørensen family, who occupied them for two generations. The rooms chart the progress of the family's escape from rural poverty, the father's work at a brewery, the parents' deaths, and how one of their eight children, their daughter Yrsa, took over the home in 1964. Be warned, it swarms with school trips on weekdays.

★ FREE Botanisk Have & Museum
Gothersgade 128 (35 32 22 40, www.botanic-garden.ku.dk). **Open** *Garden* May-Sept 8.30am-6pm daily. Oct-Apr 8.30am-4pm Tue-Sun. *Palm house* 10am-3pm daily. *Insectivorous greenhouse* 10am-3pm daily. *Cactus greenhouse* 1-2pm Wed, Sat, Sun. *Orchid greenhouse* 2-3pm Wed, Sat, Sun. *Alpine plants* 11am-2pm Wed; *New greenhouse with endangered species* 1-3pm Wed, Sat, Sun. Museum open only for exhibitions, check online or phone (35 32 22 00). Sept-May closed. **Admission** free. **Map** p247 K13.
The garden was laid out in 1871 to designs by HA Flindt, with a lake that was once part of the city moat as its centrepiece. You'll find examples of most of Denmark's flora, as well as those exotic plants that could be persuaded to grow this far north. The Botanisk Museum is open only in summer.

★ FREE Davids Samling
Kronprinsessegade 30 (33 73 49 49, www. davidmus.dk). Metro Nørreport. **Open** 1-5pm Tue, Fri; 10am-9pm Wed; 10am-5pm Thur; 11am-5pm Sat, Sun. **Admission** free. **Map** p247 L15.

This art and antiquities museum is housed in the building once home to its founder, Christian Ludvig David, as well as in a neighbouring 19th-century property. Both buildings underwent comprehensive renovation between 2005 and 2009. David was a prominent lawyer, whose collections spanned European 18th-century art, Danish Early Modern works and Islamic art and artefacts. The latter collection is the museum's largest and most important, and has grown to become one of the ten most important collections of its kind in the Western world, covering the entire classical Islamic world, from Spain to India, and from the eighth to the 19th centuries. The European items feature furniture, porcelain and paintings from the 18th century (with lots of Dutch and French portraits).

Kongens Have.

SIGHTS

SIGHTS

Geologisk Museum

Øster Voldgade 5-7 (35 32 23 45, www.geologisk-museum.dk). Metro Nørreport. **Open** 10am-1pm Tue-Fri; 1-4pm Sat, Sun. **Admission** 40kr; 25kr concessions; free to all Wed. **Credit** MC, V. **Map** p247 K13.

Head here for displays of fossils and dinosaurs. There are several English-language leaflets, but the museum is showing its age, and is really only for those with a special interest.

Den Hirschsprungske Samling

Stockholmsgade 20 (35 42 03 36, www.hirschsprung.dk). Metro Nørreport. **Open** 11am-4pm Mon, Wed-Sun; phone to check. **Admission** 50kr; 40kr concessions; free under-18s; free to all Wed. **Credit** AmEx, MC, V. **Map** p247 J14.

This art collection from the 19th and early 20th centuries is strong on the Danish Golden Age (1800-50). It was created by tobacco manufacturer Heinrich Hirschsprung (1836-1908), who crammed the paintings and sculptures into his home on Højbro Plads. Before he died Hirschsprung donated the collection to the Municipality of Copenhagen on condition that they be displayed in similarly intimate surroundings, hence the series of small rooms around three larger halls that make up the building. The museum opened in 1911 and has continued to purchase works ever since.

Nyboders Mindestuer

Sankt Pauls Gade 24 (33 32 10 05, guided tours 33, 32 79 13, www.nybodersmindestuer.dk).

Metro Kongens Nytorv. **Open** 11am-2pm Sun. Guided tours by appointment. **Admission** 15kr; 10kr concessions. **No credit cards. Map** p249 K16.

★ Rosenborg Slot

Øster Voldgade 4A (33 15 32 86, www.rosenborgslot.dk). Metro Nørreport. **Open** *Jan-Apr, Nov-mid Dec* 11am-4pm Tue-Sun. *May, Sept, Oct* 10am-4pm daily. *June-Aug* 10am-5pm daily. *Mid Dec-26 Dec* closed; *27-30 Dec* 11am-4pm. **Admission** 75kr; 50kr concessions; free under-17s. **Credit** AmEx, MC, V. **Map** p247 K14.

Though it was built at the same time as Frederiksberg Slot, Rosenborg was Christian IV's favourite residence. Towards the end of his life, Christian, aged 70, was taken by sleigh through the snow from Frederiksborg to Rosenborg to die. He literally pulled up the palace drawbridge to escape the harsh economic realities of Denmark's ruin and contemplate a bitter death.

Most of the castle was closed to the public between late 2006 and spring 2008 for a major structural restoration to reinforce the building's beams; the visible results of these works are a new marble floor in the Long Hall on the second floor and refurbished rooms on the first.

The castle started as a small summer house. Christian extended it between 1606 and 1634, finishing off with the octagonal staircase tower designed by the fantastically named Hans van Steenwinckel the Younger. Rosenborg is still jammed full of the king's fancies: toys, architectural tricks, inventions, art objects and jewellery, which he gathered from

Statens Museum For Kunst.

around Europe like a regal Mr Toad. A source of great pride was the castle basement, where his orchestra would perform, its music travelling up through a complex system of pipes connected to his living quarters. These days the basement houses the Treasury, the stronghold of the crown jewels. It's a collection in which quality, not quantity, is the watchword. The star is the Golden Crown of the Absolute Monarchy, decorated with sapphires, diamonds and rubies, made by Poul Kurtz in 1670, and used by Denmark's kings for 170 years. Christian IV's gold, pearl and jewel-encrusted saddle and crown (1595) are, as you'd expect, jaw-dropping. Newer rooms in the basement display royal weapons and objets d'art of ivory and amber.

Rosenborg was a royal residence until 1838, when these collections were opened to the public, along with the many rooms that had remained intact from the time of Christian IV (1588-1648) to Frederik IV (1699-1730); later rooms were recreated. The decision to arrange the rooms chronologically was, at the time, radical and, consequently, Rosenborg claims to be the first museum of contemporary culture in Europe. The 24 rooms (plus six Treasury rooms) currently on show offer an insight into the lives of Renaissance kings that is perhaps unparalleled in Europe for its atmosphere and intimacy. Christian IV's toilet, covered in beautiful blue Dutch tiles, for example, is as fascinating a treasure as the jewels in the basement.

Other must-sees include Christian's study with his elegant writing desk; Frederik III's marble room; the breathtaking Mirror, Porcelain and Venetian Glass Cabinets; and the last room to be completed (in 1624), the Long Hall, with an amazing throne made from narwhal horns, and guarded by three solid silver lions from 1670.

★ Statens Museum For Kunst

Sølvgade 48-50 (33 74 84 94, www.smk.dk).
Metro Nørreport. **Open** 10am-5pm Tue, Thur-Sun; 10am-8pm Wed. **Admission** 95kr; 65kr-75kr concessions; free under-18s. **Credit** AmEx, MC, V.
Map p247 J14.

As with Nationalmuseet, the world-class collection of Statens Museum For Kunst, though founded in 1824, has its origins in royal collections from centuries earlier. During the 19th century the collection was based in Christiansborg Slot, until a fire meant it had to move to the current building specially designed by Vilhelm Dahlerup (also responsible for Ny Carlsberg Glyptotek and Det Kongelige Teater) in 1896.

Unlike Henning Larsen's acclaimed extension to the Ny Carlsberg Glyptotek, Indrio's glass and stone addition has proved to be a controversial space for the museum's collection of Danish and European art from the 20th century onwards. Some say the new gallery fails to provide appropriate rooms in which to exhibit the paintings, others find its mixture of vast glass windows (overlooking Østre Anlæg park) and unrelenting stone offers a pleasing spatial puzzle. It's true that every window offers a perfectly framed vista, but it is

INSIDE TRACK
TORCH-LIT TOURS

Despite existing happily for more than a century without it, the **Rosenborg Slot** (*see left*) has now installed electricity. That's a great shame, because the palace's Stygian gloom was a major part of its appeal. But at least the special torch-lit, night-time tour still takes place here once a year on **Kulturnatten** (*see p166* **For One Night Only**).

not quite the neutral backdrop the museum claims, more a grand piece of 'event' architecture against which the art sometimes struggles to be heard.

The museum's main focus is, of course, Danish art, and, as you'd expect, the artists from the so-called Golden Age of the early 19th century figure prominently. These rooms are dedicated to Danish masters, such as CW Eckersburg and his pupils Christen Købke and Constantin Hansen. The landscapes of JT Lundbye, the stark portraits of Vilhelm Hammershøi, the powerful portraits by LA Ring and the symbolist pieces by PC Skovgaard (whose mighty canvas, *Christ in the Kingdom of Death*, a milestone in Danish art, has now been restored), and their forerunners from the 18th century, like Nicolai Abildgaard and Jens Juel, are among the best treats in the museum. The Skagen artists (Michael and Anna Ancher and PS Krøyer), who were specialists in everyday scenes and light, summery landscapes, and the Fyn painters (Peter Hansen and Frits Syberg) are also well represented. Though the works are sometimes sentimental, no one before or since has quite captured the unmistakable, crisp Danish light as these artists did, and their paintings often also depict brutal, beautiful and compelling stories concerning 'real' people's lives, be they butchers, maids, schoolchildren, farmers or fishermen. If you haven't seen them before, allow as much time as you can in these rooms.

In the new wing, the collection of 25 paintings by Henri Matisse, as well as works by Braque, Munch and Picasso, are highlights, as is the Danish modernist collection featuring the painters Giersing and Isakson, and sculptors Kai Nielsen and Astrid Noack. In the old wing the Italians are well represented by Titian, Tintoretto, Filippino Lippi, Mantegna and Guardi. Dutch and Flemish 15th- to 17th-century masters here include Rubens, Bruegel, Rembrandt, Van Dyck and Van Goyen. French 18th-century works are by Fragonard, Poussin and Lorrain. Statens Museum also has one of the world's oldest collections of European prints and drawings (some 300,000) by artists such as Degas, Toulouse-Lautrec, Picasso, Giacometti, Rembrandt and Piranesi. On the ground floor is a children's art museum with hands-on displays, and the museum also has a large bookshop and a new 2010 café with designer chairs and Paul Gernes artwork.

SIGHTS

Christianshavn

From laid-back to seriously chilled.

The people of Christianshavn will wince if you suggest that they're part of the island of Amager. The neighbourhood does indeed have a charm and a character that are charmingly unique, but there are only a few bridges separating Christianshavn from the rest of Copenhagen. The surrounding streets have a laid-back feel, as does the central canal that cuts through the middle of the area. Of course, laid-back soon becomes seriously chilled when you come to Christiania, even though events of the past few years have made the mood of the place a little more tense these days.

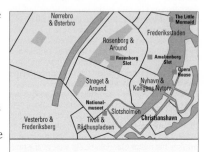

Map p252-253   **Cafés & Bars** p135
Restaurants p120

THE CANAL DISTRICT

Christianshavn was built to the east of Slotsholmen in the early 17th century to protect Christian IV's burgeoning city from attack, and to ease overcrowding within the city walls. The king's complex plan, inspired by Amsterdam's grid of canals, was eventually simplified for reasons of cost, but remains pretty much intact today following sympathetic renovation in the 1980s and '90s. Christianshavn's charming houses and courtyards also escaped most of the fires that ravaged Copenhagen over the centuries, though developers are now doing their utmost to spoil the historic ambience.

To the north of Christianshavn is Holmen, the old dockland area that was built on reclaimed land in the 17th century. Holmen still has its naval base, but has changed and now throngs with students on summer evenings at the 'beach' bars. And the recently built **Operaen** (*see p192* **Royal Danish Theatre**) has put this area at the forefront of Denmark's cultural life. Holmen is a fascinating place, best explored by bicycle.

Christianshavn's dominant landmark is the **Vor Frelsers Kirke** (Church of Our Saviour), whose fabulous 90-metre (295-foot) high spire can be seen from most parts of the city centre.

Christianshavn's other significant church is **Christians Kirke**, notable for its unique interior, laid out in the style of a theatre.

Christianshavn's importance in Denmark's naval history is attested to in **Orlogsmuseet** (Royal Danish Naval Museum), which has an extensive collection of fantastically detailed model ships. The collection was started by Christian IV and originally exhibited in Sankt Nicolaj Kirke; it was moved to the current site of Søkvæsthus, the old naval hospital, in 1989.

Further along historic Strandgade is **Dansk Arkitekturcenter** (Danish Architecture Centre). Exhibitions cover current Danish projects and international themes and, though fairly specialised, are usually worth a look for

View from **Vor Frelsers Kirke**.

those with an interest in architecture. They are often accompanied by debates and conferences in the restaurant on the main floor.

One of Christianshavn's easily overlooked sites is **Lille Mølle**, a windmill dating from 1669, situated on the ramparts south-east of Christiania. It was converted into a private home in 1916 and the interior, with numerous antiques and art objects, has been perfectly preserved by Nationalmuseet, which now owns the site. Next door is **Bastionen og Løven**, an excellent café (*see p133*) and a very popular meeting place during summer.

If you head west from Christianshavn across the old defensive ramparts, you come to **Islands Brygge** (*see p83* **Come On In, the Water's Lovely**). It's enjoying a new lease of life after trendy architects Plot were commissioned to build the city's magnificent, permanent, open-air bathing complex. The complex is moored on the waterfront beside Langebro and behind it, the lawns are packed with sunbathers, basketball players and picnickers. Various trendy independent galleries and cafés have sprung up in the area, too, putting Islands Brygge on the hipster map.

FREE Christians Kirke
Strandgade 1 (32 54 15 76, www.christians kirke.dk). Metro Christianshavn. **Open** 10am-4pm Mon-Fri; after 10am service Sun. **Admission** free. **Map** p252 P16.
The rococo structure of this church, with its neo-classical spire, was designed by Nicolai Eigtved in 1755 for the German population of Christianshavn. Financed by a lottery, it was known for a long time as the Lottery Church.

Dansk Arkitekturcenter
Strandgade 27B (32 57 19 30, www.dac.dk). Metro Christianshavn/bus 2A, 40. **Open** 10am-5pm Mon, Tue, Thur-Sun; 10am-9pm Wed.

Admission 40kr; 25kr concessions; free under-15s; free after 5pm Wed. **Credit** MC, V. **Map** p252 O16.

Lille Mølle
Christianshavns Voldgade 54 (33 47 38 38, in July phone 33 47 38 57, www.natmus.dk). Metro Christianshavn/bus 66. **Open** (guided tours only) June-Sept 1pm, 2pm, 3pm Sat, Sun. *Oct-May* closed. **Admission** 50kr; 40kr concessions, free under-18s. **No credit cards.** **Map** p252 P18.

Orlogsmuseet
Overgaden Oven Vandet 58 (33 11 60 37, www.orlogsmuseet.dk). Metro Christianshavn/bus 2A, 19, 350S. **Open** noon-4pm Tue-Sun. *July* 10am-4pm Tue-Sun. **Admission** 60kr; 40kr concessions; free under-17s. Free to all Wed. **Credit** AmEx, MC, V. **Map** p252 P17.
The oldest model in Orlogsmuseet, the Royal Danish Naval Museum, is of a man-of-war, dating from 1680, in addition and there are countless replicas of later ships (including the interior of a submarine, with sound effects), as well as a comprehensive history of the Danish Royal Navy and several historic battle scenes recreated in model form. One gallery contains a splendidly ornate state barge from 1780, another is dedicated to marine archaeology. Orlogsmuseet will delight model-making enthusiasts and naval historians; it's also popular with children, who are catered for with a well-equipped playroom.

★ Vor Frelsers Kirke
Sankt Annægade 29 (32 57 27 98, www. vorfrelserskirke.dk). Metro Christianshavn/ bus 2A, 66, 350S. **Open** *Church* 11am-3.30pm daily. *Spire* Apr-June, mid Sept-mid Nov 11am-4pm daily; July-mid Sept 11am-7pm daily; mid Nov-Dec 11am-4pm weekends only. **Admission** free for church. *Spire* 25kr; 10kr concessions. **No credit cards.** **Map** p252 P17.

Von Freslers Kirke. *See p81.*

SIGHTS

This landmark church was built by architect Lambert van Haven for Christian V in 1682 in the Palladian Dutch baroque style, from red brick and sandstone. Don't be taken in by Danes who tell you that the spire's architect, Laurids de Thurah, threw himself off the top because it wound the wrong way – he actually died in poverty seven years after its completion. The spire was inspired by the lanterns on the Church of Sant'Ivo alla Sapienza in Rome and was completed in pine with copper cladding and gilt decoration in 1752. On the day of its dedication King Frederik V climbed to the top to receive a 27-gun salute as crowds cheered below. This extraordinary spire is open to any visitors who feel they can conquer their vertigo and its 400 or so steps, which spiral ever narrower to the summit. Inside, the church is spacious, but prosaic, in the typical Lutheran manner, though its immense three-storey organ, which was completed in 1698, is stupefying

CHRISTIANIA

Christiania, or the Freetown of Christiania to give it its full title, is a residential area unlike any other in Denmark. This mess of historic military buildings, makeshift housing and ramshackle businesses, which straddles the defensive moat and 17th-century ramparts to the east of Christianshavn, is home to approximately 1,000 people (exact figures are difficult to come by). It attracts around three-quarters of a million visitors a year, which makes it one of Denmark's biggest tourist attractions.

Christiania is unique. Until very recently it was a community that existed within Copenhagen, but outside its laws and conventions. With the election of the new government, and more particularly the rise to power of right-wing factions within the coalition such as the Dansk Folkeparti, Christiania has been under threat as never before. There was talk of the whole place being torn down and the first casualty was the world-famous Pusher Street, where soft drugs were being sold openly from stalls like market produce.

In January 2004, Christiania voted to tear down the booths selling ready rolled spliffs, cannabis resin and other drugs – before the government ordered the police to do it forcibly, as they had been threatening. This came despite the fact that the police felt it would be counterproductive to send the sale of soft drugs underground – 'You don't just make a problem like this go away with a click of the fingers,' said Copenhagen's drugs tsar at the time.

The demolition of Pusher Street did turn out to be a smart move, however, as the government's final surprise ruling was that Christiania could stay, but must follow a 'legalisation' process, involving the removal of some buildings and the rental system being made more 'above board'. Despite this pressure to conform, its residents remain committed to their 'alternative' lifestyle.

Up until 1971, the 41-hectare (101-acre) site that Christiania now occupies was an army barracks. When the army moved out, a group of like-minded Christianshavn residents decided to knock down the fence on Prinsessegade and access the land as a playground and open space. Meanwhile, an exhibition at Charlottenborg, Noget for Noget (Give and Take), which examined the hippie movement, and an alternative lifestyle newspaper, *Hovedbladet* (Head Magazine), galvanised Copenhagen's experimentalists. The paper ran an article on the barracks with various proposals for its use, including as housing for the young. This was all the encouragement that hundreds of 'drop-outs' from across Denmark needed and soon the site began to fill up. On 13 November 1971, the new residents founded what they like to call the Freetown of Christiania, although it was promptly declared illegal by the authorities. However, the number of residents had already grown to the extent that, despite their best and often most violent efforts, the police failed to clear the barricades.

In subsequent years, as the community formed its own system of government, built schools, shops, cafés, restaurants, various co-operatives and music venues, and embarked on recycling programmes and nascent solar- and wind-power projects, the debate about

Come On In, the Water's Lovely

Harbour and sea spots from which to take the summer plunge.

Copenhagen has developed into an idyllic spot for summer bathing in the past few years, following the construction of the Islands Brygge section of the **Copenhagen Harbour Baths** by the architectural firm Plot in 2003, 115 metres (380 feet) south of the Langebro bridge. The opening of the baths followed a drive by local authorities to improve the quality of the harbour water, which is now as clean as that in the Øresund (and constantly monitored). Many parts have been given a Blue Flag.

Consisting of five basins (two for children), the **Islands Brygge Harbour Baths** (pictured) have been an enormous success, and are partly responsible for the regeneration of the surrounding area. Open from the first week in June to the end of August (7am-7pm Mon-Fri; 11am-7pm Sat, Sun), they mark the official start (and end) of summer for many locals.

Islands Brygge are the most popular of the Copenhagen Harbour Baths, with a capacity for 600 people, but there is also a bathing complex at Vesterbro's Havneholmen (close to the Fisketorvet shopping mall, just south of Kødbyen, the Meatpacking District) known as **Copencabana**, and another is due to open at **Sluseholmen** in the South Harbour in June 2011. All the harbour baths are part of the extensive waterfront regeneration of the past few years, which has also included the openings of several landmark buildings (*see p29* **On the Waterfront**).

But the Harbour Baths aren't the only spots for a summer dip. The pools are actually a supplement to the handful of beaches around the city. It's easy to forget that Copenhagen is bordered by coastline – but, in fact, the seaside is walking distance from the centre, making it a perfect summer city. In June 2010, a new 4,000 square-metre (13,000 square-feet) artificial beach (and pier) opened at Østerbro's **Svanemøllestranden**, and there has has been an extensive urban beach to the east of the city at **Amager Strandpark** since 2005. The latter consists of 4.6 kilometres of white sand, where you can swim in the sea, rent kayaks, eat ice-cream or light a bonfire in one of the allocated spots. Slightly further down the coast, and connected to Amager Strandpark by a long wooden bridge, is **Kastrup Søbad** ('the Snail'), while just north of Copenhagen is Klampenborg's 700-metre-long **Bellevue Beach**, five minutes' walk from Dyrehaven.

In summer 2010, the Royal Danish Theatre (*see p192* **Royal Danish Theatre**) established the temporary artificial Ophelia Beach on the Kvæsthusbroen pier next to the Royal Playhouse, bringing the beach even closer to the action. Keep your eyes peeled for its return in 2011.

SIGHTS

SIGHTS

Christiania raged. The bulldozers and batons were never far away. Charity records, concerts, PR stunts and the election to the local council of some of its residents ensured Christiania remained in the headlines and, eventually, in 1991, an uneasy truce was met with the authorities. Christiania agreed to pay rent and cover the cost of water and electricity supplies, as well as to look after the buildings that were of historical importance, while the city council agreed to allow it to continue as a 'social experiment'. In truth, were Christiania to be closed down tomorrow, the ensuing housing crisis and crime wave would prove a far greater political hot potato. The site is technically still owned by the Ministry of Defence.

Today, with the sale of drugs banished, the community earns money from its restaurants and bars, as well as the sale of its unique Christiania bicycles and handicrafts. The residents (around 70 per cent of whom receive some kind of government benefit) pay rent, which goes towards the upkeep of buildings, city taxes and services. None pays income tax.

A complex system of self-government is headed by the Common Meeting with power devolved through 15 local Area Meetings. Decisions are arrived at via consensus, as opposed to majority vote, and new arrivals must be approved by the House Meeting. A stunt by a Danish TV show showed how territorial the Freetown is, however, when they turned up and tried to build a house by the lake. Locals tore it down and assaulted the TV crew.

Christiania is divided by the moat into two distinct areas – the main commercial centre, with its music venues, shops, restaurants and bars; and Dysen, a quiet residential area on the eastern side of the moat.

'Flower power' staggers on in Christiania and, by way of evidence, no wall is left undaubed with murals, graffiti and, well, daubs, and large, shaggy dogs of indeterminate breed roam unhindered. There are a number of cafés and restaurants. **Spiseloppen** (*spise* means 'eat'; *loppen* means 'the flea'; *see p123*) and **Morgenstedet** (*see p122*) are the best. In the same building as Spiseloppen is the atmospheric music venue **Loppen** (*see venue index*), while the 2,000-capacity **Den Grå Hal** (the Grey Hall) is Christiania's largest music venue, and has hosted gigs by the likes of Blur and Bob Dylan.

All of Christiania is open to tourists (though obviously not the private dwellings). You can pass a very pleasant afternoon wandering around the quieter parts, inspecting the extraordinary variety of housing – from pyramids, railway carriages and tree houses, to sophisticated wooden chalets and the original 17th-century barracks. It's well worth taking the time to explore this remarkable community.

Christiania. *See p82.*

Vesterbro & Frederiksberg

Vibrant nightlife and sleaze meet desirable residential enclaves.

Sex and drugs have long been the claim to fame of **Vesterbro** – the area stretching west from Central Station – but this notoriously sleazy district has been gentrified in recent years. The sex shops and junkies are still here, but they are now crowded out by media people, artists and students, who appreciate the area's ethnically diverse population and exotic food shops and restaurants. As the trendies have taken over – most notably in **Kødbyen**, the city's Meatpacking District – hip cafés, bars and indie design shops have sprung up.

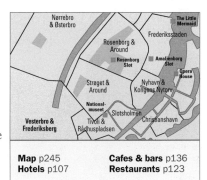

Map p245	**Cafes & bars** p136
Hotels p107	**Restaurants** p123

Though just west of Vesterbro, quiet and refined **Frederiksberg** seems worlds away from its blowsy neighbour. Its wide, leafy avenues, grand parks and elegant 18th-century royal palace make this one of the city's most desirable residential areas (slightly lower taxes for residents help), and its parks and zoo are a popular destination at weekends.

South of Frederiksberg (and west of Vesterbro) lies Valby, home to the old Carlsberg Brewery.

VESTERBRO

Vesterbro has revelled in its trashy image since the 18th century, when it was the site of numerous music halls and drinking dens, and the second half of the 19th century, when it was filled by an immense block of inhuman corridor flats (to ease overcrowding in the city).

Meat markets, literal and metaphorical, have always been Vesterbro's speciality. Their trade was centred on **Værnedamsvej**, which at one time had Europe's highest concentration of dead flesh. The street, which borders on gentrified Frederiksberg, is now one of the area's nicest, its cute food shops, boutiques and cafés, such as **Falernum** (*see p137*) and **Granola** (*see p137*), giving it a Parisian feel. The sex trade is now more centrally located, on the seedier eastern end of **Istedgade**, Vesterbro's artery. For Vesterbro's plethora of fashion and design shops, head to the western, Enghaven (park) end of Istedgade.

Halmtorvet squre, south of Istedgade, is one of the most visible symbols of the area's rejuvenation: it has had the sandblasters and decorators in and the cobbles relaid, and is a popular evening and weekend destination, boasting several good cafés. The fashionistas, however, flock to **Kødbyen**, just south of here – the new, regenerated Meatpacking District, whose low-rise former butchers' shops and slaughterhouses are now home to several cool galleries, bars, restaurants and nightspots (as well as a few remaining butchers), including late-night bar **Bakken** (*see p186*), **Mother** pizza parlour (*see p125*) and seafood restaurant-of-the-moment **Fiskebaren** (*see p124*). Many a gallery or magazine launch party takes place around here.

Vesterbro has very few traditional tourist attractions, other than the city museum and planetarium. The **Museum of Copenhagen** (*see p86*) is a 15-minute walk along Vesterbrogade from Tivoli, and gives an excellent overview of the capital's history, while **Tycho Brahe Planetarium** (*see p87*), on Gammel Kongevej, shows a variety of IMAX movies and puts on interplanetary displays.

Museum of Copenhagen

Vesterbrogade 59 (33 21 07 72, www. copenhagen.dk). Bus 6A, 26. **Open** 10am-4pm Mon, Thur-Sun; 10am-9pm Wed. **Admission** 20kr; 10kr concessions; free under-18s; free to all Fri. **Credit** MC, V. **Map** p245 Q9.

This laid-back museum charts the history of Copenhagen from fishing village to cosmopolitan capital, with lots of visual displays depicting how Copenhageners have lived over the last millennium. Its insightful temporary exhibitions have covered topics such as 'Copenhagen Underground' and 'Becoming a Copenhagener'.

▶ *The museum is behind the 'Wall' – a 12-metre outdoor multi-touch screen that can be experienced at different sites throughout the city in connection with the excavations for the new City Ring Metro.*

Brewing Up a Cultural Storm

Regenerating the site of the city's old Carlsberg Brewery.

Plans to redevelop the old Carlsberg Brewery were drawn up shortly after Carlsberg moved its beer production site to Frederica, 200 kilometres west of the capital, in 2006. Carlsberg had brewed beer on the site in Valby, south of Frederiksberg, for 160 years, and the vacant buildings and space it left behind are due to be used to create a radical new cultural, residential and small business quarter over the next decade.

The industrial site, which covers 330,000 square metres, is ripe for gentrification, featuring beautiful old buildings, cellars and warehouses, squares and gardens. To create a vision for the new quarter, Carlsberg invited citizens and professionals to enter a design competition for the new area, with sustainability, innovation and heritage key words from the start.

Local architects Entasis won the competition in May 2007. However, their plan – based on transforming the brewery's cellars to create a labyrinthine area, and organising the site around a theme of

shared space – has been put on hold since the global economic crisis of 2008.

However, the halt is apparently temporary, and local planners are still hoping to see a vibrant quarter emerging over the next decade, which will feature new shops, cafés, cultural and sporting spaces, bicycle paths (a new Carlsberg green route has already been planned), green spaces and 3,000 new, low-energy homes (for a variety of income brackets). It's an interesting example of people-focused planning that Danish urban designers are so good at.

The iconic Elephant Gate is to be preserved as part of the plan, and the Carlsberg HQ will also remain. The former is a popular spot for camera-wielding tourists and locals, who are already venturing this way to check out the first few galleries (Nicolai Wallner; *see p180*) and cafés (the excellent Elefanten, *see p136*) that have moved in, as well as to attend music venue Tap 1 (www.tap1.dk). Watch this space for more openings over the next few years.

SIGHTS

It opened in April 2010 on Kongen Nytorv, will move to Rådhuspladsen in summer 2011, and then to Gammel Strand in spring 2012. See the Museum of Copenhagen website for details.

Tycho Brahe Planetarium
Gammel Kongevej 10 (33 12 12 24, www. tycho.dk). Train Vesterport. **Open** 11.30am-8.30pm Mon; 10.30am-8.30pm Tue-Fri; 9.30am-8.30pm Sat, Sun. **Admission** (includes ticket to an IMAX screening) 135kr; 72kr-115kr concessions; 85kr under-13s. **Credit** AmEx, MC, V. **Map** p250 P10.
The largest planetarium in Western Europe, it was opened in 1989 in a cylindrical building designed by Knud Munk and is named after the great Danish astronomer (1546-1601) who painstakingly catalogued the solar system – a crucial contribution to the understanding of the laws of planetary motion.

FREDERIKSBERG

Frederiksberg's appealing character may be partially the result of its distinct political status: like Christiania, Frederiksberg is a separate town within the city of Copenhagen (and a stark contrast to the alternative Freetown). An independent municipality of just over 90,000 people, it has its own mayor, town hall and administration. Apartments tend to be larger and more expensive than elsewhere in the city, especially those along **Frederiksberg Allé**, a long tree-lined boulevard, which could have been lifted straight from an affluent arrondissement of Paris. Until the 19th century Frederiksberg lay well outside Copenhagen, with views from its hill ('berg' means 'hill') over the fields (now Vesterbro) to the city beyond. And it still has a unique sense of separateness: true, the district's conservative character doesn't make for giddy nightlife, but it does have a few sights that are worth the short bus or Metro ride from the centre of town.

The heart of the quarter is **Frederiksberg Have** (Frederiksberg Park; *see p89*), a rambling expanse that was laid out in the formal French style in the 18th century, before being given a more informal English revamp at the turn of the 19th century.

The greenery extends across Roskildevej to **Søndermarken** common, a more informal but equally picturesque park that also features one of Copenhagen's most unusual museums. Entrance to **Cisternerne – Museet For Moderne Glaskunst** (the Cisterns – Museum of Modern Glass Art; *see p88*) is gained via a Louvre-style glass pyramid in the park, opposite the rear of Frederiksberg Slot. Descend the stairs into what were once sizeable underground water tanks and you will find a remarkable glass sculpture museum with modern and classical stained glass and three-dimensional works.

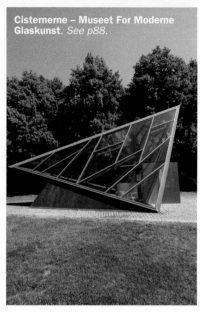

Cisternerne – Museet For Moderne Glaskunst. *See p88.*

In the south-east corner of Frederiksberg Have is **Det Kongelige Danske Haveselskabs Have** (Royal Danish Horticultural Garden; *see p89*), a formal, oriental-influenced water garden, created in 1884.

Frederiksberg has two other small parks, less frequently visited by tourists. Sheltering behind a cluster of apartment blocks on Hollændervej is the tiny **Rosenhaven** (Rose Garden), which is home to a variety of roses including the Ingrid Bergman and Queen Elizabeth. **Landbohøjskolens Have** (Agricultural University's Garden; *see p89*) on Bülowsvej was laid out in 1858 at the time of the university's foundation.

On the south side of Frederiksberg Have lies **Frederiksberg Slot** (Frederiksberg Palace; *see p89*), a royal summer residence between the early 18th and mid 19th centuries. Beside Frederiksberg Slot is the **Zoologisk Have** (Zoological Garden; *see p89*), Denmark's national zoo. Founded in 1859, it is one of the oldest in the world, and has a good reputation for breeding animals in captivity. Recent new buildings for the giraffes and the elephants have helped improve the inhabitants' lot, and there's a new savannah for African species, including a reservoir for the ever-popular hippos.

Moving around Frederiksberg Have in a clockwise direction you come to the **Royal Copenhagen Porcelain Manufactory**. Further on are two small museums that offer

SIGHTS

Frederiksberg Have.

a unique insight into the Danish sense of humour. Danes seem to be divided as to the merits of the Frederiksberg-born artist and cartoonist Robert Storm Petersen (1882-1949), better known as Storm P. For older Danes, he typifies a traditional, aphoristic strain of Danish humour; for the younger generation, he is a dusty relic of a bygone era, and about as funny as a hospital visit. At **Storm P Museet** (Storm P Museum; *see p89*) you can judge for yourself whether his social-critical cartoons display any comedic merit, or whether his symbolist-influenced paintings hold any profound philosophical meaning. There are English captions.

Behind the Storm P Museum you'll find the even more idiosyncratic **Det Danske Revymuseum** (Museum of Light; *see below*).

Opposite Frederiksberg Runddel stands the small, octagonal **Frederiksberg Kirke**, dating from 1734. The pretty Dutch Renaissance church regularly holds concerts and has an altarpiece depicting the Eucharist, painted by CW Eckersberg, while in its cemetery you'll find the grave of 19th-century poet Adam Oehlenschläger.

On the south side of Frederiksberg is **Bakkehus Museet** (Bakkehus Museum; *see below*), a converted 17th-century house containing souvenirs of Denmark's early 19th-century Golden Age. It lies literally in the shadow of the headquarters of what is Copenhagen's and probably Denmark's best-known international brand: Carlsberg. The **Carlsberg Visitors Centre & Jacobsen Brewhouse** (*see below*), in Valby, is a must for beer buffs, while the surrounding area has been ripe for redevelopment since Carlsberg moved its production plant to an area outside of Copenhagen in 2006 (*see p86* **Brewing Up a Cultural Storm**).

Bakkehus Museet

Rahbeks Allé 23 (33 31 43 62, www.bakkehus museet.dk). Train to Valby/bus 6A, 18, 26. **Open** 11am-4pm Tue-Sun. **Admission** 30kr; 1kr concessions. **No credit cards.**

This small, eclectic collection is housed in the former home of a professor of literature and publisher of the period, Knud Lyhne Rahbek. The display includes everything from death masks to Adam Oehlenschläger's dressing gown.

Carlsberg Visitors Centre & Jacobsen Brewhouse

Gamle Carlsberg Vej 11, Valby (33 27 12 82, www.visitcarlsberg.com). Bus 18, 26. **Open** *Sept-Apr* 10am-5pm Tue-Sun. *May-Aug* 10am-5pm Mon-Wed, Fri-Sun; 10am-7.30pm Thur. **Admission** 65kr; 50kr concessions; free under-12s. **Credit** AmEx, MC, V.

The centre runs guided tours through the various displays on the history of beer and the brewing processes used at Carlsberg. Naturally, visits conclude with a free sample in the Jacobsen Brewhouse bar/microbrewery (*see also p138* **A Room with a Brew**).

Cisternerne – Museet For Moderne Glaskunst

Søndermarken (33 21 93 10, www.cisternerne.dk). Bus 4A, 6A, 18, 26. **Open** *Feb-Nov* 2-6pm Thur, Fri; 11am-5pm Sat, Sun. **Admission** 40kr; 30kr concessions; free under-14s. **No credit cards.**

These former underground water tanks now house an extraordinary glass sculpture museum, featuring modern and classical stained glass and three-dimensional works. But the amazing vaulted subterranean rooms leave an equally lasting impression, still dank and wet under foot with stalactites and stalagmites surviving as evidence of their former function. This is supposedly the only art museum in Europe to do without natural light, but it manages superbly thanks to the work of theatrical effects expert John Aage Sørensen. *Photo p87.*

Det Danske Revymuseum

Allegade 5 (38 10 20 45, www.revymuseet.dk). Bus 18, 26. **Open** 11am-4pm Tue-Sun. **Admission** 35kr; 25kr concessions. **No credit cards.**

This unusual museum features 200 years' worth of memorabilia from traditional Danish revue theatre.

The assorted photographs, programmes and costumes will be largely meaningless to foreign visitors, however, as there is no English information.

★ FREE Frederiksberg Have

Main entrance: Frederiksberg Runddel (www. ses.dk). Bus 18, 26. **Open** 6am-sunset daily. **Admission** free.

With its tree-lined paths, canals and lake, this is one of the city's most romantic spaces, particularly in spring. In its grounds are a Chinese pavilion, numerous statues and an impressive avenue of stately linden trees, dating from the 1730s.

Frederiksberg Slot

Roskildevej 28 (36 13 26 00, www.ho.dk). Bus 6A. **Open** *Guided tours* Jan-May, Aug-Nov 11am, 1pm last Sat of month. **Admission** 30kr. **No credit cards**.

Frederik IV had been so taken by the villas he had seen while on a visit to Frascati that, between 1699 and 1703, he instructed architect Ernst Brandenburger to build a palace in the Italian style. The two side wings, which were designed by Laurids de Thurah, were added between 1733 and 1738, on the instruction of Christian VI. Today the palace is home to the Danish Military Academy and, as such, is not open to the public other than for the occasional guided tour.

FREE Det Kongelige Danske Haveselskabs Have

Pile Allé 6, Frederiksberg (36 44 98 99, www. haveselskab.dk). Bus 18, 26. **Open** 10am-sunset daily. **Admission** free.

In the summer this oriental water garden is one of the Copenhagen Jazz Festival's most idyllic outdoor venues, while the orange stucco Spa Room is used year-round for exhibitions and concerts.

FREE Landbohøjskolens Have

Grønnegårdsvej 15 (www.haven.life.ku.dk). Bus 14, 15, 29. **Open** sunrise-sunset daily. **Admission** free. **Map** p245 N6.

Come spring, this garden positively explodes in a riot of flora; aconite, snowdrops, crocuses and 10,000 tulips bloom each April. In summer these are succeeded by roses and 700 different summer flowers, as well as 100 or so medicinal plants and exotic trees.

Storm P Museet

Frederiksberg Runddel (38 86 05 23/www. stormp-museet.dk). Bus 18, 26. **Open** May-Sept 10am-4pm Tue-Sun; closed Mon. *Oct-Apr* 10am-4pm Wed, Sat, Sun. **Admission** 30kr; 20kr concessions; free under-18s. **No credit cards**. Closing July-Nov 2011 for refurbishment.

★ Zoologisk Have

Roskildevej 32 (72 20 02 00/72 20 02 80/www. zoo.dk). Bus 4A, 6A, 26. **Open** *Mar* 10am-4pm Mon-Fri; 10am-5pm Sat, Sun. *Apr, May, Sept* 10am-5pm Mon-Fri; 10am-6pm Sat, Sun. *June, Aug* 10am-6pm daily, 10am-9pm daily *Oct* 10am-5pm daily. *Nov-Feb* 10am-4pm daily. **Admission** 110kr-140kr; 50kr-80kr concessions. **Credit** AmEx, MC, V.

The zoo is modest by international standards, but nevertheless has an interesting selection of exotica, including polar bears, tigers, lions, giraffes and apes, plus a new elephant house designed by Lord Norman Foster. An impressive indoor zoo houses butterflies, crocodiles and tropical birds. The children's zoo is also a major attraction, and its main landmark is the 40-metre (131-foot) tower, built in 1905, which, on a clear day, affords spectacular views as far as the Swedish coast. The queues are invariably lengthy on sunny holidays.

SIGHTS

Zoologisk Have.

Nørrebro & Østerbro

Hipsters, grit and yummy mummies.

Nørrebro and Østerbro, along with Vesterbro, are often referred to as the *Brokvartererne* (literally the Bridge Quarters). These are the main residential areas outside the city's ramparts and, individual as they are, all have a flavour of 'real' Copenhagen about them that is sometimes lacking in the city centre.

Nørrebro can get a bit too real at times, hosting the odd riot, but overall remains a pulsating and attractive neighbourhood, which is now home to some of the coolest clothes shops, bars and restaurants in town. Its Assistens Kirkegård is also the final resting place for many famous Danes.

Østerbro is far more sedate and well-heeled, full of boutiques, stylish cafés and smartly-dressed young couples pushing (retro) prams.

| **Map** p248 | **Cafes & Bars** p139 |
| **Restaurants** p125 | |

NØRREBRO

Along with Vesterbro, Nørrebro is one of the hippest areas of the city, thanks to its trendy clothes shops, vibrant cafés and burgeoning nightlife. Nørrebro has its epicentre on **Sankt Hans Torv**, with its two great cafés, **Sebastopol Café** (*see p142*) and **Pussy**

INSIDE TRACK
CULINARY NØRREBRO

Nørrebro's culinary landscape has improved greatly in the past few years, and the neighbourhood is now home to some of the city's most innovative dining spots, including Michelin-starred Thai restaurant **Kiin Kiin** (*see p125*) and microbrewery-restaurant **Nørrebro Bryghus** (*see p126*), one of the pioneers of the city's recent microbrewery trend (*see p140* **A Room with a Brew**). And since 2010, the area's Jægersborggade street has welcomed in the New Nordic **Restaurant Relæ** (*see p126*), and Claus Meyer's upmarket **Meyer's Bakery** (No.9), a sister spot to his Meyer's Deli (*see p139*), selling organic bread.

Galore's Flying Circus (*see p141*), and the boutiques and cafés on pedestrianised **Blågårdsgade**, but **Ryesgade** – home to microbrewery-restaurant **Nørrebro Bryghus** (*see p126*) and café-bar **Underwood Ink** (*see p142*) – and happening **Elmegade**, lined with several good clothes shops, have spread the trendification further.

As with Vesterbro, many younger Copenhageners have found that Nørrebro's ethnic mix is a major element of its appeal as an up-and-coming residential area. But unlike Vesterbro's so-called second generation Danes, who are more established, Nørrebro's ethnic inhabitants seem less integrated into the community and are generally less prosperous. As a result, the area has suffered from that most un-Danish phenomenon, social unrest, and has even experienced some shocking violent crime, the odd riot on the occasion of a deportation or some heavy-handed policing. With its dark streets and tightly packed housing, the district is probably central Copenhagen's least safe (as opposed to 'most dangerous') neighbourhood at night – though that statement should be qualified by saying that it is still a relatively secure night-time destination, particularly compared with many other European capitals.

It is ironic, then, that Nørrebro's only museum is the **Politihistorisk Museum**

Dead Famous

Assistens Kirkegård is the final resting place of many a great Dane.

HANS CHRISTIAN ANDERSEN
Plot no: P1
Assistens' most famous lodger by far, Andersen is probably *the* most famous Dane – period. Born in Odense in 1805, he moved to Copenhagen at 14. He was a playwright, a poet and an excellent origami artist, but became world-famous first and foremost for fairytales such as *The Emperor's New Clothes* and *The Nightingale*. He died in 1875. *See also p63* **Profile**.

SØREN KIERKEGAARD
Plot no: A17
Born in Copenhagen in 1813, Kierkegaard had a life as plagued by doubt as his existentialist philosophy. Inspired by his strongly religious father, he became a pastor, but after a troubled youth and a broken engagement to the love of his life, Regine, he turned to writing philosophical masterpieces such as *Either/Or* and *The Sickness unto Death*. He died a bitter 42-year-old in 1855.

NIELS BOHR
Plot no: Q4
The 1922 Nobel Prize Winner for physics, was born in Copenhagen in 1885. Living proof that footballers aren't all dim, Bohr was a fine league player at Akademisk Boldklub. He chose to pursue physics, however, and went on to formulate the principle of atomic fission. Bohr, like thousands of Danish Jews, fled the Nazi occupation in 1943 and wound up in the US, working on the atomic bomb – though he was later to campaign against its use. He died in 1962.

MARTIN ANDERSEN NEXØ
Plot no: H2
A writer of socially minded works about the hardships of common folk around the turn of the 20th century, Nexø was born in 1869 in Copenhagen's early industrial slums. *Pelle the Conqueror* remains his best known work, not least because it was turned into an Oscar-winning movie by director Bille August. A communist, he fled occupied Denmark in 1941 and died in Dresden in 1954.

DAN TURÈLL
Plot no: B13
In his short time on earth (he died from lung cancer in 1993 at the age of 47), Turèll was the prime chronicler of Copenhagen life, ascending from a cult figure to a widely loved literary hero. His breakthrough was the 1974 *Karma Cowboy* – a collection of poems influenced by Zen Buddhism and *Lucky Luke* comics. Over the next 20 years, Turèll wrote weekly columns in the *Politiken* newspaper as well as numerous volumes of poetry and a series of 12 noir crime novels. He lived in Vesterbro and Frederiksberg.

MICHAEL STRUNGE
Plot no: V15
Alongside Turèll, Strunge was one of Copenhagen's most notable post-war writers. Strunge was a post-punk poet who committed suicide in 1986 in central Copenhagen, diving from a fourth floor window at the age of just 28. Twenty years later, his romantically bleak Cold War poems of alienation still attract new readers.

Brumleby.

(Police History Museum; *see right*). This well-presented museum would potentially be of interest to foreign visitors but for the lack of any significant information in English.

Nørrebro also has two historic cemeteries. The Jewish cemetery, **Mosaisk Kirkegård**, on Peter Fabers Gade, is surrounded by a high wall and gates, and is only open for private visits arranged through the local Jewish community. **Assistens Kirkegård** (*see p91* **Dead Famous**), on the other hand, is open year-round and, for a place of eternal rest, is fairly lively; it's used by many as a local park and picnic place (rehearsing musicians are a common sight).

Of all Nørrebro's shopping attractions, the best known are its antiques shops. The trade centres on Ravnsborggade (just south-east of Sankt Hans Torv) and its extension Ryesgade, where just about every store has a selection of old clothes, furniture, porcelain, art, glassware, silverware, gold or bric-a-brac.

★ FREE Assistens Kirkegård

Entrances on Jagtvej & Nørrebrogade (35 37 19 17, www.assistens.dk). Bus 5A. **Open** *Jan-Mar, Oct-Dec 7am-7pm daily. Apr-Sept 7am-10pm daily.* **Admission** free. **Map** p248 H8.

Buried among the hundreds of varieties of trees in this graceful cemetery is just about everyone of any note from Danish history over the last two centuries, including old rivals Hans Christian Andersen and Søren Kierkegaard; Niels Bohr; Carlsberg patriarch JC Jacobsen; and the artists Christen Købke, CW Eckersberg, Jens Juel, HW Bissen and Peter Skovgaard. *See also p91* **Dead Famous**.

Politihistorisk Museum

Fælledvej 20 (35 36 88 88/www.politimuseum.dk). Bus 5A, 350S. **Open** 11am-4pm Tue, Thur, Sun. **Admission** 30kr; free under-18s. **No credit cards. Map** p248 J10.

As well as covering the history of the police force, with old uniforms, equipment and ephemera, the building also houses the Museum of Crime, which documents Copenhagen's nefarious residents (including various infamous murderers) from past centuries.

ØSTERBRO

Østerbro, which runs from the eastern side of Nørrebro across to the docks on the coast, is dominated by Denmark's national stadium, **Parken** in Fælledparken. Bordered by Nørre

---

INSIDE TRACK
BRUMLEBY VILLAGE

Head north up Østerbrogade, turn left just before Sankt Jakobs Kirke (church) and you'll enter the tiny 'village' of Brumleby – now one of the area's most fashionable places to live. The cute yellowbrick houses were built after the city's cholera epidemic in 1853, to provide working-class Copenhageners with better housing outside the city walls. Today, it's a lovely, peaceful area for a wander and a peek inside the arty terraces.

Allé, Blegdamsvej, Østerbrogade and Jagtvej, **Fælledparken** is a large municipal park with a small lake, which is currently undergoing a massive redevelopment, sparked by its 2009 centenary. Its impressive new skatepark (*see p203* **Skate Copenhagen**) will be the biggest in Europe when it opens in summer 2011. Other new initiatives include illuminated exercise paths, playgrounds and sports areas and the planting of trees, and there's a new café in the central pavillion. A more practical open space than most of Copenhagen's other more historic or ornamental gardens, this is where locals come for a game of football or hockey, to play tennis, cycle, rollerskate, jog or skateboard. During the summer, there are often free concerts here: larger-scale pop and rock concerts by big bands and artists take place in the large concrete stadium, better known as the home of **FC København**, the country's top football team. To the west of Parken, across Nørre Allé, is the **Zoologisk Museum** (Zoological Museum; *see below*).

Østerbro itself is a prosperous residential area with a mixture of century-old apartment buildings and newer high-rise blocks. There is a good mix of shops, cafés and restaurants stretching along the length of **Østerbrogade**, and the shops along Nordre Frihavnsgade and the bars on **Bopa Plads** (such as **Café Bopa**, *see p142*) and **Rosenvængets Allé** showing clear signs of trendification. The latter is home to gourmet organic butchers/café **Gourmandiet** (*see p142*), now a popular brunch spot for well-to-do locals.

At the eastern end of Østerbro is a large dock area that in recent years has seen a considerable amount of development. Further north in Nordhavn, the docks become more industrial, though here you will find the cavernous modern furniture store **Paustian** (*see venue index*), a couple of stylish restaurants, as well as Copenhagen's yacht basins. Also nearby is the new man-made beach, Svanemøllestranden, which is well used in summer. In terms of new architecture, this is one of the most stimulating parts of the city – but bring a bike, the area is too big to cover on foot.

Zoologisk Museum
Universitetsparken 15 (35 32 22 22, www.zoologi. snm.ku.dk). Bus 18, 42, 43, 150S, 173E, 184, 185. **Open** 11am-5pm Tue-Sun. In week 7, 8 & 42 (school holidays) open 10am-5pm daily. **Admission** 75kr; 15kr-40kr concessions. **Credit** AmEx, MC, V.

Though it's a little fusty – the mammals and birds from around the world that are displayed here are all stuffed – the Zoologisk Museum is still a good place to take children if the weather is bad.

Fælledparken.

Further Afield

Head to the suburbs for educational attractions and a new concert hall.

Copenhagen's outskirts are made up (largely affluent) suburbs. Hellerup, north of Østerbro, is full of large family houses, top-notch restaurants, and the excellent **Experimentarium** children's science museum. Lyngby is another notable suburb, home to Denmark's largest open-air museum, **Frilandsmuseet**, where 110 17th-19th-century buildings from Denmark, southern Sweden and northern Germany sit. The suburb of Ishøj, meanwhile, is known for the **Arken Museum For Moderne Kunst**, one of Copenhagen's premier modern art galleries, built to celebrate the city's

year as European City of Culture in 1996. Another impressive piece of architecture now sits on the island of Amager. The **DR Koncerhuset** is the concert hall of Denmark's national broadcasting corporation, located in the new district of Ørestad.

HELLERUP & CHARLOTTENLUND

The affluent coastal suburb of Hellerup, just north of the city centre via Østerbro, has some good shops and restaurants, but the star of the show is a superb museum, **Experimentarium** (*see right*).

Continue northwards through the suburbs for **Charlottenlund Slot** (Charlottenlund Palace), the site of a royal residence since 1690. The current baroque palace was built for Princess Charlotte Amalie in 1730, but its leafy gardens subsequently found favour among city dwellers as a popular destination for Sunday outings. Various other royals have lived in the palace, but since the 1930s it has been home to the Danish Institute for Fisheries, so only the grounds, not the house, are open to the public.

Danmarks Akvarium (*see right*), located in the palace grounds, is one of Copenhagen's perennially popular attractions. It's worth a look if you are visiting **Charlottenlund Fort** (a grassy hillock with a nice campsite) and **Charlottenlund Strand** and the weather sours. Charlottenlund Strand, although small, is the nearest beach to Copenhagen heading north; though most people continue up to Bellevue Beach, the former has a large, landscaped grass area. All are a pleasant forest walk from Charlottenlund station.

Culture vultures should visit **Ordrupgaard** (*see right*), displaying French Impressionist and Danish art from the 19th and 20th centuries.

Danmarks Akvarium
Kavalergården 1, Charlottenlund (39 62 32 83, www.danmarksakvarium.dk). Bus 14, 166. **Open** *Feb-Apr, Sept-Oct* 10am-5pm daily. *May-Aug* 10.30am-6pm daily. *Nov-Jan* 10am-4pm daily. **Admission** 100kr; 55kr concessions; free under-3s. **Credit** MC, V.
Though not the most modern of aquariums, the 90 tanks contain the usual marine attractions, including sharks, piranhas, turtles and tropical fish.

★ Experimentarium
Tuborg Havnevej 7, Hellerup (39 27 33 33, www.experimentarium.dk). Bus 1A, 14, 21. **Open** 9.30am-5pm Mon,Wed-Fri; 9.30am-9pm Tue; 11am-5pm Sat, Sun. **Admission** 160kr; 70kr-100kr concessions; free under-2s. **Credit** AmEx, MC, V.
Denmark's inventive science museum is filled with imaginative displays and hands-on experiments. Though aimed at children, it attracts its fair share of adults, who are mesmerised by the virtual technology (trying a human-size gyroscope or programming robots). The museum renders mundane or esoteric topics – alternative power, genetics – fascinating and accessible. Be warned: the noise can be deafening.

Ordrupgaard
Vilvordevej 110, Charlottenlund (39 64 11 83, www.ordrupgaard.dk). Train to Klampenborg or Lyngby/bus 388. **Open** 1-5pm Tue, Thur, Fri; 1-7pm Wed; 11am-5pm Sat, Sun. **Admission** 85kr; 60kr-75kr concessions; free under-18s. **Credit** MC, V.

Zaha Hadid's stunning extension, completed in 2005, has doubled the size of the Ordrupgaard art museum, which contains works by Manet, Renoir, Matisse and Gauguin, as well as Danish art from the 19th and 20th centuries.

BISPEBJERG

The most striking landmark in Copenhagen's monotonous suburbs is **Grundtvigs Kirke** (Grundtvigs Church; *see below*) in Bispebjerg, 15 minutes' drive north-west of the city centre.

Grundtvigs Kirke
På Bjerget 14B, Bispebjerg (35 81 54 42, www.grundtvigskirke.dk). Train to Emdrup/bus 10, 16. **Open** 9am-4pm Mon-Wed, Fri, Sat; 9am-6pm Thur; *May-Sept* noon-4pm Sun. *Oct-Apr* noon-1pm Sun. **Admission** free.
The church is named after Nicolai Frederik Severin Grundtvig, the Danish priest, writer, composer and educational pioneer. And its construction was a family affair: it was designed by PV Jensen-Klint and completed after his death by his son, the designer Kaare Klint. The massive yellow-brick church took almost 20 years to complete (it was finished in 1940), and possesses a stark beauty.

LYNGBY

One of Copenhagen's greener and more attractive suburbs is **Lyngby**, eight kilometres (five miles) north of the centre, and home to Denmark's largest open-air museum, **Frilandsmuseet** (*see right*). Not to be confused with **Frihedsmuseet** (the museum of Denmark's resistance movement), Frilandsmuseet covers an area of 35 hectares (86 acres) and is home to 110 buildings from Denmark, southern Sweden and northern Germany, all dating from the 17th to the 19th centuries.

Adjacent to Frilandsmuseet is **Brede Vaerk** (*see below*), once the Brede cloth mill industrial complex (which closed in 1956), and now preserved as a complete industrial village (with workers' cottages and the owner's country house). It's run by Nationalmuseet. At one time this whole region was the centre for Denmark's industry and there were many factories and mills, stretching all the way from Lyngby to the coast.

FREE **Brede Vaerk**
IC Modewegs Vej, Lyngby (33 47 38 00, www.natmus.dk). Train to Jægersborg, then train to Brede or bus 194. **Open** *Easter-Oct* 10am-5pm Tue-Sun. Closed Oct-Easter. **Admission** free. *Guided tours* 50kr; 40kr concessions; free under-18s. **Credit** AmEx, V.
Brede House is a neo-classical manor, built in 1795 for the owner of the mill, Peter van Hemert, and has an exquisite Louis XVI interior. The house was intended to be a summer residence for his family, but van Hemert went bankrupt in 1805. Ironically, that bankruptcy, and the detailed inventory of the house that ensued, allowed Nationalmuseet to restore the interior accurately. There is also a superb restaurant, Brede Spisehuset (IC Modewegs Vej), nearby.

FREE **Frilandsmuseet**
Kongevejen 100, Lyngby (33 13 44 11, www.frilandsmuseet.dk). Train to Jægersborg, then train to Brede or bus 194. **Open** *Easter-Mid Oct* 10am-5pm Tue-Sun. Closed Mid Oct-Easter. **Admission** free. **Credit** AmEx, V.
To see and appreciate all of Frilandsmuseet's 110 houses, which date from the 17th to the 19th centuries, takes at least a day, but to get a good cross-section of architectural styles the curators suggest you visit buildings 34, 42 and 60-72. Opened in Copenhagen in 1897, and relocated to the present site in 1901 under the auspices of Nationalmuseet, the museum features wind- and watermills, farm buildings, fishermen's cottages, peasants' houses, factories, and even a 19th-century fire station, all preserved with period decor. There aren't any information signs to spoil the atmosphere. Other attractions include rare Danish cattle breeds and excellent guided tours. On the downside, thanks to poor signposting (typical of Denmark), it is difficult to find by car. However, you can get off the S-train at Jægersborg and catch the local train, which winds its pretty way to the museum at Brede station.

ISHØJ

The fourth of Sjælland's world-class art museums is found in the unprepossessing suburb of Ishøj, 15 minutes by train south along the coast from Copenhagen. **Arken Museum For Moderne Kunst** (Arken Museum of Modern Art; *see p96*) was built to celebrate Copenhagen's year as European City of Culture in 1996 and is almost as famous for its architecture as its exhibits.

Arken is a few metres from **Ishøj Strand** (Ishøj Beach), an artificial but attractive seven-kilometre (four-mile) stretch of sandy beach.

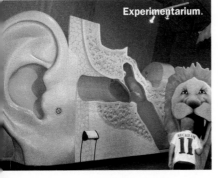
Experimentarium.

SIGHTS

Arken Museum For Moderne Kunst.

★ Arken Museum For Moderne Kunst
Skovvej 100, Ishøj (43 54 02 22, www.arken.dk).
Train to Ishøj, then bus 128. **Open** 10am-5pm
Tue, Thur-Sun; 10am-9pm Wed. **Admission** 85kr;
70kr concessions; free under-18s. **Credit** MC, V.
Arken is housed in an extraordinary concrete, glass
and steel building, designed by Danish architect Søren
Robert Lund. His compelling and perplexing construction, with its echoes of marine architecture (both inside
and out), won a competition for the design of the new
gallery in 1988, and has divided critics ever since.

Some applaud its apt maritime references (the
museum is near the beach), which give it the appearance of an abstract shipwreck; others say that an art
museum should focus on its art, not its own architecture. Most artists hate it, claiming the exhibition
spaces compete with, rather than enhance, their
work. But visitors are usually won over by Lund's
skewed vision.

Arken's permanent collection of paintings, sculpture, graphic art and installations includes 350 works
from 1990 onwards (not all of which are on display at
one time). This display, however, is augmented by
superb temporary exhibitions of both modern and contemporary Danish and international artists, often
transferred from other major European museums.
Past show have included retrospectives of Pablo
Picasso, Edvard Munch, Salvador Dalí, Joan Miró,
Andy Warhol and Christian Boltanski.

Many pieces in the permanent collection are by
Danish artists, but there are also numerous foreign
works, including those by British artist Damien Hirst
as well as pieces by Olafur Eliasson and Katharina
Grosse. Probably the most famous work in the permanent collection is the photograph *Flex Pissing/Björk er
en nar* (aka Bringing It All Back Home) by Claus
Carstensen and the art group Superflex (the mildly
controversial 'Danish Art Mob'). Arken also has a cinema, a concert hall and a café.

Arken has undergone two extensions in recent
times. The first, in 2008, provided more space for the
art, while the 2009 extension improved the facilities
for visitors. The latter extension also created an
impressive new entrance.

AMAGER

Amager is the small island immediately to
the east of Copenhagen. It is home to the city's
international airport, as well as the impressive
new **DR Koncerthuset** (concert hall; *see p197*
Profile) at DR Byen, completed in 2009 in the
new Ørestad district, just above the large
protected green space of **Amagerfælled** in
the north-west. But aside from that, it's mostly
a flat, bleak area of industrial estates, cheap
housing and farmland. However, it also boasts
the nearest (and best) beach to the centre of
town, **Amager Strandpark**.

On the east coast of Amager, among salt flats
and farmland bustling with birdlife, lies **Dragør**,
with its maze of cobbled lanes and traditional
yellow cottages. Like many coastal settlements
in this area it was founded upon the humble
herring – shipped throughout Europe before the
Reformation to provide sustenance for the Catholic
faithful abstaining from meat during Lent and on
Fridays – and prospered during the 14th century
as a fishing port. In the 19th century it found a
new lease of life as a centre for shipping and
salvage, trading through the Baltic and as far
away as England. That came to an end with the
advent of steam ships, and since then little has
changed here (part of its charm).

However, Dragør's sleepy idyll can be
misleading. Property prices here are high
– the village is popular with affluent young
professionals who commute into the city. They
ensure that Dragør remains an improbably lively,
almost cosmopolitan, village. There are also some
smart shops on its short high street, as well as
several good restaurants and beer gardens. The
town has a marina, a small cinema and an equally
small museum (**Dragør Museum**; *see below*),
housed in the town's oldest fisherman's house
(dating from 1682).

Five minutes' drive to the south, inland, is the
charming village of Store Magleby, founded by
Dutch settlers in the early 1500s. It's home to the
Amager Museum (*see below*), which traces the
history of the Dutch immigrants in the area.

Amager Museum
*Hovedgade 4 & 12, Store Magleby, Amager (32
53 93 07, www.amagermuseet.dk). Bus 30, 73,
350S (get off at St Magleby Church).* **Open** *May-
Sept* noon-4pm Tue-Sun. **Admission** 30kr; 20kr
concessions; under-18s free. **No credit cards**.

Dragør Museum
*Havnepladsen, Strandlinien 2 & 4, Dragør,
Amager (32 53 93 07, www.dragoer-
information.dk). Bus 30, 32, 81N, 75E, 350S.*
Open *May-Sept* noon-4pm Tue-Sun. Closed
Oct-Apr. **Admission** 20kr; 15 concessions;
free under-18s. **No credit cards**.

SIGHTS

Consume

Hotels   **98**
  Profile Room 606   99
  The Best Design Hotels   101
  Green Sleeps   105

Restaurants   **111**
  Where's the Beef?   116
  Profile Noma &
    Rene Redzepi   121

Cafés & Bars   **128**
  Danish Delicacies   133
  A Room with a Brew   140

Shops & Services   **143**
  Danish Designers   149
  Neighbourhood Boutiques   161

Hotels

Beds in the capital are still not cheap, but at least they're cheerful.

Copenhagen's hotel landscape has dramatically improved over the past few years. The rates still hurt, but at least now you might feel like you're staying in one of Europe's style capitals. Copenhagen can now lay claim to one of the world's most luxurious hotels (Nimb, in Tivoli Gardens), to several hotels that celebrate the city's design heritage, and to 'the fanciest youth hostel in the world'.

Most low- and mid-range Copenhagen hotels are situated in the trendy Vesterbro neighbourhood, just west of Central Station, where hip designer shops and bars rub shoulders with sex shops. Meanwhile, the more prestigious hotels (except the Radisson Blu (SAS) Royal) tend to be on the other side of the city centre, near Kongens Nytorv and Amalienborg Slot.

CONSUME

TIVOLI, RÅDHUSPLADSEN, STRØGET & AROUND

Deluxe

Copenhagen Marriott Hotel
Kalvebod Brygge 5, 1560 Copenhagen V (88 33 99 00, www.marriott.com/cphdk). Train København H. **Rates** 1,599kr-2,499kr double. **Rooms** 383. **Credit** AmEx, MC, V. **Map** p251 Q13 ❶

This relatively new five-star block of luxury is the place to go if you want to be pampered in proper American fashion. Standards are high and there are a million extras on offer, but aside from the harbour view this hotel suffers from a problem that is common in chains: you could be in any Marriott hotel anywhere in the world. Be sure to ask for a room on one of the upper floors on the water side of the building; you could sit there all day, sipping champagne and watching the aquatic goings-on down below from behind the wall of glass.
Bar. Bike rental (150kr/day). Business services. Concierge. Disabled: adapted rooms (4). Gym. Internet (Wi-Fi). Parking (200kr-250kr/night). Restaurant. Room service (24hrs). TV: pay movies.

> ❶ Red numbers given in this chapter correspond to locations marked on the street maps. *See pp245-253.*

Copenhagen Plaza
Bernstorffsgade 4, 1577 Copenhagen V (33 14 92 62, www.profilhotels.com/copenhagenplaza). Train København H. **Rates** 1,395kr-1,495kr double. **Rooms** 93. **Credit** AmEx, MC, V. **Map** p250 P11 ❷

The Plaza, commissioned by King Frederik VIII in 1913, has recently been transformed from an old English-style hotel into something a little more 'Scandinavian'. The rooms are airy and pleasant with big beds. The lobby retains a distinctive early 20th-century atmosphere. The Library Bar (*see p128*) was named 'one of the five best bars in the

> **INSIDE TRACK**
> **RESERVATIONS, RATINGS AND RATES**
>
> Note that room rates given in this chapter refer to pre-paid rates made via online booking for a standard double. Booking in advance is always a good idea, but if you arrive in the city without a reservation, the **Wonderful Copenhagen Tourist Information Bureau** (70 22 24 42, www.visitcopenhagen.com) can make same-night reservations for hotels at reduced rates. The service is available as well from the tourist information desk in Copenhagen Airport's arrivals hall.
>
> For accommodation catering primarily to a gay clientele, see p184.

Profile Room 606

The Radisson Blu (SAS) Royal Hotel room that's a must for Arne Jacobsen fans.

Arne Jacobsen (1902-71) – Denmark's most-famous architect-designer, and one of the pioneers of functionalism – is probably best known for the hotel now called the **Radisson Blu (SAS) Royal Hotel** (*see p101*), considered the pinnacle of his career. The world's first design hotel – and Denmark's first skyscraper, at 20 storeys – was designed by Jacobsen for the Scandinavian Airlines System (SAS), and completed in 1960. Jacobsen designed not only the building itself, but everything inside, from the lighting to the now-iconic chairs that still take pride of place in the lobby, to the ashtrays and the stainless steel cutlery used in the roof-top restaurant, Alberto K (named after the hotel's first director; *see p113*). The cutlery was futuristic enough for Stanley Kubrick's to use it in his film *2001: A Space Odyssey*.

The five-star hotel has undergone several refurbishments over the years, but one guest room has been left untouched for posterity: room 606, whose original 1960s design is as it was when the hotel first opened. The room, which can still be booked, contains turquoise versions of Jacoben's 'Egg' and 'Swan' chairs chairs (as well as the lesser-known, but very cool, 'Drop' chairs), which were designed especially for the hotel, sofas, dark wood-panelled walls, wengé wood sideboards, and desks with built-in make-up mirrors that light up when the desk is opened.

According to the hotel's PR, Boline Andersen Karademir, uninformed guests are sometimes intially disappointed by the room, which costs a fair bit more than a standard double (contact the hotel for details), as

it's less luxurious than modern-stay standards dictate and its bed smaller than today's supersize versions. But once guests are told its story, they start to appreciate its singularity. With the popularity of TV's *Mad Men*, and the corresponding resurgence of interest in 1960s mid-century modern furniture, the Royal is now receiving at least one request a week to view the room.

As most of the rest of the hotel has sadly been refurbished with standard furniture and fittings, the hotel, which celebrated its 50th birthday in 2010, is sometimes referred to as Jacobsen's 'Lost Gesamtkunst werk'.

CONSUME

Earn EuroBonus points with SAS' largest global hotel partner

Best Western Hotels

is SAS' largest global hotel partner. As a EuroBonus member you can earn and redeem your points while staying in one of our more than 130 hotels throughout Scandinavia or 4,000 hotels worldwide. We also offer a number of exclusive service benefits, like free internet etc.

Best Western consists of privately owned quality hotels, and offers you a solid commitment of value, quality and superior customer service. Our uniqueness is found in each hotel's charm and local appeal, so you will never find two hotels alike.

Best Western is the World´s Largest Hotel Chain®.

Visit our websites for more information or call our toll free numbers:

Sweden	www.bestwestern.se	020 792 752
Norway	www.bestwestern.no	800 11 624
Denmark	www.bestwestern.dk	80 01 09 88

The World's Biggest Hotel Family

world' by *Forbes* magazine, and a central pillar in the lounge carries plaques naming the hundreds of famous personalities who have stayed here over the years. The Plaza enjoys a good view over Tivoli across the street, but its location next to Central Station also means windows opening out on to heavy traffic or railway noise.
Bar. Business centre. Concierge. Internet (broadband). Parking (165kr/day). Restaurants (2). Room service (7am-midnight). TV: cable/pay movies.

★ **Hotel Alexandra**
HC Andersens Boulevard 8, 1553 Copenhagen K (33 74 44 44, www.hotelalexandra.dk). Train København H. **Rates** 1,745kr-2,545kr double. **Rooms** 61. **Credit** AmEx, MC, V. **Map** p250 O11 ❸
Copenhagen's only 'Danish retro design hotel' is a must for anyone interested in mid-century furniture. Housed in an historic building in an excellent location, the Alexandra blends classic Danish design with all the facilities you'd expect from a modern hotel. Furniture by the likes of Hans J Wegner and Arne Jacobsen feature in the individually designed rooms. What's more, the hotel has superb green credentials (*see p105* **Green Sleeps**).
Bike rentals, Internet (Wi-Fi). Restaurant. TV: cable/pay movies, Parking (150kr/night), Room service (7am-11pm), Spa.

★ **Nimb Hotel**
Bernstorffsgade 5, 1577 Copenhagen V (88 70 00 00, www.nimb.dk). **Rates** 2,500kr-8,500kr double. **Rooms** 13. **Credit** AmEx, MC, V. **Map** p250 P11 ❹
The five-star Nimb has featured on several 'world's best' hotels lists since opening in 2008, and is probably the most luxurious place in town to rest your head. A converted 1909 Moorish-inspired building, it has a cosy feel, with each individually decorated art-filled room containing antique furniture, fireplaces, four-poster beds and top-notch linen. Spacious bathrooms and slick mod cons are further draws, and all the rooms look out over the Tivoli Gardens (*see p47*; guests get complimentary entry passes). To top it all off, the hotel also houses one of the city's best restaurants – the Michelin-starred Herman (*see p111*) – as well as a fir[s]t-rate cocktail bar. With just 13 guestrooms (including eight suites), you'll need to book ahead.
Business centre, Bars (2). Gym, Internet (Wi-Fi). Restaurants (2). Room service (24hrs). TV: cable/pay movies.

Palace Hotel
Rådhuspladsen 57, 1550 Copenhagen K (33 14 40 50, www.palacehotel.dk). Train København H. **Rates** 1,310kr-1,790kr double. **Rooms** 161. **Credit** AmEx, MC, V. **Map** p250 O12 ❺
This large luxury hotel stands adjacent to Rådhuset (the Town Hall) and is one of Copenhagen's

landmark buildings. The Palace was built in 1907-10 in order to provide prestigious accommodation for visiting officials on business at the then-new Town Hall. The Ambassador Rooms have balconies overlooking Rådhuspladsen. While the reception and bars have kept their old-fashioned brown and dark-red Chesterfield style, the rooms have been smartened up and modernised, and the hotel has upgraded to a five-star and is now run by Scandic.
Bar. Concierge. Internet (dataport). Parking (300kr/night). Restaurant. Room service (24hrs). TV: pay movies.

★ **Radisson Blu (SAS) Royal Hotel**
Hammerischsgade 1, 1611 Copenhagen V (33 42 60 00, reservations 38 15 65 00, www.radissonblu.com). Train København H. **Rates** 1,495kr-1595kr double. **Rooms** 260. **Credit** AmEx, MC, V. **Map** p250 O11 ❻
For many years, renowned architect-designer Arne Jacobsen's modernist masterpiece was Copenhagen's only designer hotel, designed back in 1960. And, although the rooms have been revamped over the years, just entering the lounge and street-level café, with Jacobsen's 'Egg' and 'Swan' chairs and the Scandinavian Airlines desk, you're swept into a magical bygone era when airport terminals and avant-garde design were romantic and exclusive. Room 606 has legendary status (*see p99* **Room 606**). And the hotel's central location is another boon (Central Station and Rådhuspladsen are just across the street), and there are fabulous views of nearby Tivoli from the front-facing rooms – though Copenhagen is so lowrise that any room on the upper floors gives a superb view. For a spot of haute cuisine, it boasts one of the city's finest restaurants, Alberto K, on the top floor (*see p113*).
Bar. Bike rental (150kr/day). Business services. Concierge. Disabled: adapted rooms. Gym. Internet (Wi-Fi). Parking (240kr/day). Restaurants (2). Room service (24hrs). TV: pay movies.

THE BEST DESIGN HOTELS

Hotel Alexandra
For Danish modern furniture. *See left.*

Radisson Blu (SAS) Royal Hotel
For Arne Jacobsen's seminal work. *See above.*

Imperial Hotel
For Børge Mogensen designs. *See p103.*

Hotel Skt Petri
For decadent design. *See p106.*

DanHostel Copenhagen City
For design on a budget. *See p110.*

CONSUME

Expensive

Imperial Hotel

Vester Farimagsgade 9, 1606 Copenhagen
V (33 12 80 00, www.imperialhotel.dk). Train
Vesterport. Rates 1,190kr-1,290kr double. **Rooms**
267. **Credit** AmEx, MC, V. **Map** p250 O10 **7**
This 1956 hotel has been renovated and modernised
to good effect, with a major focus given to the indoor
'garden' restaurant and the bedrooms. About half of
the rooms are decorated in fine Danish contemporary style and the suites are even better – students
at the Danish Design School equip each one as part
of their final exam. For those with designer allergy,
the rest of the rooms are all far more traditional. The
hotel is centrally located near the lakes and the planetarium, in the middle of the movie theatre district,
and a short stroll from Tivoli.
Bar. Bike rental (150kr/day). Business services.
Concierge. Disabled: adapted rooms (2). Internet
(Wi-Fi). Parking (250kr/day). Restaurants (2).
Room service (6.30am-10.30pm). TV: cable/pay
movies.

Kong Frederik

Vester Voldgade 25, 1552 Copenhagen V (33
12 59 02, www.firsthotels.com). Metro Nørreport.
Rates 1,095kr-1,295kr double. **Rooms** 110.
Credit AmEx, MC, V. **Map** p250 N12 **8**
The Kong Frederik goes full tilt for the traditional
English style, with wood panelling, Chesterfields
and a blazing fireplace. In the lobby hang portraits
of all Denmark's (many) King Frederiks and the
restaurant (called, well, what do you expect,
Frederiks) is accessible straight from the street – it's
worth visiting both for its decor (imported piece by
piece from a London pub) and its haute cuisine. The
rooms are comfortable with appealing, unobtrusive
decor, although the bathrooms are a bit small.
Guests prepared to make the trek get free use of the
upmarket spa and pool at Kong Frederik's sister
Hotel Skt Petri (*see p106*).
Bar. Bike rental (120kr/day). Internet (Wi-Fi).
Parking (150kr/24hr). Restaurant. Room service
(10.30am-midnight). TV: pay movies.

The Square

Rådhuspladsen 14, 1550 Copenhagen V (33 38
12 00, www.thesquarecopenhagen.com). Train
Vesterport. Rates 1,090kr-1,160kr double. **Rooms**
267. **Credit** AmEx, MC, V. **Map** p250 O12 **9**
The Square is a moderately priced temple to elegant,
modern Scandinavian decor. The entrance area is
impressive, being part-lobby, part light-flooded art
installation, and the hotel is located right in the heart
of the action on Rådhuspladsen. Up the elevators,
you'll find 267 uniformly smart and bright rooms,
the higher ones (and the sixth-floor breakfast room)
commanding great views over the square.
Bike rental (120kr/day). Internet (Wi-Fi). Room
service. TV: movie channels/pay TV.

Moderate

DGI-Byens Hotel

Tietgensgade 65, 1704 Copenhagen V (33 29
80 50, www.dgi-byen.dk). Train København H.
Rates 945kr-1,595kr double. **Rooms**
104. **Credit** AmEx, MC, V. **Map** p250 Q11 **10**
Just around the corner from the main railway station
and part of the DGI centre (*see p 202*), this hotel makes
up for its rather desolate location among meat
markets and railroad tracks with style, comfort and
facilities. The ultra-cool *Vandkulturhuset* ('Water
Culture House'), Copenhagen's state-of-the-art swimming pool and spa, occupies one wing and guests are
admitted free. The spacious rooms are distinguished
by minimalist Scandinavian design (lots of light –
natural and artificial – and plenty of wood).
Disabled: adapted rooms. Gym. Internet (Wi-Fi).
Parking (140kr/day). Restaurant. Spa. Swimming
pool (indoor). TV: cable/pay movies.

Hotel Twentyseven

Løngangstræde 27, 1468 Copenhagen K
(70 27 56 27, www.hotel27.dk). Train København
H. Rates 990kr-1,360kr double. **Rooms**
200. **Credit** AmEx, MC, V. **Map** p251 O13 **11**
What used to be the Mermaid Hotel underwent a
massive transformation to turn it into one of the
hippest places in town. Part of the three-star
designer hotel's appeal now lies in its attached
Icebar – cool in every meaning of the word. Other
draws include the Wine Room, the cocktail lounge,
the Arne Jacobsen chairs.
Bar. Bike rental (150kr/day). Internet (Wi-Fi).
Parking (200kr/24hr). TV: cable/pay movies.

Savoy Hotel

Vesterbrogade 34, 1620 Copenhagen V (33 26
75 00, www.savoyhotel.dk). Train København H.
Rates 695kr-850kr double. **Rooms** 66. **Credit**
AmEx, MC, V. **Map** p250 P10 **12**
A recently renovated three-star hotel in a wonderful
building, with a green- and gold-decorated façade
designed by Anton Rosen – those with a fondness
for history will enjoy the original lift and staircase.
The large, bright rooms are set back from the street,
making them quiet and peaceful. The hotel has its
own restaurant with courtyard terrace open in the
summer months.
Bike rental (120kr/day). Business services.
Internet (Wi-Fi). Parking (140kr/24hr).
Restaurant. TV: cable.

Budget

Hotel Selandia

Helgolandsgade 12, 1653 Copenhagen K
(33 31 46 10, www.hotel-selandia.dk). Train
København H. Rates 595kr-640kr double.
Rooms 84. **Credit** AmEx, DC, MC, V.
Map p250 P10 **13**

CONSUME

The Selandia is located just behind Central Station and is very popular thanks to its rates and cheerful, friendly service. The 84 rooms are simple and functional, but note that the 25 'economy' rooms do not come with en suite bath.
Bar. Internet (Wi-Fi). TV.

NYHAVN, KONGENS NYTORV & AROUND

Deluxe

★ Hotel d'Angleterre
Kongens Nytorv 34, 1021 Copenhagen K (33 12 00 95, www.remmen.dk). Metro Kongens Nytorv. **Rates** 2,295kr-2,895kr double. **Rooms** 123. **Credit** AmEx, MC, V. **Map** p251 M15 ⑭
Unique in its class, Copenhagen's grand old five-star Hotel d'Angleterre is traditional to its core. The massive 18th-century building with its 123 bedrooms is located at the upmarket eastern end of Strøget right on Kongens Nytorv, facing café-lined Nyhavn. Guests vary from Robbie Williams and Ricky Martin to pals of the royal family (Amalienborg Slot, the Queen's residence, is just around the corner). For a cool 22,500kr you can feel like royalty, with a night in the Royal Suite. The spa and swimming pool (10mx12m) are a treat. Afternoon tea, served at 2.30pm, is a luxurious way to enjoy the art of Danish pastries.
Bar. Bike rental (150kr/day). Business services. Concierge. Gym. Internet (Wi-Fi). Parking (400kr/24hr). Restaurant. Spa. Swimming pool (indoor). Room service (24hrs). TV: cable/pay movies.

Expensive

71 Nyhavn
Nyhavn 71, 1051 Copenhagen K (33 43 62 00, www.71nyhavnhotel.com). Metro Kongens Nytorv. **Rates** 1,390kr-1,781kr double. **Rooms** 150. **Credit** AmEx, MC, V. **Map** p252 N17 ⑮
Perched at the end of Nyhavn within a splendid early 19th-century warehouse, this relaxed and well-regarded hotel enjoys a prime location. Thoroughly refurbished in 2001, the small, modern bedrooms have managed to keep their character, thanks in part to their wood-beamed ceilings. When you check in, be sure to ask for a view over the water or you could find yourself facing the neighbouring building at the rear. Breakfasts are generally a cut above.
Bar. Bike rental Mar-Oct (125kr/day). Business services. Concierge. Internet (Wi-Fi). Parking (195kr/24hr). Restaurant. Room service. TV: cable.

Copenhagen Admiral Hotel
Toldbodgade 24-28, 1253 Copenhagen K (33 74 14 14, www.admiralhotel.dk). Metro Kongens Nytorv. **Rates** 995kr-1,195kr. **Rooms** 366. **Credit** AmEx, MC, V. **Map** p252 M17 ⑯

You could be forgiven for thinking you're sailing in the hold of some massive wooden galley inside the Admiral. The tree-trunk-thick beams criss-crossing the huge lobby area and most of the rooms add to the already existing maritime atmosphere of this waterside hotel. A 2003 refurbishment has created appealing, cosy rooms, well appointed with solid teak furniture. About half the bedrooms have sea views. At SALT (*see p117*) the bar and restaurant downstairs, you can finger the shrapnel scars on the beams from 19th-century bombardments by the British Royal Navy, or agonise over which of the three different types of salt to pinch over your brasserie-style fare.
Bars (2). Bike rental (100kr/day). Business centre. Disabled: adapted rooms. Internet (Wi-Fi). Parking (135kr/night). Restaurant. Room service (24hrs). TV: pay movies.

Phoenix Copenhagen
Bredgade 37, 1260 Copenhagen K (33 95 95 00, www.phoenixcopenhagen.dk). Metro Kongens Nytorv. **Rates** 990kr-1,290kr double. **Rooms** 213. **Credit** AmEx, MC, V. **Map** p249 L16 ⑰
Housed in a massive building dating from 1780, the Phoenix is one of Copenhagen's most extravagant hotels: the flashy foyer has tall mirrors, a fountain, huge candelabras and paintings. Its chic location, tucked between Kongens Nytorv and Amalienborg Palace, means the hotel is surrounded by some of Copenhagen's hottest art galleries. The hotel has elegant bedrooms, decorated in Louis XVI style, and the owner, who is passionate about art, indulges that taste by displaying only originals on his walls.
Bar. Business services. Internet (Wi-Fi). Parking (250kr/day). Restaurants (2). Room service (24hrs). TV: cable/pay movies.

Scandic Front
Skt Annæ Plads 21, 1022 Copenhagen K (33 13 34 00, www.scandichotels.com). Metro Kongens Nytorv. **Rates** 1,410kr-1,695kr double. **Rooms** 132. **Credit** AmEx, MC, V. **Map** p252 M17 ⑱
While there is now an abundance of designer-chic hotels in Copenhagen, few capture a sense of decadence and fashion as sharply as the Front, which opened in 2006. You might be surprised to learn that it's owned by the most traditional hotel family in Copenhagen, though here it seems the Remmens (who also own the Hotel d'Angleterre) went for a radical and modern twist with the revamp of the Front: new name, new design, new rooms. There are MP3 players to borrow for the gym, free wireless internet, even personal yoga trainers. The design is all 'hot pink and cosy grey' and the rooms, with the finest designer furniture, combine comfort and extravagant.
Bar. Business centre. Disabled: adapted rooms. Internet (Wi-Fi). Parking (300kr/24hr). Restaurant. Room service. TV: cable/pay movies.

CONSUME

Green Sleeps

Eco-friendly places to rest your head.

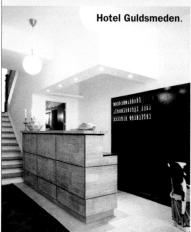

Hotel Guldsmeden.

.Copenhagen has a great many sustainably run hotels, with several listed as Green Key hotels – an internationally recognised label given to leisure organisations that fulfill an extensive list of environmentally friendly requirements.

Of the city's smaller green hotels, **Hotel Alexandra** (*see p101*) has designer second-hand furniture, an allergy-proof floor and the option of an entirely organic breakfast, while **Hotel Guldsmeden** (*see p108*) is another of the city's eco hotel warriors – its three Copenhagen locations all offer fully organic breakfast buffets along with organic toiletries in each of the rooms. Other hotels with Green Keys are the Arp-Hansen-run **71 Nyhavn** (*see left*) and **Phoenix Copenhagen** (*see left*).

Of the bigger hotel brands, Radisson rises above other chains. Its four Copenhagen hotels, including the **Radisson Blu (SAS) Royal Hotel** (*see p101*) and the **Radisson Blu Scandinavia Hotel** (*see p108*), have been awarded the Scandinavian 'Swan' eco-label, for their commitment to reduce energy and water consumption, while promoting waste generation. The Brøchner group, which includes **Kong Arthur** (*see p106*) and **Hotel Fox** (*see p108*) also became a carbon-neutral hotel chain in 2008. The greenest of them all, though, is the **Crowne Plaza Copenhagen Towers** (*see p109*), which was given the Eco-Tourism Award (in the Urban Accommodation category) in 2010. Completed in 2009, the hotel has solar-powered electricity, a groundwater-based cooling and heating system and low-energy TVs and lighting.

Moderate

Comfort Hotel Esplanaden

Bredgade 78, 1260 Copenhagen K (33 48 10 00, www.choicehotels.dk). Metro Kongens Nytorv. **Rates** 770kr-870kr double. **Rooms** 117. **Credit** AmEx, MC, V. **Map** p249 K17 ⑲

This central three-star hotel looks out on to the attractive Kastellet park on the corner of Esplanaden and Bredgade. The building dates from 1891 and has been 'gently renovated', which means it has kept its old-fashioned feel. This is a good bet for solo travellers: about a third of its 117 rooms are singles. Esplanaden was the first hotel in Denmark to become completely non-smoking.

Bar. Bike rental Mar-Oct (85kr/day). Internet (Wi-Fi). Parking (155kr/day). TV: cable/pay movies.

Hotel Opera

Tordenskjoldsgade 15, 1055 Copenhagen K (33 47 83 00, www.hotelopera.dk). Metro Kongens Nytorv. **Rates** 815kr-1,740kr single; 1,025kr-1,840kr double; 2,055kr-3,080kr suite. **Rooms** 91. **Credit** MC, V. **Map** p252 Q16 ⑳

An old-fashioned, cosy three-star hotel with 91 small but very charming rooms named after the old Opera House, not the new one; the hotel is located right next to the Royal Theatre, under the arches. There's a special cheap weekend rate as well as lots of winter offers; check the website.

Bar. Internet (broadband). TV: cable.

Sømandshjemmet Bethel

Nyhavn 22, 1056 Copenhagen K (33 13 03 70, www.hotel-bethel.dk). Metro Kongens Nytorv. **Rates** 845kr double. **Rooms** 29. **Credit** AmEx, MC, V. **Map** p252 M16 ㉑

The Sømandshjemmet Bethel is perfectly located on Nyhavn and has charming premises in a former seaman's hostel. The bright, pleasant rooms are all equipped with bath, telephone and TV. When you book in it's worth requesting a quayside view, so

long as you're not too sensitive to noise, which can come drifting across from the canal-side bars. Alternatively, you could go and visit one of them, because alcohol is not sold or allowed inside the hotel.

Internet (Wi-Fi, for a fee). TV: cable

NØRREPORT & AROUND

Deluxe

★ Hotel Skt Petri

Krystalgade 22, 1172 Copenhagen K (33 45 91 00, www.hotelsktpetri.com). Train/metro Nørreport. **Rates** from 1,611kr double. **Rooms** 268. **Credit** AmEx, MC, V. **Map** p251 M13 ㉒

Occupying a former department store in the 'Latin Quarter', this top-notch designer hotel is well located-for sights and shopping. All 268 rooms are hugely welcoming, with every feature you'd expect, including large, comfortable beds spread with soft, cool linen and a bold, bright (but not overwhelming) use of colour throughout. It's well worth trying to get one of the 55 rooms with balconies or terraces on the higher floors. The large atrium contains Bar Rouge, a swanky cocktail bar, while the street level Café Blanc is a popular stop for power-shoppers on a break. Finally, Brasserie Bleu is a luxury restaurant.

Bar. Bike rental (150kr/day). Business centre. Concierge. Disabled: adapted rooms. Gym. Internet (Wi-Fi). Parking (380kr/day). Restaurant. Room service. TV: cable/pay channels.

Expensive

Hotel Nora

Nørrebrogade 18C, 2200 Copenhagen N (35 37 20 21, www.hotelnora.dk). Train/metro Nørreport. **Rates** 950kr-1,300kr double. **Rooms** 42. **Credit** AmEx, MC, V. **Map** p248 J10 ㉓

This two-star hotel at the bottom of Nørrebrogade opened around 2002 in an old apartment block and has retained much of the old interior, meaning that the large rooms feel more like those in a flat than a hotel. To find the reception, turn into the courtyard, buzz the door immediately on your left and walk up to the first floor where the bustle of Nørrebrogade seems hardly noticeable. The design is modern yet unobtrusive, and complimentary welcome drinks can be found in the refrigerators.

Parking. Internet (broadband/wireless). TV.

★ Kong Arthur

Nørre Søgade 11, 1370 Copenhagen K (33 11 12 12, booking 33 95 77 22, www.kongarthur.dk). Train/metro Nørreport. **Rates** 918kr-1,131kr double. **Rooms** 155. **Credit** AmEx, MC, V. **Map** p246 L11 ㉔

Given a royal inauguration by King Christian IX in 1882, the Kong Arthur stands alone in its class: a charming, family-run hotel that offers quality

---

INSIDE TRACK CHAIN GAME

The **Cab-Inn** chain (www.cabinn.com) has three hotels in the city and is a good option for budget travellers. If you can, book into the Cab-Inn City, just behind Tivoli. The other two are less conveniently located, though still only a 15-minute walk from the centre. The 'cabin'-style rooms are almost identical in all three locations and have kettles and TVs, and there's free Wi-Fi internet throughout. **Choice Hotels** (www.choicehotels.com) is another good bet, with eight branches in Copenhagen, and sound green credentials, including organic breakfasts.

Kong Arthur.

accommodation at a competitive price. This beautiful, 155-room mansion, filled with antique furniture, is conveniently located, with the lakes on one side and hip Nansensgade on the other.
Bar. Bike rental (150kr/day). Business services. Concierge. Internet (Wi-Fi). Parking (175kr/24hr). Restaurants (3). Room service (24hrs). Spa. TV.

Moderate

Ibsens
Vendersgade 23, 1363 Copenhagen K (33 13 19 13, booking 33 95 77 44, www.ibsenshotel.dk). Train/metro Nørreport. **Rates** 791kr-876kr double. **Credit** AmEx, MC, V. **Map** p246 L11 ㉕
Ibsens is a lovely three-star hotel with an appealing reception, breakfast room and bar. It's a romantic place, with flowery curtains and flowers on the balconies of what is a typical Danish 19th-century building. The location (near Nørreport Station) is about as central as you can get in Copenhagen. Guests also have complimentary access to the Helle Thorup Spa next door.
Bar. Bike rental (150kr/day). Disabled: adapted rooms. Internet (Wi-Fi). Babysitting service. Restaurant. TV: cable.

Budget

Hotel Jørgensen
Rømersgade 11, 1362 Copenhagen K (33 13 81 86, www.hoteljoergensen.dk). Train/metro Nørreport. **Rates** 550kr-700kr double; 145kr-175kr dorm room. **Rooms** 25. **Credit** AmEx, MC, V. **Map** p246 L12 ㉖
This appealing, spotless budget hotel offers scrubbed wooden floors, a relaxed atmosphere and small, basic rooms with cable TV. It's an easy walk from the city centre, close to Nørreport Station, and also have dormitory rooms that sleep six-12 people for those counting the kroners.
Bar. Restaurant. TV: cable.

VESTERBRO & FREDERIKSBERG

Expensive

Avenue Hotel
Åboulevard 29, 1960 Frederiksberg C (35 37 31 11, www.avenuehotel.dk). Metro Forum. **Rates** 1,200kr-1,400kr double. **Rooms** 68. **Credit** AmEx, MC, V.

This three-star hotel is slightly out of town in Frederiksberg, but the location offers both that handsome neighbourhood and the wilder Nørrebro within easy reach, as well as a very high standard for the price. The Avenue was completely renovated in 2005, and now all 68 rooms include free internet access, cable TV and fridge.
Bar. Bike rental (120kr/day). Internet (Wi-Fi). Parking (100kr/24hr). TV: cable.

★ Hotel Guldsmeden Bertrams

Vesterbrogade 107, Vesterbro, 1620 Copenhagen V (33 25 04 05, www.hotelguldsmeden.dk). Metro Forum. **Rates** 1,299kr-1,526kr double. **Rooms** 47. **Credit** AmEx, MC, V. **Map** p245 Q7 ㉗
This intimate boutique hotel, in a cool part of town, is furnished in Guldsmeden's signature fresh bohemian-Balinese style, with four-poster beds, Persian carpets, feather duvets, organic toiletries and flat-screen TVs in the guestrooms. Other pluses are a quiet courtyard garden, a sumptuous breakfast buffet and top-notch green credentials (*see p105* **Green Sleeps**). There are two other branches in Vesterbro – both displaying the high standards of this venue.
Bike rental (120kr/day). Disabled: adapted rooms. Internet (Wi-Fi). Parking (150kr/24hr). TV: cable/pay movies.
Other locations (Axel) Helgolandsgade 7-11 (33 31 32 66); (Carlton) Vesterbrogade 66 (33 22 15 00).

Moderate

Hotel Fox

Jarmers Plads 3, Vesterbro (33 95 77 55, www.hotelfox.dk). Train/metro Nørreport. **Rates** 600kr-1,300kr small; 800kr-1,400kr medium; 800kr-1,500kr large; 1,100kr-1,695kr x-large. **Rooms** 61. **Credit** AmEx, MC, V. **Map** p250 N11 ㉓
Copenhagen's 'chic metropolis' boom reached its 'cool' zenith in 2005 with Project Fox: a multi-million-Euro event celebrating the worldwide launch of Volkswagen's new Fox car. The launch took place simultaneously in three locations: Club Fox held a 21-day party; Fox Studio was a huge art gallery; and the Hotel Fox provided all the journalists with somewhere to sleep, with rooms designed by Europe's top graphic designers, illustrators and graffiti artists. The results were more funky than functional. But today, run by the Brøchner chain, the place is a good bet if you're bored by the run-of-the-mill 'boutique' look. It also has a sushi bar, Sushitreat Fox (*see p128*).
Bike rental (125kr/day). Internet (Wi-Fi). Restaurant. TV.

Hotel Tiffany

Halmtorvet 1, Vesterbro, 1652 Copenhagen V (33 21 80 50, www.hoteltiffany.dk). Train København H. **Rates** 955kr-1,145kr double. **Rooms** 29. **Credit** AmEx, MC, V. **Map** p250 Q11 ㉒

Tiffany bills itself as 'a sweet hotel', and it is. Each spacious, modern bedroom is well equipped with the essentials and a small kitchen. Add in a friendly atmosphere (fresh rolls are placed outside your door each morning) and it's easy to see why locals often use the hotel to put up overnight guests. It's only a five-minute walk from Central Station, in one of the most attractive squares in Vesterbro.
Internet (Wi-Fi). TV: cable.

Budget

Hotel Sct Thomas

Frederiksberg Allé 7, Fredericksberg, 1621 Copenhagen V (33 21 64 64, www.hotelsct thomas.dk). Bus 6A. **Rates** 695kr-795kr double. **Rooms** 44. **Credit** MC, V. **Map** p245 P8 ㉚
This small hotel is one of our favourites: low rates, a welcoming atmosphere and a great location on Frederiksberg Allé, one of the most sought-after residential areas in town. There are 44 rooms (26 come with en suite) and, though the services offered are limited, the free internet access (in the TV room) and breakfast are much appreciated.
Internet (free lobby access/Wi-Fi for a fee). Parking (75kr/day). TV: cable.

FURTHER AFIELD
Deluxe

Radisson Blu Scandinavia Hotel

Amager Boulevard 70, 2300 Copenhagen S (33 96 50 00, www.radissonblu.com). Metro Islands Brygge/bus 5. **Rates** 1,095kr-1,295kr double. **Rooms** 542. **Credit** AmEx, MC, V.
The biggest hotel in the city houses the Copenhagen Casino, four restaurants, a large lounge bar, a conference centre for 1,200 people and a total of 542 bedrooms. Although it's only a 15-minute walk from Rådhuspladsen, the Scandinavia is not as centrally located as most other Copenhagen hotels but makes up for its location with wonderful views from its 26 floors. There are some 'theme floors' featuring different design styles, such as 'oriental', 'hi-tech' and 'Scandinavian'. Of its four restaurants, the flashy 25th-floor Dining Room, which has stunning panoramic views, is well regarded.

Bars (3). Bike rental (120kr/day). Business services. Concierge. Disabled: adapted rooms. Gym. Internet (Wi-Fi). Parking (190kr/24hr). Restaurants (4). Room service. Swimming pool (indoor). TV: cable/pay movies.

Expensive

Crowne Plaza Copenhagen Towers
Ørestads Boulevard 114-118, 2300 Copenhagen S (88 77 66 55, www.cpcopenhagen.dk).
Train/metro Ørestad. **Rates** from 1,160kr double.
Rooms 366. **Credit** AmEx, MC, V.
One of the world's greenest hotels, the 25-storey 4-star Crowne Plaza is one of the city's newest accommodation options, located close to the airport (there's a handy, complimentary airport shuttle) in Ørestad. The carbon-neutral building has solar-powered electricity, a groundwater-based cooling and heating system, low-energy TVs and lighting, and local ingredients in its restaurant dishes. The hotel, furnished in a corporate but comfortable modern style, is popular with business travellers due to its excellent conference facilities and location.
Bar. Business services. Concierge. Disabled: adapted rooms. Gym. Internet (Wi-Fi). Parking (150kr/24hr). Restaurant. Room service. TV: cable/pay movies.

Skovshoved Hotel
Strandvejen 267, 2920 Charlottenlund (39 64 00 28, www.skovshovedhotel.dk). Bus 14. **Rates** 850kr-1,150kr double. **Rooms** 22. **Credit** AmEx, MC, V (4.75% transaction fee).

Among the thatched cottages and grand residences in the charming former fishing village of Skovshoved (about 10km/six miles north of Copenhagen along the Danish Riviera; *see p216*) you'll discover the Skovshoved Hotel. It's one of the more romantic accommodation options out of town, skilfully blending modernity with tradition and style with homeliness. It has 22 double rooms, some of which have sea-facing balconies. *Condé Nast Traveller* magazine voted the hotel one of the world's 50 coolest and we'd be inclined to agree.
Bar. Bike rental (100kr/day). Business services. Internet (Wi-Fi). Parking (free). Restaurants (2). Room service (24hrs). TV: cable

HOSTELS

DanHostel Copenhagen Amager
Vejlands Allé 200, 2300 Copenhagen S (32 52 29 08, www.danhostel.dk/copenhagen). Metro Bella Center or Sundby/bus 30. **Rates** 145kr dorm; 360kr-460kr single; 390kr-490kr double; 520kr-580kr triple; 630kr-680kr 4-person room; 725kr-780kr 5-person room. **Credit** AmEx, MC, V.
This modern hostel on the island of Amager, just south-east of the centre, is 15 minutes by bus from the city centre and offers private rooms as well as dorms, with or without bathroom. Breakfast is included in the price and there's an internet café. A Youth Hostel membership card is required to stay here (160kr/per annum), but you can buy a temporary card for 35kr per night. Closed for the last half of December.
Internet (lobby access).

Hotel Fox.

DanHostel Copenhagen City.

★ DanHostel Copenhagen City

HC Andersens Boulevard 50, Vesterbro (33 11 85 85/bookings 33 18 83 32, www.dgi-byen.dk/hostel). Bus 5A. **Rates** 135kr-185kr per person; 580kr-740kr 4-person room. Buffet breakfast 74kr. **Credit** MC, V (2.75% transaction fee). **Map** p251 Q14 ⑪

Tagged as 'the largest designer hostel in Europe', the five-star DanHostel Copenhagen City opened in 2004 with trendy Scandinavian furniture all over and a sharp, modern look. It is just five minutes' walk from landmark attractions like Tivoli and the Royal Library, with a fantastic view over Langebro Bridge. You can rent a whole room for yourself by paying for empty beds. This gives you a fine room for 600kr (520kr in the low season) in a lively hostel right in the centre for less than a room in a two- or three-star hotel. This is definitely one of the best ways to stay in Copenhagen on a budget.

Bike rental (100kr/day). Internet (Wi-Fi).

APARTMENTS

Adina Apartments

Amerikaplads 7, Østerbro (39 69 10 00, www.adina.dk). **Rates** 950kr-2,750kr 1-2 person apartment; 2,400kr-3,900kr 2-4 person apartment. **Credit** AmEx, MC, V.

Located in a smart residential area, this brand new hotel/apartment building opened in 2006. A stay here offers a feeling of independence for those who like having their own set of keys and their own kitchen; but there are a wide range of hotel service options and a swimming pool to boot.

Citilet Apartments

Sankt Peders Stræde 27B, 1453 Copenhagen K (22 77 10 30, www.citilet.dk). **Rates** 5,030kr double/wk. **Credit** AmEx, MC, V.

The first hotel/apartment chain in Copenhagen is still the best, but the chain recently went down from running 27 flats to five, which means securing a booking for a short stay requires a miracle. The first-rate serviced flats (25-115 sq m), fully furnished with luxury bathrooms, are all located close to Strøget. There is a weekly maid service, low telephone charges and free wireless internet. Apartments are comparable with a large suite in a hotel, for the price of a room in a three-star hotel.

★ Hay4you

Vimmelskaftet 49, 1161 Copenhagen K (33 33 08 05, www.hay4you.dk). **Rates** from 3,500kr/wk; from 11,000kr/mth. **Credit** AmEx, MC, V.

A good bet if you're staying in Copenhagen for three nights or more, Hay4you has an interesting range of nicely furnished, fully-equipped apartments to rent on a temporary basis in central Copenhagen, as well in neighbourhoods such as Vesterbro and Østerbro and Frederiksberg. Service is top-notch, and this is a great way to experience the city from the perspective of a (comfortably off) local.

Restaurants

From the world's best restaurant to the city's best burger bars.

If Spain was declared the new France a few years ago – by the *New York Times* no less – then Nordic must surely by now be the new Spanish. That's what Ferran Adrià of Spain's legendary restaurant El Bulli predicted a couple of years back anyway, and as it turns out he was right. It all began in 2004 when a troop of young chefs from all over Scandinavia got together to form the 'New Nordic Symposium', which championed Nordic produce to create ingredient-centric fare rooted in Scandinavian tradition – with not a sniff of olive oil or sun-dried tomatoes in the

air. Fast-forward to 2010 and Rene Redzepi's Noma is named the best restaurant in the world at the prestigious San Pellegrino Restaurant awards; Rasmus Kofoed's Geranium picks up the Bocuse d'Or – the food equivalent of the Oscars – in early 2011; and the world goes crazy for a taste of New Nordic, with Copenhagen well and truly at its heart.

THE RESTAURANT SCENE

There are now more Michelin-starred restaurants in Copenhagen than in the rest of Scandinavia put together. Eleven of the city's restaurant have stars, more than half awarded for new Nordic cuisine. Destination foodies travel here just to eat these days. But for those of leaner means, what is really energising the city's restaurant scene is the good-value, contemporary Danish bistro with a short menu of surefire classics, an informal-verging-on-hip atmosphere and wines by the glass. Places like **Les Trois Cochons** (*see p125*), and **Cofoco** (*see p123*) have been so successful they've grown into empires, while more independent places like newcomers **Mêlée** (*see p125*) and **Davids Bistro** (*see p127*) are following the formula with huge success, packing the punters in night after night. That's not to say that the traditional Danish *værtshus* (pub) serving smørrebrød and shots of aquavit has gone out of fashion: on the contrary, these places still have the flavour of the old Viking about them and no visit to Copenhagen is complete without having lunch or dinner in at least one of them.

One of the pleasures of eating out in even the top restaurants in Copenhagen is their relaxed, unstuffy attitude – the snooty sommelier is a rarity here. This is probably because most waiting staff tend to be paid comparatively

well, which means that, though a tip is always welcome, you shouldn't feel obliged to load on an extra 15 per cent unless you've had a really great experience. Five per cent or 10kr for meals under 100kr should suffice.

The cost of eating out in Copenhagen is still pretty high – a meal for two with wine can easily come to around 2,000kr – but if anything it seems to have gone down slightly in the last few years. And at least now you have the cream of the world's restaurants to splurge in. Also note that many Copenhagen cafés and bars serve excellent food, from light snacks to full meals. *See pp128-142* **Cafés & Bars**.

TIVOLI & RÅDHUSPLADSEN

Herman
Bernstorffsgade 5 (88 70 00 20, www.nimb.dk). *Train København H.* **Open** noon-1.30pm 6pm-midnight Mon-Sat. **Set menus** 4 courses 795kr, 6 courses 900kr. **Credit** AmEx, DC, V. **Map** p250 11P ❶ **New Nordic**
Thomas Herman's self-named restaurant at the chic boutique hotel Nimb (*see p101*) in Tivoli Gardens

> ❶ Blue numbers given in this chapter correspond to the location of each restaurant as marked on the street maps. *See pp245-253.*

Get the local experience

Over 50 of the world's top destinations available.

earned his first Michelin star in 2009. Aside from the usual Michelin frills – white linen, smart waiters, excellent service – this is a light, bright, diaphanous space thanks to huge arched windows offering magnificent views over the fairy-tale gardens of the park. Herman's ability to reinvent classics close to Danish hearts like 'burning love' – a hearty combo of fried potatoes and fatty bacon – and his own creations such as a bisque of Scandinavian white fish with wild Karl Johan mushrooms make his some of the most accomplished cooking in town. Be warned: once you add wine, it's also one of the most expensive.

Kr Wagamama

Tietgensgade 20 (33 75 06 58, www.wagamama. dk). Bus 6A. **Open** noon-11pm Mon-Thur, Sun; noon-midnight Fri, Sat. **Main courses** 99kr-115kr. **Credit** AmEx, DC, MC, V. **Map** p250 P12 ❷

Londoners will be familiar with the Wagamama formula: cheap, simple Asian noodles, soups, rice dishes and curries eaten at communal benches in a bustling canteen atmosphere, and it has translated well to the Danish capital. As in London reservations aren't possible, so you can expect to queue at weekends. There are entrances on Tietgensgade and via Tivoli, so you don't have to pay to enter the old playpark to dine here.

STRØGET & AROUND

Alberto K

Radisson SAS Royal Hotel, Hammerischsgade 1 (33 42 61 61, www.alberto-k.com). **Open** 6pm-midnight Mon-Sat. *Food served* 6-10pm Mon-Sat. **Set menus** 650kr-795kr. **Credit** AmEx, MC, V. **Map** p250 O11 ❸ **Italian/Danish**

Named after the first general manager of the Arne Jacobsen-designed SAS Royal Hotel (*see p101*), this magnificent modern Italian/Scandinavian restaurant ranks among the best of the city's upscale/event eateries. One of the highlights of eating here is, of course, being surrounded by 'Swan' and 'Egg' chairs, but the food's pretty good too featuring luxury Danish produce such as local oysters and scallops, wild venison and winter truffles. The 360° view of the city from the 20th-floor windows helps too. Prices are relatively high, but portions are large, and the food and service are exceptional.

INSIDE TRACK DINING TIMES

Be aware that many restaurants open their doors as early as 5.30pm and it's not unusual for the kitchen to stop serving at 10pm. Last seating is often a couple of hours before the restaurant's official closing time. Also note that many of the best restaurants close for the holidays in July.

Bøf & Ost

Gråbrødretorv 13 (33 11 99 11, www.boef-ost.dk). Metro Kongens Nytorv. **Open** 11am-1am daily. **Main courses** 149kr-235kr. **Set menu** 225kr. **Credit** DC, MC, V. **Map** p251 N13 ❹ **Steakhouse**

The rustic wooden tables and stone floor of this cellar restaurant are slightly at odds with the impressive complexity and prices of its food, but the various cuts and preparations of beef (charcoal-grilled is the house speciality) are excellent, as are the game dishes. The restaurant is situated on the southern side of the square in the oldest of the so-called Fire Houses, built after the great fire of 1728 that razed Copenhagen. Note: if you pay by credit card, a 4.06% surcharge will be added to your bill.

Chit Chat Brasserie

Sankt Peders Stræde 24A (33 33 93 39). Metro Nørreport. **Open** 5-10pm Mon, Sun; 5-11pm Tue-Thur; 5pm-midnight Fri, Sat. **Set menu** 295kr. **Credit** MC, V (5.75% surcharge for foreign credit cards). **Map** p250 N12 ❺ **French**

This simply styled, split-level café-brasserie, run by Australian Christopher Howard, serves sizeable portions of creative French and telltale glimpses of the new Scandinavian table at competitive prices, including lobster bisque with truffle oil, foie gras terrine with elderflower jelly, and venison with morels and cabbage. Handy for the cool shops and bars of the trendified district of Pisserenden.

Kr Huset Med Det Grønne Træ

Gammel Torv 20 (33 12 87 86, www.huset meddetgroennetrae.dk). Bus 11A. **Open** 11.30am-3.30pm Mon, Tue; 11.30am-10pm Wed-Sat; noon-4pm first Sun of the month. **Main courses** 60kr-124kr, classic Danish lunch menu 229kr. **Credit** MC, V. **Map** p251 N13 ❻ **Traditional Danish**

A kind of working man's Ida Davidsen's (*see p119*), this old-style lunch restaurant is frequented by journalists, local businessmen and lawyers from the nearby courthouse. Offering traditional Danish *smørrebrød* in a small, spartan cellar café with yellowed ceilings and wood-panelled walls, this is an authentic taste of basic Danish cuisine. Owner Peter Damgaard has run the place for over 20 years and is happy to talk you through the menu (English version available), which includes a decent range of typical open sandwich toppings.

Kong Hans Kælder

Vingårdsstræde 6 (33 11 68 68, www.kong hans.dk). Metro Kongens Nytorv. **Open** 6pm-midnight Mon-Sat. *Food served* 6-10pm Mon-Sat. **Main courses** 450kr. **6-course menu** 1,100kr. **Credit** AmEx, MC, V. **Map** p251 N15 ❼ **French/Danish**

Kong Hans' stylish, whitewashed, vaulted cellar rooms are tucked away down a small side street.

C O N S U M E

Rice Market.

Thomas Rode Andersen is one of the most highly respected chefs in Denmark and got his first Michelin star in 2010. From his open kitchen he combines the finest regional ingredients (Danish smoked cheese, fish and seafood from the Øresund, local meats) with classic French technique. Lending gravitas to the occasion is the kælder (cellar) itself, dating from the 15th century and said to be the oldest building in the city still in commercial use. At one time it faced the waterfront and was the site of a vineyard (hence the name Vingårdsstraede, 'vineyard street'). Prices, of course, are set at the sort of high levels you'd expect, which means that the clientele tends to be older and more conservative than the norm. Hardly the grooviest of venues, and being in a cellar there's no view, but come purely for the food and you will not leave disappointed.

Den Lille Fede

Boltens Gaard, Store Kongensgade 17 (33 33 70 02, www.denlillefede.dk). Metro Kongens Nytorv. **Open** 5.30-10pm Mon-Sat. **Set menu** 5-courses 498kr. **Credit** AmEx, DC, MC, V. **Map** p251 M15 ❽ **Mediterranean**

This dark, concrete tunnel has always been problematic for the city's restaurateurs. The latest owner, Poul Erik Ferdersen, has risen to the challenge offering keenly priced modern Mediterranean-rim cuisine updated with panache: Spanish ajo blanco – almond soup – with pickled pears and shellfish cannelloni with lobster foam. As he only offers seven dishes, from which you can either choose five or all seven,

Poul keeps prices reasonable and quality high. The name means 'the little fat one', by the way. Booking is advised at weekends and there is some outside seating in summer.

Peder Oxe

Gråbrødretorv 11 (33 11 00 77, www. pederoxe.dk). Metro/train Nørreport. **Open** 11.30am-1am daily. *Food served* 11.30am-10.30pm Mon-Wed, Sun; 11.30am-11pm Thur-Sat. **Main courses** 135kr-198kr. **Credit** MC, V. **Map** p251 N13 ❾ **Steakhouse**

Peder Oxe is one of Copenhagen's best-known restaurants and it is hugely popular with domestic and overseas tourists. A wide-ranging menu covers all the bases, from steaks and burgers (made from organic and/or free-range beef), to light, fresh, Asian-influenced dishes such as tuna tartar with avocado and mango, all of which are well presented and reasonably priced. But Peder Oxe's trump card is its romantic interior, featuring original wooden floors and exquisite Portuguese tiling – ample compensation should the few outside tables be taken.

Restaurant L'Alsace

Ny Østergade 9 (33 14 57 43, www.alsace.dk). Metro Kongens Nytorv. **Open** 11.30am-midnight Mon-Sat; 11.30am-4pm 1st Sunday of mth. **Main courses** 145kr-195kr. **5-course menu** 505kr. **Credit** AmEx, MC.V. **Map** p251 M15 ❿ **French**

You can hardly move for posh and pricey French restaurants in this part of town, but L'Alsace is more authentic than most, serving such Alsatian delicacies as foie gras, goose and *choucroute*, along with excellent cheeses and wines. This curious venue combines a whitewashed cellar with a rough and ready conservatory, but it still manages to evoke the crucial *hyggelige* atmosphere so valued by the Danes.

Rice Market
Hausergade 38 (+45 35 35 75 30, www. ricemarket.dk). Metro/train Nørreport. **Open** 11.30am-midnight daily. **Main courses** 115kr-185kr. **Credit** MC, V. **Map** p247 L13 **Oriental**
This cute little basement restaurant has become a firm fixture on the city's Asian dining scene, which is understandable since it comes from the same hands as Michelin-starred Kiin Kiin (*see p125*). Consequently, it gets rammed, especially at weekends. Tucked into an L-shaped space, the main dining section is pedestrian with conventional tables and chairs given a lift by outsize raffia lanterns, but the place to be is in one of the draped-off, private cubicles in the VIP section. Food-wise think crowd-pleasing classics such as Chinese steamed dumplings; Thai soups, salads and curries; satay, tempura and stir-fries. It's all good quality fare, though ordering lots of starters and eating your way around Asia, tapas-style, is the way to go.

Riz Raz
Kompagnistræde 20 (33 15 05 75, www.riz raz.dk). Bus 2A, 1A, 15, 40. **Open** 11.30am-midnight Mon-Fri; 9.30am-midnight Sat, Sun. **Main courses** 85kr-125kr. **Buffet** 79kr-99kr. **Credit** AmEx, MC, V. **Map** p251 O13 **Mediterranean**
The southern Mediterranean food at this convivial cellar restaurant is a favourite with tourists and Copenhageners and consistently wins over reviewers from the Danish press. Riz Raz always seems to be packed to the rafters with an eclectic range of diners, in for a quick bite before heading somewhere groovier. The buffet, which in many other places is just an excuse to stuff punters with cheap salads, is, in Riz Raz's case, fresh and tasty, as is their latest innovation of veggie and meat brochettes.
Other locations Store Kannikstraæde 19 (33 32 33 45).

Kr Slotskælderen Hos Gitte
Fortunstræde 4 (33 11 15 37). Train København H. **Open** 11am-5pm Tue-Sat. **Main courses** 55kr-100kr. **Credit** AmEx, MC, V. **Map** p251 N14 **Traditional Danish**
Everyone who comes to Copenhagen should try authentic, traditional Danish food, at least once. And it doesn't come much more authentic than Slotskælderen (the castle cellar). This old-school smørrebrød restaurant is just across the canal from Christiansborg Slot (home to the Danish parliament), which means this atmospheric, low-lit venue, run by the eponymous Gitte, attracts a fair number of politicians. Simply choose sandwiches, *frikadeller* (meatballs) and *sild* (herring) from the counter, and the attentive staff bring them to your table. Fried plaice and pickled herring are two top choices here, classically washed down with a beer and schnapps.

Sushitarian
Gothersgade 3 (33 92 30 54, www.sushitarian.dk). Metro Kongens Nytorv. **Open** noon-11pm Mon-Thur; noon-midnight Fri, Sat; 4-11pm Sun. **Main courses** 175kr. **Credit** MC, V. **Map** p251 M15 **Japanese**
The first of the new wave sushi bars to hit town and still the best. The soothing, tatami dining room is great for groups on a night out or a date, while the funkier downstairs dining room is perfect for a quick in and out. They offer a massive range of nigiri, sashimi and maki rolls, but it's the more innovative dishes that get tongues wagging: 'hairy scallop' fried in kataifi batter, perchance? Or how about a snow-crab or spicy lobster roll?

NYHAVN & KONGENS NYTORV
1.th
Herluf Trollesgade 9 (33 93 57 70, www.1th.dk). Metro Kongens Nytorv. **Open** from 6.30pm Wed-Sat. **Set menu** (includes wine) 1,250kr. **No credit cards.** **Map** p252 N16 **Modern Scandinavian**
This unique and really rather splendid restaurant behaves more as if it were a private dinner party (or a piece of performance art) than a commercial catering enterprise. You pay when you book (two to three

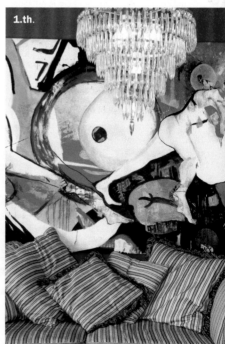

CONSUME

Where's the Beef?

Gourmet burger bars have taken Copenhagen by storm.

Copenhagen maybe getting international column inches for its New Nordic Michelin-starred restaurants, but many locals are currently more wrapped up in a rather more prosaic culinary phenomenon – that of the gourmet burger. The upmarket burger bar trend was fairly slow to hit these shores, but since it took hold a year or so ago there has been an explosion of new openings in the city – all of which compete to out-do each other in the beef and bun stakes. Most of the burger bars listed here also have a takeaway option as well as vegetarian choices and a selection of sides (fries, onion rings and baked or mashed potato).

Burger & Bun, on Vesterbro's Istedgade (No.60, 35 35 75 50, www.burgerbun.dk), opened in September 2010 and is the go-to spot for local celebs. Run by the people behind the Michelin-starred Kiin Kiin (*see p125*), it has just 12 seats, and uses top-quality ingredients (prime Danish beef, buns from the city's Andersen Bakery, own-made ketchup and organic milk in the delicious shakes). Burgers don't come cheap here (125kr for the large version), but there's no denying the quality of the ingredients. Even the beer here is artisanal, from a local microbrewery.

Hot on its heels was **Cocks and Cows**, rwhich opened a month later on the more central Gammel Strand (No.44, 33 22 82 39, www.cocksandcows.dk), quickly becoming one of Copenhagen's most popular burger bars. The affordable burgers, of which there are eight to choose from, contain 100 per cent Danish beef, and are stuffed full of relish and salad.

Nothing to do with the UK chain, **Haché**, on a side street near the Botanical Gardens (Rømersgade 20, 33 12 21 16, www.hache.dk) is fast becoming the city's burger bar of choice. The list of 15 burgers (95kr each) includes some original choices (such as the Iberian burger with manchego cheese and aïoli) and all beefburgers are made with organic meat.

Nearby is the Frederiksborggade branch of mini-chain **Halifax** (No.35, 33 32 77 11, www.halifax.nu), considered the Copenhagen pioneer of the gourmet burger. Named after the Canadian city, where the Danish owners first met and conceived the concept, all the burgers, relishes, dips and salads are made from scratch, there are two original veggie burgers (based on chickpeas and celery root), and the service is renowned. There are additional branches on Larsbjørnsstræde (No.9, 33 93 80 90), not far from Tivoli, and on Falkoner Plads 1 in Frederiksberg.

All of these spots are good bets for a top-notch burger. But first prize in the best gourmet burger awards must go to upmarket steakhouse **MASH** (*see p117*), open in Nyhavn since summer 2009. It's more restaurant than burger bar, but the burgers are fat, juicy and filling, helping to justify the 160kr price tag. Enjoy one with a premium ice-cold beer on the side.

Finally, for a cheaper bite, there's **Sporvejen**, located in an old tram car on Gråbrødretorv (*see p134*) in the centre. Open since the 1970s, the bistro has specialised in beef for aeons, and its burgers are half the price of many of the above spots.

weeks in advance is best in order to be sure of a table) and receive an invitation by return of post. When you arrive ('promptly at seven'), you buzz a discreetly labeled intercom on the door of an ordinary, turn-of-the-19th-century apartment block in the quiet residential area behind the Kongelige Teater, before being shown into a drawing room in which other 'guests' are mingling over an aperitif. After a while doors are opened with a theatrical flourish to reveal a spacious dining room with an open kitchen. The eight innovative, contemporary, but unfussy Scandinavian dishes on the fixed menu more than live up to this elaborate preamble. A truly singular experience.

Cap Horn

Nyhavn 21 (33 12 85 04, www.caphorn.dk). Metro Kongens Nytorv. **Open** *Jan-Mar* 10am-midnight Mon-Fri; 9am-midnight Sat, Sun. *Apr-Dec* 9am-1am daily. **Main courses** 139kr-195kr. **Credit** MC, V. **Map** p252 M16 ⓰ **Traditional Danish**
When Danes think of Nyhavn, they usually think of herring and smørrebrød, and for that you need a proper Danish *værtshus* (pub). Nowhere along this postcard perfect, but very touristy stretch of canal does it better than Cap Horn. Situated in one of these beautiful old town houses built by King Christian IV in the 17th century, the place oozes old world atmosphere and was a popular haunt for sailors and ladies of easy pleasure before reaching its current rather more salubrious state. It's popular for Jazz brunches (150kr) on Sundays when tourists and locals gather round a log fire, clinking glasses and generally making merry. Smørrebrod is good value at 65kr-69kr. There's outdoor seating from April to September.

Els

Store Strandstræde 3 (33 14 13 41, www. restaurant-els.dk). Metro Kongens Nytorv. **Open** 11am-midnight daily. **Main courses** 185kr-265kr. **3-course menu** 348kr. **Credit** AmEx, MC, V (4.75% surcharge for foreign credit cards). **Map** p252 M16 ⓱ **French**
There is no doubting the excellence of the kitchen at this posh (and a tad stuffy) restaurant, but you come here largely for a taste of Copenhagen past. Els has been around since Hans Christian Andersen's day (he wrote a poem in appreciation of its hospitality) and the original mid 19th-century interior underscores the mood, which is more 'well-heeled tourist on a spree' than 'regular local in for a treat'. Food-wise, expect classical French cuisine, rich, buttery and utterly decadent with dishes like lobster soup topped with slivers or smoked butterfish, grilled veal liver with lentils and cheese, and chocolate crème brûlée. You wouldn't want to eat this rich food every day, but when it's cold outside it goes down a treat.

★ MASH

Bredgade 20, Frederiksstaden (33 13 93 00, www.mashsteak.dk). Metro Kongens Nytorv. **Open** noon-3pm, 5.30-10pm Mon-Wed; noon-3pm,

5.30pm-11pm Thur-Sat; 5.30pm-10pm Sun. **Main courses** 165kr-395kr. **Credit** AmEx, MC, V. **Map** p252 M16 ⓲ **Steakhouse**
Another winner from long-time Copenhagen resident and veteran chef Francis Cardenau (also of Umami, *see p120*, and Le Sommelier, *see p119*) MASH, meaning Modern American Steak House, is all that and more. Head down a corridor lined with glass-fronted fridges stocked with steaks so deeply marbled and tender-looking you could scoff them down raw, and into a darkly glamorous setting of intimate leather booths, soft lighting and lots of red. Start as you mean to go on with a signature margarita followed by Cardenau's extraordinarily crisp-on-the-outside, gooey-in-the-middle grilled veal sweetbreads, followed by a dry-aged Danish steak – hung for 90 days until spoon tender – with onion rings, and all-American cheesecake to finish.

Restaurant d'Angleterre

Hotel d'Angleterre, Kongens Nytorv 34 (33 37 06 45/www.remmen.dk). Metro Kongens Nytorv. **Open** noon-4pm, 5.30-11pm Mon-Thur; noon-4pm, 5.30-midnight Fri, Sat; noon-3pm, 5.30-11pm Sun. **Main courses** 265kr-595kr. **3-course menu** 385kr. **Tasting menu** 700kr. **Credit** AmEx, MC, V. **Map** p251 M15 ⓳ **French**
This ornate room overlooking Kongens Nytorv in the city's grandest hotel was given a facelift a few years ago – from the rather nutty inspiration of the whimsical Danish artist Bjørn Wiinblad – to an altogether more restrained style that involved a major rebuild of the hotel frontage, while keeping the glamorous gold panelling on the walls and ankle deep carpets. It's now an extremely pleasant place to be and perfectly matches a brilliantly executed menu of such dishes as monkfish on wild watercress with warm mayonnaise and hazelnuts, and *canard à la presse* (the French classic of pressed duck served in a sauce of its own blood and marrow). The clientele, however, a bit like the duck, remains resolutely antediluvian.

Salt

Toldbodgade 24-28 (33 74 14 48, www.salt restaurant.dk). Metro Kongens Nytorv. **Open** noon-4pm, 5-10.30pm daily. **Main courses** 85kr-265kr. **Set menus** 315kr-445kr. **Credit** AmEx, DC, V. **Map** p252 M17 ⓴ **French/ Modern Danish**
Sir Terence Conran's first foray into design-conscious Denmark was a helping hand in this modern Franco-Danish eatery housed in a converted corn-drying warehouse dating from 1787. The chunky wood beams of the dining room give it a pleasingly warm and rustic air in the dead of winter, while the terrace on the waterfront is a firm favourite through the summer, and year-round the team offer an interesting menu that changes every three weeks. Imaginative dishes like salt-cured tuna with organic eggs, sea buckthorn and spinach, and beer fried pork tenderloin with celeriac and tarragon mash, and dark chocolate

CONSUME

toffee with gin and yogurt cream make this one of the best-value dining experiences in town. What's more, the lunchtime smørrebrod is good value (from 65kr). Service is a little brisk, but who cares when your sitting on top of the world with the sun on your face and the gentle waters of Copenhagen's grand canal at your toes. For special occasions, you might also like to take advantage of an evening cruise on the restaurant's own antique barge (915kr for 3 courses, plus champagne; groups of eight).

Kr Wokshop Cantina

Ny Adelgade 6 (33 91 61 21, www.wokshop.dk).
Metro Kongens Nytorv. **Open** noon-2pm, 5.30-
1pm Mon-Fri; 6-10pm Sat. **Main courses** 65kr-
145kr **Credit** AmEx, MC, V. **Map** p251 M15 ㉑
Oriental
This excellent little cellar restaurant just around the corner from Kongens Nytorv is loosely modelled on the Wagamama concept (*see p113*), with long tables and cheap, fresh and delicate dishes. The food is mostly Thai, with some other regional influences, and includes the usual noodle- and rice-based bowls. A second branch recently opened in Osterbro.

SLOTSHOLMEN

Søren K

Søren Kierkegaards Plads 1 (33 47 49 49, www.
soerenk.dk). Metro Kongens Nytorv. **Open** noon-
4pm, 5pm-midnight Mon-Sat. **Main courses**
Lunch 75kr-175kr. *Dinner* 165kr-225kr. **Set**
menus 385kr-590kr. **Credit** AmEx, MC, V.
Map p251 P15 ㉒ **Contemporary**
This supercool minimalist Scandinavian restaurant on the ground floor of the Black Diamond was awarded its first Michelin star in 2010. It's a very

---

INSIDE TRACK NEW NORDIC

The New Nordic food movement started to take shape about ten years ago, with Noma's Claus Meyer and Rene Redzepi as key players; but it's only recently that it's gained international attention. It consists of dishes made from the freshest produce grown exclusively in the Nordic regions, and is inspired by traditional Scandinavian techniques and recipes. Potatoes, fish, root vegetables, grains and wild berries feature heavily, as does porridge, pickling and salting. As a food movement focused on local, organic produce, it is inherently sustainable – and healthy to boot. The majority of Copenhagen's Michelin-starred restaurants – of which there are currently 11 – serve truly sensational New Nordic cuisine.

---

popular lunch venue, and dining here is a great way to get an interior perspective of the building's design. Although there are probably more atmospheric destinations for a night out in the city, this is one of the surprisingly few restaurants to take full advantage of Copenhagen's waterside location (but be warned, a stiff sea breeze can blight alfresco dinners even in summer) and the food is refreshingly light, imaginatively prepared and highly regarded by locals. Style, substance and a view – what more could you ask for?

FREDERIKSSTADEN

★ AOC

Dronningens Tværgade 2 (33 11 11 45, www.
premisse.dk). Metro Kongens Nytorv. **Open** 6-
10pm Tue-Sat. **4-course menu** 595kr. **7-course**
menu (incl wine) from 1,795kr. **Credit** AmEx,
MC, V. **Map** p249 L16 ㉓ **New Nordic**
The iceberg white arches of this unique-looking restaurant could be chilly, but in fact it oozes a certain cathedral-like serenity. The school of thought being that the cleaner the backdrop, the more attention you pay to the food and these dishes certainly make an impact. Although the reference point is clearly Noma (with a bit of El Bulli thrown in), AOC chef Ronny Emborg oozes talent with his precision cooking and clever, largely Nordic, flavour combinations. He won a Michelin star in 2010 for inspired creations like beetroot and razor clams with horseradish cream and dill oil, buttery halibut sashimi with cress and cod roe, and tart buckthorn granita with yogurt cream and raw egg yolk.

Kr Cascabel Madhus

Store Kongensgade 80-82 (33 93 77 97). Metro
Kongens Nytorv. **Open** 9.30am-6pm Mon-Wed;
9.30am-7.30pm Thur, Fri; 10am-6pm Sat, Sun.
Main courses 50kr-125kr. **Credit** MC, V.
Map p249 K16 ㉔ **Vegetarian**
Notable mainly as one of the few veggie restaurants in a town that favours carnivors, it may not look much from the outside, or on the inside for that matter, but Cascabel is reliable for fresh, light, vegetarian food. Above all, it's cheap. You can fill up on healthy pastas, salads and muffins for under 90kr – the sun-dried tomato pasta salad with aubergine, olives, jalapeño peppers and sunflower seeds (50kr) is a meal in itself. Understandably, Cascabel draws a loyal, local crowd of Danes and expats. Lunch only.

★ Kr Madklubben

Store Kongensgade 66 (33 32 32 34, www.
madklubben.info). Metro/train Kongens Nytorv.
Main courses 100kr-200kr. **Open** 5.30pm-
midnight Mon-Sat. **Credit** AmEx, MC, V.
Map p249 L16 ㉕ **Modern Danish**
A contemporary Danish bistro for the wallet-conscious isn't something that you come across too often in Copenhagen, especially once you throw in drinks, so Madklubben is a welcome addition to the

CONSUME

Le Sommelier.

scene. The dining room is typically Danish, in that it's smart yet casual, furnished with long, canteen-style tables sympathetically lit to define spaces, and with wood-panelled walls and floorboards softening the effect. It's boisterous enough for a large group, yet fun enough for a date and, most importantly, a good meal is guaranteed. The menu changes monthly, but generally features classics like steak on Jerusalem artichoke purée and catch of the day with roasted fennel.

★ Rasmus Oubæk

Store Kongensgade 52 (33 32 32 09, www. rasmusoubaek.dk). Metro Kongens Nytorv. **Open** noon-3pm, 6pm-midnight Mon-Fri; 6pm-midnight Sat. **Main courses** 95kr-190kr. **4-course menu** 425kr. **Credit** AmEx, MC, V. **Map** p249 L16 **㉖**
French
Having bagged a Michelin star, Rasmus Oubæk's bistro defines itself from the rest of the contemporary Danish bistro scene by sticking rigidly to French classics, although he does prides himself on sourcing locally (check out the website for a look at the prime Danish ingredients). Likewise, rather than fiddling around making endless changes, he sticks to what he knows and does it extremely well, whether you're tucking into a platter of lusty French charcuterie, a bowl of snails dowsed in garlic and parsley, or a classic boeuf béarnaise. Add impeccable presentation and a starkly elegant utilitarian interior and this is one of the most solid modern restaurants in town.

Restaurant Ida Davidsen

Store Kongensgade 70 (33 91 36 55, www.ida davidsen.dk). Metro Kongens Nytorv. **Open** 10.30am-4pm Mon-Fri. **Main courses**
smørrebrød 45kr-155kr. **Credit** AmEx, MC, V. **Map** p249 L16 **㉗ Traditional Danish**
Ida Davidsen is the undisputed queen of smørrebrød and a visit to her warm and cozy little cellar restaurant is the perfect introduction to the art of the open sandwich. Ida, who works behind the counter most days, is the fifth generation of her family to run this 100-year-old lunch restaurant, concocting ornate open-topped sandwiches that could rank as works of art in any gourmand's book. Home-made rye bread is piled high with lovingly tended toppings such as smoked salmon and caviar, home-cured pickled herring with slivers of raw red onion and dill, silky beef tartar with a fresh egg yolk plopped into the middle. From the 250 or so sandwiches on offer, the Victor Borge, is a monster featuring fresh salmon, lumpfish roe, shrimps, crayfish and dill mayonnaise, and a royal favourite who pop in from their gaff round the corner in Amalienborg.

Le Sommelier

Bredgade 63-65 (33 11 45 15, www.lesommelier. dk). Metro Kongens Nytorv or train to Østerport. **Open** noon-2pm, 6-10pm Mon-Thur; noon-2pm, 6-11pm Fri; 6-11pm Sat; 6-10pm Sun. **Main courses** 185kr-225kr. **3-course set menu** 395kr. **Credit** AmEx, MC, V. **Map** p249 K16 **㉘**
French/Danish
Big, warm and bustling Le Sommelier is staffed by people who love and know good food and draws customers who know and love good restaurants. It's a very happy marriage. Spread over three dining rooms, the first surrounds the bar area and has a couple of large, round tables for groups, the second is more intimate and closely packed, annd the third is tucked-away and discreet for special occasion

dining. It's won awards for its wine list and has one of the finest cellars in Copenhagen, stocked with over 800 bottles (more than 20 reds are sold by the glass) – *Wine Spectator* magazine has given the place an award of excellence – while veteran restaurateur Francis Cardenau continues to deliver lovingly prepared dishes that fuse the best of France and Denmark: bavette of beef with braised salsify, cassoulet with pork shank and foie gras, and a mean zarzuela (fish and seafood stew enriched with saffron). Booking is advised at weekends and in the evenings.

★ Umami

Store Kongensgade 59 (33 38 75 00, www. restaurantumami.dk). Metro Kongens Nytorv. **Open** 6-10pm Mon-Thur; 6-11pm Fri, Sat. **Main courses** 175kr-245kr. **Set menu** 545kr-700kr. **Credit** AmEx, MC, V. **Map** p249 L16 ㉙ Japanese

Looking like the backdrop for a *Wallpaper** magazine shoot, this Danish take on Nobu offers an eclectic range of Asian-influenced dishes, from classic sushi in the large sushi bar on the first floor, to unexpected fusions of classic French and Japanese cuisine (seared foie gras with eel, dashi pear, black beans and seaweed salad). Fusion has become something of a dirty word these days, but ask any of the Michelin-starred chefs in the city where they like to eat when off-duty, and this is the place they most often mention. Everyone in Copenhagen who has anything to do with food has the highest respect for chef Francis Cardenau – also behind Le Sommelier – and several years on still nothing has trumped it. The interior, by Orbit of London (who also count Louis Vuitton among their clients), is seductive with dark stone walls, walnut floors and ebony tables, and there is a saké and cocktail bar on the ground floor where mixologists come up with some seriously new wave drinks including long-aged cocktails and delicate boozy infusions.

ROSENBORG & AROUND

Kokkeriet Spisehus & Catering

Kronprinsessegade 64 (33 15 27 77, www. kokkeriet.dk). Train Østerport. **Open** 6pm-1am Tue-Sat. **3-course menu** 500kr. **6-course menu** 700kr. **Credit** AmEx, MC, V. **Map** p247 K1 ㉚ French/Danish

Tucked away in Nyboder, this small but seductive modern French restaurant is really a multifunctional food space that includes a catering company, and more recently monthly cooking classes for 1,500kr. It won its first Michelin star in 2006 and is still going great guns to impress. Loved by locals and hidden away from the tourist trail, Kokkeriet has thrived thanks to its superb kitchen and lively combinations, such as veal with Swedish lumpfish roe and marinated beetroot, and wild boar with apples and celery purée. Exceptional quality and worth hunting out.

Sticks 'n' Sushi

Nansensgade 47 & 59 (33 11 70 30, www. sushi.dk). Metro/train Nørreport. **Open** 11am-11pm Mon-Thur, Sun; 11am-midnight Fri, Sat. **Set menu** 179kr-225kr. **Credit** AmEx, MC, V. **Map** p246 L11 ㉛ Japanese

If you can forgive the heinous abbreviation in the name, you will find this to be one of Copenhagen's most stylish sushi restaurants (it was also the first), with branches in two of the city's coolest residential streets. Sticks 'n' Sushi's menu varies, depending on the fish of the day, but the quality remains generally high (as do the prices). There is a well-stocked rack of magazines to peruse as you await the arrival of your sashimi.

Other locations Øster Farimagsgade 16B (35 38 34 63); Strandvejen 195, Hellerup (39 40 15 40); Istedgade 62, Vesterbro (33 23 73 04).

Sult

Filmhuset, Vognmagergade 8B (33 74 34 17, www.sult.dk). Metro Kongens Nytorv. **Open** noon-10pm Tue-Sat; noon-9pm Sun. **Main courses** 115kr-250kr. **Credit** AmEx, MC, V. **Map** p247 L14 ㉜ Global

The Danish Film Institute's magnificent film centre has another draw. Chef Margrethe Kofoed Olsen successfully fuses southern European food with global influences in handsomely modern, New York-ish surroundings (high ceilings, wooden floors, tall windows). Sult is short for *sulten*, which means 'hungry' in Danish, and is not to be confused with the equally good Salt (*see p117*), which means 'salt' in both English and Danish.

CHRISTIANSHAVN & CHRISTIANIA

Era Ora

Overgaden Neden Vandet 33B, Christianshavn (32 54 06 93, www.era-ora.dk). Metro Christianshavn/bus 2A. **Open** noon-3pm, 7pm-midnight Mon-Sat. **6-course set menu** 880kr. **Credit** AmEx, MC, V. **Map** p252 P16 ㉝ Italian

The dedication of the chefs here is evident in the complex yet light Umbrian dishes, using ingredients flown in from Italy. This beautifully decorated restaurant, with its goldleaf lighting, burnt sienna walls and open courtyard to the rear, only serves set menus, with a choice of fish or meat for the main course. The wine list remains as impressive and expensive as ever, the service efficient and formal making it the best Italian in town by a long shot. If your wallet doesn't stretch to these gastronomic heights there's always the restaurant's sister bistro L'Altro (Torvegade 62, 32 54 54 06, www.laltro.dk) across the canal.

Kr Morgenstedet

Fabriksområdet 134, Christiania (www. morgenstedet.dk). Metro Christianshavn/bus 8,

Profile Noma and Rene Redzepi

Do believe the hype.

Rene Redzepi is that killer combination of hard-work, diligence and innate passion that talent scouts dream of, and has single-handedly done more for the cult of Nordic than any new cuisine could hope for. Yet, his emergence at the age of 32 as one of the planet's greatest chefs – Noma (*see p122*) is now world famous – is largely accidental, he says, with characteristic deference. He came to the job not through any burning desire, but because catering college was what you did if you couldn't do anything else. Along the way he discovered he quite liked it, and quickly worked his way through the ranks starting at a Michelin-starred eatery in Copenhagen, ending up at Ferran Adrià's El Bulli in Catalonia.

It was not until he returned to Copenhagen at the age of 24, and under the careful direction of Danish food guru, restaurateur and celebrity chef Claus Meyer, that Redzepi blossomed and quickly became one of the most vocal advocates of New Nordic (*see p118* **Inside Track**). Redzepi took it further. He began foraging the coast and

forests of Denmark and Sweden for wild herbs, plants and fungi that could take the place of basil, mint and coriander. He tapped sap from birch trees and served it like water. And he turned the concept of 'fine dining' upside down much to the befuddlement of Michelin inspectors: Noma's tables bear no linen, hunting knives cut the meat and many of the dishes are eaten with the hands. 'I want people to reconnect with food,' Redzepi said in an early interview, 'to become more aware of it in its raw and natural state.'

Slowly word began to spread of a young Danish chef working out of an old fishing warehouse in an obscure part of Copenhagen who was doing wondrous and unexpected things. Among the early highlights was Greenlandic musk ox served like steak tartar and studded with crunchy rye croutons and an edible garden of baby vegetables. Today you might get 'oyster and ocean' or 'potatoes with milk skin'. Noma now boasts two Michelin stars (it might even be three by the time you read this), won San Pelegrino's title of best restaurant in the world in 2010, and released a cookbook, *Noma: time and place in Nordic cuisine*, declared the most important cookbook of the year by critics.

CONSUME

72E. **Open** noon-9pm Tue-Sun. **Main courses**
75kr. **No credit cards.** Map p253 P19 ㉞
Vegetarian

This cute clapboard cottage in the heart of the Free
City of Christiania serves organic, vegetarian food
at rock-bottom prices. Most of the produce comes
from the owner's nearby farm, and the menu changes
daily featuring wholesome potato gratins, bean stews
and mushroom and tofu stirfries depending on the
season. It is a great place to fill up while on a tour of
the old hippy quarter and you can be sure you won't
eat quite like this anywhere else in the city.

★ Noma

*Strandgade 93, Christianshavn (32 96 32 97,
www.noma.dk). Metro Christianshavn.* **Open**
noon-4pm, 6.30-10pm Tue-Sat. **7-course menu**
1,095kr. **12-course menu** 1,395kr. **Credit**
AmEx, MC, V. **Map** p252 N18 ㉟ **New Nordic**

Having worked at legendary Spanish restaurant El
Bulli and the French Laundry in California,
Denmark's most innovative chef, Rene Redzepi, has
tried to focus their kind of out-of-the-box thinking
and meticulous attention to detail on Nordic ingredients, with sensational results. Redzepi is a tireless
forager, unearthing extraordinary 'substitute' ingredients, such as sea grasses that taste like coriander
from beaches in Sweden, truffles from Gotland and
herbs from the banks of Christianshavn's ramparts.
Recent highlights include dried scallops with grains
and watercress, a poetic sounding oyster and ocean,
and Gammel Dansk and sorrel. Expect to be amazed,
delighted and intrigued – often all at the same time.
The interior of this converted 18th-century warehouse
has a raw, diaphanous quality provided by bleached
wood rafters and large picture windows over the
canal, yet the Icelandic sheepskin rugs thrown over
chairs and candles on scrubbed table-tops add
warmth to a dazzlingly Nordic atmosphere. All in all
it's excellent value for an experience you'll remember
the rest of your life. *See also p121* **Profile**.

Restaurant Kanalen

*Wilders Plads 2, Christianshavn (32 95 13 30,
www.restaurant-kanalen.dk). Metro Christianshavn.*
Open 11.30am-midnight Mon-Sat. **Main courses**
128kr-275kr. **Lunch menus** 360kr-495kr. **Dinner
menus** 360kr-495kr. **Credit** AmEx, MC, V.
Map p252 O17 ㊱ **Danish**

Tucked away beside the canals in a particularly idyllic corner of Christianshavn, Restaurant Kanalen
(which means 'the Canal') strikes a happy balance
between traditional and modern Danish cooking.
You'll find excellent herring and frikadeller alongside more intricate dishes that blend the freshest
local ingredients with deliciously light sauces and
surprise ingredients from around the world, like
pickled mushrooms and pimientos piquillos (the
sweet little red peppers from Spain). With alfresco
dining in summer, sweet service, and accessible
prices Kanalen is a great all-rounder.

Fiskebaren. *See p124.*

CONSUME

Kr Spicey Kitchen
Torvegade 56 (32 95 28 29). Metro Christianshavn. **Open** 5-11pm Mon-Sat; 2-11pm Sun. **Main courses** 30kr-75kr. **No credit cards.** **Map** p252 Q17 ❸ **Indian**
The number of customers usually found waiting for a table inside this frantic and cramped one-room curry house is testament to its excellent value. The choice of chicken, lamb or fish curries might be a little limited (the chicken and spinach curry is recommended), but that hasn't stopped Spicey Kitchen building a reputation as one of Copenhagen's best cheap and fast eats.

Spiseloppen
Loppen building, 2nd floor, Bådsmandsstræde 43, Christiania (32 57 95 58, www.spiseloppen.com). Metro Christianshavn. **Open** 5-10pm Tue-Sun. **Main courses** 135kr-250kr. **Credit** MC, V. **Map** p252 P18 ❸ **Global**
What do you get when you cross an Englishman, an Irishman, a Scotsman, a Dane, a Lebanese and an Italian? Spiseloppen's constantly changing rota of international kitchen staff create a different menu every night but, for once, this isn't a case of 'too many cooks' – the myriad influences at work here rarely fail to conjure something special (the vegetarian dishes are particularly impressive). The entrance to Spiseloppen, through an anonymous door and up some shabby stairs in one of Christiania's warehouses, promises little, but once you enter its low-ceilinged, candlelit dining hall its true worth becomes clear. Diners tend to be young and arty, not minding the occasional waft of exotic cheroot.

Viva
Langebrogade Kajplads 570, Christianshavn (27 25 05 05, www.restaurantviva.dk). Metro Christianshavn or bus 5A. **Open** 10.30am-4pm, 5.30-midnight daily. **3-course menu** 310kr. **4-course menu** 365kr. **Credit** AmEx, MC, V. **Map** p251 Q14 ❸ **Global**
Viva is a floating restaurant housed aboard a ship moored next to Langebro, across the water from the Black Diamond. Noted for its shellfish dishes, it is owned by Thomas Veber and Paolo Guimaraes (the half-Portuguese chef), and is the sister restaurant to Aura. Like Aura, the dishes are tapas-sized, while the interior is similarly contemporary and furnished by Gubi. During the summer the rooftop deck is a great place for a pre-dinner cocktail with views across the harbour.

VESTERBRO & FREDERIKSBERG

Bio Mio
Halmtorvet 19, Vesterbro (33 31 20 00, http:// biomio.dk). **Open** noon-11pm Mon-Thur; noon-midnight Fri; 11am-midnight Sat; 11am-11pm Sun. **Main courses** 115kr-185kr. **Credit** MC, V. **Map** p250 Q10 ❹ **Organic**
Bio Mio opened in February 2009 in the city's trendy Meatpacking District, and is a key element in the explosion of the organic movement in Copenhagen (*see below* **Inside Track**). The creative cooking covers roasted root vegetables, local steamed and smoked fish, delicious salads, stir-fries, curries, pasta and hearty brunch options, while the set-up is equally innovative: there are no waiters here – instead, you order directly from one of the chefs (it's an open kitchen) from a 'mood-based' menu, and then collect your meal via a buzzer system. As well as organic and locally sourced food, the restaurant's green credentials extend to its ecologically certified woodwork, paraben-free soap in the bathroom and eco-friendly gas and electric policy. The weekend brunch buffet is 165kr per person.

Cofoco
Abel Cathrinsgade 7, Vesterbro (33 13 60 60, www.cofoco.dk). Train København H. **Open** 5.30pm-midnight Mon-Sat. **4-course menu** 275kr. **Credit** AmEx, MC, V. **Map** p250 Q10 ❹ **French/Danish**
Such has been the success of the Copenhagen Food Consulting People that their stable has now grown to seven restaurants (see website), all of them top quality and great value. Cofoco along with Les Trois Cochons (*see p125*) and bargain takeaway place Le Marché (Værndemsvej 2), were among the first to make eating out fun and affordable in the Danish capital and they continue to offer some of the most solid cooking around. The interior at Cofoco is rustic, cosy and casual with wooden tabletops and a blackboard marked up with the day's specials, while the menu offers rather more than the usual confit and entrecôte. Try baby new potatoes with berries and winter truffles, and pork braised for 14 hours and served with lemon-scented Jerusalem artichoke purée. Hearty portions, easy prices and a general atmosphere of bonhomie have made this a regular night out for locals and it's a great place to tap into the Danish concept of 'hygge'.

> ### INSIDE TRACK ORGANIC STAR
> Denmark's consumption of organic goods is now the highest in the world, partly due to new pro-organic governmental policies. Many restaurants and cafés are part of this positive movement that has pushed the city to a new level of eco-consciousness and spurred the rise of New Nordic cuisine (*see p118* **Inside Track**). Apparently some 75 per cent of food in Copenhagen's eateries is now organic, making it the most eco-friendly city in the world when it comes to food. The Danish mark of inspection for organic products is a red 'ø' symbol.

CONSUME

Les Trois Cochons.

★ Fiskebaren

*Flæsketorvet 100, Vesterbro (32 15 56 56, www.
fiskebaren.dk). Train København H.* **Open**
5.30pm-midnight Wed, Thur; 5.30pm-3am Fri, Sat.
Main courses 135kr-225kr. **Credit** AmEx, MC,
V. **Fish/Seafood**
Located in the heart of Copenhagen's ultra trendy, yet
rough and ready, Meatpacking District, Fiskebaren
is a shrine to the deliciousness of the deep. The vast,
industrial space arranged around a U-shaped bar
glows a deep sea blue that seems exactly right for the
food: plump, pearl-grey oysters from the icy depths
of Limfjorden, Øresund mussels with raspberry and
walnut vinaigrette, and fish 'n' chips using white fish
from Østersøen, chips from sweet Gotland potatoes
and a hearty remoulade. It's locavoring at its very best
with a snappy, largely Northern European – including
some Danish – wine list to match. *Photos p122.*

formel B

*Vesterbrogade 182, Frederiksberg (33 25 10 66,
www.formel-b.dk). Bus 6A.* **Open** 6pm-1am Mon-

INSIDE TRACK HOME COOKING

Posh restaurants and groovy cafés
are all very well, but if you really want
to get to know what makes Danes tick,
it could be worth getting in touch with
Dine with the Danes (26 85 39 61, www.
dinewiththedanes.dk). Since 1998 this
organisation has offered visitors the
chance to spend an evening in the home
of local people, sampling traditional Danish
food and getting to know more about
Denmark and Danish culture over the
dinner table.

Sat. **Main courses** 120kr. **Credit** AmEx, MC, V.
Map p245 Q6 ⓬ **Contemporary**
Several of Denmark's best-known chefs have passed
through the kitchen of this small, marble-lined cellar
restaurant at the western end of Vesterbrogade (a
very long walk from the centre of town) and it's held
a Michelin star since 2004. Like so many other places
in the city, the concept is a riff on French and Danish
classics, but they do it so well, taking the notion of
modernism in cooking to a whole new level. It's not
strictly speaking a fish restaurant, but this is where
it shines. Try a dollop of caviar on a scoop of
Jerusalem artichoke ice-cream, then go on to more
robust dishes like shellfish salad with rouille, skate
wing with tarragon foam and pickled potatoes, or
west coast turbot with braised veal tails. Ingredients
are always locally sourced and seasonal, and with
these foodie credentials you'd expect a rather serious
crowd. In fact, it draws the city's young and beautiful
so dress up and make a night of it.

Lê Lê

*Vesterbrogade 56, Vesterbro (33 22 71 35,
www.lele-nhahang.com). Bus 6A.* **Open** 11.30am-
11pm Mon-Thur; 11.30am-2am Fri; 10am-2am Sat;
10am-1pm Sun. **Main courses** 135kr-165kr.
Credit MC, V. **Map** p245 P9 ⓭ **Vietnamese**
One of the city's best oriental restaurants and also
one of its better bargain eats, serving up authentic,
complex Vietnamese dishes – everything from soups
and noodles to curries and rice dishes. The venue is
cool too, with high ceilings and massive glass windows. It's popularity has grown to the extent that it
can be almost impossible to get in at weekends, but
a little take-out outlet with a handful of tables for
eating in has opened a couple of doors along at number 46 (open daily 11am-9.30pm). If anything it's
even better than Lê Lê and is a great place for a quick
bite, especially if you're dining alone.

★ Mêlée

Martensens Allé 16, Frederiksberg (35 13 11 34, www.melee.dk). Metro Frederiksberg. **Open** 5.30pm-10.30pm Tue-Fri. **3-course set menu** 375kr. **Credit** AmEx, MC, V. **Map** p245 O6 ⓐ
Modern Danish Bistro

This newcomer to Copenhagen's thriving Nordic-does-French bistro scene is a *hygge* little spot on a residential street in chichi Frederiksberg. In the summer there are a couple of tables outside, but its best to be in the warm bosom of the dining room (tables are tiny) to soak up the celebratory atmosphere. The wine list is carefully put together to match a man-sized menu. Slabs of home-baked bread and butter accompany cod with pears and caper butter; lusty stews served straight from the pot come with mash; and a memorable 'onglet à l'echalote' – the Bordeaux classic of the gamey, diaphragm cut, topped with raw, red shallots.

★ Mother

Høkerboderne 9-15, Vesterbro (22 27 58 98, www.mother.dk). Train København H. **Open** 11am-11pm Mon-Wed, Sun; 11am-1am Thur-Sat. **Pizzas** 75kr-125kr. **Credit** MC, V. **Pizza**

This trendy pizza parlour in Kødbyen (the Meatpacking District) has been packed since opening a year or so ago. The secret is in the organic sourdough pizza bases (which are apparently easier to digest than conventional bases), top-quality toppings and an authentic wood-fired oven, which combine to produce simply delicious pizzas. Starters and sides such as bruschetta made from manitoba flour are also excellent.

▶ *Being in the heart of the nightlife scene, Mother is a good bet if you want a bite to eat before moving on to one of the area's cool bars, such as Bakken (see venue index).*

PatéPaté

Slagterboderne 1, Vesterbro (39 69 55 57, http://patepate.dk). Train København H. **Open** 8am-midnight Mon-Wed; 8am-1am Thur; 8am-3am Fri; 10am-3am Sat; 10am-midnight Sun. **Main courses** 185kr-250kr. **Credit** MC, V. **Mediterranean/Danish**

PatéPaté, situated next door to Bio Mio (*see p123*) in Kødbyen, is a wine bar, restaurant, tapas bar and delicatessen that was opened in summer 2009 by the group that run Bibendum (*see p135*) and Falernum (*see p137*). The restaurant's name was inspired by the building's previous incarnation as a liver pâté factory. Rustic cuisine is the name of the game, with lots of hearty meat and fish dishes, as well as an excellent wine list. Candlelight and homely decor create a convivial mood.

Les Trois Cochons

Værnedamsvej 10 (33 31 70 55, www.cofoco.dk). Metro Forum. **Open** noon-3pm, 5.30pm-midnight daily. **2-course lunch menu** 185kr. **3-course**

menu 295kr. **Credit** AmEx, MC, V. **Map** p245 P8 ⓐ **French/Danish**

Run by the folk behind Franco-Danish Cofoco (*see p123*), Les Trois Cochons dishes up similarly priced, superb value three-course French meals with locally sourced ingredients and an enjoyable lack of formality. Decor is a bit more luxe than the sister restaurant, with generous armchairs that invite lingering and chandeliers lighting the dining tables. Dishes are a cut above the usual bistro offerings too featuring the likes of rabbit cooked in smoked bacon, salsify and wine, or saffron scented fish. Puddings are just as good and satisfyingly – think retro rhubarb crumble and ice-cream.

NØRREBRO

Kiin Kiin

Guldbergsgade 21 (33 35 75 55, www.kiin.dk). Bus 5A. **Open** 5.30pm-1am Mon-Sat. Last reservation 9pm. **5-course menu** 775kr. **Credit** AmEx, MC, V. **Map** p248 H9 ⓐ **Modern Thai**

Mother.

CONSUME

Formerly of the Paul, chef Henrik Yde Andersen has put five years spent living in Thailand to good effect in this new three-storey Nørrebro restaurant, close to Sankt Hans Torv. Weary of being served the same five dishes in the city's Thai restaurants, Andersen's mission has been to get Danes eating new and interesting Thai food, and vegetables and shellfish feature strongly in dishes like orchid-lemon grass salad, and scallops with young ginger. The menu changes daily and there is a well-chosen wine menu for 675kr. Kiin Kiin is now one of the few Thai restaurants in Europe to boast a Michelin star.

★ Nørrebro Bryghus
Ryesgade 3, Nørrebro (35 30 05 30, www.noerre brobryghus.dk). Bus 5A. **Open** 11am-midnight Mon-Thur; 11am-2am Fri, Sat. **Main courses** 189kr-198kr. **5-course set menu** (incl drinks) 500kr. **Credit** DC, MC, V. **Map** p246 J11 ⓸
Gastropub
This super-stylish, split-level modern Scandinavian take on a microbrewery serves not just great home-brewed beers and ales but also some excellent, gastro-pub style fare. The medium-priced menu changes monthly but will typically include plenty of fresh fish, such as fried pepper mackerel with summer cabbage, plus a choice of roast meats. All washed down, of course, with some of the best beers in town.
▶ *For information on Copenhagen's microbreweries, see p138* **A Room with a Brew**.

★ Relæ
Jægersborggade 41, Nørrebro (36 96 66 09, www.restaurant-relae.dk). Bus 18. **Open** 5.30pm-10pm Wed-Sat. **4-course menu** 325kr. **Credit** MC, V. **Map** p248 H6 ⓸ **Modern Danish Bistro**
Not many restaurants would have the balls to serve you a raw, pickled carrot with a glass of champagne and call it an amuse bouche. Then again Relae is no ordinary restaurant. Founded by Christian Puglisi (chef) and Kim Rossen (front-of-house), both previously at Noma, it looks all quietly cool with an open kitchen and wrap-around bar, yet rocks to an eclectic sound track: a welcome antidote to more po-faced 'serious' restaurants. Relae serves one meat, one vegetarian menu, both adventurous but accessible, featuring Nordic dazzlers like barley porridge with cauliflower 'crumbs' and wild mushrooms, and silky slow-cooked veal heart on Jerusalem artichoke puree.

ØSTERBRO

★ Aamanns Etablissement
Øster Farimagsgade 12, Østerbro (35 55 33 10, www.aamanns.dk). Metro Østerport. **Open** noon-4pm, 6-11pm Wed-Sat. **Smørrebrød plate** 165kr. **Set menus** 235kr-405kr. **Credit** MC, V. **Map** p247 J13 ⓸ **Modern Danish**
At last, a modern spin on the nation's beloved smørrebrød. It's well worth travelling to this elegant, light-filled restaurant of scrubbed wood floors and dove grey walls to sample Adam Aamann's moreish open-topped sandwiches at lunchtime, or a heartier Modern Danish meal, based on local, seasonal ingredients (poached haddock with local veg, say, or braised pork cheeks with creamy speltgrains) in the evening. If you're here for the smørrebrod, choose from inspired combinations like home-cured herring on leek salad and parsley cream, thick slices of slow-cooked belly pork topped with zingy cranberry purée, and organic Danish blue cheese with hazelnut butter.
▶ *Next door, at No.12, is Aamanns smørrebrødsdeli/takeaway (33 55 33 44), where you can pick lunchtime smørrebrod of your choice to eat in on the small café table or take away in a beautifully packaged box.*

Aamanns Etablissement.

Restaurant Jacobsen

★ Davids Bistro

Århusgade 22, Østerbro (46 32 13 21, www.davids deli.dk). Bus 1A, 18. **Open** 5.30pm-midnight Tue-Sat. Last orders 9pm. **Main courses** 100kr. **3-course menu** €200. **5-course menu** 900kr. **Credit** AmEx, MC, V. **Map** p248 C14 ⑳ **French/Danish.**

Owner-chef David came from a stellar kitchen at Kong Hans Kælder, but went for a more down-to-earth atmosphere when he reopened his deli as a bistro in 2010. There is no standing on ceremony by staff, no lengthy menu descriptions. The bar is built from salvaged doors, none of the chairs match, and the plates are a hodgepodge of antique Danish china. It's a place to have fun and make merry over magnificent food: no-nonsense French bistro classics with a sprinkling of Danish magic. Try lightly salted salmon with licorice, or chicken liver terrine with home-made pickles and chutneys, followed by a robust pot of boeuf bourguignon.

Geranium 2

Per Henrik Lings Allé 4, 8 (69 96 00 20, www. geranium.dk). Bus 1A. **Open** 6pm-1am Wed-Sat. Last seating 9pm. **Tasting menu** 998kr. **Credit** AmEx, MC, V. **Map** p248 D12 ㉛ **New Nordic**

In January 2011, chef Rasmus Kofoed earned himself the Bocuse d'Or award for culinary greatness, and in so doing firmly established Copenhagen's position as one of the most exciting places in the world to eat. Kofoed – like every leading chef in Denmark these days – has if not an entire crusade, than at least a manifesto to shake things up a bit – in his case a predilection for food that is 'light', 'lucid' and provides 'enriching challenges'. It changed location in 2010 from Kongens Have gardens to the more immense parkland of Faelledparken, getting you closer to 'nature' and if anything an even finer plate of food. Dishes veer towards molecular gastronomy, but

remain recognisable and change with the seasons. Expect sybaritic intrigue along the lines of smoked potatoes, dried peas and lovage, and roast monkfish with 'elements of the sea and ocean'. It doesn't come cheap though: if you go for the wine pairing too you're looking at spending around 2,000kr per head.

Le Saint-Jacques

Sankt Jakobs Plads 1 (35 42 77 07, www.le saintjacques.dk). Bus 1A, 14. **Open** noon-3pm, 6-10pm Mon-Fri; 11am-4pm, 6-10pm Sat, Sun. **Main courses** 195kr. **3-course menu** 345kr. **4-course menu** 395kr. **Credit** MC, V. **Map** p248 C13 ㉜ **French**

This pricey but inviting French restaurant is across the street from the national stadium, Parken, in a quiet square just off busy Østerbrogade. Impeccable service, crisp white linen tablecloths and candlelight that flickers across the glittering gold of the religious icons on the walls ensure that this is a place that the locals return to again and again for special treats or that well-earned blow-out. Home-smoked salmon is a speciality. Also popular for weekend brunch.

FURTHER AFIELD

Den Gule Cottage

Staunings Plæne, Strandvejen 506, Klampenborg (39 64 06 91, www.dengulecottage.dk). Train Klampenborg. **Open** noon-10pm Mon-Thur, Sun; noon-midnight Fri, Sat. **3-course menu** 300kr. **Credit** AmEx, MC, V.

With its fairytale location in a thatched, half-timbered cottage, set beneath oak trees on lawns that roll down to Bellevue beach, this tiny restaurant could probably get away with serving hot dogs (in fact, it used to be an ice-cream kiosk). But this is one of the finest restaurants in the region, serving elegant, fabulously choreographed modern Danish dishes from the freshest seasonal ingredients. Expect local game, fish and meats, funky foams and extravagant desserts in this definitive *hyggelige* venue. Highly recommended.

Restaurant Jacobsen

Strandvejen 449, Klampenborg (39 63 43 22, www.restaurantjacobsen.dk). Train Klampenborg. **Open** noon-3pm, 5.30-10pm Tue-Sat; 10.30am-4pm Sun. **Set menus** 550kr-850kr. **Credit** AmEx, MC, V.

When Arne Jacobsen designed the Bellavista housing complex and theatre, he didn't quite have the chutzpah to name the restaurant after himself. But with his designs now as trendy as ever, the current owners have done just that. Jacobsen 'Ant', 'Swan' and 'Egg' chairs decorate the light, white interior with views of the Øresund Sea. The food is Danish-Asian-French fusion, and the service can be sloppy, but there is outside seating in summer and, architecturally, it can't be beaten. The restaurant has started offering picnic baskets and bike rental so, if the weather is fine, you can head to Dyrehaven for an alfresco lunch or dinner.

CONSUME

Cafés & Bars

Summer alfresco café culture and cosy winter bars.

Copenhageners have been addicted to coffee for centuries. Despite this, café culture has only really flourished in the city in the last decade or so. In that time, dozens of venues have opened up, growing in sophistication over the years from the original, grand, French-style Café Norden on Amagertorv to the quirky coffee bars on Istedgade and Halmtorvet, encompassing ambitious gourmet places and painfully hip vodka bars along the way.

Virtually all cafés serve alcohol and food of some description, and so the line between café, bar and restaurant is often blurred. To add to the confusion, many change as the day progresses. Some become more bar-like, others transform into full-blown restaurants, or have DJs playing at weekends (see chapter Nightlife).

The better Copenhagen cafés can be a match for many of the city's restaurants both in terms of the quality of food they serve and the atmosphere. Brunch is still the most important meal of the day for many Copenhagen cafés, which vie to see who can offer the most elaborate and exotic mid-morning platter.

TIVOLI & RÅDHUSPLADSEN

Tivoli itself has around 30 restaurants and cafés, some good, most average, and all expensive, so be advised to seek sustenance outside.

Bjørgs
Vester Voldgade 19 (33 14 53 20, www.cafe bjorgs.dk). Train Vesterport. **Open** 9am-midnight Mon-Wed; 9am-1am Thur; 9am-2am Fri; 10am-2pm Sat; 10am-midnight Sun. **Credit** AmEx, MC, V. **Map** p250 N12 ❶
This L-shaped café-bar does a passable impression of an Edward Hopper painting, with its large windows, red sofas and mirrored walls. Although it's from the same stable as Sommersko (*see p128*) and Dan Turèll (*see p129*), Bjørgs is less pretentious, and serves as both a local bar and a trendy Saturday night stop-off.

Library Bar
Sofitel Plaza Copenhagen Hotel, Bernstorffsgade 4 (33 14 92 62). Train København H. **Open** 4pm-midnight Mon-Thur; 4pm-1am Fri, Sat. **Credit** AmEx, MC, V. **Map** p250 P11 ❷
Though members of some of the more salubrious gentlemen's clubs in London's St James's will be underwhelmed by the scale of this quiet and faux-exclusive bar within the Sofitel Plaza Copenhagen Hotel, most visitors are taken by its characterful wood panelling, crystal chandeliers, book-lined walls and Chesterfield-style sofas. This was once voted one of the finest gentlemen's bars in the world by *Forbes* magazine. If you've any money left over, you may care to nibble on sybaritic snacks like oysters and Parma ham. Cocktails start at 80kr.

Sushitreat Fox
Jarmers Plads 3 (28 74 51 20, www.hotelfox.dk). Bus 5A, 6A. **Open** 4.30pm-10pm Fri, Sat; 4.30pm-9pm Sun. **Credit** AmEx, MC, V. **Map** p250 N11 ❸
Every night the lobby of the funky Fox Hotel draws the city's sophisticates as it transforms into the Sushitreat, serving cocktails and sushi until the wee hours. Guests lounge on low-slung sofas, slowly slipping into a kaleidoscopic haze thanks to the psychedelic lighting and ultra-chilled ambience. Needless to say, there's a DJ on hand at weekends. Takeaway sushi is also available.

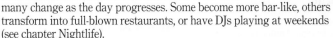

❶ Green numbers given in this chapter correspond to the location of each bar as marked on the street maps. *See pp245-253.*

Ultimo
Tivoli, Vesterbrogade 3 (33 75 07 51, www.
cafeultimotivoli.dk). Train København H.
Open noon-10pm daily during Tivoli opening.
Credit AmEx, MC, V. **Map** p250 O11
The latest addition to the portfolio of Copenhagen
restaurant mogul Torben Olsen is this glorious conservatory restaurant in the old pleasure garden. One
of the most beautiful dining rooms in the city now
serves contemporary, high-end Italian food – crab
ravioli with tomato sauce, chilli, orange and grilled
Norwegian lobster; vitello tonnato; posh pizzas.
There's outside seating if the weather allows.

STRØGET & AROUND

42°Raw
Pilestræde 32 (32 12 32 10, www.42raw.com).
Metro Kongens Nytorv. **Open** 10am-8pm Mon-Fri;
10am-6pm Sat; 11am-5pm Sun. **Credit** AmEx,
MC, V. **Map** p251 M14 ❺
Devoted to raw cuisine (no food sold here is heated
to more than 42 degrees – the temperature at which
enzymes are destroyed), 42°Raw is a new and popular concept for the city. Smoothies and juices, cook-
ies made with 'raw' chocolate, super fresh salads,
and dishes such as an unusual but very tasty version
of lasagna are served in the petite, slick space. It's
also good as a healthy takeaway spot.

Atlas Bar
Larsbjørnsstræde 18 (33 15 03 52, www.atlas
bar.dk). Metro Nørreport. **Open** noon-midnight
Mon-Sat. Kitchen closes at 10pm. **Credit**
MC, V. **Map** p250 N12 ❻

42°Raw.

Atlas Bar serves 'food from the warm countries', which
in practice means its influences range from Asia (it
does a decent Manila chicken) to Mexico (humungous
burritos). To underscore the point, the tabletops are
decorated with maps. This welcoming cellar bar is well
located in the heart of bustling Pisserenden and so is
great for a mid-shop lunch, and popular with vegetar-
ians. Upstairs is Flyvefisken, its sister Thai restaurant.

Bloomsday Bar
Niels Hemmingsgade 32 (33 15 60 13,
www.bloomsdaybar.com). Metro Nørreport.
Open noon-2am daily. **Credit** MC, V.
Map p251 M13 ❼
This small, low-ceilinged Irish cellar pub, owned by
Englishman Phil and Irishman Jonathan, is open until
2am every night, and offers a warm welcome with a
good range of Irish and British draught beers. There
is live Irish music on Sunday afternoons. Big with
expats but also draws keen local øl (beer) enthusiasts.

Cafeen På 4
Illum, Østergade 52, Strøget (33 18 28 63,
www.illum.dk). Metro Kongens Nytorv. **Open**
10am-7pm Mon-Fri; 10am-6pm Sat. **Credit**
AmEx, MC, V. **Map** p251 N14 ❽
To escape the madding crowds on Strøget, take the
Willy Wonka-style glass elevator to the spacious,
light and airy top floor of the Illum department store
(the name means 'the café on 4'). There have been
various attempts to turn this into a café/restaurant
over the years: right now it is Kåre Find Jensen's turn
to have a go with sandwiches, salads and brunches.

Café Europa
Amagertorv 1 (33 14 28 89,
www.europa1989.dk). Metro Kongens Nytorv.
Open 7.45am-11pm Mon-Thur; 7.45am-1am Fri;
7.45am-midnight Sat; 9am-11pm Sun. **Credit**
AmEx, MC, V. **Map** p251 N14 ❾
With a location right in the heart of the shopping
district on Amagertorv, Café Europa is one of the
city's most popular meeting places. Its prices can be
high and service frosty, but the food isn't bad and
it's a nice place to stop off for a drink during an afternoon's shopping. Sandwiches are reasonable value.
There is seating outside in summer.

CONSUME

CONSUME

Café Norden.

Café Norden

*Østergade 61, Strøget (33 11 77 91, www.
cafenorden.dk). Metro Kongens Nytorv.* **Open**
9am-midnight daily. **Credit** AmEx, MC, V.
Map p251 N14 ⑩

This grandest and largest of all Copenhagen's cafés
(it seats 350 on sunny days) overlooks Amagertorv
in the heart of Strøget, but despite its vast, two-
storey, Parisian-style interior (with chandeliers and
wood panelling), it's usually a challenge to find a
table. The service here is often fairly grouchy (in
fact, there is no table service and you have to order
at the bar), but the food is adequate (salads, sandwiches, steaks and so forth), though you will pay
around 20% more for everything by virtue of Café
Norden's prime location.

Café Sommersko

*Kronprinsensgade 6 (33 14 81 89, www.cafe
sommersko.dk). Bus 11A.* **Open** 8am-midnight
Mon-Thur; 8am-2am Fri; 9am-2am Sat; 9am-
midnight Sun. **Credit** AmEx, MC, V. **Map**
p251 M14 ⑪

Sommersko was one of Copenhagen's café pioneers
back in the 1980s (it opened in 1976, when a strong
café culture hadn't yet reached the city) and things
have moved on since then, but its wonderfully glamorous kitsch decor (mirror mosaics, baby grand
piano, red vinyl banquettes) is distinctive, which is
more than you can say for many cafés. The menu is
rather predictable (mussels, burgers, salads, et al),
however, and the food can be disappointing. Service,
too, often leaves plenty to be desired.

Café Victor

*Ny Østergade 8 (33 13 36 13, www.cafevictor.dk).
Metro Kongens Nytorv.* **Open** *Café* 8am-1am
Mon-Wed; 8am-2am Thur-Sat; 11am-11pm Sun.
Restaurant 11.30am-4pm, 6-10.30pm Mon-Thur;
11.30am-4pm, 6-11pm Fri, Sat; 6-10pm Sun.
Credit AmEx, MC, V. **Map** p251 M15 ⑫

A Copenhagen institution, Café Victor is one of the
city's prime see-and-be-seen venues for celebrities,
football stars, politicians, journalists and the jet set.
Midday it is packed with lunching ladies, wrapped
in fur or Gucci. The food is ultra-classic French fare
– lobster americaine, sole meunière – of a high standard. However, you don't come here just for the food,
but more to soak up the atmosphere, marvel at the
mirrored, art deco interior and do battle with the
supercilious staff. If you don't fancy a full meal, half
a dozen oysters at the bar (150kr) washed down with
a glass of champagne will give you a taste of the
Victor experience. A 4.2-5.7% surcharge is added to
credit card payments (Visa excepted).

Café Zeze

*Ny Østergade 20 (33 14 23 90, www.cafe-zeze.dk).
Metro Kongens Nytorv.* **Open** 8am-midnight Mon-
Thur; 8am-2am Fri; 9am-2am Sat. **Credit** AmEx,
MC, V. **Map** p251 M15 ⑬

Some cafés spend thousands on design, finding the
right chairs and the right lighting, but ultimately it's
the clientele who decides if a place succeeds or fails,
and for all its spartan appearance, there is something
about Zeze that continues to draw a dream café
crowd. Models, ad folk, actresses, musicians – all
young and beautiful – cram this place just about
every night of the week. The food is fancier than the
standard café fare, but hardly remarkable, and there
is limited outdoor seating in summer. A great place
to start an evening, and located near to Kongens
Nytorv and Strøget.

★ Copenhagen JazzHouse

*Niels Hemmingsens Gade 10 (33 15 26 00/33 15
47 00, www.jazzhouse.dk). Metro Kongens Nytorv.*
Open 6.30-5am concert nights. **Credit** AmEx,
MC, V. **Map** p251 N14 ⑭

A stalwart of the Copenhagen nightlife scene, this
superb live jazz venue has two storeys with a bar on

INSIDE TRACK
ALFRESCO DRINKING

Good spots for a sup in the sunshine
include **Karriere** (*see p136*), which has
outdoor tables in summer; the bars of
Nørrebro's **Sankt Hans Square**; the
Traktørstedet café of Rosenbourg Castle
(*see p78*); the courtyard of the **Museum
of Industrial Art** (*see p75*) and **Kaffesalonen**
(*p139*) next to the Dronning Louises lake.

Café Zeze.

Det Elektriske Hjørne

*Store Regnegade 12 (33 13 91 92, www.
elhjoernet.dk). Metro Kongens Nytorv.* **Open**
11am-midnight Mon-Wed; 11am-2am Thur; 11am-
5am Fri, Sat. *Food served* 11.30am-8pm Mon-Fri.
Credit AmEx, MC, V. **Map** p251 M15 ⑰
This grand corner café, with an ornate frontage dating from the 1890s, is well located, with dozens of
the city's best bars and restaurants nearby. Wisely,
the Hjørne doesn't attempt to outdo its neighbours
on the food front, but instead trades on its welcome
spaciousness and comfy sofas. The basement has
table football, darts and pool.

Flottenheimer

*Skindergade 20 (35 38 32 12, www.cafe
flottenheimer.dk). Train/metro Nørreport.*
Open 10am-11pm Mon-Wed; 10am-1am Thur;
10am-2am Fri, Sat; 11am-5pm Sun. **Credit** MC, V.
Map p251 M13 ⑱
Based just round the corner from the lovely
Gråbrødretorv square, Flottenheimer is a feminine
space (think fairy lights, vintage tables and a tango
soundtrack) appealing to fashionable ladies
who lunch and discerning tourists. The diverse
menu offers a good range of sandwiches and small
bites (nachos, soup, tzatziki and bread), as well
as pasta dishes.

Galathea Kroen

*Rådhusstræde 9 (33 11 66 27, www.galathea
kroen.dk). Bus 14.* **Open** 6pm-2am Tue-Thur;
6pm-4am Fri, Sat. Kitchen closes 9pm daily.
Credit AmEx, MC, V. **Map** p251 O13 ⑲
Galathea opened in 1953 and was named after a ship
that was used as a base for exploration of Pacific sea
life. Inside it is decorated with mementos from the
ship's journeys. The moment you enter this charismatic, eclectic mess of a bar, past the totem poles
that guard the entrance, you know that Galathea
Kroen is not one of Copenhagen's more style-con-
scious places. Maybe it's the jazz on the turntable
(this is a strictly vinyl-only joint) or the affable and
intriguing clientele, from trendy teens to bohemian
oldies; or perhaps it's the engagingly dishevelled
decor. Galathea changed owners in 2005 but, happily, the bar and its unique atmosphere remain
unchanged.

La Glace

*Skoubogade 3 (33 14 46 46, www.laglace.com).
Bus 11A.* **Open** 8.30am-5.30pm Mon-Thur;
8.30am-6pm Fri; 9am-5pm Sat; 11am-5pm Sun
(closed Sun Apr-Sept). **No credit cards.**
Map p251 N13 ⑳
Copenhagen's most vaunted and venerable bakery
and pâtisserie was founded in 1870 and is famous
for its delectable cream cakes, which would tempt
even the most fanatical of calorie-counters. The speciality is the Sports Kage (Sport Cake), an over-the-
top cream, caramel and nougat mousse confection.

each, a large dancefloor downstairs and is a dead
cert most nights for an excellent atmosphere, interesting clientele and great music. Jazz aficionados
head here on Friday and Saturday nights (although
it's occasionally open on weeknights) for the best
concerts in town, but despite this the Copenhagen
JazzHouse remains blessedly free of jazz snobs.
See also p190.

Dan Turèll

*Store Regnegade 3-5 (33 14 10 47, www.dan
turell.dk). Metro Kongens Nytorv.* **Open** 9.30am-
midnight Mon-Wed; 9.30am-1am Thur; 9.30am-
2am Fri, Sat; 10am-10pm Sun. **Credit** AmEx,
MC, V. **Map** p251 M15 ⑮
One of Copenhagen's most famous cafés, Dan Turèll
is named after a well-known poet, writer and icono-
clast and has been one of *the* places to visit on a
Friday or Saturday night for as long as anyone can
remember. But the food here is middling (salads and
sandwiches during the day), the staff snobby and
the drinks expensive.

Drop Inn

Kompagnistræde 34 (33 11 24 04). Bus 14.
Open noon-5am daily. **Credit** MC, V. **Map**
p251 O13 ⑯
With live music every night (jazz, blues and folk),
and an open front with pavement seating in summer,
Drop Inn is one of those places that never seems to
take a rest. Hardly cool or trendy, the place tends
instead to attract the more dedicated drinkers, so
things can get lively towards the end of the evening.

CONSUME

Skoubogade is just off the west end of Strøget, which makes it perfect for weary shoppers, but also means that you have to fight your way through a scrum of devoted cocoa bean groupies most afternoons.

Kafe Kys

Læderstræde 7 (33 93 85 94, www.kafekys.dk). Metro Kongens Nytorv. **Open** 8.15am-11pm Mon-Wed; 8.15am-midnight Thur; 8.15am-2am Fri, Sat; 11am-6pm Sun. **Credit** MC, V. **Map** p251 N14 ④

This enduringly popular bar is unremarkable other than for its pleasant location and its sandwiches, which are slightly more exotic than the usual café fare. That and the fact that it seems, for some reason, to draw an unusually attractive clientele. Friday night is the hottest of the week for Kys when it is usually packed with the young and the beautiful bar-hopping their way along Copenhagen's most charming street.

K-Bar

Ved Stranden 20 (33 91 92 22, www.k-bar.dk). Metro Kongens Nytorv. **Open** 4pm-1am Mon-Thur; 4pm-2am Fri, Sat. **Credit** AmEx, MC, V. **Map** p251 N14 ④

This low-slung, flirty cocktail bar is just how you imagine all Scandinavian bars will be: very cool, beautifully designed and with a short but sweet cocktail list featuring tempters like 'Very Berry Caipirinha' and 'Rude Cosmopolitan'. Bartender Kirsten is a dab hand at Martinis and there are 13 to try on the menu. This jewel of a place is tucked away just around the corner from Højbro Plads, a few moments from Strøget.

Kreutzberg Café & Bar

Kompagnistræde 14A (33 93 48 50). Bus 11A, 14. **Open** 9am-midnight Mon-Thur; 9am-2am Fri, Sat; 11am-6pm Sun. **Credit** MC, V. **Map** p251 N13 ④

Kreutzberg has carved a niche as a friendly, buzzing basement venue serving classic café food. It's one of several cosy, cool places on the pedestrianised street that runs parallel to Strøget.

Peder Oxe Vinbar

Gråbrødretorv 11 (33 11 00 77, www.peder oxe.dk). Bus 11A. **Open** 11.30am-1am daily. **Credit** MC, V. **Map** p251 N13 ④

This stylish, spacious wine bar near the centre of Strøget opened in 1978 and is located in the vaulted cellars beneath the venerable Peder Oxe restaurant (*see p111*). It is one of the city's more sociable, cosy cellar venues.

★ Royal Café

Amagertorv 6 (33 12 11 22, www.theroyalcafe.dk). Train/metro Nørreport. **Open** 10am-7pm Mon-Fri; 10am-6pm Sat; 11am-5pm Sun. **Credit** AmEx, MC, V. **Map** p251 N14.④

Royal Copenhagen's stylish café opened in its (refurbished) flagship store in 2007, and is known for its contemporary sushi-style open-faced sandwiches ('smushi') and classic desserts. The upmarket, feminine space features royal portraits on the walls and fixtures, fittings and furniture from famous Danish design brands, such as Bang & Olufsen and Fritz Hansen. You might need to wait for a table.

Studenterhuset

Købmagergade 52, Copenhagen University (35 32 38 61, www.studenterhuset.com). Bus 11A. **Open** 9am-6pm Mon; 9am-midnight Tue; noon-1am Wed, Thur; noon-2am Fri. **No credit cards**. **Map** p251 M13 ④

This subsidised student drinking den and music venue is a few steps from the Rundetårn. The decor is grotty-chic to match the clientele's dress sense, and prices are set for those on a government-grant budget. The beer is cheap and there is usually something fun happening of an evening – most notably, a gay evening on Tuesdays; 'International Night' on Wednesdays; jazz on Thursdays; and rock on Fridays. It is also a participating venue in the annual jazz festival.

Thé à la Menthe

Rådhusstræde 5B (33 33 00 38). Bus 11A, 14. **Open** 10am-9pm Mon-Thur; 10am-10pm Fri, Sat. **Credit** MC, V. **Map** p251 O13 ④

This charming little cellar café and teahouse sells couscous, salads and curries alongside its exotic teas. Laid-back sofas and scatter cushions complete the chilled Moroccan vibe. An oasis in the heart of the shopping district.

★ Zirup

Læderstræde 32 (33 13 50 60, www.zirup.dk). Metro Kongens Nytorv. **Open** 10am-midnight Mon-Thur, Sun; 10am-2am Fri, Sat. **Credit** MC, V. **Map** p251 N14 ④

Our choice of all the many excellent cafés on this pretty pedestrian street parallel to Strøget, with its beautifully lit interior, good value and slightly more adventurous fusion menu (everything from stroganoff to curry to Mexican wraps). Tables go outside when the weather permits. All in all, a pleasant place to pass time. The Sunday morning hangover brunch should be available on prescription.

Zoo Bar

Sværtegade 6 (33 15 68 69, www.zoobar.dk). Metro Kongens Nytorv. **Open** 11am-midnight Mon-Wed; 11am-4am Thur-Sat. **Credit** AmEx, MC, V. **Map** p251 M14 ④

Zoo Bar recently relocated to a larger new space on Sværtegade, and has upgraded its decor in the process. A favourite hangout for the fashion crowd, the bar has DJs at weekends, decent food (try the Zoo burger) and an excellent cocktail list (Zoo Passionfruit Martini anyone?).

CONSUME

Danish Delicacies

The nation's classic dishes and foodstuffs demand to be sampled.

Traditional Danish cuisine (if that's not too grand a term for it) has, until recently, with the rise of New Nordic, endured a rather bad press. And it is true that a blend of hard-to-digest rye bread, vinegary herring, fried pork and processed meats holds little obvious appeal for visitors from, say, France or Spain. But Danish food can be delicious, and is definitely worth trying.

Smørrebrød.

SILD

Locally caught *sild* (herring) in some form or other is the archetypal Danish ingredient. This dense, oily fish is usually salted and pickled in vinegar with a touch of sugar, some onion, white peppercorns and a bay leaf (or, for reasons best known to the Danes, a curry-style sauce), and served on buttered rye bread with chopped red onion.

SMØRREBRØD

Herring is one of the classic toppings for the traditional Danish lunch option of *smørrebrød* (literally 'buttered bread'), which has undergone a renaissance in the past few years as part of the general revival of Nordic cuisine. *Smørrebrød* is the name given to the classic Danish open sandwich, and toppings can vary from highly elaborate gourmet confections featuring caviar, prawns and egg (as at **Ida Davidsen**, *see venue index*, and **Aamanns**, *see venue index*), to the more prosaic liver paste and cucumber. Basically anything

goes as long as it's savoury, but toppings will typically include boiled egg and dill, prawns, beetroot, tinned mackerel, cucumber, roast onions, various cold meats and goose or pork dripping. A good place for a smørrebrød initiation is cool café-bar **Dyrehaven** (*see p135*) in Vesterbro.

STEGT FLÆSK

With over 20 million pigs bred each year in Denmark, pork naturally features heavily on most menus. A classic dish is *stegt flæske* – consisting of fatty, fried pork strips (often translated as bacon) served with potatoes and parsley sauce. Try it at **Dyrehaven** (*see p135*) and **Madklubben** (*see p117*). Danes also mince pork to make *frikadeller* (meatballs), which are usually served without sauce and, as with many meals, accompanied with a small glass of schnapps and a beer or two.

PØLSER

Danish street food is limited to *pølser*, a kind of hot dog served from mobile kiosks and ladled with vivid coloured sauces and fried onions. *See also p59* **Profile**.

WIENERBRØD

Bizarrely there is no such thing as Danish pastry in Denmark. What we call Danish pastry, the Danes call *wienerbrød* (directly translated as 'Viennese bread'), made from sweet, buttery, flaky pastry topped with nuts, custard, stewed apple, chocolate or cinnamon. A particularly delicious pastry is snegle, a spiral (hence 'snail') cinammon pastry often topped with chocolate. The other classic Danish dessert is the unpronounceable *rødgrød med fløde*, a currant and raspberry or strawberry coulis mixed with fresh cream. **Meyer's Deli** (*see p136*) is a good, if expensive, spot to sample Danish pastries and desserts.

Wienerbrød.

CONSUME

CONSUME

NYHAVN & KONGENS NYTORV

Café à Porta

Kongens Nytorv 17 (33 11 05 00, www.cafea porta.dk). Metro Kongens Nytorv. **Open** 11.30am-11pm Mon-Sat. **Credit** AmEx, MC, V. **Map** p251 M15 ㉚

This glorious Viennese café is one of the city's oldest and grandest – it opened in 1792 – with a perfectly restored, mirrored 19th-century interior (Hans Christian Andersen lived upstairs for a while and was a regular). The service is brisk, but not brusque, and the reliably tasty French/Danish bistro cooking (with ample portions) ensures it's packed with a mix of tourists and older locals. On Fridays and Saturdays the restaurant now becomes a nightclub between 11pm and 3am.

Fisken

Nyhavn 27 (33 11 99 06/www.skipperkroen-nyhavn.dk). **Open** 8.30am-1am Mon-Thur; 8.30am-2am Fri, Sat; 8.30am-midnight Sun. *Food served* until 10.30pm Mon-Thur, Sun; 11pm Fri, Sat. **Credit** AmEx, MC, V. **Map** p252 M16 ㉛

One of Nyhavn's most *hyggelige* (cosy) pubs is in the cellar underneath Skipperkroen. The decor is heavy on maritime references (although it's hard to tell how authentic any of it really is) and there's live folky, guitar-based music every evening.

Palæ Bar

Ny Adelgade 5 (33 12 54 71, www.palaebar.dk). Metro Kongens Nytorv. **Open** 11am-1am Mon-Thur; 11am-3am Fri, Sat; 4pm-1am Sun. **No credit cards. Map** p251 M15 ㉜

This esteemed boho bar, just around the corner from the Hotel d'Angleterre, tends to appeal to more mature drinkers who prefer its unrushed, understated mood and rich, old-fashioned Parisian-style boozer atmosphere. Popular with journalists and writers, Palæ exudes a kind of old-world intellectualism (or so it seems after a few glasses of wine).

Quote

Kongens Nytorv 16 (33 32 51 51, www.cafe quote.dk). Metro Kongens Nytorv. **Open** 9am-midnight Mon-Wed; 9am-1am Thur; 9am-2am Fri; 10am-2am Sat; 11am-midnight Sun. **Credit** AmEx, MC, V (2.5% transaction fee). **Map** p251 M15 ㉝

One of the largest café-bar-restaurant places to open in Copenhagen for a long time is this chic, two-floor venue next door to the national newspaper *Jyllands Posten*. With black banquettes, white walls, mirror-tiled columns and a *Get Shorty*-style central staircase, there is an enjoyable theatricality about the place. The food, by chef Patrick de Neef, is equally showy, with regulars such as stuffed Bresse chicken with braised cabbage or pumpkin and chilli soup with tiger shrimp. There is outdoor seating overlooking the city's grandest square in summer. A more contemporary alternative to the inns of nearby Nyhavn.

Sporvejen

Gråbrødretorv 17 (33 13 31 01, www.sporvejen.dk). **Open** 11am-10pm Mon-Sat; noon-10pm Sun. **Credit** MC, V. **Map** p251 N13 ㉞

This burger bar is housed in an old tram of the type that used to run in the city (before they were all flogged out to Egypt), but is now embedded in a wall in this historic cobbled square just off Strøget. As you'd expect, it is rather cosy inside, but there is outside seating in summer.

FREDERIKSSTADEN

Oscar Bar & Café

Bredgade 58 (33 12 50 10, www.oscarbarcafe.dk). **Open** 9.30am-11pm daily. **Credit** AmEx, MC, V. **Map** p249 K16 ㉟

A welcome refreshment stop in what is otherwise a café-free quarter, Café Oscar is located on a corner site near to Amalienborg, Kunstindustrimuseet, Kastellet and the other main sights of the area. This light, spacious and relaxed establishment serves the usual beverages and sandwiches, plus a short crêpe menu and a more substantial selection of beef, fish and pasta dishes. There are a few outside tables for summer munching.

ROSENBORG & AROUND

★ Bankeråt

Ahlefeldtsgade 27-29 (33 93 69 88, www.bankeraat.dk). Metro Nørreport. **Open**

Bankeråt.

9.30am-midnight Mon-Fri; 10.30am-midnight Sat, Sun. **No credit cards**. **Map** p246 L11 ⑯
Monster brunches, great tortillas and pasta dishes, plus the quirkiest decor of all Copenhagen's cafés, set this grungy boho cave apart. Brace yourself for a sobering encounter when you descend to the basement loos, as you're confronted by a ghoulish assortment of Gothic taxidermy tableaux – animals standing upright wearing long leather coats are a favourite. And parents beware, porn awaits. A weird and wonderful place.

MJ Coffee
Gothersgade 26 (33 32 01 05, www.mj-coffee.dk). Metro Kongens Nytorv. **Open** 8am-11pm Mon-Thur; 8am-midnight Fri; 9am-11pm Sat; 10am-11pm Sun. **Credit** MC, V. **Map** p247 L13 ㉟
It may have changed its name from Mojo (to avoid confusion with the similarly named blues bar across town), but the quality of the coffee, the lengthy options and the wonderful cakes thankfully remain the same. This corner café located on bustling Gothersgade is very popular and a great place to ruminate while sipping coffee and watching the world go by, thanks to its floor to ceiling windows. It's owned and run by an American émigré from Chicago, so you know that this is the real deal. Also serves soups, salads and smoothies.

Vincaféen Bibendum
Nansensgade 45 (33 33 07 74, www.loveof foodnwine.dk/bibendum). Metro Nørreport. **Open** 4pm-midnight Mon-Sat. **Credit** MC, V. **Map** p246 L11 ㉚
Playing a leading role in the gentrification of Nansensgade, this cosy, sexy wine bar complements its more rough and ready neighbour Bankeråt (*see left*) with an extensive range of wines by the glass (unusual in beer-minded Copenhagen) and a flirty cellar ambience. The tapas plates are excellent and the staff knowledgeable. Argentinian wines are a speciality.

CHRISTIANSHAVN

Aristo
Islands Brygge 4 (32 95 83 30, www.restaurant aristo.dk). Metro Islands Brygge. **Open** 11am-midnight Mon-Thur; 11am-2am Fri; 10am-2am Sat; 10am-11pm Sun. **Credit** MC, V. **Map** p251 Q14 ㊴
Located in the hip Islands Brygge area beside Langebro, this light, modern harbourside café serves contemporary European/global food (everything from sandwiches to five-course menus) and really comes into its own in the summer when the nearby harbour baths fill up with local sun-worshippers.

Bastionen og Løven
Christianshavns Voldgade 50 (32 95 09 40, www.bastionen-loven.dk). Metro Christianshavn/ bus 2A, 40, 66. **Open** 11am-midnight Thur-Sat; 11am-6pm Sun. **Credit** AmEx, MC, V. **Map** p252 Q18 ㊵
This delightful, if rather hard to find, garden café is situated in an extension of Nationalmuseet's Lille Mølle (Little Windmill) on the ramparts of Christianshavn. It's set well off the tourist trail and during summer is usually packed with locals, but if you fancy trying one of the city's great culinary institutions – traditional Copenhagen brunch (a simple but satisfying array of cheeses, herring, bread, fruit and cold meats) – in idyllic surroundings, this is the best place to visit.

Café Luna
Sankt Annæ Gade 5 (32 54 20 00, www.cafe luna.dk). Metro Christianshavn/bus 2A, 40, 66. **Open** 9.30am-midnight Mon-Thur; 9.30am-1am Fri, Sat; 9.30am-midnight Sun. **Credit** AmEx, MC, V. **Map** p252 P17 ㊶
If you can't get a table at Café Wilder opposite (*see p134*), Café Luna offers good, simple food, including cheap salads, pasta dishes and more traditional Danish café fare. It's a good vegetarian option, and has an extensive wine list.

CONSUME

Café Wilder.

★ Café Wilder

*Wildersgade 56 (32 54 71 83, www.cafewilder.dk).
Metro Christianshavn/bus 2A, 66, 350S.* **Open**
9am-11pm Mon-Thur; 9am-1am Fri, Sat; 9am-
10pm Sun. **Credit** MC, V. **Map** p252 P17 ❷
Christianshavn's loveliest café-bar is located just a
short walk from the chaos of Christiania. The food
is fresh, cheap and simple (pasta, salads and sandwiches), and the service charming. This small, L-
shaped room is usually crowded to bursting point
with trendy, arty locals at weekends, so arrive early
to be sure of a seat. Supermodel Helena Christensen
lives nearby and is allegedly a regular when in town.
Brunch is 119kr.

VESTERBRO & FREDERIKSBERG

Apropos

*Halmtorvet 12, Vesterbro (33 23 12 21,
www.cafeapropos.dk). Bus 10, 84N.* **Open** 10am-
midnight Mon-Thur, Sun; 10am-1am Fri, Sat;
10am-9pm Sun. **Credit** MC, V. **Map** p250 Q10 ❸
Probably the best of the trendy café-restaurants to
have opened on the rejuvenated Halmtorvet in the

INSIDE TRACK COSY BARS

In winter, Danes become obsessed with the
concept of *hygglige* – the unique brand of
amiable cosiness which helps to get them
through the cold, dark months. Many of
Copenhagen's cafés and bars elicit a
cosy feel through soft lighting, candles and
blankets, and hot chocolate (always with
cream) and *glögg* (mulled wine) on the menu.

---

last few years, Apropos offers mid-priced, southern
European café food (the 129kr tapas plate, for example), more substantial French à la carte dishes, and
a limited drinks menu. What makes Apropos and its
neighbours particularly popular is their great location, and the fact that Halmtorvet is now a see-and-
be-seen-in place, especially at weekends. There is
plenty of outdoor seating in summer. Tables can be
reserved online.

Bang og Jensen

*Istedgade 130, Vesterbro (33 25 53 18, www.
bangogjensen.dk). Bus 10, 84N.* **Open** 8am-2am
Mon-Fri; 10am-2am Sat; 10am-midnight Sun.
No credit cards. **Map** p245 R8 ❹
This Vesterbro café has been a mainstay of the quarter's nightlife scene for years and the area's plentiful
fashion victims can usually be relied upon to serve
up a bit of life most nights. Though the food is the
usual Copenhagen café fare, it doesn't detract from
Bang og Jensen's appeal as an alluring place to while
away an evening (slumped, if you're lucky, in its
great squashy sofas). Breakfast, with a fine disre-
gard for the dictates of the clock, is served until 4pm
daily. The laptop brigade are in abundance during
the daytime – it's the classic popular spot for office-
less freelancers and bloggers.

Barbar Bar

*Vesterbrogade 51, Vesterbro (33 31 88 89,
www.barbarbar.dk). Bus 10, 84N.* **Open** 10am-
midnight Mon-Thur, Sun; 10am-2am Fri, Sat.
Credit AmEx, MC, V. **Map** p245 Q9 ❺
This funky Vesterbro café and bar lies in shadow
during the day, but it is lively at night when it is usually packed with cool locals. It serves sandwiches
and salads at reasonable prices.

Café André Citroën

*Vesterbrogade 58 (33 23 62 82, www.andre
citroen.dk). Bus 5A, 14.* **Open** 10am-11pm Mon;
10am-midnight Tue, Wed; 10am-1am Thur; 10am-
2am Fri, Sat; 10am-11pm Sun. **Credit** MC, V.
Map p245 P9 ❻
With its mirrors, red banquettes and classic
brasserie menu, this is like a little bit of Paris trans-
planted on to busy Vesterbrogade. The food, service
and people-watching are all top notch. Like so many
places in town, it serves up a traditional Danish
lunch but more mixed bag of French, Italian and
Mexican fare in the evening.

Café Elefanten

*Pasteursvej 20, Vesterbro (88 81 08 11,
www.elefantennet.dk). Bus 3A.* **Open** 10am-5pm
Mon-Fri. **Credit** AmEx, MC, V. **Map** p245 S5 ❼
This friendly, laid-back café is located on the ground
floor of an old Carlsberg Brewery warehouse, which
also houses (upstairs) the rehearsal space for the
Dansescenen (*see p199*) contemporary dance company – so expect to see lots of lithe-looking figures

in sweatpants and leg-warmers, as well as plenty of arty/media types. Top-quality sandwiches are the name of the game here, as well as very fresh salads, and decent coffee.

▶ *Elefanten is a taste of what might be to come in the evolving Carlsberg area; see p86* **Brewing Up a Cultural Storm**.

Café Viggo

Værnedamsvej 15, Vesterbro (33 31 18 21). Bus 10, 14. **Open** 10.30am-1am Mon-Wed; 10.30am-2am Thur-Sat; 11am-6pm Sun. **No credit cards. Map** p245 P8 ㊽

This cheap, characterful French café on what was once Copenhagen's 'food street' is a gathering place for the city's French community, which is usually a good sign. Sandwiches, omelettes and salads are served during the day, while the dinner menu includes heartier bistro fare like rabbit stew and roast duck.

Det Gule Hus

Istedgade 48, Vesterbro (33 25 90 71, www.cafedetgulehus.dk). Train København H.
Open 9am-midnight Mon-Thur; 9am-2am Fri; 10am-2pm Sat; 10am-11pm Sun. **Credit** AmEx, MC, V. **Map** p245 Q9 ㊾

One of the more spacious and attractive of Istedgade's hip cafés, Det Gule Hus is light, airy and welcoming, with great people-watching potential via the gritty daily life on Copenhagen's sleaziest street. Some tables outside in summer.

★ Dyrehaven

Sdr. Boulevard 72 (33 21 60 24, www.dyrehavenkbh.dk). Train to Dybbølsbro. **Open** 9am-midnight Mon-Wed; 9-2am Thur, Fri; 10-2am Sat; 10am-6pm Sun. *Food served* 10am-9pm Mon-Wed; 10am-10pm Thurs-Sat. **Credit** MC, V. **Map** p245 S8 ㊿

Dyrehaven is a stylish spot owned by three young locals that attracts small groups of sociable twenty- and thirtysomethings. The appeal is good design, friendly staff, a laid-back atmosphere and top-notch food and drink. The menu specialises in Danish classics, such as smørrebrød and *stegt flæsk* (for both, *see p131* **Danish Delicacies**). The wooden walls and bar, old mounted deer heads, vintage pictures and separate dining cubicles give the bar a distinct 1970s feel, and the space is as popular for weekend brunch as it is for decent beer and wine, and evening cocktails, when DJs add to the vibe.

▶ *Other good places for smørrebrød and other classic Danish cuisine are Madklubben (see p117) and Aamanns (see p125).*

Falernum

Værnedamsvej 16, Frederiksberg (33 22 30 89, www.falernum.dk). Bus 6A, 14, 15. **Open** 8am-midnight Mon-Thur; 8am-2am Fri, Sat; 10am-midnight Sun. **Credit** MC, V. **Map** p245 P8 (51)

Located on one of Frederiksberg's nicest streets, this popular, cosy wine bar/café has plenty of character, thanks to its old wooden tables, candles and agreeable, loyal punters. The wine list is extensive and well thought out, and tapas plates are served in the evening. It's also a good spot for a light breakfast.

▶ *Falernum is part of a successful mini-chain that includes Pánzon (see p140), Vincaféen Bibendum (see p133) and PatéPaté (see venue index).*

★ Granola

Værnedamsvej 5 (33 25 00 80). Bus 14 or metro Forum. **Open** 9am-5.30pm Mon-Fri; 9am-4pm Sat. **Credit** MC, V. **Map** p245 P8 (52)

This small café, on the area's most genteel street, has a loyal following. The space evokes the 1930s with its retro decor, and it's one of the few places where you can order the Danish fruit dessert *rødgrød med fløde* (stewed red fruit, usually strawberries, with cream). It also serves classic milkshakes and delicious ice-cream, and stocks an excellent range of top-quality teas and coffee. It's a popular spot for brunch.

Dyrehaven.

CONSUME

CONSUME

Kaffe & Vinyl.

★ Kaffe & Vinyl

Skydebanegade 4, Vesterbro (61 70 33 49,
www.sortkaffevinyl.dk). Bus 10. **Open** 8am-
7pm Mon-Fri; 10am-6pm Sat; 11am-6pm Sun.
No credit cards. Map p245 R9 ㊳
Serving some of the best coffee in town (from local
brand Risteriet), this friendly place draws in a cool
bunch of caffeine and vinyl addicts, many of whom
get here early in the day for a pre-work boost. The
varied collection of records runs the gamut from
electronica to rock.

Karriere

Flæsketorvet 57-67, Vesterbro (33 21 55 09,
www.karrierebar.com). Train København H.
Open *Cocktail bar* 4pm-midnight Thur; 4pm-
4am Fri, Sat. *Restaurant* 6-10pm Thur-Sat.
Credit AmEx, MC, V. **Map** p250 Q10 ㉞
This ambitious art gallery/cocktail bar/restaurant
opened in a former slaugherhouse in Kødbyen in 2007,
the brainchild of artist Jeppe Hein and his sister
Lærke. The interior is designed by renowned contemporary artists (Ulrik Weck, for instance, created lampshades for the bar made of pots, pans and bowls
turned upside down), who also supply works for the
permanent and temporary exhibitions. Head chefs in
the restaurant are Astrid Baadsgaard and Lena Lee
Jørgensen, who worked together at restaurant-of-the-
moment Noma (*see venue index*). Concerts, gigs, lectures and cultural events are also held here.

★ Meyers Deli

Gammel Kongevej 107 (33 25 45 95,
www.meyersdeli.dk) Bus 14, 15. **Open** 8.30am-
10pm daily. **Credit** MC, V. **Map** p245 O7 ㉟
Klaus Meyer is one of the leading foodie figures in
Denmark. Entrepreneur, TV personality and restaurateur (he is the man behind Noma), Meyer opened
this magnificent deli-café in the heart of bourgeois
Frederiksberg back in 2005 and his healthy, innovative eat/heat/cook takeaways have proved popular
with time-poor yuppie locals. There's also a branch
in Magasin department store.
Other locations Meyer's Bakery,
9 Jægersborggade, Nørrebro (no phone).

Ricco's Coffee Bar

Istedgade 119 (33 31 04 40, www.riccos.dk).
Bus 10. **Open** 8am-11pm Mon-Fri; 9am-11pm
Sat, Sun. **Credit** MC, V. **Map** p245 R8 ㊱
This tiny, narrow coffee bar and boutique, owned by
Ricco Sørensen, has a devoted following among
Vesterbro's dedicated coffee addicts. They take their
coffee very seriously here, selling a wide range of beans,
syrups and paraphernalia. There is a comfortable room
out back with long sofas and vinyl-only sounds.
Other locations throughout the city.

Vinstue 90

Gammel Kongevej 90 (33 31 84 90, www.vinstue
90.dk). Metro Forum or bus 14. **Open** 11am-1am

Vinstue 90.

CONSUME

Mon-Wed, Sun; 11am-2am Thur-Sat.
Credit AmEx, V. **Map** p245 O8 ⑤
Something of a local legend, this small bar – founded in 1916 – is famous for its 'slow beer'; it takes 15-20 minutes to pour a glass, so customers often order a 'normal' beer while they wait. It's all about the pouring – standard Carlsberg pilsner is on tap – but poured very slowly from unpressurised kegs, a smoother taste is produced. Although they don't serve food, the friendly owners will happily order smørrebrod (or anything else) for you if you call in advance. They'll even provide you with plates and cutlery. A gem.
▶ *Copenhagen is home to a good number of microbreweries; see p138* **A Room with a Brew**.

NØRREBRO

Bodega
Kapelvej 1, off Nørrebrogade (35 39 07 07, www.bodega.dk). Bus 5A. **Open** 10am-midnight Mon-Thur; 10am-2am Fri, Sat; 10am-6pm Sun.
Credit AmEx, MC, V. **Map** p248 J9 ⑤
Formerly Barstarten, this tucked away café-cocktail bar reopened as Bodega in 2006, with pretty much the same set-up (albeit with better food). The food is contemporary southern European fare, the coffee excellent and the interior effortlessly hip, with low ceilings, white walls, expensive leather chairs and a striking wooden bar and tables. DJs play soul, funk and R&B at weekends, and in summer there is limited seating outside, across the road from Assistens Kirkegård (*see venue index*). The graveyard here is Denmark's most prestigious, providing a final resting place to Hans Christian Andersen, Søren Kierkegaard and Niels Bohr.

Café 22
Sortedam Dossering 21 (35 37 38 27, www.cafe22.dk). Bus 5A. **Open** 9am-midnight Mon-Wed, Sun; 9am-2am Thur-Sat. **Credit** MC, V. **Map** p248 J11 ⑤
It remains something of a mystery why there aren't more cafés and bars located beside Copenhagen's elegant man-made lakes to the west of the city centre, since it seems such an obviously picturesque spot to dine and drink. Perhaps the reason lies hidden in the long cold of Copehagen's winter which can whip across the open water here. But we should be grateful for Café 22, an appealing cellar café/bar (with outdoor tables during summer), serving excellent sandwiches, pasta dishes, tapas, burgers and desserts.

Harbo Bar
Blågårdsgade 2D (no phone). **Open** 8.30am-midnight Mon-Thur; 8.30am-2am Fri; 9.30am-2am Sat; 9.30am-midnight Sun. **Credit** MC, V. **Map** p248 K10 ⑥

INSIDE TRACK DRINKS PRICES

Though it's not as costly as in the other Scandinavian countries, alcohol is still expensive in Denmark, with spirits especially so (though, by some curious quirk of excise, wine is cheaper in Danish supermarkets than British ones). As a rule, the further the café or bar is from the centre, the cheaper the booze. Nyhavn is one of the dearest spots for a nipple.

A Room with a Brew

Head to the city's microbreweries for freshly brewed beer and decent grub.

Nørrebro Bryghus.

The golden era of Denmark's microbrewery explosion in the first decade of the 21st century may now be over, but Copenhagen is still a great place to sample a wide range of beers from small-scale, non-industrial brewers using traditional techniques.

Since 2005, Denmark has had a higher percentage of breweries per capita than any other European country, with many locals' renewed interest in beer (called 'øl' in Danish) stemming from the opening of several microbreweries in the early noughties, which led to the microbrewery explosion a few years' later. Regrettably, everal of these small businesses haven't survived the recession. That their beers are inevitably more expensive than standard brews means that some were forced out of business when consumers started counting the kroners. Yet, despite this, there are still far more microbreweries in Copenhagen today than there were in 2000. What's more, as well as their rich, malty brews, many offer brewery tours and decent grub.

Copenhagen's first microbrewery was **Bryggeriet Apollo** (Vesterbrogade 3, 33 12 33 13, www.bryggeriet.dk), close to Tivoli; established in 1990, and still pumping out litres of the brown stuff today, to be enjoyed alongside its organic food. Apollo's (mainly pilsner) beer is brewed according to the German 'purity law', meaning only hops, yeast, malt and water are used. If you're paying a trip to Tivoli itself, be sure to check out its legendary **Færgekroen Bryghus** (Vesterbrogade 3, 33 75 06 80, www. faergekroen.com), which has had its own microbrewery since 2005. Enjoy one of its two house beers (blonde and amber lagers) with the bryghus's smørrebrød.

One of the most dynamic microbreweries in the city – and central to the microbrewery explosion – is **Nørrebro Bryghus** (*see p124*), located in one of the coolest parts of town. Here you can enjoy modern Nordic cooking with a wide selection of beers (both in the food, and as perfectly suited accompaniments). The artisanal beers include Belgian white beer, pre-Prohibition-style New York lager and English-style stout, all of which are brewed on the premises. The place was awarded two gold medals and one silver at the 2010 World Beer Cup in Chicago, and also recently released Denmark's first carbon-neutral beer, Globe Ale.

Vesterbro has its equivalents in the more recently established **Vesterbro Bryghus** (Vesterbrogade 2B, 33 11 17 05, www.vesterbrobryghus.dk) and **Mikkeller** (Viktoriagade 8, www.mikkeller.dk). The former, known for its long bar, brews five special beers from traditional Austrian recipes. The award-winning Mikkeller, run by young 'Gypsy-brewer' Mikkel Borg Bjergsø, is one of the most-talked about breweries/microbars in the city. Its 15 taps (ten of which pump house brews) include the recently launched Vesterbro Coffee stout ('black as hell, lots of toasted notes and a razor sharp coffee taste').

In 2005, keen not to miss out on the fun, Carlsberg opened a new 'artisanal' brewhouse – called **Husbryggeriet Jacobsen** (www.jacobsenbryg.dk) in the Carlsberg Visitors' Centre in Valby. Here Carlsberg brews special beers aimed at connoisseurs. A ticket to the Visitors' Centre include two complimentary glasses of beer in the brewery bar overlooking the production area.

Other spots for beer fans include Nørrebro's **Ølbaren** pub (Elmegade 2, www.oelbaren.dk), offering one of the best selections in the city; Frederiksberg's **Vinstue 90** (*see p136*), a local fave since 1916, and a proponet of 'slow beer'; and the excellent Vesterbro beer shop **Ølbutikken** (*see p156*), which stocks some 250 rare artisanal brands, including Mikkeller. If you're in town in May, don't miss the Copenhagen Beer Festival (*see p164*), now in its 11th year. Nyhavn is also host to an annual beer festival in September.

CONSUME

Designed with a laid-back 'living room' concept in mind, Harbo Bar opened in late 2009, and reflects the fact that multicultural Nørrebro is now home to the city's hipster community. Retro fittings, a plethora of laptops (the place is buzzing with freelancers in the daytime), grazing-oriented food and decent beer create a vibe more readily associated with Berlin than Copenhagen. The place is also known for its organic walnut brandy. A cornerstone of the 'hood.

▶ *Pedestrianised Blågårdsgade is home to several good independent shops and cafés, including vegetarian spot Cafe N at No.17.*

Kaffesalonen

Pebling Dossering 6 (35 35 12 19, www. kaffesalonen.com). **Open** 8am-midnight Mon-Fri; 10am-midnight Sat, Sun. **Credit** AmEx, MC, V. **Map** p248 K10 ⬤
Salonen is blessed with an ideal location close to the lakes, which allows it to expand on to a large floating deck during summer. It's the perfect place for a long, leisurely sundowner, followed by a selection from the accomplished Franco-Danish menu.

★ Laundromat Café

Elmegade 15 (35 35 26 72, www.thelaundromat cafe.com). Metro Nørreport or bus 5A. **Open** 8am-midnight Mon-Fri; 10am-midnight Sat, Sun. **Credit** AmEx, MC, V. **Map** p248 J10 ⬤
The Laundromat Café – an original concept that mixes coffee shop with launderette – has been a big local hit since opening in 2004. Stick your laundry in the washing machine, then take a seat in the stylish space (think wood-panelled walls and designer lampshades) to enjoy a grilled sandwich, a salad or a sweet snack while your clothes are being washed. What's more, there's a good range of coffees and a plentiful supply of reading material. It's also a nice spot for weekend brunch. Another branch in Østerbro, similarly stylish but lacking the washing machines, opened in 2006. **Other locations** Århusgade 38, Østerbro (35 55 60 20).

Oak Room

Birkegade 10 (38 60 38 60, www.oakroom.dk). Bus 3A, 5A. **Open** 8pm-midnight Tue, Wed; 8pm-2am Thur; 4pm-4am Fri; 6pm-4am Sat. **No credit cards. Map** p248 J10 ⬤
This cramped venue just off trendy Elmegade is always packed and sweaty, with crowds spilling on to the pavement at weekends. After opening in 2004 it became the place to drink in Nørrebro, popular with pre-clubbers on their way to Rust nearby, or movie-goers emerging from the Empire Cinema round the corner. Happy hour is until 9pm.

Pussy Galore's Flying Circus

Sankt Hans Torv 30 (35 37 68 00, www.pussygalore.dk). Bus 3A, 5A. **Open** 8am-midnight Mon-Wed; 8am-1am Thur; 8am-2am Fri; 9am-2am Sat; 9am-midnight Sun. **Credit** MC, V. **Map** p248 H10 ⬤
Located in the centre of one of the hippest parts of Copenhagen (around Sankt Hans Torv) lies Pussy Galore's Flying Circus, the archetypal modern Copenhagen café which kick-started Nørrebro's popularity. This busy L-shaped bar and dining area, decorated in requisite 1990s minimalist style (replete with Arne Jacobsen chairs), is the trendy counterpart to the more conventional French food offered by Sebastopol next door (*see p140*). The menu is fusion-heavy, with salads and hearty burgers, but the quality can be variable. As with Sebastopol, come spring Pussy Galore's tables move on to the square. The cocktails are reasonably priced compared with bars in the centre of town. *Photo p142.*

CONSUME

Laundromat Café.

Sebastopol Café

Sankt Hans Torv 32 (35 36 30 02, www.sebastopol. dk). Bus 3A. **Open** 8am-midnight Mon-Wed; 8am-2am Thur, Fri; 9am-2am Sat; 9am-midnight Sun. **Credit** AmEx, MC, V. **Map** p248 J10 ⑮

Sebastopol's French staples offer tempting, good-value competition to the more erratic offerings of Pussy Galore's next door. A young and hip clientele (musicians, journalists, advertising types) from this super cool part of town provides constant visual entertainment. Sebastopol gets very crowded on summer weekends when, like Pussy's, it bursts exuberantly on to the square.

★ Underwood Ink

Ryesgade 30A (35 35 55 53, www.underwood-ink.com). Bus 5A, 6A. **Open** 4pm-2am Wed-Sat. **Credit** AmEx, MC, V. **Map** p246 J11 ⑯

Saved from closure by new investment, Underwood Ink is a characterful, bohemian spot. Literature lovers should feel right at home; the shelves are stacked with books (mostly English-language) by novelists of the Bukowski ilk, and there's also a range of international magazines. A cool yet cosy spot in which to hang out, quietly chat or get into that holiday novel with the help of a warming coffee. Expanded opening times are planned for summer 2011.

► *Ryesgade is one of Nørrebro's coolest streets, and also home to excellent restaurant/ microbrewery Nørrebro Bryghus (see p138).*

ØSTERBRO

Café Bopa

Løgstørgade 8 (35 43 05 66, www.cafebopa.dk). Train Nordhavn. **Open** 9am-midnight Mon-Wed,

Pussy Galore's Flying Circus. *See p141.*

Sun; 9am-2am Thur; 9am-5am Fri, Sat. **Credit** MC, V. **Map** p248 C14 ⑰

Dark and arty by day, pulsating by night, Bopa is at the heart of this leafy square's young scene. At the weekends DJs ensure the place is packed and sweaty. Unusually late opening hours are another plus, as are cheap cocktails.

Dag H

Dag Hammarskjölds Allé 36-40 (35 27 63 00, www.dagh.dk). Bus 1A, 14, 15. **Open** 8am-11pm Mon-Wed; 8am-midnight Thur, Fri; 10am-midnight Sat; 10am-10pm Sun. **Credit** AmEx, MC, V. **Map** p248 F14 ⑱

Formerly the coffee cathedral Amokka, this mainstay of Østerbro's café life on Lille Trianglen (Little Triangle, just along from the American Embassy) reopened with chefs Brian Damkvist and Peter Andersen in the kitchen. The coffee is still great, but not the centre of attraction as it once was. The emphasis is more on the excellent food now, which includes fancy burgers and more mod-Med food.

Fru Heiberg

Rosenvængets Allé 3 (35 38 91 00, www.fru heiberg.dk). Bus 1A, 3A. **Open** 5-10pm Tue-Thur, Sun; 5-11pm Fri, Sat. **No credit cards.** **Map** p248 E14 ⑲

This local Danish/French/Mediterranean restaurant has proved immensely popular since opening in 2006, thanks to excellent ingredients prepared with diligence and imagination. Cosy and old-fashioned but with a young, hip clientele.

★ Gourmandiet

Rosenvængets Allé 7 (39 27 10 00, www. gourmandiet.dk). Bus 1A, 3A, 14. **Open** 11am-3pm Mon-Wed; 11am-3pm, 5.30-midnight Thur-Sat. Kitchen closed at 10pm Thur-Sat. **Credit** AmEx, MC, V. **Map** p248 E14 ⑳

The upmarket organic butcher/café has been a big hit with the gentrified neighbourhood's residents, who come here for top-quality steaks and biodynamic wine. The walls are adorned with murals of pastoral scenes, while nicely arranged displays showcase the shop's tempting array of products, including a range of organic charcuterie products. A popular spot for Saturday brunch, Gourmandiet also opens as a restaurant on weekend evenings.

► *Another Østerbro gem, cosy wine bar Pánzon (see below), sits opposite.*

★ Panzón

Rosenvængets Allé (35 38 98 00, www.falernum. dk/panzon). Train Østerport. **Open** 4pm-midnight Mon-Thur; 4pm-2am Fri, Sat. **Credit** MC, V. **Map** p248 E14 ㉑

Similar in atmosphere to its sister spot, Falernum (*see p135*), in Frederiksberg, this is a nice cosy bar in which to enjoy quality wine and a tapas plate. Decent beer too

Shops & Services

There's something for everyone in Scandinavia's top shopping city.

Copenhagen is a shopper's paradise, thanks to the locals' devotion to quality goods and innovative style. The city's shopping landscape reflects Denmark's egalitarian and inclusive society, offering something great for every budget. You'll find bustling branches of international high-street chains, thriving specialist shops and luscious boutiques all vying for your attention, with retailers largely clustered by type in various parts of the city.

The majority of retail therapy can be had on and around the seemingly endless **Strøget**, although shopping opportunities aren't limited to the city centre: in recent years several of Copenhagen's suburbs have become fashionable, including Vesterbro, Nørrebro, Østerbro and Frederiksberg (*see p161* **Neighbourhood Shops**).

ONE-STOP SHOPPING
Department stores

★ Illum
Østergade 52, Strøget (33 14 40 02, www. illum.dk). Metro Kongens Nytorv. **Open** 10am-7pm Mon-Thur; 10am-8pm Fri; 10am-6pm Sat; 11am-4pm Sun. **Credit** AmEx, MC, V. **Map** p251 M15.
Illum's interior design and magnificent glass dome make it the more modern of the city's two department stores. The ground floor is home to cosmetics, accessories and a fabulous range of womenswear by Scandinavian designers (Acne Jeans, J Lindeberg, Bruuns Bazaar), while the basement houses a branch of supermarket Irma. More high-end fashion is found on the first and second floors.

Magasin
Kongens Nytorv 13 (33 11 44 33, www. magasin.dk). Metro Kongens Nytorv. **Open** 10am-7pm Mon-Thur; 10am-8pm Fri; 10am-5pm Sat; noon-4pm 1st & last Sun of month. **Credit** AmEx, DC, MC, V. **Map** p251 M15.
This was Scandinavia's first department store and remains its largest, with five floors of clothes, high-class cosmetics, toys, household goods, books and fine food. Womenswear is a strong point, while families will find a Hamleys toy store, two juice bars and a comprehensive childcare area. *Photo p145.*
Other locations Field's Mall, Arne Jacobsens Allé 12 (32 47 06 00).

★ Royal Copenhagen
Amagertorv 6, Strøget (33 13 71 81, www. royalcopenhagen.com). Metro Kongens Nytorv or bus 1A, 2A, 6A, 15, 350S. **Open** 10am-6pm Mon-Fri; 10am-5pm Sat; noon-5pm Sun. **Credit** AmEx, MC, V. **Map** 251 N14.
With its big refurbishment in 2007, Royal Shopping spilt into three separate shops, all of which are interconnected. The Royal Copenhagen flagship, housed in a 16th-century building, is the place to head for the famous porcelain, whose designs span the traditional to the modern and include the world-famous 'Flora Danica' collection; Georg Jensen sells silverware and jewellery (*see p159*); and Illums Bolighus (*see p157*) is for furniture and designer homewares. To complete the royal shopping trip, head to the Royal Café (*see p132*), in the same building.

INSIDE TRACK SALES TAX

Sales tax is high at 25%, so if you live outside the EU and spend over 300kr at any of the places displaying a Global Refund Tax Free Shopping sign, it is worth asking the shop for a VAT refund cheque. When leaving Denmark, remember to make time before your flight to go to customs (Terminal 3, Arrivals hall) and get your forms stamped; they can then be cashed at the Global Refund office for a refund of 19% of your total purchases.

CONSUME

4

Apartments in Copenhagen
for days, weeks & months

Malls

Field's
Arne Jacobsens Alle 12, Ørestad (70 20 85 05, www.fields.dk). Metro/train Ørestad. **Open** 10am-8pm Mon-Fri, 10am-6pm Sat; 10am-5pm 1st & last Sun of month. **Credit** varies.
This shopping and leisure centre is Scandinavia's largest, boasting a branch of Magasin department store, a Bilka supermarket and 70 high-street shops, including H&M and Zara.

Fisketorvet
Kalvebod Brygge 59, Vesterbro (33 36 64 00, www.fisketorvet.dk). Train Dybbølsbro or bus 1A, 30, 65E. **Open** 10am-8pm Mon-Fri, 10am-6pm Sat; 11am-5pm 1st & last Sun of month. **Credit** varies.
With 120 shops, a supermarket, 16 restaurants and a ten-screen cinema, this enormous mall has something for all ages. All the usual chains are here (H&M, Mango, Vero Moda), plus there's a Lego store.

ANTIQUES, CLASSICS, DECORATIVE ART

Bredgade is where all the serious antiques stores, art dealers and auction houses are located. Alternatively, **Ravnsborggade** has over 20 specialist antiques stores catering to a range of budgets (www.ravnsborggade.dk).

Antikhallen
Sortedams Dossering 7C, Nørrebro (35 35 04 20). Bus 5A. **Open** 2-6pm Mon-Fri; 11am-3pm Sat. **No credit cards.** **Map** p246 H12.

INSIDE TRACK
OPENING HOURS

Late risers are in for a surprise in Copenhagen, with Denmark's weekend opening hours fleeting to say the least. Most stores close early on Saturdays – often around 2pm – and almost all are closed on Sundays, but late opening on Fridays provides some compensation.

An unpretentious treasure trove of second-hand and antique furniture. The shop is bursting with eye-catching curiosities, from 19th-century mahogany tables to 1970s moulded orange plastic chairs.

★ Antique Toys
Store Strandstræde 20 (33 12 66 32, www.antique-toys.dk). Metro Kongens Nytorv. **Open** 3-6pm Wed-Fri and by appointment. **No credit cards.** **Map** p252 M16.
This has to be one of Copenhagen's cutest stores, selling a huge range of antique toys in all shapes and sizes (model cars, train sets, doll's houses), some dating from as far back as the 17th century.

H Danielsen's Successors
Læderstræde 11 (33 13 02 74). Metro Kongens Nytorv. **Open** 10am-5.30pm Mon-Fri; 10am-2pm Sat. **Credit** AmEx, MC, V. **Map** p251 N14.
Founded in 1907, this family firm owns the original moulds of countless cutlery designs, allowing it to reproduce long extinct silverware to order.

CONSUME

Magasin. *See p143.*

Green Square Copenhagen

Strandlodsvej 11B (32 57 59 59, www.greensquare. dk). Metro Lergravsparken, then 7min walk. **Open** 10am-5.30pm Mon-Thur; 10am-6pm Fri; 10am-4pm Sat. **Credit** AmEx, MC, V (transaction fee 6%).

Green Square occupies a massive aircraft hangar of a building south of the city, and claims to be northern Europe's single largest antiques dealer, selling a vast range of 18th- to 20th-century furniture.

Gregory Pepin's Danish Silver

Bredgade 12 (33 11 52 52, www.danishsilver. com). Metro Kongens Nytorv. **Open** 10am-5.30pm Mon-Fri; 10am-2.30pm Sat. **Credit** AmEx, MC, V. **Map** p249 K16.

Pepin claims to stock the largest amount of antique Georg Jensen creations in the city, from jewellery to more formal sculpted pieces, as well as items from the likes of Hans Hansen and Evald Nielsen.

Kim Anton

Ravnsborggade 14C, Nørrebro (35 37 06 24). Bus 5A. **Open** 9.30am-5.30pm Mon-Fri; 11am-2pm Sat. **Credit** V. **Map** p248 J10.

A two-floor emporium of ornate 18th- and 19th-century European furniture, plus a selection of fine fabrics from Bevilacqua.

Soelberg Kunst & Antikvitetshandel

Knabrostræde 15 (33 12 79 77, www.soelberg-antik. dk). Bus 14. **Open** 10.30am-4.30pm Mon-Fri; 11am-2pm Sat. **Credit** AmEx, MC, V. **Map** p251 O13.

Designer Zoo.

One of the city's most eclectic stores, Soelberg boasts the likes of Russian Orthodox icons, military memorabilia and Inuit cultural artefacts – there's even a small shrine to *Star Wars* merchandise. Bizarre.

Sølvkælderen

Kompagnistræde 1 (33 13 36 34). Bus 14. **Open** 9am-5.30pm Mon-Thur; 9am-6pm Fri; 10am-2pm Sat. **Credit** AmEx, MC, V. **Map** p251 N13.

A century-old purveyor of Danish silver. Certain pieces date back as far as 1700, but there are also more modern candlestick holders, plates and cutlery.

ART & DESIGN

The annual **Danish Arts and Crafts Association market** (www.kunsthaand vaerkermarkedet.dk) takes place every August in Vor Frue Plads.

★ Designer Zoo

Vesterbrogade 137, Vesterbro (33 24 94 93/ www.dzoo.dk). Bus 6A, 26. **Open** 10am-5.30pm Mon-Thur; 10am-7pm Fri; 10am-3pm Sat. **Credit** MC, V. **Map** p245 Q7.

The brainchild of six young artisans who work in full view of ogling visitors (hence the name), and with furniture, glass, handmade clothes, jewellery and ceramics among the output.

Galerie Stamkunsten

Sankt Peders Stræde 27B (33 12 25 90, www.stamkunsten.dk). Train/metro Nørreport. **Open** varies; call for details. **No credit cards**. **Map** p250 N11.

This charming workshop and gallery offers one-off paintings and ceramics from a team of largely non-professional in-house artists. Opening times depend on who is in the workshop.

ART SUPPLIES, HOBBIES & CRAFTS

Nordatlantens Brygge

Strandgade 91 (32 83 37 00, www.bryggen.dk). Metro Christianshavn. **Open** 10am-5pm Mon-Fri; noon-5pm Sat, Sun. **Credit** MC, V. **Map** p252 O17.

The best source for Greenlandic handicrafts and information, this small shop attached to the cultural centre sells books, jewellery, exquisitely forged, hand-ground knives, art and – animal rights supporters beware – seal fur products.

Københavns Farvehandel

Badstuestræde 9 (33 11 16 81, www. kobenhavnsfarvehandel.dk). Bus 14. **Open** 10am-5.30pm Mon-Fri; 10am-1pm Sat. **No credit cards**. **Map** p251 N13.

Established in 1909, this charming shop caters to the most demanding of fine artists with a comprehensive range of creative raw materials.

Arnold Busck.

Uldstedet
Fiolstræde 13 (33 91 17 71, www.uldstedet.dk).
Train/metro Nørreport. **Open** 10am-5.30pm
Mon-Fri; 10am-3pm Sat. **Credit** MC, V.
Map p251 M13.
A well-stocked knitting shop with quality yarns
from Italy to Norway. A second branch, in suburban
Lyngby, boasts an in-house knitting café.
Other locations Gl Jernbanevej 7, Lyngby
(45 88 10 88).

AUCTIONS

Bruun Rasmussen Kunstauktioner
Bredgade 33 (33 43 69 11, www.bruun-
rasmussen.dk). Metro Kongens Nytorv. **Open**
11am-4pm Tue-Thur; 11am-3.30pm Fri. **Credit**
MC, V. **Map** p249 K16.
Denmark's premier auction house also happens to
be one of the world's top ten auctioneers, serving
the prime end of the antiques and arts market.
Usually themed, Rasmussen's sales of art, antiques,
furniture, wine and just about everything else that
could go under the gavel take place at least a couple
of times each week. A second house at Havnen
focusing on online auctions has a younger vibe,
with a large selection of modern furniture and
decorative art.
Other locations Sundkrogsgade 30 (88 18 11 11).

BEAUTY

Illum and **Magasin** (*see p143*) both have
good cosmetics departments. **Matas**, meanwhile,
offers beauty products to suit all budgets and has
branches throughout the city.

★ Pure Shop
Grønnegade 31 & 36 (33 17 00 70, www.pure
shop.dk). Metro Kongens Nytorv. **Open** 10am-6pm
Mon-Thur; 10am-7pm Fri; 10am-4pm Sat. **No
credit cards.** **Map** p251 M15.
All-natural and hypoallergenic cosmetics, skincare
and beauty products. Brands available include Dr
Hauschka, Jurlique and Weleda. The new store at
No.36 is the flagship, and has a make-up department.

BOOKS

The Latin Quarter boasts a large number
of bookshops, although those people seeking
second-hand and vintage volumes should head
to Fiolstræde.

Antiquarian/second-hand

Peter Grosell
Læderstræde 15 (33 93 45 05, www.grosell.dk).
Metro Kongens Nytorv. **Open** 10am-5pm Mon-Fri;
10am-1pm Sat. **Credit** AmEx, MC, V.
Map p251 N14.
This large dealer in rare, second-hand and antiquar-
ian books is particularly strong on art and design
books, as well as Scandinavian first editions.

General

Arnold Busck
Købmagergade 49 (33 73 35 00, www.arnold
busck.dk). Train/metro Nørreport. **Open** 10am-6pm
Mon-Thur; 10am-7pm Fri; 10am-4pm Sat; noon-
4pm 1st & last Sun of month. **Credit** AmEx, MC,
V. **Map** p251 M14.

CONSUME

Busck is one of Denmark's leading book retailers, and this three-storey branch – its biggest – has a large department dedicated to English-language paperbacks and guides. *Photo p147.*

Other locations Købmagergade 50 (33 15 44 66); Fiolstræde 24 (33 73 35 45); Statens Museum For Kunst, Sølvgade 48-50 (33 74 86 68).

Politikens Boghallen
Rådhuspladsen 37 (33 47 25 60, www.politikens boghal.dk). Train København H. **Open** 10am-7pm Mon-Fri; 10am-4pm Sat. **Credit** AmEx, DC, MC, V. **Map** p250 O12.

Along with Arnold Busck (*p147*), Politikens Boghallen is one of the city's biggest bookshops, with a huge range of English-language titles available in store.

Newsagents

The two best sources of international magazines and newspapers are **Magasin**'s vast basement newsstand (*see p143*) and the newsagent at **Central Station** (København H).

Specialist

Cinematekets Bog og Videohandel
Filmhuset, Vognmagergade 8B (33 74 34 21, www.dfi.dk). Metro Kongens Nytorv. **Open** noon-6pm Tue-Fri; 11am-5pm Sat, Sun. **Credit** AmEx, MC, V. **Map** p251 M14.

There's no safer haven for cinephiles than Filmhuset – headquarters of the Danish Film Institute – and its affiliated bookshop is the best place to pick up that elusive tome on Scandinavian cinema.

Diamantboghandlen
Det Kongelige Bibliotek, Søren Kierkegaards Plads 1 (33 47 49 47, www.diamantboghandlen.dk). Metro Kongens Nytorv. **Open** 9.30am-5.30pm Mon-Fri; 10am-5pm Sat. **Credit** MC, V. **Map** p251 P15.

The glittering waterfront Black Diamond building is home to the Royal Library bookshop, one of Copenhagen's most reliable sources of English-language books about Danish culture.

Nordisk Korthandel
Studiestræde 26-30 (33 38 26 38, www. scanmaps.dk). Train/metro Nørreport. **Open** 10.30am-6pm Mon-Fri; 9.30am-3pm Sat. **Credit** MC, V. **Map** p250 N12.

Copenhagen's best source of maps, travel books and globes, staffed by knowledgeable travel enthusiasts.

CERAMICS

Butik for Borddækning
Møntergade 6 (33 32 61 01). Metro Kongens Nytorv. **Open** 11am-6pm Mon-Fri; 11am-4pm Sat. **Credit** MC, V. **Map** p251 M14.

A reputable purveyor of handmade ceramics from the prosaic to the positively outlandish, with everything from sleek sushi sets and enigmatic espresso cups to artfully wonky water pitchers.

Helbak/Scherning
Kompagnistræde 8 (20 61 04 77, www.helbak-scherning.dk) Metro Kongens Nytorv. **Open** 11am-5.30pm Wed, Thur; 11am-6pm Fri; 10am-4pm Sat. **Credit** AmEx, MC, V. **Map** p251 N13.

High-quality earthenware vessels and delicate porcelain jewellery by Malene Helbak and Mette Scherning, all hand-decorated in playful colours.

FASHION
Budget & international chains

Cos
Østergade 33-35, Strøget (36 97 88 81, www.cos.com). Metro Kongens Nytorv. **Open** 10am-6pm Mon-Thur; 10am-7pm Fri; 10am-5pm Sat. **Credit** AmEx, MC, V. **Map** p251 M15.

The grown-up sister to H&M sells Scandinavian-led clothes characterised by simple, stylish cuts and muted tones.

H&M
Amagertorv 21, Strøget (70 10 23 31, www.hm.com). Metro Kongens Nytorv. **Open** 10am-6pm Mon-Thur; 10am-7pm Fri; 10am-5pm Sat. **Credit** AmEx, DC, MC, V. **Map** p251 N14.

This Swedish retail giant needs no introduction. With two branches on Strøget alone, H&M is a Danish favourite for affordable fashion.

Other locations throughout the city.

Urban Outfitters
Østergade 42, Strøget (33 17 05 00, www.urbanoutfitters.co.uk). Metro Kongens Nytorv. **Open** 10am-6pm Mon-Thur; 10am-7pm Fri; 10am-6pm Sat; noon-4pm 1st & last Sun of mth. **Credit** AmEx, MC, V. **Map** p251 M15.

Denmark's is the 100th branch of this popular US fashion and homewares chain.

Casual, street & menswear

For the city's excellent skate shops, *see p203* **Skate Copenhagen**.

Adidas Originals
Pilestræde 6-8, Strøget (33 93 63 60, www.adidas.com). Metro Kongens Nytorv. **Open** 10am-6pm Mon-Thur; 10am-7pm Fri; 10am-4pm Sat. **Credit** AmEx, MC, V. **Map** p251 M14.

This place is a sanctuary for Adidas classics, with hard-to-find trainers, clothing (Carlo Gruber skiwear, for example) and accessories with an emphasis on the golden years of Adidas from the 1960s to the '80s.

Diesel
Købmagergade 19 (39 27 56 55, www.diesel.com).
Metro Kongens Nytorv. **Open** 10am-6pm Mon-
Thur; 10am-7pm Fri; 10am-5pm Sat. **Credit**
AmEx, MC, V. **Map** p251 M14.
An impressive showcase for Diesel's slightly skewed,
self-proclaimed 'haute couture of casual' streetwear.

★ **Norse Store**
Pilestræde 4 (33 93 26 26, www.norsestore.com).
Metro Kongens Nytorv. **Open** 10am-6pm Mon-

Thur; 10am-7pm Fri; 10am-4pm Sat. **Credit** MC,
V. **Map** p251 M14.
Norse Projects was established in 2004, and has
since become one the most popular shops in town
for style savvy young men. The clothes combine
street fashion, classic workwear and contemporary
designs, with a hand-picked selection of clothing
and footwear from its own clothing collection as
well as other labels from around the world, including Ally Capellino, Folk, Acne, Lee, Levis, Adidas
and Penfield. *Photos p150.*

Danish Designers

Know your Goyas from your Stærks.

What do you get if you combine well-funded
art colleges with a national heritage
for clothes-making and an affinity for
innovation? The answer is Denmark, a
country that has produced one of Europe's
most dynamic fashion industries, which is
finally making waves the world over. Styles
and prices vary, but the following designers
share an emphasis on quality and originality.

SILAS ADLER
Menswear designer of the moment Silas
Adler is behind local label Soulland. Adler
came into the fashion business via an
unconventional route – a keen skateboarder,
he started off creating street-style T-shirts,
and in so doing found his calling. His
designs are clean and simple, with his
2011 autumn/winter collection inspired by
the American Civil War. His US Import shop
(*see p150*), which stocks Soulland garb, as
well as other Scandinavian brands, opened
in late 2010. **www.soulland.eu**

STINA GOYA
Founded in 2006, Stine Goya has
established herself as one of the most
interesting female designers on the Danish
market, developing the brand onto the
international scene. With her bold designs,
interesting silhouettes and dominant use
of colour she manages to create collections
with a distinct mood. Through seasonal
collaborations with artists and use of her
own textile designs, Goya has managed
to set a new visual expression within
Scandinavian fashion. **www.stinegoya.com**

JENS LAUGESEN
London-based and Paris-trained, this
critically acclaimed Danish designer is
known for his cerebral yet highly wearable
takes on fashion classics. A master of

streamlined formalwear in black, white and
neutrals, his clothes are sold at Selfridges
and Antipodium in London and in countless
boutiques across Japan.
www.jenslaugesen.com

CAMILLA STÆRK
London-based Camilla Stærk's dark, edgy
yet eminently feminine womenswear has
been featured in Paris *Vogue, Grazia* and
UK *Elle*. Her trademark contrast of black
and neutrals with delicious splashes of
colour has made her work much coveted
in the world's fashion capitals.
www.camillastaerk.co.uk

HENRIK VIBSKOV
Beck's Futures prize winner and Central St
Martin's-trained Henrik Vibskov is one of
Denmark's hottest young designers. His
streetwise clothes, recognisable for their
distinctive prints, are sold all over the world
in fiercely cool shops such as Colette in
Paris, Oak in New York and Pineal Eye in
London. **www.henrikvibskov.com**

Silas Adler.

CONSUME

Norse Store. *See p149.*

US Import

Gammel Kongevej 37 (www.usimportstore.com). Train København H. **Open** 11am-6pm Wed-Fri; 11am-4pm Sat. **Credit** MC, V. **Map** 245 P9.

This tiny shop on Gammel Kongevej stocks Scandinavian designers including owner Silas Adler's Soulland, Stina Goya, Ann Sofie Back from Sweden and Veronica B Vallenes from Norway. US workwear brands such as Pendleton as also represented. The shop is something of a hub for the city's hipsters. *See also p149* **Danish Designers**.

★ Wood Wood

Krystalgade 4 & 7 (33 93 62 64, www. woodwood.dk). Train/metro Nørreport. **Open** 11am-6pm Mon-Thur; 11am-7pm Fri; 11am-4pm Sat. **Credit** AmEx, MC, V. **Map** p251 M13.

Wood Wood started life as a graphic T-shirt brand, moving on to becoming one of Copenhagen's most stylish streetwear-influenced labels. Its a first port-of-call for casual shoes, jackets, T-shirts and more, and now also stocks womenwear too.

Childrenswear

Pluto Børne Sko

Rosengården 12 (33 93 20 12). **Open** 10am-5.30pm Mon-Fri; 10am-2pm Sat. **No credit cards.** **Map** p251 M13.

For nascent foot fetishists everywhere, this children's shoe shop sells trendy footwear for kids whose parents are prepared to pay designer prices.

Designer & boutiques

★ Acne Jeans

Gammel Mønt 10 (33 93 93 28, www.acne jeans.com). Metro Kongens Nytorv. **Open** 11am-7pm Mon-Fri; 10am-5pm Sat. **Credit** AmEx, MC, V. **Map** p251 M14.

A flagship store for this increasingly popular Swedish brand of men's and women's clothing. Streetwise denim is the order of the day, although suits, shoes and plenty of T-shirts are also on offer.

Birger Christensen

Østergade 38, Strøget (33 11 55 55, www.birger-christensen.com). Metro Kongens Nytorv. **Open** 10am-6pm Mon-Thur; 10am-7pm Fri; 10am-5pm Sat. **Credit** AmEx, MC, V. **Map** p251 M15.

Mens- and womenswear, shoes and accessories from a range of top international designers including YSL, Prada, Chanel and Paul Smith, as well as a selection of ostentatious seal and sable furs.

Bruuns Bazaar

Kronprinsensgade 8-9 (33 32 19 99, www. bruunsbazaar.com). Metro Kongens Nytorv.

Open 10am-6pm Mon-Thur; 10am-7pm Fri; 10am-4pm Sat; 10am-5pm 1st & last Sun of mth. **Credit** AmEx, DC, MC, V. **Map** p251 M14.
Set up by the two brothers Bruun in the mid 1990s, Bruuns Bazaar has since found its way on to catwalks around the world. Its mainstays are creative but wearable designs in attractive colours and top-of-the-range fabrics. The women's shop also sells a good range of tiny, delicate, deliciously colourful footwear.

By Malene Birger
Antonigade 6 (35 43 22 33, www.bymalene birger.dk). Metro Kongens Nytorv. **Open** 10am-6pm Mon-Thur; 10am-7pm Fri; 10am-5pm Sat; noon-4pm 1st Sun of mth. **Credit** AmEx, MC, V. **Map** p251 M14.
Luxurious ready-to-wear clothing is the remit of Malene Birger's elegant flagship store, with glamorous but highly wearable designs in beautiful fabrics that have taken the fashion world by storm.

Companys
Frederiksberggade 24, Strøget (33 11 35 55). Train København H. **Open** 10am-7pm Mon-Thur; 10am-8pm Fri; noon-4pm Sat. **Credit** AmEx, MC, V. **Map** p251 O12.
Highlights include By Malene Birger clothing, Marc Jacobs shoes, Miu Miu bags for women and Tiger of Sweden for men. Lower-priced Danish brands InWear, Part II and Matinique can also be found at this one-stop shop for label lovers of both sexes.

DAY Birger et Mikkelsen
Pilestræde 16 (33 45 88 80, www.day.dk). Metro Kongens Nytorv. **Open** 10am-6pm Mon-Thur; 10am-7pm Fri; 10am-5pm Sat; noon-4pm 1st Sun of mth. **Credit** AmEx, MC, V. **Map** p251 M14.
DAY's flagship store is the only place offering every one of the brand's bohemian glamour lines under one roof, from sophisticated mens- and womenswear to a charming range of cool clothing for kids.

Filippa K
Ny Østergade 13 (33 93 80 00, www.filippa-k. com). Metro Kongens Nytorv. **Open** 10am-7pm Mon-Thur; 10am-8pm Fri; 11am-6pm Sat. **Credit** AmEx, MC, V. **Map** p251 M15.
Filippa Kihlborg creates understated clothes with a distinct but internationally relevant Scandinavian style, which many other Copenhagen designers have since struggled (and largely failed) to imitate.

Henrik Vibskov
Krystalgade 6 (33 14 61 00, www.henrikvibskov.com). Train/metro Nørreport. **Open** 11am-6pm Mon-Thur; 10am-7pm Fri; 11am-5pm Sat. **Credit** AmEx, MC, V. **Map** p251 M13.
Henrik Vibskov's cutting-edge designs are top of every Danish fashion insider's wish list. This flagship store offers the complete Vibskov experience, with the full collection of his coveted, edgy designs on sale.

J Lindeberg
Christian IX Gade 1 (33 13 11 77, www. jlindeberg.com). Metro Kongens Nytorv. **Open** 11am-6pm Mon-Thur; 11am-7pm Fri; 10am-4pm Sat. **Credit** AmEx, MC, V. **Map** p251 M14.
A Swedish lifestyle brand with a deep-seated rock 'n' roll aesthetic, J Lindeberg's quality men's and women's tailoring is perennially popular with those seeking unfussy fashion with an underground edge.

Mads Nørgaard
Amagertorv 15, Strøget (33 32 01 28, www. madsnorgaard.dk). Metro Kongens Nytorv. **Open** 10am-6pm Mon-Thur; 10am-7pm Fri; 10am-5pm Sat. **Credit** AmEx, DC, MC, V. **Map** p251 N14.
A wide range of international labels – Prada, Miu Miu, Dries Van Noten, John Smedley and Carhartt – alongside Mads Nørgaard's own-brand clothing. **Other locations** Frederiksberggade 24, Strøget (33 12 18 28).

Moshi Moshi
Dag Hammarskjolds Allé 34, Østerbro (35 38 70 78, www.moshimoshi.dk). Bus 1A, 14. **Open** 11am-6pm Mon-Fri; 11am-3pm Sat. **Credit** AmEx, MC, V. **Map** p247 G14.
Effortlessly stylish womenswear from the likes of Sonia Rykiel, Vanessa Bruno and Acne Jeans. A second, more spiritual branch, Moshi Moshi Mind (Dag Hammarskjolds Allé 40, 35 38 70 79), sells everything from yoga costumes by Filippa K to skincare products from the Organic Pharmacy.

Munthe plus Simonsen
Grønnegade 10 (33 32 03 12, www.muntheplus simonsen.dk). Metro Kongens Nytorv. **Open** 10am-6pm Mon-Thur; 10am-7pm Fri; 10am-4pm Sat. **Credit** AmEx, DC, MC, V. **Map** p251 M15.
Luxurious muted colours abound at Munthe plus Simonsen. The shop is reportedly a favourite of supermodel Helena Christensen and Crown Princess Mary.

★ Parterre
Gammel Kongevej 103 (31 54 43 13, www. parterre.dk). Metro Forum. **Open** 11am-6pm Mon-Fri; 10am-3pm Sat. **Credit** AmEx, MC, V. **Map** p245 O7.
Parterre stocks surpremely tasteful, top-quality and hard-to-find womenswear labels that can't be found elsewhere in Copenhagen, such as Sofie d'Hoore. Simple but stylish cuts are a speciality.

Sabine Poupinel & Co
Kronprinsensgade 12 (33 14 44 34). Metro Kongens Nytorv. **Open** 11am-6pm Mon-Fri; 11am-4pm Sat. **Credit** AmEx, MC, V. **Map** p251 M14.
The old adage that 'if you have to ask how much it costs, you probably can't afford it' gets a shot in the arm at this store, which dispenses with price tags altogether. Hand-crafted, individually tailored, reassuringly expensive clothing.

CONSUME

CONSUME

Sand

Østergade 40, Strøget (33 14 21 21, www.sand-europe.com). Metro Kongens Nytorv. **Open** 10am-6pm Mon-Thur; 10am-7pm Fri; 10am-5pm Sat. **Credit** AmEx, MC, V. **Map** p251 M15.

Divine men's and women's clothes from this archetypal Copenhagen designer store. Sand's simple, elegant style is the epitome of high-end Scandinavian clothing design, but it doesn't come cheap.

Stig P

Kronprinsensgade 14 (33 14 42 16). Metro Kongens Nytorv. **Open** 10am-6pm Mon-Thur; 10am-7pm Fri; 10am-5pm Sat. **Credit** AmEx, DC, MC, V. **Map** p251 M14.

Home to local names like Dico, MAVI and Ganni next to Cacharel, Paul & Joe and Marc Jacobs, not to mention Stig P's highly desirable own-label products. The Nørrebro branch has men's clothing too. **Other locations** Ravnsborggade 18, Nørrebro (35 35 75 00).

★ Storm

Store Regnegade 1 (33 93 00 14). Metro Kongens Nytorv. **Open** 11am-5.30pm Mon-Thur; 11am-7pm Fri; 10am-4pm Sat. **Credit** AmEx, DC, MC, V. **Map** p251 M15.

Line Storm's high-end boutique offers labels like Dries Van Noten, Dior Homme and Raf Simons for the men, plus women's clothes from the likes of Veronique Branquinho, Balenciaga, Chloé and APC. The clean, sparse atmosphere gives the featured clothing the space it needs to breathe, and you may need to take a bit of a deep breath when you see some of the prices.

Wettergren & Wettergren

Læderstræde 5 (33 13 14 05). Metro Kongens Nytorv. **Open** 11am-6pm Mon-Fri; 11am-4pm Sat. **Credit** MC, V. **Map** p251 N14.

Beautifully made womenswear from Danish brands Graumann and Tara Jarmon alongside a small collection of vintage cocktail dresses, every one of them altered to bring them bang up to date.

★ Whyred

Pilestræde 35 (33 69 00 68, www.whyred.com). Metro Kongens Nytorv. **Open** 10am-6pm Mon-Thur; 10am-7pm Fri; 10am-5pm Sat. **Credit** AmEx, MC, V. **Map** p251 M14.

Cool Swedish label Whyred is a combination of clean lines, neat shapes and quirky details. Urban clothing for women and men that's eminently wearable.

Zone 1

Nikolaj Plads 7 (33 12 13 43). Metro Kongens Nytorv. **Open** 11am-6pm Tue-Fri; 11am-4pm Sat. **Credit** AmEx, MC, V. **Map** p251 N15.

Proprieter Jan Machenhauer's own sharply tailored men's and women's clothes are complemented by T-shirts from John Smedley, shoes by Emma Hope and the lavish scarves of French designer Epice.

Erotic

Lust

Mikkel Bryggers Gade 3A (33 33 01 10, www.lust.dk). Train København H. **Open** 11am-7pm Mon-Thur; 11am-8pm Fri; 11am-6pm Sat. **Credit** AmEx, DC, MC, V. **Map** p250 O12.

Lust took Copenhagen's sex shop scene out of the dark ages when it opened in 1999, with a mainstream attitude, central location and an eminently female-friendly atmosphere.

Lingerie

There are comprehensive lingerie departments at both **Illum** and **Magasin** (*see p143*).

Agent Provocateur

Pilestræde 6 (33 91 99 31, www.agent provocateur.com). Metro Kongens Nytorv. **Open** 10am-7pm Mon-Fri; 10am-2pm Sat. **Credit** AmEx, DC, MC, V. **Map** p251 M14.

Agent Provocateur's Copenhagen debut allows Danish women to spice up their underwear drawers with some of the sexiest smalls on the planet.

Fogal

Østergade 2, Strøget (33 14 86 84, www.fogal.com). Metro Kongens Nytorv. **Open** 10am-6pm Mon-Thur; 10am-7pm Fri; 10am-5pm Sat. **Credit** AmEx, MC, V. **Map** p251 M15.

This Swiss purveyor of fine hosiery – a favourite of Queen Margrethe – is the place to find tights and stockings in exactly the right shade, sheerness or size.

Mid-range

Invasion

Vestergade 10 (33 11 00 26, www.invasion.dk). Train/metro Nørreport. **Open** 10am-6.30pm Mon-Thur; 10am-7pm Fri; 10am-5pm Sat. **Credit** AmEx, MC, V. **Map** p250 O12.

Invasion has a huge stock of painfully trendy clothes that, in one of life's tragic ironies, only skinny teenagers can get away with wearing, but only the over-20s are able to afford. **Other locations** Frederiksborggade 12 (33 93 79 77); Falkoner Allé 45, Frederiksberg (38 33 35 34).

InWear/Matinique

Østergade 27, Strøget (33 14 20 41, www.inwear.com). Train/metro Kongens Nytorv. **Open** 10am-6pm Mon-Thur, Sat; 10am-8pm Fri. **Credit** AmEx, MC, V. **Map** p251 M15.

A quality mens- and womenswear chain, offering affordable alternatives to current designer trends and a great line in stylish suits and eveningwear.

Vero Moda

Østergade 7-9, Strøget (33 15 88 15, www.veromoda.dk). Metro Kongens Nytorv. **Open**

10am-6pm Mon-Thur; 10am-7pm Fri; 10am-5pm Sat; noon-4pm 1st Sun of mth. **Credit** AmEx, MC, V. **Map** p251 M15.

With three branches along Strøget alone, this Danish chain is clearly making a name for itself among women who want wearable, work-friendly versions of catwalk trends at high-street prices. **Other locations** throughout the city.

Second-hand & vintage

Head to Vestergade for the widest selection of second-hand and vintage clothes shops.

Atelier Décor

Rømersgade 9 (33 14 80 98, www.decorvintage. dk). Train/metro Nørreport. **Open** noon-6pm Tue-Fri; 10am-4pm Sat. **Credit** V. **Map** p246 L12. Located next to the Israels Plads Saturday flea market, this wonderful store offers Copenhagen ladies the chance to unearth quality vintage clothing

at bargain prices, while Edith Piaf sets a suitably nostalgic tone on the shop stereo.

Boutique Chic

Naboløs 4 (33 11 42 60). Metro Kongens Nytorv. **Open** 10am-5pm Tue-Sat. **No credit cards.** **Map** p251 N14.

This dress agency sells quality used clothing and accessories for women by designer labels, including suits by Chanel, Escada and Max Mara.

Kitsch Bitch

Læderstræde 30 (33 13 63 13). Metro Kongens Nytorv. **Open** noon-6pm Mon-Fri; noon-5pm Sat & 1st Sun of mth. **Credit** MC, V. **Map** p251 N14.

A fabulous little treasure trove of a shop, loaded with 1950s, '60s and '70s fashion gems. There's also the kind of kitsch Swedish kitchenware that would have caused death by social embarrassment any time earlier than the 21st century.

Time's Up Vintage. *See p154.*

CONSUME

CONSUME

Bruno & Joel.

★ Time's Up Vintage

Krystalgade 4 (33 32 39 30, www.times-up.dk).
Train/metro Nørreport. **Open** 11am-6pm
Mon-Fri; 11am-5pm Sat. **Credit** AmEx, MC, V.
Map p251 M13.
Located on a lovely street in central Copenhagen,
Time's Up has a well-edited selection of designer vin-
tage clothing, with art deco pieces (with a particu-
larly good jewellery range) and couture from Chanel,
Dior and Givenchy all appearing. The variety of
shoes is also strong. *Photos p153.*
Other locations Blågårdsgade 2A (35 10 61 89).

FASHION ACCESSORIES

Bags

Gucci, Hermès, Mulberry and Louis
Vuitton all have shops on Strøget; Loewe
and Burberry can be found at **Magasin** and
Illum respectively.

Friis & Company

Købmagergade 41 (33 91 01 70, www.friis-co.dk).
Metro Kongens Nytorv. **Open** 10am-6pm Mon-
Thur; 10am-7pm Fri; 11am-5pm Sat. **Credit**
AmEx, MC, V. **Map** p251 M14.
Affordable bags, shoes and accessories adorned
with the distinctive fleur-de-lys motif and diamanté
crown of this popular Danish brand. Staff here are
particularly helpful, so don't be afraid to ask them
for advice or recommendations.

Neye

Vimmelskaftet 28, Strøget (33 69 28 33, www.
neye.dk). Metro Kongens Nytorv. **Open** 10am-
Mon-Thur; 10am-7pm Fri; 10am-5pm Sat; 11am-
4pm 1st Sun of mth. **Credit** AmEx, MC, V.
Map p251 N13.
The city's largest bag shop, with handbags, luggage
and rucksacks to suit most mainstream tastes. Well-
known brands include Samsonite, Carlton and
Florentine manufacturer Bridge, which offer a nice
line in leather suitcases and satchels.

Hats

Chapeaux Petitgas

Købmagergade 5 (33 13 62 70). Metro Kongens
Nytorv. **Open** 10am-5.30pm Mon-Fri; 10am-1pm
Sat. **Credit** AmEx, MC, V. **Map** p251 N14.
Nothing much has changed over the century-and-a-
half that Chapeaux Petitgas has been furnishing the
heads of Copenhagen's gentlemen – but that, of
course, is all part of its charm.

Samarkand

Dag Hammarskjölds Allé 32 (35 38 14 45,
www.samarkand.dk). Train/metro Østerport or
bus 1A, 14, 40. **Open** noon-6pm Mon-Fri; 11am-
3pm Sat. **Credit** AmEx, MC, V. **Map** p247 G14.
Eberlein makes only 100 luxurious Mongolian-style
embroidered silk and fur hats a year, and Queen
Silvia of Sweden and Hillary Clinton are among the
well-to-do heads she has covered in the past.

Susanne Juul

Store Kongensgade 14 (33 32 25 22). Metro Kongens Nytorv. **Open** 11am-5.30pm Tue-Thur; 11am-6pm Fri; 10am-2pm Sat. **Credit** MC, V. **Map** p249 L16.

Designs range from Tibetan-inspired wool beanies to wide-brimmed chic chapeaux from the milliner of Denmark's Crown Princess Mary.

Shoes

A Pair

Ny Østergade 3 (33 91 99 20, www.apair.dk). Metro Kongens Nytorv. **Open** 10am-6pm Mon-Thur; 10am-7pm Fri; 10am-5pm Sat. **Credit** AmEx, MC, V. **Map** p251 M15.

One of Copenhagen's most popular mid- to high-end shoe shops, selling shoes, boots and bags, with own-brand designs on offer alongside international labels. **Other locations** Nansensgade 39 (33 33 99 24); Copenhagen airport (32 51 99 24).

Bruno & Joel

Kronprinsensgade 2 (33 13 87 78, www.bruno-joel.com). Bus 11A. **Open** 11am-6pm Mon-Fri; 10am-4pm Sat. **Credit** AmEx, MC, V. **Map** p251 M14.

Unbelievably chic Danish-designed, Italian-made foot candy for quality shoe junkies. Both women's and men's styles are also sold here.

FOOD & DRINK

Bakeries & pâtisseries

Conditoriet La Glace

Skoubougade 3-5, Strøget (33 14 46 46). Bus 11A, 14. **Open** 8.30am-5.30pm Mon-Thur; 8.30am-6pm Fri; 9am-5pm Sat. **No credit cards**. **Map** p251 N13.

The city's oldest pâtisserie and tea salon is an institution among Danes with a taste for the sweeter things in life. Generous slices of the dozen or so fairytale-sized cakes in the window are available to take out, as are the delightfully dainty cream cakes and traditional Danish pastries.

Emmerys

Vesterbrogade 34, Vesterbro (33 22 77 63, www.emmerys.dk). Bus 6A, 26. **Open** 7am-6pm Mon-Fri; 7.30am-3pm Sat, Sun. **Credit** MC, V. **Map** p250 P10.

One bite of chewy Emmerys bread and you'll be sold. The ingredients (only organic flour, salt and water) sound about as exciting as a piece of dry cracker, but Emmerys claims to use a 5,000-year-old method in its production. The same bread is used for the (pricey) lunchtime sandwiches with fillings like serrano ham, marinated artichokes and parsley pesto.
Other locations throughout the city.

Lagkagehuset Bageri og Konditori

Torvegade 45, Christianshavn (32 57 36 07, www.lagkagehuset.dk). **Open** 6am-7pm daily. **No credit cards**. **Map** p252 P16.

Fresh bread, cakes and divine pastries are sold at this busy Christianshavn bakery, which has expanded into a chain over the past few years. The perfect place to sample an authentic Danish pastry. *Photos p157.*
Other locations Vesterbrogade 4A (33 11 36 07); Falkoner Alle 4 (33 23 07 10); Frederiksberggade 21 (72 48 47 77).

Butchers

Upmarket butchers/café **Gourmandiet** (*see p142*) in genteel Østerbro sells top-quality, organic meat, and has a great brunch menu.

Slagteren ved Kultorvet

Frederiksborggade 4 (33 12 29 02, www.kultorvet. dk). Train/metro Nørreport. **Open** 8am-5.30pm Mon-Thur; 8am-7pm Fri; 8am-2pm Sat. **Credit** MC, V. **Map** p247 L13.

Butcher Jens Slagter – whom you'll often find quoted in the Danish media for his 'you are what you eat' views – has built up a huge customer base for his quality products. This is a great place to try one of the several types of Danish salami or bacon — the smell of the place alone (the smoking oven is in the back) will make your stomach rumble.

Chocolate & confectioners

Peter Beier

Skoubougade 1 (33 93 07 17, www.peterbeier chokolade.dk). Bus 11A, 14. **Open** 10am-6pm Mon-Thur; 10am-7pm Fri; 10am-4pm Sat. **Credit** AmEx, MC, V. **Map** p251 N13.

The essence of chocolate chic, this modern shop, run by the charming Bagger family, offers premium quality chocolates in customisable gift boxes, plus dessert and port wines to accompany more refined tasting sessions. Prices start at 52kr for 100g.

Sømods Bolcher

Nørregade 24 & 36 (33 12 60 46, www.soemods-bolcher.dk). Train/metro Nørreport. **Open** 9.15am-5.30pm Mon-Thur; 9.15am-6pm Fri; 10am-2.30pm Sat. **Credit** AmEx, DC, MC, V. **Map** p250 M12.

There has been a traditional boiled candy factory and shop here on Nørregade since 1891, and you can still watch the multicoloured sweets being made by the fourth generation of the Sømod family.

Coffee & tea

★ AC Perchs Thehandel

Kronprinsensgade 5 (33 15 35 62, www.perchs-the.dk). Metro Kongens Nytorv. **Open** 9am-5.30pm Mon-Fri; 9.30am-4pm Sat. **Credit** MC, V. **Map** p251 M14.

CONSUME

Copenhagen's most venerated and venerable tea emporium dates from 1834 and is currently in the hands of the sixth generation of the Perch family. The glorious, wood-panelled interior is lined with old-fashioned jars of tea leaves (own blends as well as some more exotic brands), and the staff are only too happy to help you choose. Also the Darjeeling First Flush comes highly recommended. Note that the café has separate opening times:11.30am-5.30pm Mon-Fri; 11am-5.30pm Sat.

Østerlandsk Thehus

Nørre Voldgade 9 (33 13 10 00, www. osterlandskthehus.dk). Train/metro Nørreport. **Open** 10am-6pm Mon-Fri; 10am-3pm Sat. **Credit** AmEx, MC, V. **Map** p246 L12.

What Perchs is to tea, Østerlandsk Thehus is to Copenhagen's coffee scene. The interior of the shop has recently been restored to its former glory, originally decorated by the designer behind Tivoli's chinoiserie decor. The stock incorporates the finest coffee beans from around the world, own blends and a dazzling assortment of gleaming coffee makers and equimpment.

Delicatessens

Værnedamsvej (*see p85*) in Frederiksberg has lots of gourmet food shops.

Løgismose

Nordre Toldbod 16 (33 32 93 32, www.loegismose. dk). Train Østerport. **Open** 10am-7pm Mon-Fri; 10am-3pm Sat. **Credit** AmEx, DC, MC, V. **Map** p249 J18.

What started out as a wine importer attached to the renowned restaurant Kong Hans Kaelder has grown into the best gourmet supermarket in town, with an eclectic mix of items, from Harvey Nichols tins and jars to delicious Valhrona chocolates. The shop also produces its own serve-yourself meals and there is an in-house butcher's and baker's as well.

Fish

Gammel Strand stall

Gammel Strand (no phone). Metro Kongens Nytorv. **Open** 10am-2pm Mon-Fri. **No credit cards.** **Map** p251 N14.

INSIDE TRACK CUPCAKES

The cupcake trend has finally reached Copenhagen. **Agnes Cupcakes** (Sværtegade 2, 31 20 60 00, www. agnescupcakes.com) has been a sugar-laden hit since it opened its alluring shop in 2010, and lays claim to being Denmark's first cupcake bakery.

The last remnant of Gammel Strand's fishing heritage is this sole fish seller. Strange to think that this single stall is all that remains of a city that was founded on herring landed from the Øresund.

Health & organic food

Egefeld

Gammel Kongevej 113, Frederiksberg (33 28 20 20, www.egefeld.dk). Metro Forum. **Open** 10am-7pm Mon-Fri; 10am-5pm Sat, Sun. **Credit** MC, V. **Map** p250 O7.

An award-winning, comprehensively stocked one-stop shop for the city's eco-friendly. As wide a selection of organic products as you'll find anywhere.

International

Abigail's

Peder Hvidtfeldts Stræde 17 (33 16 41 79). Train/metro Nørreport. **Open** 10.30am-5.30pm Mon-Thur; 10.30am-6pm Fri; 10am-4pm Sat. **No credit cards. Map** p251 M13.

Who'd have thought there'd be a market for selling British sweets, tinned food and crisps to the Danes? This is the place to come when only British teabags, sausages and baked beans will do.

Wines, beers & spirits

Kjær og Sommerfeldt

Gammel Mønt 4 (33 93 34 44, www.kogs.dk). **Open** 10am-5.30pm Mon-Thur; 10am-6pm Fri; 10am-2pm Sat. **Credit** AmEx, MC, V. **Map** p251 M14.

Sommerfeldt's wood-panelled interior is more akin to a gentlemen's club than an off-licence. The shop speciality is Bordeaux wines, but it also has an entire room dedicated to Scottish and Irish single malts.

★ Ølbutikken

Oehlenschlægersgade 2, Vesterbro (33 22 03 04, www.olbutikken.dk). Bus 6A. **Open** 3-7pm Wed-Fri; 11am-3pm Sat. **Credit** MC, V. **Map** p245 Q8.

The microbrewery movement exploded in Copenhagen a few years' back (*see p138* **A Room with a Brew**), and this beer shop rose to the challenge magnificently, selling a selection of Danish micro beers and international alternatives.

FURNITURE

Casa Shop

Store Regnegade 2 (33 32 70 41, www.casa group.com). Metro Kongens Nytorv. **Open** 10am-5.30pm Mon-Thur; 10am-6pm Fri; 10am-3pm Sat. **Credit** AmEx, MC, V. **Map** p251 M15.

Casa is one of the country's premier retailers of contemporary furniture, but there are plenty of smaller, quirkier pieces to catch, such as Nemo lamps and Ron Arad's flexible Bookworm bookshelf.

Lagkagehuset Bageri og Konditori.
See p155.

Hay CPH
Pilestræde 29-31 (99 42 44 00, www.hay.dk).
Metro Kongens Nytorv. **Open** 11am-6pm
Mon-Fri; 10am-4pm Sat. **Credit** AmEx, MC, V.
Map p251 M14.
Walking into Hay's you might be forgiven for think-
ing you've stumbled on a chic version of the
Teletubbies house. Simple, rounded forms and mod-
ular, felt-covered units in primary colours abound.
Tinky Winky is no fool, however, for these Danish
designs are supremely comfortable. There's a second
showroom upstairs and the website gives a good
idea of what's in store. *Photos p158.*

Illums Bolighus
*Royal Shopping, Amagertorv 10, Strøget (33
14 19 41, www.illumsbolighus.com). Metro
Kongens Nytorv.* **Open** 10am-7pm Mon-Fri;
10am-6pm Sat; noon-5pm Sun. **Credit** AmEx,
MC, V. **Map** p251 N14.
The homeware arm of department store Illum boasts
a selection of premium brands including Orrefors,
Arabia and Alessi, while connecting doors lead into
the Royal Copenhagen, Holmegaard and Georg
Jensen shops.

★ Paustian
*Kalkbrænderiløbskaj 2, Østerbro (39 16 65 65,
www.paustian.dk). Train Nordhavn or bus 26.*
Open 10am-6pm Mon-Fri; 10am-3pm Sat.
Credit AmEx, MC, V.

It's a bit of a trek to get over here, but Paustian's
stunning warehouse – designed by Jørn Utzon of
Sydney Opera House fame – makes the trip worthwhile. Inside, you'll find the likes of Aalto, Eames,
Starck and Jacobsen.

HI-FI/HOME ENTERTAINMENT

Bang & Olufsen
*Kongens Nytorv 26 (33 11 14 15/www.bang-
olufsen.com).* **Open** 10am-6pm Mon-Thur; 10am-
7pm Fri; 10am-4pm Sat. **Credit** AmEx, DC, MC,
V. **Map** p251 M15.
Danes are justifiably proud of this top-notch brand
of televisions, stereos and telephones, the minimalist modern masterpieces of which constantly dominate the world's fashion and design bibles.
Other locations Nørre Voldgade 8 (33 12 33 08);
Fisketorvet shopping centre, Kalvebod Brygge
59, Vesterbro (33 11 34 50).

Fona
*Østergade 47, Strøget (33 15 90 55, www.
fona.dk). Metro Kongens Nytorv.* **Open** 10am-6pm
Mon-Thur; 10am-7pm Fri; 10am-5pm Sat. **Credit**
AmEx, MC, V. **Map** p251 M15.
Denmark's largest home entertainment chain stocks
plenty of well-known home entertainment and com-
puter brands, including the likes of Apple and Bang
& Olufsen.
Other locations throughout the city.

CONSUME

HOMEWARES

Kaiku
Kompagnistræde 8 (33 11 19 07, www.kaiku.dk).
Metro Kongens Nytorv. **Open** 11am-5.30pm
Mon-Thur; 11am-6pm Fri; 10am-3pm Sat.
Credit AmEx, MC, V. **Map** p251 N13.
Affordable, design-led homewares and knick-knacks
are sold in this friendly, popular shop, on a lovely
central street (*see p159* **Inside Track**). It's a good
bet for original presents.

Le Klint
Store Kirkestræde 1 (33 11 66 63, www.le
klint.com). Metro Kongens Nytorv. **Open** 10am-
6pm Tue-Fri; 10am-4pm Sat. **Credit** MC, V.
Map p251 N14.
This is the main stockist for Kaare Klint's trademark
concertina-style lampshades, including his perennially popular 'Model 1', folded by hand since 1943.

Normann Copenhagen
Østerbrogade 70, Østerbro (35 55 44 59, www.
normann-copenhagen.com). Bus 1A, 14, 15, 650S.
Open 10am-6pm Mon-Fri; 10am-4pm Sat. **Credit**
AmEx, MC, V. **Map** p248 E14.
Normann Copenhagen's home accessories take centre stage in this former theatre, with a huge range
of effortlessy sleek and streamlined domestic
designware, from arty vases to achingly modern
salad sets.

Søstrene Grene
Amagertorv 29, Strøget (no phone, www.
grenes.dk). Metro Kongens Nytorv. **Open** 10am-
7pm Mon-Fri; 10am-5pm Sat; 11am-4pm 1st Sun
of mth. **No credit cards**. **Map** p251 N14.
People either love Søstrene Grene's lucky dip potential or loathe its often brazenly poor-quality stock,
but there's no denying that there are gems aplenty
lurking among its collection of oddball crockery,
toys, bedding, glassware and miscellaneous gifts.

Tom Rossau Showroom
Istedgade 59, Vesterbro (51 92 47 17, www.
tomrossau.dk). Bus 10. **Open** 11am-6pm Mon-Fri;
11am-3pm Sat. **Credit** MC, V. **Map** p245 R9.
Tom Rossau's beautiful lamps are made from sustainable, natural wood veneers, with retro stylings.

Vi Ses
Valkendorfsgade 3 (33 12 33 15, www.blindes-
arbejde.dk). Metro Kongens Nytorv. **Open** 11am-
5.30pm Mon-Fri; 10am-2pm Sat. **Credit** AmEx,
MC, V. **Map** p251 N13.
Whether it's for bottles, hair or nails, Vi Ses has the
brush for you, plus there's a nice line in wooden toys
to amuse kids while parents browse the bristles.
Great for obsessive compulsives with a cleaning
complex. A large part of the stock is made up of
brushes made by blind people.

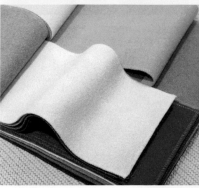

Hay CPH. *See p157.*

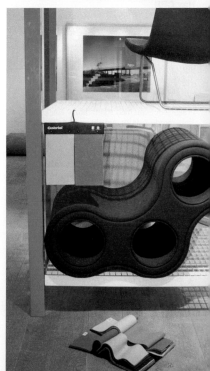

JEWELLERY

★ Georg Jensen
Amagertorv 4, Strøget (33 11 40 80, www. georgjensen.com). Metro Kongens Nytorv. **Open** 10am-6pm Mon-Thur; 10am-7pm Fri; 10am-5pm Sat. **Credit** AmEx, MC, V. **Map** p251 N14.
The undisputed daddy of Danish silver design, Jensen's showroom boasts elaborate flower arrangements artfully complementing the ornate jewellery on display. There's also a museum at the back showcasing the history of the company.

Halberstadt
Østergade 4 (33 15 97 90, www.halberstadt.com). Metro Kongens Nytorv. **Open** 10am-5.30pm Mon-Fri; 10am-3pm Sat. **Credit** AmEx, MC, V. **Map** p251 M15.
Since 1846 Halberstadt has been selling elaborate, often bespoke jewellery with an emphasis on Danish amber. Even if you don't feel like stepping inside, it's worth checking out the Golden Train, a solid gold, diamond-encrusted toy pulling a cargo of real rubies, sapphires and emeralds inside the window.

Monies
Nordre Toldbod 17 (33 91 33 33, www.monies. dk). Bus 1A. **Open** 10am-5pm Mon-Fri. **Credit** AmEx, MC, V. **Map** p249 J18.
Spectacular formal jewellery by designer couple Gerda and Nikolai Monies, who use jade, bone, wood and amber, among other materials, to create truly original sculptural statements.

MUSIC

Accord
Vestergade 37 (70 15 16 17, www.accord.dk). Train København H. **Open** 10am-6pm Mon-Thur; 10am-7pm Fri; 10am-4pm Sat; noon-5pm Sun. **Credit** AmEx, MC, V. Note there is a 10% surcharge for foreign credit cards. **Map** p250 O12.
Stacks of old and new vinyl, including a whole floor of 78s, along with hundreds of CDs and DVDs make this a good hunting ground for those who want to pick up a bit of music. Techno, house, rock, pop and world music are the main genres. There's also a good selection of new release titles and the prices are competitive as well.

Danacord
Vognmagergade 9 (33 11 22 51, www. danacord.dk). **Open** 10am-5.30pm Mon-Thur; 10am-6pm Fri; 10am-2pm Sat. **Credit** AmEx, MC, V. **Map** p251 M14.
Unpretentious, mildly chaotic but as comprehensive as you'll get, this is supposedly Scandinavia's largest classical music store. Stock is mainly new CDs, but there's some second-hand vinyl available too. The shop has recently undergone a significant facelift, after being taken over by a Danish record label.

Sex Beat Records
Studiestræde 18 (33 12 82 92, www.sexbeat records.dk). Train/metro Nørreport. **Open** 11am-6pm Mon-Fri; 11am-4pm Sat. **Credit** MC, V. **Map** p250 N12.
New and used British and American indie rock and metal is the speciality at Sex Beat Records, where the staff are extremely knowledgeable about everyone from 16 Horsepower to White Zombie. It's also one of the best places in town to pick up tickets for local gigs.

OPTICIANS & EYEWEAR

Poul Stig Briller
Østergade 24, Strøget (33 15 52 52, www. poulstigbriller.dk). Metro Kongens Nytorv. **Open** 10am-6pm Mon-Thur; 10am-7pm Fri; 10am-4pm Sat. **Credit** AmEx, MC, V. **Map** p251 M15.
Smart, minimal and consistently cool eyewear in the only boutique in Denmark offering products from the venerable Poul Stig.

OUTLET SHOPPING

Langelinie Pier
Langelinie Alle. **Open** 11am-6pm daily. **Credit** varies. **Map** p249 H18.
There are over a dozen outlet stores under the arches of Langelinie Pier. Casual clothing by Danish labels such as Noa Noa and Friis Company mingle with international brands like Diesel and Miss Sixty, with the end result that only the most obstinate meanie will be able to leave empty-handed.

Royal Copenhagen Factory Outlet
Søndre Fasanvej 9, Frederiksberg (38 34 10 04, www.royalcopenhagen.com). Metro Fasanvej or bus 14, 15. **Open** 10am-7pm Mon-Fri; 10am-5pm Sat. **Credit** AmEx, MC, V.
Reduced prices on items from the prestigious Royal Copenhagen group (including silver from Georg Jensen and glass by Holmegaard), mostly end-of-line products or seconds with no discernible flaws.

PHARMACIES

Steno Apotek
Vesterbrogade 6C (33 14 82 66). Train København H. **Open** 24hrs daily. **Credit** AmEx, MC, V. **Map** p250 P10.

CONSUME

Steno Apotek is a 24-hour chemist facing Central Station. Please note that there is a small surcharge (15kr) on any purchases made outside normal business hours.

PHOTOGRAPHY & FILM PROCESSING

Kontant Foto

Købmagergade 44 (33 12 00 29, www.kontant foto.dk). Metro Kongens Nytorv. **Open** 10am-6pm Mon-Thur; 10am-7pm Fri; 10am-4pm Sat. **Credit** AmEx, MC, V. **Map** p251 M14.

Konstant Foto is a conveniently located film processors and camera stockist.

★ Photografica

Skindergade 41 (33 14 12 15, www.photografica. com). **Open** 9.30am-5.30pm Mon-Thur; 9.30am-6pm Fri; 9.30am-3pm Sat. **Credit** AmEx, MC, V. **Map** p251 N13.

An Aladdin's cave of top brands (Hasselblad, Leica), equipment and accessories.

SERVICES/REPAIRS

Dry cleaning & alterations

Schleisner Rens

Vester Voldgade 12 (33 11 00 37). Train/metro Vesterport or København H. **Open** 8am-5.30pm Mon-Fri; 10am-2pm Sat. **No credit cards**. **Map** p250 O12.

This dry cleaners offers same-day cleaning on items brought in before 10am.

Key cutting & shoe repairs

Hælebaren

Østergade 16, Strøget (33 91 02 20). Metro Kongens Nytorv. **Open** 10am-6pm Mon-Fri; 10am-4pm Sat. **Credit** MC, V. **Map** p251 M15.

Hælebaren is a centrally located key cutter and shoe repairer.

SPORT/CYCLING

Christiania Cykler

Refshalevej 2, Christiania (32 95 45 20, www. pedersenbicycle.dk). Metro Christianshavn. **Open** 10am-5.30pm Mon-Fri. **No credit cards**. **Map** p253 O19.

Christiania Cykler's most interesting item is the idiosyncratic Pedersen bike. Based on a design from the early 20th century, the bike was the work of Mikael Pedersen, who was tired of getting a sore backside from riding. He devised a swinging hammock-like leather seat, then built a unique pyramid-style frame to support it. Today, the shop builds 40 to 50 specially ordered Pedersen bikes a year, about half of which are shipped abroad.

★ Cykelfabrikken

Istedgade 92 (27 12 32 32, www.cykelfabrikken. dk). Train København H. **Open** 1-6pm Tue-Fri; 11am-3pm Sat. **Credit** AmEx, MC, V. **Map** p245 T9.

These well-designed, simple bikes are a perfect blend of track and Scandinavian upright frames. The stylish shop opened in 2009, and fits in perfectly on independents-heavy Istedgade.

Eventyr Sport

Nørre Voldgade 9 (33 93 66 21, www.eventyr sport.dk). Train/metro Nørreport. **Open** 10am-6pm Mon-Fri; 10am-3pm Sat. **Credit** AmEx, MC, V. **Map** p250 L12.

Eventyr Sport sells camping equipment, climbing gear, clothing for heavy duty outdoor use and all the usual accoutrements required for survival in the wilderness (or Copenhagen in winter).

★ Sögreni of Copenhagen

Sankt Peders Stræde 30A (33 12 78 79, www. sogreni.dk). Train/metro Nørreport. **Open** noon-6pm Mon; 10am-6pm Tue-Thur; 10am-7pm Fri; 11am-3pm Sat. **Credit** AmEx, MC, V. **Map** p250 N12.

This high-end bicycle maker produces a limited quantity of traditional-looking yet ultra-modern bikes, several of which have been featured in *Wallpaper** magazine and sell at the Conran Shop in London. Prices start at around 6,000kr and go up to 12,000kr.

STATIONERY

Ordning & Reda

Grønnegade 1B (33 32 30 18, www.ordning-reda.com). Metro Kongens Nytorv. **Open** 10am-6pm Mon-Fri; 10am-4pm Sat. **Credit** AmEx, MC, V. **Map** p251 M15.

Delectable designer paper, folders, photo albums and other stationery from this stylish Swedish chain. **Other locations** Magasin department store (*see p143*).

SUPERMARKETS

Irma

Nørre Voldgade 78 (33 15 10 94, www.irma.dk). Train/metro Nørreport. **Open** 8am-8pm Mon-Fri; 9am-8pm Sat. **Credit** MC, V. **Map** p250 O12.

A high-end central supermarket with a good selection of fine food and wine. **Other locations** Irma City, Vesterbrogade 46 (33 79 02 39).

REMA 1000

Hammerichsgade 1 (33 93 68 63). **Open** 8am-8pm Mon-Sat; 8am-5pm Sun. **Credit** MC, V. **Map** p250 O11.

Well stocked and centrally located.

Neighbourhood Boutiques

The city's main residential districts are all bursting with independent shops.

Cykelfabrikken.

CONSUME

FREDERIKSBERG

Værnedamsvej is fit to burst with specialist food stores, including gourmet butchers, bakers and bagel makers, while Gammel Kongevej offers a mix of clothing and accessory shops to rival the best in the city centre, including **Parterre** (*see p151*), **nué** (Gammel Kongevej 111, 33 24 33 02, www.nuecph.com) and **B.APS** (No.91; 33 21 58 00), the latter selling a gorgeous selection of quality women's brands including Chloé, Cacharel and D&G. Foodies, meanwhile, should head for **Meyer's Deli** (*see p138*), the gourmet food shop and café of celebrity chef Claus Meyer.

ØSTERBRO

Østerbro is the height of chic. Classensgade has plenty of quality fashion and jewellery boutiques, and eminently stylish homeware accessories from **Weber Furniture** (No.25; 33 23 77 17). Beside the lake, Østerbrogade is home to the flagship store of **Normann Copenhagen** (No.70; 35 55 44 59), a veritable temple to modern Danish design housed in a former theatre, while neighbouring Nordre Frihavnsgade offers a variety of shops – from traditional grocers and antiques dealers to trendy gift shops. There are also tons of high-end childrenswear shops.

VESTERBRO

Vesterbrogade, the main street, is teeming with shopping opportunities, although Istedgade has an interesting collection of smaller, more streetwise fashion shops. Highlights include **Donn Ya Doll** (No.55; 33 22 66 35, www.donnya doll.dk), which offers a mix of quirky gift items, casual clothes and accessories; **Asfalt** (No.83; 33 22 51 74), which boasts second-hand and customised clothing; and **Cykelfabrikken** (*see p160*), which sells simple, retro-style bikes.

NØRREBRO

Ravnsborggade, best known for its antique and second-hand furniture shops, has become a thriving fashion centre with **Stig P** (No.18; 35 35 75 00) and **Dico** (No.21; 35 34 24 90) among its biggest designer emporiums, while **LLLP** (No.18; 35 36 60 04), on nearby Fælledvej, has hip brands like Camilla Stærk and Jens Laugesen alongside its functional custom furniture. Elmegade, meanwhile, has an abundance of trendy clothing shops, such as **Velour** (No.21, 35 35 60 64) for men's and women's threads, as well as excellent retro homewares shop **Bruun's Indretning** (No.24, 26 16 99 01).

CONSUME

Lego Flagship.

TICKET AGENTS

BilletNet (www.billetnet.dk) is Denmark's online ticket agent; **Sex Beat Records** (*see p159*) also sells tickets to local concerts.

TOYS

Build-a-Bear Workshop

Vesterbrogade 3 (33 13 80 30, www.builda bear.dk). Train København H. **Open** 11am-6pm Mon-Thur; 11am-7pm Fri; 10am-6pm Sat, Sun. **Credit** MC, V. **Map** p251 O11.
A wildly successful stuffed toy shop where visitors put together their own furry friends from scratch.

Dansk Håndværk

Kompagnistræde 20 (33 11 45 52). Bus 11A, 14. **Open** 11am-5.30pm Mon-Thur; 11am-6pm Fri; 11am-3pm Sat. **Credit** AmEx, MC, V. **Map** p251 O13.
Local craftsman Lars Jensen has been producing traditional wooden toys for almost 30 years, and this small cellar shop is full of hand-crafted, brightly coloured playthings for under-fives.

Fætter BR

Frederiksberggade 11 (35 26 21 24, www.br-leg. dk). Train/metro Nørreport. **Open** 10am-6pm Mon-Thur; 10am-7pm Fri; 10am-5pm Sat. **Credit** AmEx, MC, V. **Map** p250 O12.
Denmark's biggest toyshop chain, with lots of Lego as well as international brands.
Other locations Bremerholmen 4 (35 46 21 14); Købmagergade 9 (35 46 21 06).

Faraos Cigarer

Skindergade 27 (33 32 22 11, www.faraos.dk). Train/metro Nørreport. **Open** 11am-5.30pm Mon-Thur; 10am-4pm Fri; 10am-3pm Sat; 10am-4pm 1st & last Sun of mth. **Credit** AmEx, MC, V. **Map** p251 N13.
Copenhagen's answer to London's Forbidden Planet is a meeting place for people who collect comics, role-playing figures and *Star Wars* merchandise.

★ Lego Flagship

Vimmelskaftet 37, Strøget (www.lego.dk). Metro Kongens Nytorv. **Open** 10am-6pm Mon-Thur; 10am-7pm Fri; 10am-4pm Sat; noon-4pm 1st Sun of mth. **Credit** MC, V. **Map** p251 N13.
See p173 **Follow the Lego-brick Road**.

Solspejlet

Frederiksborggade 41 (33 33 72 12, www. solspejlet.dk). Train/metro Nørreport. **Open** 11am-5pm Mon-Fri; 11am-2pm Sat; 10am-4pm 1st & last Sun of mth. **Credit** AmEx, MC, V. **Map** p246 L12.
Handmade toys including painted wooden fruit and veg for budding shopkeepers and miniature wicker shopping baskets for aspiring shopaholics.

Arts & Entertainment

The Queen's Birthday. *See p164.*

Calendar	**164**
For One Night Only	166
Children	**168**
Profile Christiana Bike	170
Follow the Lego-brick Road	173
Film	**174**
Galleries	**178**
See and Be Seen	181
Gay & Lesbian	**182**
Nightlife	**185**
Performing Arts	**191**
Profile Royal Danish	
Theatre	192
Profile DR Koncerthuset	197
Sport & Fitness	**200**
Skate Copenhagen	203

Calendar

From summer fun to winter blues bars, Copenhagen loves to celebrate.

Scandinavians aren't exactly renowned for their love of festivals or public expressions of joy, but Copenhagen nevertheless has a wealth of annual cultural, artistic and festive events that hold a great appeal for visitors. The events listed in this chapter are just the highlights: individual chapters have a wider selection and more information. For further details and precise dates of the year's events in the city, the lavishly named **Wonderful Copenhagen Tourist Information Bureau** (70 22 24 42, www.visitcopenhagen.dk) has a superb English website with up-to-the minute listings and reviews of sporting and cultural events.

For those who want to avoid the queues, Danish school holidays begin around the end of June and finish in the first week of August. For a list of public holidays, *see Directory*.

SPRING

The Queen's Birthday
Date 16 Apr.
The Danes are united by their fondness for their multi-talented Queen Margrethe II and her birthday is cause for celebration across the country. The Queen herself makes an appearance on a balcony at Amalienborg Slot at noon, while the Royal Life Guards mark the occasion by parading in their finest ceremonial dress.

CPH:PIX
33 12 00 05, www.cphpix.dk.
Date Mid-Apr to early May.
CPH:PIX represents the merging of Denmark's two premier film festivals (NatFilm Festivalen and the Copenhagen Film Festival). Day and night for two weeks in mid April the city's many cinemas showcase over 200 films, with directors often turning up to talk about their work after the screenings.

May Day
Fælledparken, Østerbro. Bus 1A, 95N.
Map p248 E12. **Date** 1 May.
Head to Østerbro for this trades unions-led festival of the working man, complete with live music and ethnic food.

Ølfestival (Beer Festival)
TAP 1, Ny Carlsbergvej 91 (www.beerfestival.dk). Train to Enghave. **Tickets** 100kr-200kr (with tastings) available in advance from BilletNet (www.billetnet.dk). **Date** 3 days late May.
The growth of microbreweries has finally challenged the stronghold of Carlsberg and interest in beer is growing fast in Denmark. This is the country's leading festival, drawing crowds of over 10,000. Tastings, talks and, of course, monster hangovers are all part of this annual three-day event.

Copenhagen Marathon
35 26 69 00, www.copenhagenmarathon.dk.
Admission 600kr-650kr, 300kr student concession.
Credit MC, V. **Date** 3rd weekend in May.
Professional and amateur runners from around the world pound the cobbles from Vesterbro to Nørrebro to Østerbro and Vester Voldgade.

Copenhagen Whitsun Carnival
Østerbrohuset, Århusgade 103, Østerbro (29 40 45 57, www.copenhagencarnival.dk). **Admission** free. **Map** p248 E12. **Date** Whitsun weekend.
This is Copenhagen's stab at a Rio Carnival-type event, with lashings of South American spirit, costumes, parades and floats. The three-day festivities are centred on Østerbro's Fælledparken.

SUMMER

Sankt Hans Aften
Date 23 June.
Sankt Hans Aften (St Hans Night) is one of the biggest celebrations of the festival calendar for

Danes, who have marked the longest day of the year since pagan times with bonfires and songs. The major gatherings are usually held on the beaches or in the parks.

Danish Derby

Klampenborg Galopbane, Klampenborgvej, Klampenborg (39 96 02 13, www.galopbane.dk). Train to Klampenborg/bus 388. **Admission** 100kr; 50kr concessions; free under-18s. **No credit cards. Date** late June.
Denmark's leading equine event takes place at Klampenborg racecourse, to the north of the city.

Roskilde Festival

Roskilde (46 36 66 13, www.roskilde-festival.dk). Train to Roskilde. **Tickets** 70 26 32 67 (weekdays 10am-5pm), www.billetnet.dk. **Credit** varies. **Date** late June/early July.
Held over four days, Roskilde is renowned as Scandinavia's largest outdoor music event. In 2010 crowds of 80,000 enjoyed headline acts including Patti Smith, The Prodigy, Muse and Them Crooked Vultures. The festival is famous for its relatively crime-free party atmosphere, and for many teenage Danes their first Roskilde Festival is an important coming-of-age milestone. A shuttle bus runs from Roskilde Station to the festival grounds on the outskirts of this ancient town in the centre of Sjælland.

Round Sjælland Yacht Race

Helsingør (www.sjaellandrundt.dk). Train to Helsingør. **Date** early July.
Sailors compete in one of Europe's major yacht races over three days.

Copenhagen Jazz Festival

33 93 20 13, 33 93 25 45, www.jazzfestival.dk. **Tickets** vary. **Credit** varies. **Date** 1st Fri-2nd Sun in July.
As soon as Roskilde is over, the Copenhagen Jazz Festival gets under way. The Danes love their jazz, and, thankfully, that passion isn't limited to the Dixieland tourist-fodder you'll hear on Nyhavn of a summer's afternoon. The festival is delightfully ad hoc, with impromptu gigs, jam sessions, improvisations, free outdoor concerts and street parades happening all over the city. Naturally, you need to book early for any big names.

Metropolis (formerly Sommerscene)

33 15 15 64, www.kit.dk. **Tickets** phone for details. **Credit** varies. **Date** Aug.
Flagship project of the Copenhagen International Theatre, Metropolis is an annual festival of international theatre, circus and dance happening in streets and venues across the city. The line-ups are impressive and have included Philip Glass and the RSC.

Shakespeare at Kronborg

Kronborg Slot, Helsingør (49 21 69 79, www. hamletscenen.dk). Train to Helsingør. **Tickets** phone for details. **Credit** varies. **Date** Aug.
Productions of *Hamlet* have been staged at Kronborg since 1816, many by British companies. Laurence Olivier and his wife Vivien Leigh played here in 1937, but John Gielgud's 1939 Hamlet is generally regarded as the definitive performance. Since then, Richard Burton, Michael Redgrave, Derek Jacobi, Kenneth Branagh and Simon Russell Beale have all given notable Hamlets.

ARTS & ENTERTAINMENT

Copenhagen Jazz Festival.

For One Night Only

The city's top attractions open their doors until midnight.

Although autumn can be beautiful in Copenhagen as the trees on Kongens Nytorv change colour, there is no mistaking the hint of foreboding in the air as the long, dark, wet Danish winter approaches. To help stave off the gloom each year, around the middle of October (14 Oct 2011) Copenhagen lets rip with one last cultural hurrah during **Kulturnat** (Culture Night; www.kulturnatten.dk). For one night only the festival sees many of the city's museums and palaces stay open until midnight. Around 300 venues take part in the night, inaugurated in 1992, including churches, galleries and other exhibition spaces – even Parliament and the Supreme Court open their doors. There is usually a craft fair in Rådhuspladsen, performances galore on Strøget, countless concerts and performances, and rare displays of historic weaponry at the Tøjhusmuseet. Kulturnat brings a singular atmosphere to the venues and the city. It is the epitome of the Danish *hygge* ('cosiness') phenomenon – in which visitors, usually including a good proportion of very excited children, get to see a new side of familiar institutions. Leading up to the event, you can buy a Kultur pass which includes access to the majority of the venues, plus bus and local train travel.

Kulturhavn (Culture Harbour)
Islands Brygge, central Copenhagen (33 66 38 50, www.kulturhavn.dk). Metro Islands Brygge. **Date** 1st weekend in Aug.
Over 80 events from diving to dance, water polo to dragon boat races, and theatrical performances to fireworks, on and around the water beside Islands Brygge.

Copenhagen Pride
Throughout Copenhagen (www.copenhagen-pride.dk). **Date** mid Aug.
Previously known as Mermaid Pride, this is the festival of the year for the city's gay and lesbian community, drawing crowds of up to 50,000.

DCCD Images Festival
Nytorv 17 (33 17 97 00, www.dccd.dk). **Tickets** vary; phone for details. **Credit** varies. **Date** Aug-Sept.

An annual celebration of the non-Western world, including theatre, dance, visual arts, handicrafts, photography, music, architecture and literary events, held in various venues around Denmark.

Art Copenhagen
Forum, Julius Thomsens Plads, Frederiksberg (32 47 20 00, www.artcph.com). Metro Forum. **Date** late Sept.
This annual contemporary art fair features around 60 galleries from Scandinavia, as well as discussions and artist interviews.

Copenhagen Blues Festival
Venues throughout the city (70 15 65 65, www.copenhagenbluesfestival.dk). **Date** late Sept.
The city's leading blues event featuring local and international blues musicians in over 60 concerts. Main venues include Mojo (*see venue index*).

AUTUMN

Kulturnatten
33 25 74 00, www.kulturnatten.dk. **Tickets** vary.
Date 1st night of autumn half-term in mid Oct.
See left **For One Night Only**.

Tivoli Halloween Opening
Vesterbrogade 3 (ticket centre 33 15 10 12,
www.tivoli.dk). Train København H. **Tickets**
phone for details. **Credit** AmEx, MC, V.
Date mid-late Oct. **Map** p250 P12.
Tivoli opened for Halloween for the first time in 2006
with special spooky activities for children and a
Halloween market.

Mix Copenhagen
(LesbianGayBiTrans Film Festival)
33 93 07 66, www.cglff.dk. **Tickets** online, prices
vary. **Credit** varies. **Date** late Oct.
Ten days of mainstream and underground gay and
lesbian films arranged by the Danske Film Institut.

Junge Hunde
86 19 00 79, www.entrescenen.dk; tickets:
BILLETnet 70 15 65 65. **Tickets** call weekdays
10am-4pm or see online, prices vary. **Credit** MC,
V. **Date** Oct-Nov.
Previously confined to Copenhagen, the Junge
Hunde (Young Dogs) international dance festival
now takes place simultaneously in Århus and
Malmö. It features many of the stars of tomorrow
and has a reputation for being avant-garde.

WINTER

CPH:DOX
Axeltorv 12 (33 93 07 34, www.cphdox.dk).
Date mid Nov.
Copenhagen's International Documentary Festival
takes place in cinemas throughout the city for a week
during mid November. Established in 2003, the festival has already grown into the third largest of its
kind in northern Europe.

Tivoli Christmas Season
Tivoli (33 15 10 01, www.tivoli.dk). Train
København H. **Admission** 75kr, 125kr
Fri after 8pm, children under 7 free.
Credit AmEx, MC, V. **Map** p250 P12.
Date mid Nov-Christmas.
From mid November Tivoli turns into a vast
Christmas grotto with a special Christmas market,
ice skating, Yuletide grub and an infestation of
nisser (Danish Christmas pixies). Expect crowds.

Christmas Fairs & Parade
www.visitcopenhagen.dk. **Date** from end Nov.
Like most European cities, Copenhagen is decked
out in decorations and illuminations at this time
of year. But, unlike most, the atmosphere is less

commercial and more authentically 'Christmassy'
(maybe the sub-zero temperatures have something
to do with it). At the end of November Father
Christmas parades through the city in the Great
Christmas Parade. Look out too for the Hotel
d'Angleterre's spectacular Christmas decorations.

Christmas
www.visitcopenhagen.dk. **Date** 24 Dec.
The Danes give a great Christmas, both in the pri-
vacy of their own homes, with elaborate rituals,
feasting and decorations, and on a more grand public scale. Like all Danes, Copenhageners celebrate on
Christmas Eve. Having already gone out into the
woods to chop down their own tree, Danes will decorate it the night before Christmas and hang it with
real candles. Once these are lit, the family dances
around the tree holding hands and singing carols,
before settling down to a traditional Christmas dinner of roast duck, potatoes and red cabbage followed
by rice pudding with a hidden almond (whoever gets
the almond wins a present).

New Year
Date 31 Dec/1 Jan.
Rådhuspladsen is the place Danes gather on New
Year's Eve for the traditional celebration. In recent
years, the firework displays throughout the city
(private and public) have been ever more breathtaking, but be warned: the Danes are not too hot on
firework safety.

Winter Jazz Festival
33 93 20 13, www.jazzfestival.dk. **Tickets**
see online for details. **Credit** varies.
Date end Jan-early Feb.
This is a smaller, more low-key ten-day version of
the famous summer jazz festival.

Wondercool Copenhagen
Venues vary, see tourist office website for
all details. **Tickets** see online for details.
Credit varies. **Date** Feb.
Umbrella name for four winter festivals and designed
to lure visitors to the city in the dark days of February:
events are based around the Copenhagen Jazz
Festival, Copenhagen Fashion Festival, Copenhagen
Cooking and the new FROST rock festival.

Fastelavn
www.karneval.dk. **Date** late Feb/early Mar.
Fastelavn could be considered the Danes' Halloween,
in which children dress up in costumes and gather
together wielding sticks with which they beat the
hell out of a wooden barrel. This is mild compared
with what used to happen when the barrel, containing a live cat, would be suspended from a tree by a
rope so that the youths of a town could gallop past
on a horse and wallop it until the bottom fell out.
These days, the traumatised feline has been replaced
by hundreds of sweets.

ARTS & ENTERTAINMENT

Children

With a theme park and Lego flagship at its centre, this is a city built for kids.

One almost wonders if Copenhagen was created just for children. The city is full of imaginatively designed play parks and fairytale palaces; there are several museums just for kids and many others have special departments for children; every restaurant has high chairs; every bus can take prams (they favour the Victorian Mary Poppins-style ones here); the Metro has lifts (are you listening, Paris and London?); and every bicycle seems to have a kid's seat on the back. During the holidays there are dozens of performances laid on for children in the theatres and parks. There are nappy-changing facilities in most public buildings and much of the city centre is pedestrianised. And then, of course, there is Tivoli, the world's cosiest amusement park.

GREAT DAYS OUT

A good way to see Copenhagen with a child is to adopt a geographical approach and base a day's activities around one area of the city.

Tivoli & Rådhuspladsen

A must for every child visiting Copenhagen is **Tivoli** (*see p44*), open throughout the summer. Located right next to Central Station, the old amusement park can still make every child's heart beat faster. The world's tallest carousel (80 metres/262 feet), the shooting galleries,

Valhalla Castle and the Pantomime Theatre are among the attractions that provide action and fun for kids (and many adults), while the flowers and gardens, open-air cafés and restaurants offer parents tranquillity and time to breathe. Food is expensive in Tivoli (take advantage of the plentiful picnic areas) and rides cost extra, but the fireworks on Saturday nights (and some Wednesdays) are free, as are many performances on the open-air stage. For children of nappy age, there's a family amenity centre with baby-changing tables, free nappies and microwave ovens for heating baby food.

Across Rådhuspladsen from here is the fun **Ripley's Believe It or Not Museum** (*see p53*) and the not so impressive **Hans Christian Andersen Museum** (*see p52*).

Nationalmuseet (National Museum; *see p51*) can be an interesting place to take children (after all, who can resist the Vikings?). Every new exhibition is accompanied by a children's area, with specially designed activities, plus a toy museum on the top floor and an excellent hands-on children's museum in the basement.

West of Tivoli is the **Tycho Brahe Planetarium** (*see venue index*), with its small exhibition on astronomy and space travel, but the real attraction here is the **IMAX cinema** (*see p177*) which is just as likely to show films about skateboarding or skydiving as the stars. (Ask for headphones with English narration at the ticket office – children must be over three.)

South of Tivoli, older kids will definitely get something from a visit to the renovated **Ny Carlsberg Glyptotek** (*see p51*), especially if they are promised a trip to the popular nearby swimming centre **Vandkulturhuset** (within the DGI-Byen sports complex; *see p202*), which contains a baby pool with fountains, a swimming pool, waterslides, diving boards, climbing walls and a spa where parents can recharge their batteries.

The magnificent open-air **Islands Brygge** (*see p83*) harbour pools near Langebro ('Long Bridge') are open throughout the summer, as are the pools at **Fisketorvet**; both have a children's area. Alternatively, a short bus ride away is the **Amager Strand** lagoon (*see index*), a spectacular sandy beach development with gently sloping shallows and plenty of children's entertainment laid on during the summer.

Strøget & around

The long pedestrian street **Strøget** can be fun for kids, partly because of its shops (there's a toy store, Fætter BR, near the Rådhuspladsen end, as well as the new **Lego flagship**; *see p173* **Follow the Lego Brick Road**), but mostly because of the street performers. Towards the Kongens Nytorv end are the **Guinness World Records Museum** and **Mystic Exploratorie** (*see p55*), which children seem to enjoy.

Get away from the noise of the street by climbing the 17th-century **Rundetårn** (Round Tower; *see p57*) on Købmagergade. Instead of steps, there is a 209-metre (686-foot) long ramp, that spirals up inside the tower: a real challenge for buggy pushers.

For something completely different, rent out a kayak from **Kajak-Ole** (www.kajakole.dk) on Gammel Strand (*see p58*). A guide leads the group through the canals, telling anecdotes on the way; a drink at a café in Christianshavn is included in the price. No experience is necessary, as the kayaks are very stable, but children must be 11 or older for a two-person kayak, and 15 for a single-person kayak.

South of Gammel Strand on Slotsholmen, the double-handed swords, suits of armour and other military paraphernalia at **Tøjhusmuseet** (Royal Arsenal Museum; *see p70*) are usually a hit, especially with boys. The charismatic **Thorvaldsens Museum** (*see p70*) is surprisingly interesting for kids too. Also on Slotsholmen, older children might like the spooky atmosphere of the **Ruinerne Under Christiansborg** (Ruins Under Christiansborg; *see p70*). The excavated ruins of the original castle of Bishop Absalon (the founder of Copenhagen), jumbled together with those of later castles on the site, are situated directly below the current Christiansborg Slot.

Tivoli.

ARTS & ENTERTAINMENT

Profile Christiania Bike

This Danish design icon can be seen on bike lanes all over the city.

Almost synonymous with the word 'cargo bike' in Denmark, the Christiania has been an element of daily life in Copenhagen for over 25 years, becoming one of the city's unofficial emblems. In fact, the bike was recently awarded the Classics Prize for the Danish Design Centre's (*see p50*) Danish Design Awards 2010/11, where it was recognised as having 'proven its durability through many years of daily transport of shopping bags and children. The bicycle is a beautiful example of design that springs from a simple, good idea that stays viable due to function and charm.'

Invented in 1984 by Lars Engstrøm, in the car-free commune of Christiania, the bike is essentially a back-to-front tricycle with a plywood box on the front for shopping or kids. The bikes have a fitted rain cover (with window), and Danish children are often carted to and from school in the front box, which comes complete with seats and safety belts; two or three youngsters can often be seen happily snuggled up together in the den-like space.

Copenhagen's flat terrain and safe bike lanes make for ideal conditions for the Christiania (a Christiania-based school run in Lisbon or San Francisco, say, would be a decidedly more difficult affair). As well as using the bikes for school runs, locals use Christiania bikes for shopping, taking their dogs to the park and moving and buying tools, equipment, Christmas trees... whatever large items you might need to transport. Denmark's postmen even use a specially designed Christiania bike for deliveries, while enterpreneurial types have recently begun using them as mobile drinks and snack stalls.

Christiania Bikes aren't cheap, costing between 10,300kr and 14,000kr – but you're paying for a high level of craftsmanship and a genuine alternative to the car. What's more, the bike would soon pay for itself when you consider the savings in transport and petrol costs. If you're in Copenhagen with kids, and fancy carting them around in this most convenient and pollution-free way, they can be rented from **Baisikeli** and **Københavns Cykler** (for contact details, *see p42*).

WEBSITE
www.christian
iabikes.com/
english/uk_
main.htm

Rosenborg & around

Five minutes' walk north of the east end of Strøget lies **Kongens Have**. This is a really wonderful place to stop for a picnic. The park has a unique wooden playground for one- to four-year-olds, and alongside is one of the most charming traditional attractions in Copenhagen: the **Marionet Teater** (Marionette Theatre; see p195). Performances for children aged two and upwards take place every day in the summer (except Monday) at 2pm and 3pm.

Across the park, **Rosenborg Slot** (Rosenborg Palace; see p78) is packed with historical treasures, and is also the place to watch the Queen's Life Guards (who live in barracks next door) in training. The rooms of special interest to children are the Treasury, the Long Hall and Room 10. The atmospheric Treasury, in the basement, houses the Danish crown jewels, while the impressive Long Hall is decorated in golden stucco and has three silver lions guarding the thrones of the king and queen. Room 10 (on the first floor, in the castle's northern end) features a curious picture by Gaspard Antoine de Bois-Clair in 1692, which shows Frederik IV and his sister Sophie; made on a zig-zag folded canvas, when you look at it from the left, you see a girl; from the right, you see a boy.

Two minutes' walk south of Rosenborg is the **Musikhistorisk Museum** (Musical History Museum; see p76), worth visiting with a musically minded child. Audio sets play the sounds of old instruments, including Highland pipes from Scotland, launeddas from Greece and hurdy-gurdys from the Czech Republic. You cannot play the historical instruments, but the museum does have a kids' room where children can use up some of their energy on drums, stringed instruments and xylophones.

A couple of minutes' walk north of Rosenborg is the excellent **Statens Museum for Kunst** (National Gallery; see p79). It features a children's gallery and a workshop, and offers free guided tours for children aged four to 12 at 1pm on Saturdays, Sundays and throughout the Danish school holidays. These are mainly in Danish, but English speakers can also be accommodated. Young children can also participate in the workshops (30kr per child) that are held between 10.30am and 4.30pm on the same days, where children can sculpt, draw and paint (budding Rodins may even take their work home with them).

If you need a little down-time from the kids, behind the gallery stretches **Østre Anlæg park** which contains some of the best playgrounds in Copenhagen.

INSIDE TRACK CARNIVAL

For information on the range of children's activities available during Copenhagen's annual carnival, visit **www.karneval.dk**. The website also has details of the children's biennial festival in Kongens Have and several other events.

Christianshavn

Vor Frelsers Kirke (Church of Our Saviour; see p81), close to Christianshavns Kanal, has a tower with a spiral staircase twisting around the outside of the spire. It's a fun (if a little scary) climb up 400 steps, and you're rewarded with a great view. But be warned: when windy, the tower can start to sway a little. Back on terra firma, the kids will love a trip to the **Orlogsmuseet** (Royal Danish Naval Museum, see p81). While you may be drawn to the wonderful collection of model ships and maritime art, the kids might prefer to climb aboard the submarine Spækhuggeren, the interior of which has been partially recreated so that visitors can enter the command centre, the radio/radar room and the officers' mess, and even have a peep through the periscope.

From nearby Holmen you have a lovely view from the Opera House across the water to **Amalienborg Slot**, the royal palace (see p71), which can be reached by hopping on one of the harbour buses. The changing of the guards takes place at Amalienborg every day at noon.

Frederiksberg

To the west of central Copenhagen lies **Frederiksberg Have** (see index), a beautiful garden that is perfect for a picnic, with its dozens of secluded, leafy corners. To find out more about the royal gardens, take one of the guided boat trips on the lake. The neighbouring **Zoologisk Have** (Zoological Garden; see venue index) is one of the most attractive in Europe, with plenty of space for its animal residents plus a new elephant house designed by Lord Norman Foster. It has a special petting zoo where the smallest children can touch and play with the usual range of not-so-dangerous beasties. Other attractions include pony rides, climbing the zoo tower or just looking at the numerous baby animals. Be warned, though: queues can be long on sunny summer days.

Opposite the rear of Frederiksberg Slot, beneath the lawns of Søndermarken park, is a subterranean glass museum, **Cisternerne – Museet for Moderne Glaskunst** (The Cisterns – Museum of Modern Glass Art; see venue index), housed in former water cisterns. Though not aimed at kids, it's dank, spooky and rather fun.

ARTS & ENTERTAINMENT

Dyrehaven.

Østerbro & further north

Just outside the city centre, north along the harbour front, are the ancient battlements and moat surrounding **Kastellet** (*see p75*), a base for the Danish army for several centuries and still a fun and atmospheric place for kids. Nearby is the much maligned **Den Lille Havfrue** (The Little Mermaid, *see p73*).

In Østerbro lies the extensive **Fælledparken** (*see p93*), which has several playgrounds, a new skate park and an indoor swimming pool. In summer, several festivals, carnivals and playdays for children are held here. Another summer attraction in the park is Pavillionen, an outdoor café and restaurant that does very good barbecues. Østerbrogade, Østerbro's main street, is lined with a host of upmarket children's clothes boutiques. It's also home to the excellent **Park Bio** cinema (*see p177*), which offers 'Babybio' screenings for parents with small children at 10.30am every Friday (except during July).

Older children might find the stuffed animals a little static, but for younger kids the **Zoologisk Museum** (Zoological Museum; *see p93*), just west of Fælledparken, is a real hoot (especially the full-size replica mammoth).

The **Experimentarium** (*see venue index*), further north in Hellerup, is one of Copenhagen's great children's attractions. This science centre explores nature and technology, the environment and health issues through more than 300 interactive exhibits. In the kids' pavilion – aimed at children between three and six – are crazy mirrors, water wheels and other delights.

In **Danmarks Akvarium** (Danish Aquarium; *see venue index*) in Charlottenlund, you can learn about the sea life that inhabits polar seas and tropical waters. On Saturdays and Sundays, when the touch pool is open, children can get up close with marine life of all kinds. Don't miss feeding time at 1.30pm on weekdays, and 11.30am and 2pm on weekends and bank holidays. During the school holidays there are daily activities but the aquarium does get crowded at weekends. The aquarium's creatures are set to be rehoused once the city's futuristic new **Blue Planet** aquarium opens in 2013; designed by innovative architectural firm 3XN, the aquarium – which is currently being constructed on the island of Amager, near the airport – is set to be northern Europe's largest and most spectacular. For more information, visit www.denblaaplanet.dk.

The oldest amusement park in the world, **Bakken** (*see venue index*), is located in the forest of **Dyrehaven**, further north of the city at Klampenborg. Open from late spring to early autumn, Bakken has all the usual amusement park attractions, including rollercoasters, shooting galleries and daily shows for children, but note that, although entrance to the park is free, the attractions are not. A pleasant way to see the rest of Dyrehaven (which means 'deer park') is by pony. Little ponies, which can be led by parents, are available at **Fortunens Ponyudlejning** (*see below*). Alternatively, take a horse and cart ride or simply stroll around in the forest. Right next to Dyrehaven is one of the best beaches in the Copenhagen area – **Bellevue** (*see p83* **Come On In, the Water's Lovely**).

Further north, just a short train journey from the centre of town, the beautifully situated **Louisiana Museum For Moderne Kunst** (Louisiana Museum of Modern Art; *see venue index*) has a children's wing offering daily artistic activities such as drawing and model making. Louisiana also has a wonderfully designed park, perfect for a picnic, and there's a small swimming beach in front of the museum.

Fortunens Ponyudlejning

Ved Fortunen 33, Lyngby (45 87 60 58, www. fortunensponycenter.dk). Train to Klampenborg, then bus 388 towards Lyngby or train to Lyngby, then bus 388 towards Helsingør. **Open** noon-6pm Mon-Fri; 9am-6pm Sat, Sun. *School holidays* 9am-6pm daily. **Rates** 180kr/hr; 150kr under-11s. **No credit cards**.

Follow the Lego-brick Road

A long overdue flagship store for one of Denmark's most famous brands.

Although it's just about possible to do a daytrip from Copenhagen to the original Legoland (www.legoland.dk) – which lies three-and-a-half hours away by train, on the other side of the country in Billund, Jutland – it requires something of a heroic effort, getting up at an ungodly hour. The theme park – Denmark's second most popular tourist attraction after Tivoli – is also only open between April and October. A more straightforward option for Lego-obsessed kids is the new Lego flagship store, which opened in central Copenhagen in December 2010, just in time for Christmas.

The Lego brand (the word comes from the Danish 'Leg godt', 'play well') was founded in 1932 by carpenter Ole Kirk Christiansen. In 1949, Christiansen began producing plastic building bricks with eight studs on the top and he never looked back. In the late 1950s, the company added the tubular supports that gave the bricks their strength and usability; it created the double-size Duplo sets for younger children in the late '60s; opened Legoland in Billund in 1968; and introduced the iconic Lego man

in 1973. In 2000, the British Association of Toy Retailers named the Lego brick the Toy of the Century.

The impressive new store, in the middle of Strøget, is one of 14 in Europe, and consists of three main areas: a 'Pick-a-Brick' wall showcasing the famous bricks; an interactive play area in the centre of the store; and the 'brand ribbon', which runs the circumference of the store, and which features displays and presentations of fun facts. Exclusive and hard-to-find sets are for sale, as well as new Lego games, Harry Potter-themed sets, the Creator and City lines, Lego Duplo sets for pre-school children, and the full selection of classic Lego products and branded merchandise.

What the store (or website) won't tell you is that the toy brick concept was in fact invented by an Englishman, Hilary Harry Fisher Page, and originally built by his company Kiddicraft as 'self-locking building bricks'. Page was one of the first people to approach toy design from an educational and psychological point of view. Lego got their hands on some Kiddicraft bricks in the 1940s, saw the potential and began manufacturing their own version. Page committed suicide in 1957 and Lego introduced its bricks to the English market a year later, finally buying the rights to the Kiddicraft system in 1981 – a rather dark element of the toy that millions of children grew up with.

Lego developed the idea beyond Page's wildest imaginings, of course, creating an absorbing and educational toy system that would be sold around the world. The Christiansen family, today headed by Ole's grandson Kjeld, remains one of the wealthiest in Denmark and the company still has its base in Billund.

Lego Flagship, Vimmelskaftet 37, Strøget (www.lego.dk). **Open** 10am-6pm Mon-Thu; 10am-7pm Fri; 10am-4pm Sat; noon-4pm 1st Sun of mth. **Credit** MC, V. **Map** p251 N13.

ARTS & ENTERTAINMENT

Film

Documentary, social realism and children's films still reign supreme.

The Danes have a prodigious movie-making history. From the silent era of black-and-white film with piano accompaniment through the Dogme collective to the more recent spate of intelligent feature films and controversial documentaries, Danish film-makers have had an impact on cinema disproportionate to the country's size and population. This can be credited to the Danes' true love of and devotion to film, as well as government subsidies to create quality products for the international market; the Danish Film Institute, reorganised in 2008, provides a strong supportive and promotional role. In recent times, however, film-makers have had to jump through more and more hoops to gain funding.

There is also the famous Danish Film School (Den Danske Filmskole) with its steady flow of talented graduates, who have brought Danish cinema several notable triumphs during the last three decades.

PIONEERS AND FUNDING

Denmark's film-makers were among the key pioneers in European cinema and in the decades leading up to World War II had a notable influence on its development. The establishment of the Nordisk Film Kompagni in 1906 galvanised the industry, and in 2006 it celebrated its centenary. **Nordisk Film** was the first studio in Europe to focus solely on feature films and it thrived (until the emergence of the American film industry, from around 1913), thanks to its technical superiority and the talent of its directors. As extraordinary as this may sound, in the early days of cinema Denmark was the world's biggest producer of films.

After facing near bankruptcy with the advent of sound, Nordisk Film re-established itself in 1929 as a producer of talkies. It is still the oldest working film studio in the world and its polar bear logo is said to have inspired the use of a lion as MGM's symbol.

Among the most important innovators of early cinema were film-makers **Benjamin Christensen** and **Carl Theodor Dreyer**. In front of the camera, the world fell in love with **Asta Nielsen**, one of the first great movie stars.

The popularity of cinema – particularly documentary, which is still one of Denmark's strongest genres – exploded in Denmark during the 1930s and, as a result, a Film Act was passed in 1938, establishing the Film Council, the Film Fund and the National Film Board.

Between World War II and the early 1980s, Danish cinema experienced something of a lull in international terms, with the country's film-makers focusing their energies on television production. When feature films were made, they were often worthy social dramas or soft pornography (the industry having been derestricted in 1969). Yet in this period, director **Henning Carlsen** created the masterful *Knud Hamsun's Hunger* (1964), which is one of the ten official film entries in the 'canon' of Danish culture (www.kulturkanon.kum.dk).

Government subsidies for film production started in the 1960s, and by the mid '70s most Danish films were made with some element of government aid. By 1989 an even more radical system was introduced, whereby a film-maker could demand 50 per cent of the film's budget (with no creative strings attached) from the government if the director could match it with private funding.

INTERNATIONAL SUCCESS

In 1988, **Gabriel Axel**'s film adaptation of Karen Blixen's short story *Babette's Feast* won the Oscar for Best Foreign Language Film, which led the way to many more international successes for Danish cinema, including the unprecedented double triumph when **Bille August**'s *Pelle the Conqueror* won in the same category the following year. The great Swedish actor, Max von Sydow, received a nomination in the Best Actor category. The film, adapted from Martin Andersen Nexø's novel telling the bleak tale of Swedish immigrants coping with life on 19th-century Bornholm (the Danish island in the Baltic), also won the Palme d'Or at Cannes.

ENFANT TERRIBLE

Danish cinema continued to hog the limelight in the 1990s with the international success of director **Lars von Trier**, and the advent of Dogme 95. Von Trier's (the 'von' is an aristocratic affectation) successes over the last couple of decades has earned him a virtually unrivalled reputation for stylistic experimentation, provocative scripts as well as less than reverential treatment of actors. He established his name on the international art house circuit with such films as *The Element of Crime* (1984), *Epidemic* (1987) and *Europa* (1991).

Von Trier's spooky and disturbing 1994 TV series, *The Kingdom*, set in Copenhagen's main hospital, was a huge international success. However, it was his 1996 feature, *Breaking the Waves*, that finally launched him on the world stage. A torrid and occasionally crudely manipulative film (the first of his so-called 'Trilogy of Goodness'), the film set the scene for his future relationship with the world's film critics, who continue to be violently polarised in their opinions of his work.

More controversy followed with his 1998 Dogme release, *The Idiots*, featuring explicit sex and a less than politically correct look at mental illness. Von Trier's 2000 feature, the bleak musical *Dancer in the Dark*, starred Björk, who famously ate her costume in frustration at working with the obsessive director. Again the film divided critics, but it went on to win the Palme d'Or at Cannes.

Dogville (2004), starring Nicole Kidman, was a barely concealed attack on American culture and again very well received. It was intended to spawn two further films starring Kidman, who instead pulled out of Lars' flop, *Manderlay* (2006).

2009's *Antichrist*, starring Willem Dafoe and Charlotte Gainsbourg, was Von Trier's first attempt at an all-out horror (although he later said he shouldn't be labelled as such). The story of a couple who retreat to a cabin in the woods following the death of their child, the film contained graphic scenes of grotesquely violent sex (four people reportedly passed out at the film's premiere in Cannes), making it as dark and controversial as any of the director's works.

His upcoming film, *Melancholia* – described by the director as a 'psychological disaster movie' – will star Kirsten Dunst and Kiefer Sutherland.

Von Trier created his own film company, Zentropa, which has been part-owned by Nordisk Film since 2008.

DOGME STYLE

Von Trier was one of the film-makers behind the internationally famous Dogme collective, a movement founded in Copenhagen by four Danish directors – von Trier, **Thomas Vinterberg**, **Søren Kragh-Jacobsen** and **Kristian Levring**. Dogme's mission was to discard the 'trickery' of modern film-making to refocus on the characters' emotional journey.

The Dogme directors declared that Hollywood movies deceived their audience by mythologising the process of film-making. But to set themselves aside from all the other bleating, under-funded independent directors, they made it clear that their creed (called the Vow of Chastity) need not preclude Hollywood-sized budgets. As Vinterberg commented: 'The Dogme 95 Manifesto does not concern itself with the economic aspects of film-making. A Dogme film could be low-budget or it could have a $100m budget.' The 'Vow' included such draconian commandments as 'Shooting must be on location only', 'The director can receive no credit' and 'Films cannot be of a specific genre'. No dubbing, tripods, artificial lighting or optical effects were allowed either.

The movement spawned several notable successes, prime among them Vinterberg's successful second feature film, *Festen (The Celebration)* (1998), a disturbing tale of family secrets, set against the backdrop of a 60th birthday party.

However, the movement, which broke up in 2005, also had many critics, who saw it as a pretentious experiment that became as conventional as the genres it criticised.

RECENT SUCCESSES

Resonant dramas such as *Facing the Truth* (2002), *Inheritance* (2003), *After the Wedding* (2006) and *In a Better World* (2010) are key examples of the intelligent and high-quality movies made by established directors such as **Nils Malmros**, **Per Fly**, **Susanne Bier** and **Anders Thomas Jensen**, who continue to make waves internationally. Meanwhile a new generation of young

INSIDE TRACK METROPOLE

Summer 2010 brought the sad closure of Copenhagen's Metropole cinema – one of the city's oldest (it first opened its doors in the 1930s). This was due to the redevelopment of the Industriens Hus building, in which it was housed.

film-makers is redefining genre-oriented films with forceful stories told in highly aesthetic packages, such as **Nikolaj Arcel**'s political thriller *King's Game* (2004), **Nicolas Winding Refn**'s raw and violent drug trilogy which began with *Pusher* (1996), and **Christoffer Boe**'s modern romances such as *Allegro* (2005), and his thriller *Everything Will Be Fine* (2010).

Danish children's films have a very long tradition of winning international awards, and have rolled with the times to deliver first-class CGI animation movies such as *Terkel in Trouble* (2004) and *The Ugly Duckling and Me* (2006). And documentary, meanwhile, continues to be a major strand of Danish film; the ambitious **CPH:DOX** festival (*see Calendar*) continues to make waves internationally, while **Mads Brügger**'s *Red Chapel*, a comic documentary about about a visit to Korea, won Best Foreign Documentary at the 2010 Sundance Film Festival. **Janus Metz**'s controversial *Armadillo*, meanwhile – a brutal documentary on Danish soldiers in Afghanistan – provoked shock among local audiences and the Danish press when it was released in May 2010.

In 2006, the creation of a fund called **New Danish Screen**, based on a subsidy scheme of risk capital, provided a solid financial platform for innovative ideas in film-making (both fiction and documentary).

CINEMA-GOING & FESTIVALS

There are plenty of top-quality screens in Copenhagen's city centre, with a choice of multiplexes and art houses as well as the dynamic **Filmhuset** (*see below*). This all points to the locals' insatiable cinemania, which means even the largest cinema in Scandinavia, the **Imperial** (*see p177*), is usually packed to capacity during blockbuster openings.

Copenhagen hosts several excellent film festivals. **CPH:PIX** (www.cphpix.dk) is the international feature film festival (the result of a merger between NatFilm Festival and Copenhagen International Film Festival). Held in April annually, the innovative ten-day festival screens some 180 films from around the world.

The International Documentary Film Festival **CPH:DOX** (www.cphdox.dk) has gone from strength to strength since it started in 2003.

As the largest documentary film festival in Scandinavia, the ten-day event draws an engaged international crowd to Copenhagen every November, attracted both by the screenings and the professional seminars.

October's annual Copenhagen Gay & Lesbian Film Festival changed it's name to **MIX COPENHAGEN/LesbianGayBiTrans Film Festival** in 2011. As one of the longest-running festivals of its type (it celebrated its 25th anniversary in 2010) it attracts gay-centric films from around the world.

★ Filmhuset/Den Danske Filminstitut Cinemateket

Gothersgade 55, Rosenborg & Around (33 74 34 00, www.dfi.dk). Metro/train/bus Nørreport. **Open** *Café* 10am-midnight Tue-Sat; 10am-10pm Sun. Closed July. *Bookshop* noon-6pm Tue-Fri; 11am-5pm Sat, Sun. *Documentary archive & library* noon-7pm Tue, Thur; noon-4pm Wed, Fri. **Tickets** prices vary for cinema. **Map** p251 M15. This world-class film complex is devoted to Danish and international cinema. Among its facilities are a shop selling difficult-to-find film books, posters and videos, a restaurant, a documentary archive (open to non-members) and three cinemas.

MULTIPLEXES

CinemaxX

Fisketorvet Shopping Center, Kalvebod Brygge 57, Slotsholmen (70 10 12 02, www.cinemaxx.dk/koebenhavn). Train Dybbølsbro. **No credit cards**. **Map** p251 Q13. This multiplex in a shopping mall has Copenhagen's biggest screen. Comfortable but costly.

Dagmar Teatret

Jernbanegade 2, Tivoli & Rådhuspladsen (70 13 12 11, www.dagmar.dk). Bus Vesterport. **Credit** DC, MC, V. **No credit cards**. **Map** p250 O11. A multiplex devoted to projecting quality films. The main cinema is decent, the smaller screens less so.

Empire Bio

Guldbergsgade 29F, Nørrebro (35 36 00 36, www.empirebio.dk). Bus 5A. **No credit cards**. **Map** p248 H9. Nørrebro's local multiplex manages to show both art-house movies and blockbusters. Comfortable double seats are available in the back row.

★ Falkoner Biografen

Sylow Allé 15, Frederiksberg (70 13 12 11, www.kino.dk). Metro Frederiksberg. **Credit** DC, MC, V. Part of the Nordisk chain, this six-screen cinema is one of Copenhagen's newest, open since 2007. Its stylised interior design is matched with top-notch facilities, like the comfortable sofa seats.

Palads

★ Imperial
Ved Vesterport 4, Tivoli & Rådhuspladsen
(70 13 12 11, www.kino.dk). Train Vesterport.
Credit MC, V. **Map** p250 O10.
The Imperial is Copenhagen cinema par excellence.
A large, old-fashioned theatre that used to be the
biggest screen in Scandinavia before the CinemaxX
(*see p177*) giant came to town. Many films
premiere here.

Palads
Axeltorv 9 (70 13 12 11, www.kino.dk). Train
Vesterport. **Credit** MC, V. **Map** p250 O11.
Copenhagen's family multiplex is nicknamed 'the
birthday cake' for its pink exterior.

Park Bio
Østerbrogade 79, Østerbro (35 38 33 62,
www.parkbio-kbh.dk). Bus 1A, 14. **Credit** V.
Map p248 C13.
A charming neighbourhood cinema showing three
different movies a day. There are special baby
screenings every Friday at 10.30am (except during
July), which are great for parents with small children to entertain.

ART HOUSE CINEMAS

Gloria
Rådhuspladsen 59, Tivoli & Rådhuspladsen
(33 12 42 92, www.gloria.dk). Bus 95N, 96N.
No credit cards. Map p250 O12.
Small underground art house cinema located in the
heart of town.

★ Grand Teatret
Mikkel Bryggers Gade 8 (33 15 16 11,
www.grandteatret.dk). Metro Nørreport or bus
95N, 96N. **Credit** AmEx, MC, V. **Map** p250 O12.

This beautiful old building is home to a distinguished cinema screening an impeccable selection
of international and art house titles.

Husets Biograf
2nd Floor, Huset, Magstræde 14, Slotsholmen
(33 69 32 00, www.husetmagstraede.dk).
No credit cards. Map p251 O13.
Art house, student-oriented cinema with a predilection for the unusual.

Posthus Teatret
Rådhusstræde 1 (33 11 66 11, www.posthus
teatret.dk). Bus 11A, 14. **No credit cards.**
Map p251 O13.
Travel back in time in this tiny cinema, which from
the outside could almost be mistaken for a puppet
theatre. Screens international art house films.

Vester Vov Vov
Absalonsgade 5, Vesterbro (33 24 42 00, www.
vestervovvov.dk). Bus 6A. **No credit cards.**
Map p245 Q9.
Vesterbro's charming local cinema has a really cosy
feel to it, with comfortable reclining airline seats in
its screening rooms.

IMAX

Tycho Brahe Planetarium Omnimax
Gammel Kongevej 10 (33 12 12 24, www.
tycho.dk). Bus 14, 15. **Credit** AmEx, MC, V.
Map p250 P10.
This ultra-modern landmark contains an exhibition
space and also features Copenhagen's spectacular
IMAX cinema, projecting family-friendly science
and nature films.
► *The IMAX is housed in the same building at the*
city's planetarium; see venue index.

Galleries

A dynamic gallery scene means lots of art parties.

The interest, and thus the market, for contemporary art in Denmark has had a remarkable growth over the past decade. Copenhagen has always had a strong portfolio of galleries dealing in art from all ages, but in recent years the opening of several new galleries in the formerly unloved areas of **Islands Brygge** and industrial **Valby** (in particular the up-and-coming Carlsberg area) has reinvigorated the scene, as has September's Kopenhagen Contemporary festival, now in its fourth year.

In the centre, **Bredgade** is the street to head to, home to lots of interesting galleries, which sit in-between the cutesy antiques shops; the fact that David Risley set up shop here in 2009, relocating from London's Vyner Street, reflects the fact that Copenhagen is now an important player on the international art scene.

Not surprisingly, Copenhagen's trendy Meatpacking District, **Kødbyen**, is also a key area to visit for galleries – in particular Flæsketorvet Square, home to V1 Gallery, one of the city's top spots for art parties and events.

CENTRE

Charlottenborg Udstillingsbygning
Nyhavn 2 (33 13 40 22, www.kunsthal charlottenborg.dk). Metro Kongens Nytorv. **Open** 11am-6pm Mon, Tue, Thur-Sun; 11am-9pm Wed. **Admission** 60kr; 40kr concessions. **No credit cards. Map** p252 M16.
This huge gallery alternates between Danish and international exhibitions of contemporary art, architecture and decorative arts. The hall was built in 1883 at the request of an influential group of Danish artists and is now run by the Ministry of Culture.

Clausens Kunsthandel
Toldbodgade 9 (33 15 41 54, www.clausens kunsthandel.dk). Metro Kongens Nytorv. **Open** 11am-5pm Tue-Sat. **Admission** free. **No credit cards. Map** p249 K17.
Clausens has been working in the art trade since 1953 and the two-floor gallery houses an impressive selection of graphic work by some of Denmark's most established artists.

Fotografisk Center
Amaliegade 28 (33 93 09 96, www.photography.dk). **Open** 11am-5pm Tue-Sat. **Admission** 15kr; 10kr concessions. **Credit** MC, V. **Map** p249 K17.

Holding six annual exhibitions of mostly contemporary photography, the Fotografisk Center is also the only art bookshop in Denmark that specialises solely in the photographic arts. The gallery now also includes the Digital Room, a well-equipped digital darkroom and workshop available to artists.

Galerie Asbæk/Martin Asbæk Projects
Bredgade 23 (33 15 40 04, www.asbaek.dk, www. martinasbaek.dk). Metro Kongens Nytorv. **Open** 11am-6pm Tue-Fri; 11am-4pm Sat. **Admission** free. **Credit** DC, MC, V. **Map** p249 K16.
Since its inception in 1975, Asbæk has been one of Denmark's leading galleries. Patricia and Jacob Asbæk have collected an impressive stable of modern artists and their prices are commensurately high, with works running up to 100,000kr. In the gallery's shop, graphic works, books, posters, and international art magazines line the walls. Martin Asbæk Projects is an independent extension of the gallery, working exclusively with the younger artists represented.
► *Also on Bredgade are Gallerie Birch, Denmark's oldest gallery for contemporary art; Galerie Mikael Anderson (see below); Gallerie Christoffer Egelund; and the new Secher Scott Scandinavian Auction & Gallery. The Peter Lav Gallery (see p180) is located just round the corner on Esplanden.*

★ Galerie Mikael Andersen

Bredgade 63 (33 33 05 12, www.mikaelandersen. com). Bus 1A. **Open** noon-6pm Tue-Fri; 11am-3pm Sat. **Admission** free. **No credit cards.** **Map** p249 K17.

Mikael Andersen opened in 1989 and is now a major force in the Copenhagen art scene, representing a number of artists who debuted in the mid 1980s and who have gone on to become internationally significant. Works on show come from the likes of Kaspar Bonnén, Mogens Andersen, Günther Förg, Poul Gernes and Øivind Nygård.

Galerie Pi

Borgergade 15D (35 43 82 84, www.galeriepi.dk). Metro Kongens Nytorv. **Open** noon-6pm Tue-Fri; 11am-2pm Sat. **Credit** MC, V. **Map** p247 G14.

Galerie Pi's new space features contemporary art of all genres, with a particular focus on painting and graphics by emerging talent.

Galleri Specta

Peder Skrams Gade 13 (33 13 01 23, www. specta.dk). Metro Kongens Nytorv. **Open** noon-5.30pm Tue-Fri; 11am-2pm Sat. **Admission** free. **Credit** V. **Map** p252 N16.

Gallery owner Else Johannesen was one of the most well-respected figures in the art scene in Århus, Denmark's second largest city. She moved to Copenhagen in 1992, establishing Galleri Specta. She represents the likes of Sylvie Fleury, Clay Ketter, Anders Moseholm and Sven Daalskov. Specta sells well, thanks to its collection of smaller works by some of the more cutting-edge Danish artists.

Galleri Susanne Ottesen

Gothersgade 49 (33 15 52 44, www. susanneottesen.dk). Metro Kongens Nytorv.

Open 10am-6pm Tue-Fri; 11am-3pm Sat. **Admission** free. **No credit cards.** **Map** p247 L14.

Like Galerie Asbæk (*see below*), Susanne Ottesen represents the established generation of contemporary artists. The gallery opened back in 1989 and has had an impressive string of exhibitions, including Per Kirkeby, Kirsten Ortwed, Cindy Sherman and Kehnet Nielsen.

Galleri Tom Christoffersen

Skindergade 5 (33 91 76 10, www.tom christoffersen.dk). Metro Nørreport. **Open** noon-6pm Wed-Fri; 11am-4pm Sat. **Admission** free. **No credit cards.** **Map** p251 N13.

Tom Christoffersen's gallery positions itself at the heart of the Scandinavian contemporary art scene. It aims to work with the youngest, most forward-thinking artists on the international scene, and does so by putting on roughly ten exhibitions every year.

Helene Nyborg Contemporary

Ground Floor, Store Kongensgade 40H, Skt Annæ Passage (30 23 23 07, www.helenenyborg.com). Metro Kongens Nytorv. **Open** 11am-5pm Tue-Fri; 11am-2pm Sat. **No credit cards.**

Helene Nyborg's gallery was established in 2006 in a giant industrial estate in Valby. Now in a new central space, the gallery pushes a mix of funky and futuristic creations from an army of Nordic and international artists, including Judit Ström, Peter Rune Christiansen and Ida Kvetny.

Kunstforeningen

Gammel Strand 48 (33 36 02 60, www.glstrand. dk). Bus 1A, 2A, 6A, 15, 26, 29. **Open** 11am-5pm Tue, Thur-Sun; 11am-8pm Wed. **Admission** 55kr; 40kr concessions; free under-16s. **Credit** MC, V. **Map** p251 N14.

Kunstforeningen was built in 1825 and has been an institution in Danish art ever since. With five exhibitions a year, it focuses attention on presenting shows reflecting our age, often through retrospectives or by importing group shows from abroad.

Nikolaj – Copenhagen Contemporary Art Center

Nikolaj Plads 10 (33 18 17 80, www.nikolaj-ccac.dk). Bus 2A, 5A. **Open** noon-5pm Mon-Wed, Fri-Sun; noon-9pm Thur. **Admission** 20kr; 10kr concessions; free under-15s and all Wed. **No credit cards.** **Map** p251 N14.

The former Sankt Nikolaj Kirke has long been associated with contemporary art. Carlsberg Brewery founder Carl Jacobsen turned the church into a cultural centre in 1917 and it was the location of a number of avant-garde happenings during the 1960s, including some of Fluxus's first international performances. With a small permanent collection and four exhibition spaces, Nikolaj certainly has room for the constant flow of (mostly group) shows that

---

INSIDE TRACK
BRAVE NEW SPACES

A novel concept in the trendy Meatpacking District, Kødbyen, is **Butcher's Lab** (www.butcherslab.dk), a space that opened in 2009 and which combines a gym with a gallery. The idea behind it is to enable people to work out in an inspiring space. The 1,000-sq-m former slaughterhouse holds a gym, Crossfit equipment, a Weng Chun martial arts school and a shop, with temporary exhibitions and provocative graphics providing the backdrop. Meanwhile, **Karriere** (*see p138*), also in Kødbyen, combines an art gallery with a café/bar. The artworks are communicative pieces and the space aims to provide a new take on public art.

ARTS & ENTERTAINMENT

pass through its doors. Fluxus artist Eric Andersen created a fascinating permanent installation here, the Crying Room, which is adorned with all kinds of things that make you cry (onions, needles, etc).

Peter Lav Photo Gallery

Esplanden 8D (28 80 23 93, www.plgallery.dk). Metro Kongens Nytorv. **Open** 5-7pm Wed-Fri; noon-3pm Sat. **Admission** free. **Credit** MC, V. **Map** p250 N12.

This is the first gallery in Copenhagen to focus exclusively on contemporary photography. Peter Lav's exhibition space profiles both up-and-coming and more established photographers.

CHRISTIANSHAVN & AMAGER

Andersen S Contemporary

Amager Strandvej 50B (46 97 84 37, www. andersen-s.dk). Metro Øresund. **Open** noon-5pm Mon-Fri; noon-3pm Sat during exhibitions. **Admission** free. **No credit cards**.

Situated right on the habour of Islands Brygge, this gallery features the most succesful Danish artist of recent years, Olafur Eliasson, alongside works by many of his national contemporaries and the occasional international exhibition.

Frederiks Bastion

Refshalevej 80 (31 16 32 05, www.frederiks bastion.dk). Bus 48. **Open** noon-9pm Mon, Wed-Sat; 11am-7pm Sun. **Admission** free. **No credit cards**. **Map** p253 M21.

This is one of a series of bastions, built in 1744 to defend the city against (usually British) naval attack. Now that Admiral Nelson is no more, it's been turned into a gallery with a large permanent collection and various temporary exhibitions, concentrating on Nordic art in a wide variety of styles. The gallery also houses a restaurant and is sometimes hired for events, so call in advance if you're planning a special trip.

INSIDE TRACK
DENMARK'S BANKSY

Copenhagen's best-known street artist is **HustMitNavn**, whose name translates as 'RememberMyName'. The artist's graffiti and illustrations, celebrated for their humorous social commentary, now sell for thousands – making comparisons with Banksy unavoidable (even though his style is much more cartoon-like – and arguably less orginal – than Bristol's elusive one). The artist's launch party for his solo show at V1 Gallery (*see p181*) in autumn 2010 attracted the city's scenesters in their droves. To get a taste of his work, visit www.huskmitnavn.dk.

Galleri Christina Wilson

Sturlasgade 12H, Islands Brygge (32 54 52 06, www.christinawilson.net). Metro Islands Brygge or bus 40. **Open** noon-5pm Tue-Fri; noon-3pm Sat. **No credit cards**.

This gallery deals in installations, photography and paintings by emerging Danish and foreign artists. Wilson's mission is to present a range of ambitious international shows.

Overgaden

Overgaden Neden Vandet 17, Christianshavn (32 57 72 73/www.overgaden.org). Metro Christianshavn or bus 2A. **Open** 1-5pm Tue, Wed, Fri-Sun; 1-8pm Thur. **Admission** free. **No credit cards**. **Map** p252 P16.

Overgaden is a two-floor open exhibition space for younger experimental artists. A three-person committee has the task of panning through hundreds of applications for artistic gold, but the shows it selects often strike the motherlode.

VESTERBRO & CARLSBERG/VALBY

★ Galleri Bo Bjerggaard

Flæsketorvet 85A, Vesterbro (33 93 42 21, www. bjerggaard.com). Train København H. **Open** 1-6pm Tue-Fri; noon-4pm Sat. **Admission** free. **Credit** MC, V.

Bjerggard represents Denmark's most celebrated painter, Per Kirkeby, who had retrospectives at Louisiana (*see venue index*) and London's Tate Modern in 2008 and 2009 respectively. Founded in 1999, the gallery recently moved to a new, larger space, on the same square as V1 Gallery (*see right*).

★ Galleri Nicolai Wallner

NY Carlsberg Vej 68, Carlsberg (32 57 09 70, www.nicolaiwallner.com). Bus 1A, 3A, 10. **Open** noon-5pm Tue-Fri; noon-3pm Sat. **Admission** free. **No credit cards**.

One of the most significant contemporary art galleries in Copenhagen, Wallner changed the local art scene in the early 1990s, and was one of the galleries that kicked-off the rejuvenation of Islands Brygge. Since 2009, the gallery has been based in an 800sq-m space in an old garage in the industrial area of Carlsberg (*see p86* **Brewing Up a Cultural Storm**).

▶ *The gallery shares the building with four other galleries and a publishing house: Nils Stærk (www. nilsstaerk.dk), artist-run space IMO (www.imo- projects.com), and BKS Garage (bksg.kunstakade miet.dk), a space run by the Royal Danish Academy of Fine Arts, and Kopenhagen Publishing.*

Øksnehallen

Halmtorvet 11, Vesterbro (33 86 04 00, www.oeksnehallen.dk). Train København H. **Open** times vary; call for details. **Admission** free. **Credit** MC, V. **Map** p250 Q10.

See and Be Seen

Art festivals, events and parties.

V1 Gallery.

Copenhagen's most significant art events take place annually in September. The well-established **Art Copenhagen** (www.artcopenhagen.dk) – the leading art show in Scandinavia, now in its 15th year – set a visitor record in 2010, attracting 13,000 guests, and reflecting Copenhagen's increased profile on the international art scene. Around 80 Nordic galleries took part in the show, held in Forum Copenhagen, representing some 500 artists.

The younger **Kopenhagen Contemporary** (www.kopenhagencontemporary.com) takes place in the same month, and involves small cutting-edge galleries, as well as established art museums, including Louisiana (*see venue index*) and Arken (*see venue index*). Now in its fourth year, it's a lively weekend event with parties, debates, talks, guided walks and, of course, exhibitions, which in 2010 focused on the Carlsberg art scene.

Many of the city's galleries and artists' studios also take part in October's **Kulturnat** (Culture Night; *see p166* **For One Night Only**), when the city's museums, churches and cultural and performing arts institutions open their doors to the public during the evening; the event creates a great atmosphere around town.

Hob nob with Copenhagen's creative crowd, and you'll hear mention of **V1 Gallery** (*see listing below*) – one of the fave spots in town for art parties and magazine launches. Located in a space in hip Kødbyen (the Meatpacking District) since 2007, the gallery has a reputation for showcasing work by emerging names and street artists.

For general updates on small art festivals and events, visit **www.kultunaut.com**, which has information on established, museum-oriented art and culture news, and **www.kopenhagen.dk** for details of openings and interviews with artists. Comprehensive listings can also be found at **www.aok.dk**, **www.kunstonline.dk**, or the website of the English-language newspaper, *Copenhagen Post*, at **www.cphpost.dk**. Meanwhile, for information about online art, software art and other computer based art forms, check out **www.artificial.dk**.

This was once the largest slaughterhouse in town but, after many dormant years, it was turned into a cultural centre in 1996. At a massive 5,000sq m (53,700sq ft), Øksnehallen is ideal for larger events, such as trade shows and conventions. Exhibitions tend to concentrate on photography and design.

★ V1 Gallery

Flæsketorvet 69–71, Vesterbro (33 31 03 21, www.v1gallery.com). Train København H. **Open** noon-6pm Wed-Fri; noon-4pm Sat; or by appointment. **Admission** free. **No credit cards**.

One of the best-known of Copenhagen's commercial galleries, V1 has a reputation for showcasing work by emerging names – Mads Lynnerup, Kasper Sonne, Carl Krull, Søren Solkær Starbird – and street artists, including Banksy, Shepherd Fairy and Denmark's own HustMitNavn (*see p180* **Inside Track**), who held a solo exhibition here in November 2010. Owners Jesper Elg, Peter Funch and Mikkel Grønnebæk strive to challenge audiences and established norms through visual art, installations, video and sculpture. The gallery was given the FEAGA award for creativity and innovation at ART BASEL 2010.

Gay & Lesbian

Small is beautiful – and very progressive.

Denmark has long been a great place for gays and lesbians. Homosexual sex was legalised way back in 1933, the age of consent equalised in 1977 and registered same-sex partnerships have been available since 1989. This also isn't a nation dragging its heels when it comes to promoting gay culture. In 2009, Denmark hosted the gay and lesbian sporting Outgames, **Copenhagen Pride** is every August (www.copenhagenpride.dk) and the annual **Gay Lesbian Bi Trans Film Festival, Mix Copenhagen** is held in October (www.cglff.dk). Perhaps then, with such a
so-what attitude to sexuality it's unsurprising that the city's nightlife scene is fairly mixed and its gay scene – concentrated around Studiestræde in the centre – small. But what it lacks in size it makes up for with a warmth that few cities can match.

ORGANISATIONS

LGBT Danmark – Landsforeningen for Bøsser, Lesbiske, Biseksuelle og Transpersoner (LGBT)
Nygade 7, 1164 Copenhagen K (33 13 19 48, www.lgbt.dk). Bus 11A. **Open** *for phone enquiries* 2pm-5pm Thur. **Map** p251 N13.
Denmark's national gay and lesbian association for gays, lesbians, bisexuals and transgender persons was founded in 1948, and prides itself on being at the vanguard of gay politics. The LGBT runs an English-language website, www.panbladet.dk.

Stop Aids
Amagertorv 33, 1160 Copenhagen K (33 11 29 11, www.stopaids.dk). **Open** *Phone enquiries* 10am-4pm Mon-Fri. **Map** p251 N14.
Stop Aids has been promoting safe sex in Denmark since 1986. Its refreshing approach has included putting up condom-and-lube compartments in cruising parks, offering numerous free workshops and courses, distributing safe sex kits in gay bars and larger one-off parties, and providing free massages in exchange for a chat about safe sex.

BARS & CLUBS

Admission is free unless otherwise stated.

Amigo Bar
Schønbergsgade 4, Frederiksberg (33 21 49 15). Bus 6A, 14. **Open** 10pm-6am Mon-Thur, Sun; 10pm-7am Fri, Sat. **Credit** AmEx, DC, MC, V. **No credit cards**. **Map** p245 P8.
Amigo Bar attracts an unpretentious mixed crowd of gay men, lesbians and straights. It's a bit of a trek to get to, but then it is one of the very few karaoke venues in town, with plenty of late-night singalongs catering to off-key amateurs. Be prepared for a late one as things only start to hot up at around midnight.

BLUS at Studenterhuset
Købmagergade 52 (35 32 38 60, www.blus.dk). Bus 11A. **Open** *Sept-June* 8pm-1am Tue. **No credit cards**. **Map** p251 M13.
Gay students meet weekly for Tuesday GayDay, although you don't have to be studying to join in with the laidback poetry readings, political discussions, lectures and music performances. Biannual gay parties pack the place to the rafters.

★ Café Intime
Allégade 25, Frederiksberg (38 34 19 58, www.cafeintime.dk). Metro Frederiksberg. **Open** 6pm-2am daily. **No credit cards**.
This pint-sized but eminently popular piano bar has been around since 1920, and these days draws everyone from older Marlene Dietrich obsessives to younger jazz connoisseurs.

★ Centralhjørnet
Kattesundet 18 (33 11 85 49, www.centralhjornet. dk). Bus 11A, 14. **Open** noon-2am daily. **No credit cards**. **Map** p250 N12.

INSIDE TRACK DINNER DATING

Also associated with Dine with the Danes is **Meet Gay Copenhagen** (www. meetgaycopenhagen.dk), which offers dinners and socialising organised by local gay couples.

Copenhagen's most famous gay bar has been around for more than a century, offering a friendly pub atmosphere that's popular with everyone from the local 'countessa' to gay carpenters downing a pint or three after work. Holidays see the owner's notorious taste for wild decoration come to the fore.

Club Christopher
Knabrostræde 3 (www.clubchristopher.dk). Bus 2A, 1A, 15, 40. **Open** midnight-5am Sat. **Credit** Phone for details. **Map** p251 N13.
Named after New York's famed homo street, Christopher is a weekly party on the ground floor of what used to be PAN. At the time of going to press the club was operating on an open bar (drink-as-much-as-you-like) basis for 200kr – expect messiness.

Cosy Bar
Studiestræde 24 (33 12 74 27, www.cosybar.dk). Train København H. **Open** 10pm-6am Mon-Thur, Sun; 10pm-8am Fri, Sat. **Credit** AmEx, MC, V. **Map** p250 N12.
If you're still out and about after a long evening on the town, chances are you'll end up in this dark, boisterous and cruise-oriented bar, where the tiny dancefloor gets ridiculously packed at weekends.

Jailhouse Copenhagen
Studiestræde 12 (33 15 22 55, www. jailhousecph.dk). Train København H. **Open** *Bar* 3pm-2am Mon-Thur, Sun; 3pm-5am Fri, Sat. *Restaurant* 6pm-midnight Thur-Sat (kitchen closes 11pm). **Credit** AmEx, MC, V. **Map** p250 N12.
Jailhouse Copenhagen is a two-level gay bar and restaurant, which is decorated with prison bars and jail-related paraphernalia. Not nearly as hardcore as it sounds, the downstairs bar is noted for being surprisingly relaxed. As a bonus, staff are friendly and easy-going, despite being dressed in full prison guard regalia.

Masken
Studiestræde 33, 1455 København K (33 91 09 37, www.maskenbar.dk). Train København H. **Open** noon-2am Mon-Thu, Sun; Fri-Sat noon-5am.
A giant mural of Scarlett O'Hara and Rhett Butler watches over a diverse, friendly crowd of boys and girls on two floors. As far as the crowd goes, it's a mixed bag of ages and types, though wallet friendly prices and '80s tunes make it particularly popular with students.

Men's Bar
Teglgårdsstræde 3 (33 12 73 03, www. mensbar.dk). Metro/train Nørreport. **Open** 3pm-2am daily. **Credit** AmEx, MC, V. **Map** p250 N12.
The only real men's bar on the scene: jeans, semi-leather, dimly lit. You know the sort of thing. Diluting the saucy vibe slighty is the free brunch from 6pm on the first Sunday of every month.

Copenhagen Pride. *See p184.*

ARTS & ENTERTAINMENT

INSIDE TRACK WEBSITES

For an excellent English overview of gay life in Copenhagen, visit www.copenhagen-gay-life.dk or www.out-and-about.dk.

Never Mind

Nørre Voldgade 2 (33 11 88 86, www.nevermind bar.dk). Metro/train Nørreport. **Open** 10pm-6am daily. **Credit** AmEx, MC, V. **Map** p250 N11.
A lively bar churning out pop and disco hits to a mainly male crowd with late-night revellers tending to bounce between this place and Cosy. Being situated just across from Copenhagen's cruisiest park boosts its appeal dramatically.

★ Oscar Bar & Café

Rådhuspladsen 77 (33 12 09 99, www.oscar barcafe.dk). Metro Kongens Nytorv. **Open** 9.30am-2am daily. **Credit** AmEx, MC, V. **Map** p250 O12.
Take some sexy bartenders, mix with reliable café food and garnish with talented DJs spinning some of the funkiest house and dirtiest disco around, and you're some way to understanding the popularity of Oscar. The atmosphere here is trendy but laidback, and people-watching is always at the top of the menu, making this a must for both first-timers and seasoned pros in Copenhagen.

EVENTS

For details of the **Copenhagen Gay & Lesbian Film Festival** and **Copenhagen Pride**, *see pp164-167* **Calendar**.

FITNESS & SAUNA

Amigo Sauna

Studiestræde 31 (33 15 20 28, www.amigo-sauna.dk). Train Vesterport. **Open** noon-7am Mon-Thur, Sun; noon-8am Fri, Sat. **Admission** 100Kr. **Credit** MC, V. **Map** p250 N12.
Copenhagen's largest gay sauna is very dark, very lively and definitely a place for some serious action, especially on weekends.

Copenhagen Gay Center

Istedgade 34-36 (33 22 23 00, www.copenhagengaycenter.com). Train København H. **Open** 10am-10pm Mon-Thur, Sun; 10am-11pm Fri, Sat. **Credit** MC, V. **No credit cards.** **Map** p250 P10.
A small sauna and gay shop in Copenhagen's red light district complete with an intimate cinema for gay film screenings.

HOTELS

Carsten's Guest House

5th floor, Christians Brygge 28, Slotsholmen, 1559 Copenhagen V (33 14 91 07, www.carstens guesthouse.dk). Train København H or metro Christianshavn. **Rates** 180kr dormitory; 480kr-495kr single; 510kr-585kr double; 892kr-1,185kr studio or apartment. **Credit** AmEx, MC, V. **Map** p251 Q14.
Queens will definitely fall in love with this gay and lesbian guest house: from the outside, it looks just like a cake castle; inside, it's a luxurious (but surprisingly affordable) B&B. Past guests have only good things to say about the amiable proprietors and their warm, personal service.
Non-smoking rooms. Parking. TV.

Oscar Bar & Café.

Nightlife

Let the goodtimes roll.

For such a small city, Copenhagen's nightlife is surprisingly vibrant. Sure, there isn't the same diverse range of sub-cultural 'scenes' that flourish in other European capitals – crate-digging audiophiles are largely notable by their absence – but various forms of electronic music are well represented, with top-name international DJs being regularly booked at clubs such as Culture Box, Rust and Vega.

Those looking for the most happening zones should make a beeline for **Kødbyen**, Copenhagen's regenerated Meatpacking District, and **Nørrebro**. Kødbyen's low-rise butchers' shops and slaughterhouses have been transformed into a host of cool bars and laid-back clubs since 2005, while Nørrebro is home to some of the edgiest bars in town.

THE LOWDOWN

First-time visitors may initially find Copenhagen's party scene a little elusive. There are a few superb clubs and a multitude of über-stylish venues packed with armies of attractive punters, but the best nights are mainly promoter-rather than venue-led, which means that it's possible to turn up randomly on an off-night even at some of the more dedicated clubs – including **Rust** (*see p189*) and **Vega** (*see p190*) – and find the place a little lacking in atmosphere and people.

As with everywhere else this side of the millennium, Copenhagen is experiencing a blurring of the boundaries between pre-clubbing restaurant, café, bar and lounge venues that don't fit into the typical club mould, but which can be equally worthy of a night out in themselves. **Boutique Lize** (*see p186*), **Barbarellah** (*see p186*) and **Gefährlich** (*see p187*) are just a few such hybrids, where it's as easy to throw down a few cocktails before heading elsewhere as it is to spend the whole evening partying there in the bar, if you don't have the inclination to move on.

The places listed here are the city's main nightlife venues, but clubs come and go and places fall in and out of fashion so it's also worth checking the local press for updates on regular nights and one-offs. Online resources with info in English on venues, cafés and bars is **www.aok.dk**. For up-to-date information on forthcoming events, check out the *Copenhagen Post* (www.cphpost.dk) – a Danish newspaper in English, available from kiosks and cafés.

For more regular visitors, **Human Productions** (www.humanwebsite.com), a group of organisers, artists and party people, sends out a weekly email that keeps a finger on the pulse of underground art, culture and nightlife events, while the Danish website **www.hifly.dk** puts flyers for electronic and house music up on its calendar. As always, record stores are another good place to pick up flyers, as are the more streetwear-oriented clothing stores: check out Amoeba Records on Hyskenstræde and Wasteland clothing store on Studiestraede.

Finally, a word about stimulant use: it may not be as rampant as in other European capital cities, but toilets without lids and one-in-a-cubicle policies demonstrate that it's definitely present. Remember that security do search for drugs and will expel you immediately if they find any.

INSIDE TRACK LATE STARTS

Due to the price of alcohol, locals usually don't get going until late, preferring to pre-party at home, so don't expect to hang with the hipsteratti before midnight. Luckily, there is a plethora of places to begin the night and once they get started, many clubs and large bars stay open until 5am on Friday and Saturday nights.

Bakken i Kødbyen.

LOUNGE & MUSIC BARS

★ Bakken i Kødbyen

Flæsketorvet 19-21, Kødbyen (no phone, www.bakkenkbh.dk). Train København H or Dybbølsbro. **Open** 9pm-4am Thur-Sat. **Admission** free. **Credit** AmEx, MC, V.

One of the trendiest nightspots of the moment, Bakken is located in the cool Meatpacking District (Kødbyen). The area's restaurants and bars, this one included, are all housed in former butchers' shops and slaughterhouses; in fact, some of the district's original tennants remain, so don't be surprised if you bump into some men in white coats carrying carcasses, if you stay out till dawn. Bakken's smoky, dark interior is packed with a fashion-conscious revellers, who pile in to the small space to socialise, get drunk and move to the dance and indie-rock tunes provided by resident DJs.

Barbarellah

Nørre Farimagsgade 41 (33 32 00 61, www. barbarellah.dk). Metro or train to Nørreport. **Open** 3pm-2am Wed-Thur; 3pm-4am Fri, Sat. **Admission** free. **Credit** AmEx, MC, V. **Map** p250 M11.

Right in the heart of the boho Nansensgade quarter, Barbarellah is a large, friendly café lounge-cum-cocktail bar, with good vibes and DJs dropping beats until the small hours.

Bar Rouge

Hotel Skt Petri, Krystalgade 22 (33 45 98 22, www.hotelsktpetri.com). Metro or train to Nørreport. **Open** 5pm-midnight Mon-Wed, Sun; 5pm-1am Thur; 5pm-2am Fri, Sat. **Admission** free. **Credit** AmEx, MC, V. **Map** p251 M13.

Hosting everything from the main MTV Music Awards after-party to regular gatherings of top-end model agencies, it's all been happening at Hotel Skt Petri, and that's probably all thanks to the svelte trappings of Bar Rouge. It's good to note that members and hotel guests have priority when it comes to entry, although a timely email can usually secure a much coveted place on the guestlist even on a weekend. Music-wise, evenings ususally start with a bit of Buddha Bar chill and work their way up to Ibiza-style house.

Boutique Lize

Enghave Plads 6 (33 31 15 60). Bus 10. **Open** 8pm-3am Thur; 8pm-4.30am Fri, Sat. **Admission** free. **No credit cards**. **Map** p245 S7.

Boutique Lize is one of the best cocktail bars in the city, with queues of people trying to get in from 11pm onwards. It attracts a lot of the area's more mature trendsetters with its hip Vesterbro ambience and reasonably priced cocktails. There is a happy hour from 8-11.30pm on Thursday and 8-10pm on Fridays and Saturdays.

Café Bopa

Løgstørgade 8, Østerbro (35 43 05 66, www. cafebopa.dk). Train Nordhavn or bus 1A, 14. **Open** 9am-midnight Mon-Wed, Sun; 9am-2am Thur; 9am-5am Fri, Sat. **Admission** free. **Credit** MC, V. **Map** p248 B14.

A friendly café, bar and restaurant popular with trendy locals. Disco and mainstream dance comprise the tunes, and in summer the café spills out on to Bopa Plads, with deckchairs, rugs and pétanque.

Gefährlich

Fælledvej 7, Nørrebro (35 24 13 24, www.gefahrlich.dk). Bus 3A. **Open** 5pm-1am Tue, Sun; 5pm-2am Wed; 5pm-3am Thur-Sat. **Admission** free. **Credit** AmEx, MC, V. **Map** p248 J10.

Gefährlich (German for 'dangerous') claims to be a restaurant, bar, art gallery, coffee shop, record store, cultural centre and nightclub all rolled into one. It may sound a bit over-conceptualised and ambitious, but in reality it's a rather small, low-key affair with an eclectic programme of regular and one-off events, including a rare soul night on the first Saturday of every month.

Ideal Bar

Enghavevej 40, Vesterbro (33 25 70 11, www. vega.dk). Bus 3A, 10. **Open** 10pm-4am Wed; 10pm-5am Thur-Sat. **Admission** free. **Credit** MC, V. **Map** p245 S7.

Part of the Vega complex (*see p190*), this classic lounge bar is ideal for pre-club drinks or even after-partying. Thursdays are especially popular, with gypsy punk and Balkan grooves on offer, Saturdays cater to hipster kids with electro-indie at Svedhytten, which means sweat-lodge or sauna. Delightful.

Isola Bar

Israels Plads 16 (33 13 61 13, www.isolabar.dk). Metro Nørreport. **Open** 8pm-5am Thur-Sat. **Admission** free. **Credit** MC, V. **Map** p246 L12.

As Stereo Bar, this was a long-time cornerstone of Copenhagen revelry. Now called Isola, it's a rock bar and live venue, pitching itself as an alternative club to the city's electronic after-dark hangouts. Expect a rock crowd and a bar that mainly sells beer.

Oak Room

Birkegade 10, Nørrebro (38 60 38 60, www.oak room.dk). Bus 3A, 5A. **Open** 8pm-midnight Tue,

Rust. *See p189.*

Wed; 8pm-2am Thur; 4pm-4am Fri; 6pm-4am Sat.
No credit cards. **Map** p248 J10.
A tiny, stylish lounge bar tucked around the corner
from trendy Sankt Hans Torv, the Oak Room is
literally that: a single, narrow room dominated by a
huge wooden bar. When it's packed (which seems
to be every weekend), it's very hard to sit in the
little wooden booths opposite the bar without
getting your drinks knocked over by passers-by;
for some, this seems to be a legitimate means for
meeting members of the opposite sex. Happy hour
is until 9pm.

Zoo Bar

Sværtegade 6 (33 15 68 69, www.zoobar.dk).
Metro Kongens Nytorv. **Open** 11am-midnight
Mon-Wed; 11am-2am Thur-Sat. **Admission**
free. **Credit** AmEx, DC, MC, V. **Map** p251 M14.
It might no longer be the most fashionable bar in
the city, but Zoo is still a popular central spot to
meet and warm up with a few drinks before heading out clubbing, and it occasionally throws a
decent party in its own right. It's intimate (read:
small) and the excellent window seats are
perfect for a spot of people-watching on trendy
Kronprinsensgade. At the weekends there are DJs
from 7pm.

CLUBS

Celcius

Rådhuspladsen 16, 1st Floor (70 33 35 55,
www.celcius.dk). Train København H. **Open**
midnight-5am Fri, Sat. **Admission** by guestlist
only, price varies by event, typically 100kr.
Credit AmEx, MC, V. **Map** p250 O12.

INSIDE TRACK
COPENHAGEN DISTORTION

Started out by hosting mobile raves
in unusual locations (buses and boats,
for example), but has since grown into a
week-long festival of music and conceptual
art every June, with occasional one-off
parties throughout the year. Visit
www.cphdistortion.dk for details.

With amazing views over the main square of
Rådhuspladsen, Copenhagen's answer to Piccadilly
Circus, Celcius is the latest club to hit the city centre
and was already garnering a painfully trendy crowd
of regulars at the time of going to press. That said,
Celcius's craving for glamour could ultimately be its
downfall. See website for details of events, and to
sign up for the mandatory guestlist.

★ Culture Box

Kronprinsessegade 54A (33 32 50 50,
www.culture-box.com). Metro Nørreport
or Kongens Nytorv. **Open** varies; typically
midnight-6am Fri, Sat. **Admission** 50kr-90kr.
Credit AmEx, MC, V. **Map** p247 K15.
Copenhagen's premier techno palace regularly plays
host to DJ legends like Derrick May and Jeff Mills.
The sound system has by far the most penetrating
bass in town, the VJ shows are superb and the more
sedate downstairs dancefloor is perfect for those
who don't want to sweat for hours on the main floor
of 'the Box'. Their next-door pre-clubbing bar,
Cocktail Box, is open from 8pm.

Søpavilionen. *See p190.*

Vega. *See p190.*

★ Jolene

*Flaesketorvet 94, Kødbyen (no phone,
www.myspace.com/jolenebar). Train København
H or Dybbølsbro.* **Open** 5pm-2am Mon-Thur,
Sun; 5pm-3am Fri, Sat. **Admission** varies.
Credit AmEx, MC, V.

Jolene recently relocated from Sorgenfrigade to
this former slaughterhouse in Kødbyen. And, of all
the bars in the district, it probably is the one that
most lives up to its 'meat market' tag – albeit with
a studenty, fun-packed vibe. The small club has a
diverse line-up of DJs that get the tightly packed
crowds moving.

NASA

*Boltens Gård, Kongens Nytorv (33 93 74 15/
www.nasa.dk). Metro Kongens Nytorv.* **Open**
11pm-6am Fri; midnight-6am Sat **Admission**
100kr, subject to doorman's discretion. **Credit**
AmEx, MC, V. **Map** p251 M15.

A long time ago (in a galaxy far, far away), NASA
supposedly represented the cream of the cream of
Copenhagen clubbing. These days that accolade
seems to refer only to the bio-morphic, all-white interior, inspired by the glamour of space travel and
Stanley Kubrick's sanitised visions of the future.
While it used to be a members-only nightspot with
a reputation for being even harder to get into than a
pair of hotpants, the trendy patina has worn off and
it's now a far less discriminatory venue, swearing
instead by a policy of 'massclusivity': namely, if you
can afford to pay for a table there, then you're in.

Nevertheless, NASA remains one of the most
amazing-looking clubs in the world, with some
nights – including those hosted by party legend Jean
Eric von Baden – that are still good enough to eclipse
the air of studied self-consciousness.

Park Café

*Østerbrogade 79, Østerbro (35 42 62 48,
www.parkcafe.dk). Bus 1A, 14, 83N, 85N, 95N.*
Open 11pm-5am Fri; 11pm-6am Sat. **Admission**
100kr. **Credit** AmEx, MC, V. **Map** p248 B13.

With three dancefloors, a restaurant and a capacity
of 2,000, it's not surprising that Park attracts a more
mature, dressed-up crowd. On Friday and Saturday
(after the restaurant closes), the whole venue turns
into a nightclub, featuring mainstream house, pop
and R&B.

★ Rust

*Guldbergsgade 8, Nørrebro (35 24 52 00,
www.rust.dk). Bus 5A.* **Open** 9pm-5am Wed-
Sat. **Admission** 40kr Wed, Thur; 60kr Fri,
Sat; 50kr Fri, Sat; prices vary according to
events. **Credit** MC, V. **Map** p246 H10.

Rust is one of the city's best venues for both concerts and clubbing, and an integral part of
Copenhagen's nightlife. Its evolution over the years
(from political café through to dubious rock club
and finally the more polished venue seen today) is
all the more impressive for its retention of an experimental edge and an ability to roll with the times.
Photo p187.

The small cocktail bar, Living Room, is a minimalist interpretation of a 1970s lounge, complete with groovy low seating, mellow lighting and a chilled ambience. There's also the sweaty downstairs area, Bassment, living up to its name with plenty of growling beats.

Søpavillionen

Gyldenløvesgade 24 (33 15 12 24, www.soepavillionen.dk). Metro Forum or Nørreport. **Open** 11pm-5am Fri, Sat. **Admission** 90kr-125kr. **Credit** MC, V. **Map** p246 M10.

This beautiful white pavilion on the lake holds one of the meatiest Saturday night meat markets in town: a seventh heaven for divorced thirtysomethings looking to groove to innocuous pop hits. The building, designed by architect Vilhelm Dahlerup in the 1890s, is spectacular, especially when it's lit up at night. *Photo p188.*

★ Vega

Enghavevej 40, Vesterbro (33 25 70 11, www.vega.dk). Bus 3A, 10. **Open** varies, nightclub 11pm-5am Fri, Sat; concerts typically start 7-8pm. **Admission** nightclub 60kr-150kr; concerts 100kr-400kr. **Credit** MC, V. **Map** p245 S7.

Vega, opened in 1996, is the queen of Copenhagen's nightlife, a listed landmark building featuring a large and small concert hall, Big Vega and Little Vega (1,200 and 550 capacity respectively), the latter of which doubles up as a nightclub, plus a lounge and cocktail bar, the Yankee Bar and the street-level Ideal Bar, a party institution in itself. The list of famous names to have played at Vega in recent years is a testament to its popularity, from secret gigs by Prince and David Bowie to concerts from the likes of Björk. The interior is superb, the service professional and the DJs among the best in town. Gig tickets are also available online. *Photo p189.*

LIVE MUSIC VENUES

See also *p188* **Clubs**.

Jazz, blues, folk & world

★ Copenhagen JazzHouse

Niels Hemmingsens Gade 10 (33 15 26 00, www.jazzhouse.dk). Metro Kongens Nytorv. **Open** *Concerts* 6.30pm-5am Thur-Sat; open when concerts on Mon-Wed, Sun. *Club* JazzHouse midnight-5am Thur-Sat. **Admission** *Club* JazzHouse free Thur; 60kr after midnight Fri, Sat. *Concerts* prices vary. **Credit** AmEx, MC, V. **Map** p251 M13.

The JazzHouse builds on the legacy of the legendary but long gone Copenhagen Montmartre jazz club of the 1960s. Now the country's premier jazz venue, JazzHouse is subsidised by the government and showcases both international and local musicians.

It offers consistently good gigs on Thursdays, Fridays and Saturdays (and sometimes on other nights of the week) throughout the year. When concerts finish, the large downstairs dancefloor is filled by a younger disco-loving crowd, while celebs can occasionally be spotted in the upstairs bar area.

La Fontaine

Kompagnistræde 11 (33 11 60 98, www.lafontaine.dk). **Open** 7pm-5am daily. *Metro Kongens Nytorv.* **Admission** free Mon-Thur, Sun; 60kr Fri, Sat. **No credit cards.** **Map** p251 O13.

Though it has a capacity of only 60 people, this cosy, low-key jazz venue is well known for its legendary jam sessions and late, late nights. It attracts music students and other jazz lovers to its weekend swing and mainstream concerts. It's also one of the few bars in town that are open until 5am every night.

Global

Nørre Alle 7 (50 58 08 41, www.globalcph.dk). Bus 5A. **Open** varies. **Admission** varies. **No credit cards.** **Map** p246 H10.

This new Nørrebro venue, near Sankt Hans Torv, hosts bands from Denmark and abroad, encompassing nu-folk, jazz, fusion, reggae, blues and more. DJ-led club nights are also on the menu.

Mojo

Løngangstræde 21C (33 11 64 53, www.mojo.dk). Bus 14. **Open** 8pm-5am daily. **Admission** varies according to event. **Credit** MC, V. **Map** p251 O13.

Grubby but friendly little blues venue, featuring live entertainment every night.

Rock & pop

Amager Bio

Øresundsvej 6 (tickets Billetnet 70 15 65 65, information 32 86 02 00, www.amagerbio.dk). Metro Lergravsparken, then 5min walk. **Open** varies according to event. **Admission** varies according to event. **Credit** AmEx, MC, V.

One of the largest concert spaces in Copenhagen, with a capacity of 1,000. The programme is strong on old-school rock, blues and country.

★ Loppen

Christiania (32 57 84 22, www.loppen.dk). Metro Christianshavn, then 5min walk. **Open** 9pm-2am Mon-Sun. **Admission** 50kr-200kr. **Credit** V. **Map** p252 P18.

Since opening in 1973, Loppen has built an excellent reputation for live music despite its dilapidated surroundings, and its predilection for rock predates Copenhagen's rock revival. The booking policy is adventurous, covering the whole spectrum from jazz to rock, but with a strong emphasis on alternative sounds. Loppen is unconcerned with refinement, wallowing languorously in the unique environment of Copenhagen's former hippie enclave.

ARTS & ENTERTAINMENT

Performing Arts

New architectural marvels have boosted an already strong cultural scene.

Copenhagen is known the world over for its jazz scene, but the city also has much to offer the classical music lover. Not only can you enjoy professional outfits like the **Danish National Symphony Orchestra** – housed in the new Jean Nouvel-designed **DR Koncerthuset**, now Scandinavia's top concert hall – but the seemingly limitless number of atmospheric churches offer a range of regular concerts.

The language barrier means that much of what happens in Copenhagen's dramatic arts arena remains inaccessible to visitors – aside from a shared architectural awe for the new waterside **Royal Danish Playhouse**. However, as many of the city's most interesting directors come from abroad, it is possible for non-Danes to enjoy a night at the theatre, especially in some of the more experimental venues, or in Vivienne McKee's **London Toast Theatre**. Opera fans, meanwhile, are in for a treat with the impressive **Operaen**, which gave a new lease of life to the opera scene when it opened in 2005. The city's dance scene, too, has been reignited in the past few years, both in terms of small modern dance venues and as a result of the reorganisation of the Royal Danish Theatre.

Classical Music & Opera

ENSEMBLES

Foremost among the professional choirs is **Musica Ficta** (www.ficta.dk), a chamber choir led by composer and conductor Bo Holten and performing mostly Renaissance and contemporary music. **Camerata Chamber Choir** (www.camerata.dk) is one of Denmark's oldest choirs; founded in 1965, it has attracted some of the best choral singers in the country, many of them students at the musical department of the University of Copenhagen. For something completely different, try **Concerto Copenhagen** (www.coco.dk), Scandinavia's leading baroque orchestra and one of the more interesting early music groups in Europe.

COMPETITIONS

Relative to its size, Denmark hosts an impressive range of competitions. The most important one for conductors is named after Nikolai Malko, a conductor who brought the Danish National Symphony Orchestra to prominence after World War II. The **International Nikolai Malko Competition for Young Conductors** (www.malkocompetition.com) happens every three years, with the next due to take place in 2012.

Denmark's highest musical honour is the **Léonie Sonning Music Prize** – a 600,000kr award given out annually to an internationally acknowledged composer, musician, conductor or singer. This prestigious prize has previously been given to such artists as Keith Jarrett, Leonard Bernstein, Gidon Kremer, Janet Baker and flautist Michala Petri. The last Dane to win it was Lars Ulrik Mortensen in 2007.

ARTS & ENTERTAINMENT

Profile Royal Danish Theatre

The Royal Danish Theatre's stages have expanded dramatically over the past few years.

Originally confined to one building – the Royal Danish Theatre (Det Kongelige Theater) at Kongens Nytorv – the Royal Danish Theatre has now been split into three different venues. The original building (now named Gamle Scene – 'Old Stage') is now used principally for ballet, while two spectacular, purpose-built architectural marvels – the Opera House, which opened in 2005, and the Royal Danish Playhouse, completed in 2008 – occupy opposite sides of Copenhagen's waterfront.

Additional Royal Danish Theatre performances also take place at the new DR Koncerthuset (*see p194*). Productions and information for all of the venues can be found at **www.kglteater.dk**.

Skuespilhuset.

SKUESPILHUSET (ROYAL DANISH PLAYHOUSE)

This stunning (but initially controversial) purpose-built three-stage playhouse opened in February 2008 (with a production of *Hamlet*) on the harbourfront at Kvæsthusgade, round the corner from Nyhavn. Designed by Danish architectural practice Lundgaard & Tranberg (which was awarded a RIBA European Award for the building), its

arrival marked the broadening and modernising of the Royal Theatre's role in Danish performing arts. The 20,000-square-metre building, consisting of three stages, is now the principal venue for dramatic theatre in Denmark, but also hosts a small number of music, dance and children's events.

Emmet Feigenberg has been artistic director since 2008; he took over from Mikkel Harder Munck-Hansen, who did much to reinvigorate the company.

Operaen.

ARTS & ENTERTAINMENT

As this is the national theatre, tickets are subsided by the government. Note, however, that most works at the Playhouse are in Danish.

OPERAEN (COPENHAGEN OPERA HOUSE)

Opera got a new lease of life in Copenhagen after the inauguration of the stunning new harbourside Opera House in January 2005 – purpose-built for the opera wing of the Royal Danish Theatre. Designed by Henning Larsen, the building is nine floors high, covers 41,000 square metres (376,000 square feet) and is home to two separate stages: the grandiose main stage and the neighbouring 'Takkelloftet', the latter used for more experimental productions and opera for younger audiences. Meanwhile, artistic director Kasper Bech Holten continues to strengthen contemporary Danish opera while remaining loyal to the classics, with everything from Tchaikovsky to hip hop fusion on the programme.

The Operaen's 2010/11 season includes a number of classics, such as Puccini's *Madame Butterfly*, and four operas that have never before been presented by the Royal Danish Theatre: Verdi's *Nabucco*; Alban Berg's *Lulu*; Richard Strauss's *Die Frau ohne Schatten*, as well as Danish composer Poul Ruder's new opera *Dancer in the Dark*.

Concerts, ballet and plays are also performed here.

DET KONGELIGE TEATER, GAMLE SCENE (ROYAL DANISH THEATRE, OLD STAGE)

With the opening of Operaen in 2005, the Royal Theatre shifted for the first time in its history. When the Playhouse

Det Kongelige Teater, Gamle Scene.

opened in the 2008, it modernised further, and its original building near Kongens Nytorv (renamed 'Old Stage') is now principally used for ballet (being the home of the Royal Danish Ballet, see p199), although dramatic theatre and concerts also still take place here. The building also houses the Royal Danish Theatre's costume department.

The building started life in 1748, but was largely replaced in 1874. Its baroque interior, with crystal chandeliers, red velvet, golden angels and frescoed ceilings reflects the lavishness of the time. Two bronze statues are situated in front of the building's exterior (which was undergoing restoration works at the end of 2010), a tribute to Danish dramatists Adam Oehlenschläger and Ludvig Holberg.

Stærekassen – originally the 'new stage' of the theatre, added as an annexe in 1931 – was so named because of the way it hangs over Tordenskjoldsgade street (it translates as 'Nesting Box'). This stage is now owned by the Ministry of Finance, Palaces and Properties Agency, and used for one-off events.

HIDDEN MEANINGS?

Against the foyer's red background, the Operaen's chandeliers bear an uncanny resemblance to the flag of Christiania, with its three yellow circles.

GUIDED TOURS

Tours can be booked for each venue; contact the individual venue directly for details. All houses also have excellent restaurants and bars.

ARTS & ENTERTAINMENT

FESTIVALS

Copenhagen hosts a number of festivals. In the summer you can usually find organ festivals, a baroque festival and Tivoli Koncertsal's season of mini festivals (from April to September). Every other year national broadcaster Danmarks Radio puts on a competition for young ensembles and chamber musicians at DR Koncerthuset, while the **Copenhagen Summer Festival** (www.copenhagensummerfestival.dk) is an annual showcase for both young talents and established names in the classical music world. The festival takes place in late July/early August in the Charlottenborg Festival Hall in Kongens Nytorv, and boasts 12 concerts in 12 days, many with free admission.

Contact the **Wonderful Copenhagen Tourist Information Bureau** (70 22 24 42, www.visitcopenhagen.com) for further details of all the above, as well as information on its free Wednesday concert series, held at various venues at 5pm throughout the year.

MAJOR VENUES

Black Diamond

Søren Kirkegaards Plads 1 (33 47 47 47/ www.kb.dk). Bus 66. **Box office** 1hr before performances (or from BILLETnet 70 15 65 65). **Credit** MC, V. **Map** p250 P15.
The concert hall in the Black Diamond is panelled with Canadian maple and ornamented with black tapestries woven with quotations from Hans Christian Andersen's fairytales. The ensemble in residence plays six times a year, with a repertoire covering everything from modern classics and newly composed works to experiments in the borderlands between musical styles.

★ DR Koncerthuset

Emil Holms Kanal 20, Ørestad (35 20 30 40, 35 20 62 62, www.dr.dk/Koncerthuset). Metro DR-Byen. **Box office** 2-5pm Wed-Fri. Note that tickets can also be bought from BILLETnet (70 15 65 65). **Credit** MC, V.
See p198 **Profile**.

★ Operaen (Copenhagen Opera House)

Ekvipagemestervej 10 (33 69 69 69, www.kgl teater.dk). **Box office** 10am-4pm Mon-Sat. **Credit** DC, MC, V. **Map** p249 L18.
See p192 **Profile**.

Royal Danish Academy of Music (Konservatoriets Koncertsal)

Julius Thomsens Gade 1, Frederiksberg (72 26 72 26, www.dkdm.dk). Metro Forum or bus 2A, 68. **Box office** (by phone) 9am-3pm Mon-Fri. **Admission** free. **Credit** MC, V. **Map** p248 M9
This Functionalist architectural gem, built in 1945, housed the Danish Broadcasting Corporation's

Radiohusets Koncertsal until the summer of 2008. It's now the venue for the Royal Danish Academy of Music's 200 annual public concerts, many of which are free of charge. The Academy's Concert Hall is also the new winter residence of the Copenhagen Philharmonic Orchestra.

Tivolis Koncertsal

Tivoli, Vesterbrogade 3 (Tivoli information line 33 15 10 01, ticket centre 33 15 10 12, www. tivoli.dk). Train København H. **Box office** *Mid Apr-mid Sept, mid Nov-23 Dec* 9am-11pm daily. *Mid Sept-mid Nov, 24 Dec-mid Apr* 9am-5pm Mon-Fri. Note that the phone line is open 10am-8pm daily. **Credit** AmEx, MC, V. **Map** p250 P12.
Throughout summer (mid April to late September) there is jazz and other popular music in the various little pavilions dotted around the park, while the concerts in the Koncertsal vary from musicals to chamber music. Visit the website for up-to-date information as seasonal times do vary.

Other venues

Christianskirke

Strandgade 1 (32 54 15 76, www.christians kirke.dk). Metro Christianshavn or bus 2A, 40, 66, 350S. **No credit cards**. **Map** p252 P16.
Concerts in this 16th-century church cover the full spectrum of musical genres, from gospel to chamber music, and are held throughout the year.

Garnisons Kirken

Skt Annæ Plads 4 (33 91 27 06/www.garnisons kirken.dk). Metro Kongens Nytorv. **No credit cards**. **Map** p252 M16.
The venue itself is unremarkable, but this church hosts a number of enjoyable concerts throughout the year. The gaudy gold and red organ may not be easy on the eye, but it rarely fails to please the ear.

Holmens Kirke

Holmens Kanal (33 13 61 78/www.holmens kirke.dk). Metro Kongens Nytorv. **No credit cards. Map** p252 O15.

Every Easter and Christmas Holmens Kirke hosts performances of Bach's sublime Passions – both the *St John* and the *St Matthew* – and Handel's *Messiah*. There's also music throughout the evening on the annual Culture Night in October (*see p166* **For One Night Only**).

Kastelskirken

Kastellet 15 (33 91 27 06/www.kastelskirken.dk). Bus 15, 19. **No credit cards. Map** p249 H17.

This beautifully restored yellow-painted church has unique acoustics and is often used for recordings as well as concerts. Sometimes a military brass band performs on the square outside the church, mixing the usual military marches with the occasional ABBA number.

Musikteatret Undergrunden

Åkandevej 20, Værløse (44 47 49 44/ www.undergrunden.com).

Underground Music Theatre is a touring opera company for children founded in 1977 by Niels and Kaja Pihl. The theatre works in a wide range of styles, from avant-garde experiments to repertory works, with puppet operas a regular fixture since 1989.

Theatre

What follows is an overview of the organisations, venues, groups and festivals that make up the Copenhagen theatre scene. More general information can be found at **www.kultur naut.dk**, **www.aok.dk** and **www.cphpost.dk**.

VENUES

With the opening of the Operaen and Royal Danish Playhouse, the 'Old Stage' (Gamle Scene; *see p192* **Profile**) of the Royal Danish Theatre on Kongens Nytorv is now mainly used for dance performances.

Folketeatret

Nørregade 39 (33 12 18 45, administration 38 34 55 55, www.folketeatret.dk). Metro Nørreport. **Box office** 1-6pm Mon-Fri; noon-4pm Sat. **Credit** MC, V. **Map** p250 M12.

Despite starting out as a down-to-earth competitor to the Royal Theatre, the 'People's Theatre' – which celebrated its 150th birthday in 2007 – now offers an eclectic mix of more modern performances across three stages.

Grønnegårds Teatret

Bredgade 66 (33 16 22 12, box office 33 32 70 23, www.groennegaard.dk). Bus 1A. **Box office**

Mid June-Sept Times vary; call or check online. **Credit** AmEx, MC, V. **Map** p249 K17.

Grønnegårds Teatret enjoys a unique outdoor location, nestling under linden trees in the garden of the Danish Museum of Art and Design. The season runs throughout the summer and features a visit by the Royal Danish Ballet each July, with pre-performance picnic baskets from the museum's restaurant.

Køpenhavns Musikteater

Kronprinsensgade 7 (33 32 38 30, booking 33 32 55 56, www.kobenhavnsmusikteater.dk). Metro or train Nørreport. **Box office** 1hr before performances. **No credit cards. Map** p251 M14.

This 'music theatre' seems to have gone through an identity crisis in the past five years: in 2006, it changed its name from Den Anden Opera to Plex, in order to reflect a more international profile; then in 2008 it changed its name again to Køpenhavns Musikteater. The theatre still fills every floor of its beautiful old Pentecostal church with installation and sound art, video, dance and experimental music performances. Note that there is an additional box office in Tivoli (9am-5pm Mon-Fri).

Mungo Park

Fritz Hansensvej 23, Allerød (48 13 13 00, box office 48 13 13 09, www.mungopark.dk). Train Allerød. **Box office** 4-8pm Thur, Fri; 3-5pm Sat. Bookings can also be made by email: billet@mungopark.dk. **No credit cards.**

A small theatre in a former furniture store in a leafy suburb 30 minutes north-west of Copenhagen by train may seem of little relevance, but Mungo Park's fearlessness in tackling difficult topics has attracted a lot of attention since the theatre was established in 1979; *Women Know Your Body*, for example, was a 2010 adaptation of an iconic set of Scandinavian feminist manuals from the 1970s.

▶ *Mungo Park opened a new theatre in the town of Kolding, a 2.5-hour journey by train, in 2008.*

Det Ny Teater

Gammel Kongevej 29, Vesterbro (box office 33 25 50 75, www.detnyteater.dk). Train København H. **Box office** noon-6pm Mon; noon-7.30pm Tue-Fri; noon-8pm Sat; noon-4pm Sun. Note that it's only open on weekends during performance runs. **Credit** AmEx, MC, V. **Map** p245 P8.

The misleading New Theatre (it opened in 1908) is best known for staging Danish versions of money-making international musicals (the Danish premiere of *Wicked* opened in January 2011), but it also has a restaurant, Teater Kælderen, where actors wait on tables and perform routines between servings.

Østre Gasværk Teater

Nyborggade 17 (39 27 71 77, www.oestre-gasvaerk.dk). Bus 18, 865. **Box office** 2-6pm Mon-Fri. Bookings can also be made online. **Credit** AmEx, MC, V. **Map** p248 A14.

This old building – a former gas storage facility – regularly plays host to visually dazzling, big-budget productions often with plenty of international performers, but English-language pieces are few and far between.

Plan-B Teater

Huset, Magstræde 14 (33 91 11 77, box office 33 12 58 14, www.plan-b-teater.dk). **Box office** 4-6pm Tue-Fri. **No credit cards**. **Map** p248 A14.
Plan-B was founded in 2002, but theatre has been performed in Huset since its days as a hub of the grass roots radicalism that engulfed Copenhagen in the 1960s and '70s. Premieres from the likes of Teater Grob and Mammutteatret are staged alongside works by smaller, more experimental groups.

Republique

Østerfælled Torv 34-37 (33 23 31 00, box office 70 20 10 31, www.republique.dk). Bus 1A, 14, 18 or train Svanemøllen St. **Box office** 2-6pm Mon-Fri; 2-4pm Sat. **Credit** AmEx, MC, V. **Map** p248 B13.
Republique opened its doors for the first time in June 2009, as an independent institution that's nonetheless supported by State funds. As part of Copenhagen Theater's collective strategy, the theatre is dedicated to new interpretations of classic works, international theatre arts and family productions, and has a constant aim of challenging the limitations of theatre. Music events are also held here.

★ Skuespilhuset (Royal Danish Playhouse)

Sankt Annæ Plads 36 (main box office 33 69 69 69, www.kgl-teater.dk). Metro Kongens Nytorv or bus 11A, 29. **Box office** 2-6pm Mon-Sat. **Credit** MC, V. **Map** p252 N16.
See p192 **Profile**.

COMPANIES

Cantabile 2

55 34 01 19, www.cantabile2.dk.
Many of Cantabile 2's pieces are site-specific, while those performed in theatres can often see the space totally transformed. The company is responsible for the biennial Waves festival, which gathers performers from around the world in the town of Vordingborg every other August.

Copenhagen Theatre Circle

www.ctcircle.dk.
The only amateur English-language theatre group in Denmark, composed of non-professionals working in their spare time and aiming to stage at least one production per year. Recently performed playwrights include Dario Fo and Harold Pinter.

Holland House

35 55 26 40, www.hollandhouse.dk.

Holland House was founded in 1988 by Danish artist Ane Mette Ruge and Dutch opera director Jacob Schokking. Since then the company has pushed at the boundaries of both modern theatre and opera, generating a buzz the world over.

Hotel Pro Forma

32 54 02 17, www.hotelproforma.dk.
Kirsten Dehlholm, the founder of HPF, has a background in textile design as well as the hippie movement of the 1960s – both factors that have influenced the group's shows, which are often radical in subject matter and performed in the most unconventional of theatrical spaces.

London Toast Theatre

33 22 86 86, www.londontoast.dk.
The enormously successful LTT was established in 1982 by British actress, writer and director Vivienne McKee and her Danish husband Søren Hall. Its ecclectic English-language repertoire spans everything from the moderns and Shakespeare to stand-up comedy and murder mysteries. Its lighthearted Christmas cabarets have become a fixture of the Tivoli Christmas season.

Meridiano Teater

45 20 20 90, www.meridiano.dk.
Italian director Giacomo Ravicchio has earned a reputation for visual design and ingenious stagecraft at Meridiano, which he founded in 1995 with actors Elise Müller and Lars Begtrup. Many of the performances are aimed at audiences from six years upwards.

Odin Teatret

97 42 47 77, www.odinteatret.dk.
Denmark's oldest surviving contemporary theatre company. In 2006 Odin was chosen to perform the annual reinterpretation of *Hamlet* at Kronborg Castle in Helsingør.

Signa

www.signa.dk.
Venues for Signa's performance installations are as likely to be abandoned buildings or campsites as established theatres. With topics like fictitious cults and eastern European prostitution cropping up in recent pieces, Signa's work has created something of a stir in the city.

That Theatre Company

33 13 50 42, www.that-theatre.com.
Known for his satirical tragi-comic monologues, Ian Burns co-founded That Theatre Company in 1997. Since 2001, one or two productions a year have been staged at Østerbro's small Kruddttønden venue and the repertoire ranges from thought-provoking dramas to lighter mood pieces. However, all are highly professional despite being made on a shoestring and are worth seeking out by those who like theatre with bite to it.

ARTS & ENTERTAINMENT

Profile DR Koncerthuset

Scandinavia's premier classical concert hall.

Selected as the Wallpaper* 2010 Design Award's Best New Public House, Danmarks Radio (DR) Koncerthuset (*see p194*) is one of Copenhagen's most exciting architectural projects of the past few years, and a new landmark for the city.

Designed by French architect Jean Nouvel (known for Madrid's Reina Sofía extension and London's One New Change), the concert hall was inaugurated in early 2009 after six years in construction. The building makes use of its location in Ørestad North: the bright blue of its exterior blends with the waterfront setting, while images are projected on to the surface of its semi-transparent frontage when an event is being held – projections relating to the specific event, as well as reflections from the clouds and the surrounding area. The idea is for the building to appear to be in motion, blending with its environment and changing with the weather and the light. Nouvel proposed that, 'At night the [building] will come alive with images, colours and lights expressing the life going on inside.'

Consisting of four concert halls, the Koncerthuset's main auditorium (Studio 1) accommodates 1,800 concert-goers, and is already renowned for its world-class acoustics (the work of Japan's Yasuhisa Toyota), as you might well expect for the most expensive concert hall ever built (the project's final figure ran to the tune of some $300 million). As the home of the Danish National Symphony Orchestra (which provide concerts every Thursday), the building is now the city's – in fact, Scandinavia's – premier venue for classical concerts; as well as symphony concerts, this is also the place to head to for chamber music and

choral performances by all of Denmark's national musical ensembles, as well as a host of concerts by international names. A key aim of the Koncerthuset, however, is for its musical scope to be broad – thus, small-scale jazz concerts also take place in the foyer, and rock and pop acts are sometimes held in the three small concert halls.

Even if you don't make it to a concert here, it's worth a trip down to DR Byen ('byen' means 'town' in Danish) to see the area, which, since 2007, has also been home to the rest of the Danmarks Radio – the national broadcasting corporation – headquarters. 'Architecture is like music,' Nouvel stated in reference to the project, 'it is made to move and delight us.' See the building when a big event is on, and you can judge yourself whether the architect succeeded.

ARTS & ENTERTAINMENT

ORGANISATIONS

Danish International Theatre Institute & Theatre Union (DITITU)
Nørre Voldgade 12 (33 86 12 10, www.dititu.dk).
Open *Office* 10am-2pm Mon-Fri; call to make an appointment. **Map** p245 Q7.
Established in 1948 to support Danish theatre groups and venues.

Copenhagen International Theatre (KIT)
33 15 15 64, www.kit.dk.
Since its foundation in 1979, KIT has organised more than 40 international festivals in Denmark. It's most visible in the summer, when the annual Sommerscene circus festival showcases some of Europe's best acrobatic talents, while Hamletsommer brings a production of *Hamlet* to the prince's 'true' home, Kronborg Castle in Helsingør (Elsinore).

Dance

The Royal Danish Theatre's dance monopoly was broken in 1979 with the foundation of the Patterson independent dance group. In 1981 Patterson changed its name to Nyt Dansk Danse Teater (New Danish Dance Theatre). In 1982 American dancer and choreographer Warren Spears joined the company and began a tradition of inviting choreographers and dancers from abroad, which has since become the lifeblood of contemporary Danish dance. Brit Tim Rushton took over as artistic director at Nyt Dansk Danse Teater (NDDT) in 2002, shortening the company name to **Danish Dance Theatre** and helping to popularise contemporary dance with lavish multimedia productions like *Requiem*, which took over the entire Opera House with its enormous video backdrop in 2005.

Dansescenen (*see below*) remains the city's sole venue entirely dedicated to modern dance performance, while the **Royal Danish Ballet** (based at the Royal Theatre) is recognised as one of the world's top five ballet companies.

VENUES

Bellevue Teatret
Strandvejen 451, Klampenborg (39 63 64 00, www.bellevueteatret.dk). Bus 14, 85N, 185, 388
Box office 4-8pm Mon-Fri. **No credit cards**.
Since 2003 the seafront Bellevue Theatre has broadened its appeal by collaborating with Copenhagen International Ballet to produce the famous Summer Ballet under the careful direction of choreographer Alexander Kølpin.

Dansescenen
Pasteursvej 20 (33 29 10 10, box office 33 29 10 29, www.dansescenen.dk). Bus 18, 26.
Box Office 2-4pm Mon-Fri and 1hr before performances. **Credit** MC, V. **Map** p245 S6.
The heart of the city's dance milieu, Dansescenen puts on more than 130 performances a year, including an annual competition for young choreographers, Dansolution, where the audience get to vote for their favourite. Dansescenen also organises development programmes for young artists, and its Junior Company regularly performs at youth festivals. It is now based in the old Carlsberg factory (*see p86* **Brewing Up a Cultural Storm**).

Dansescenen.

Det Kongelige Teater, Gamle Scene.

★ Det Kongelige Teater, Gamle Scene (Royal Danish Theatre, Old Stage)

Kongens Nytorv (main box office 33 69 69 69, www.kgl-teater.dk). Metro Kongens Nytorv or Bus 11A, 29. **Box office** 2-6pm Mon-Sat. **Credit** MC, V. **Map** p252 N16.
See p192 **Profile**.

Tivoli

Vesterbrogade 3 (information 33 15 10 01, www.tivoli.dk). Bus 6A, 26. **Box office** 9am-5pm out of season. Bookings can be made online. **Credit** AmEx, MC, V. **Map** p250 P12.

Tivoli's concert hall hosts some of the biggest international dance companies, including the New York City Ballet. The Plænen open-air stage holds many international events, while the Pantomime Theatre is a favourite for children's shows.

COMPANIES

Åben Dans Productions

35 82 06 10, www.aabendans.dk.

Åben Dans (Open Dance) is one of the most well-toured modern dance companies in Denmark. The majority of performances are accompanied by a series of lectures, workshops and audience debates.

Danish Dance Theatre

35 39 87 87, www.danskdanseteater.dk.

Over the course of its 25-year history, Danish Dance Theatre has redefined modern dance and experimental ballet in Denmark with its high-quality productions, and, as artistic director, Tim Rushton, continues to take this incredibly prolific company from strength to strength.

Granhøj Dans

86 19 26 22, www.granhoj.dk.

Choreographer Palle Granhøj founded Granhøj Dans in 1989 with set designer Per Victor in Århus, Jutland, where the company still has its own theatre.

Peter Schaufuss Ballet

97 40 51 22, www.schaufuss.com.

One of the country's biggest ballet stars, Peter Schaufuss has had a profound influence on the development of modern ballet in Denmark. His company, based in Jutland, presents several full-length productions every year on the most eclectic topics: 2010's *The Boys from Liverpool*, for example, was based on the life and work of the Beatles.

Royal Danish Ballet

www.kglteater.dk.

The Artistic Director of the Royal Danish Ballet is currently Nikolaj Hübbe, previously principal dancer of the New York City Ballet. Most productions are performed at the Old Stage of the Royal Danish Theatre (*see above*).

(Stilleben)

52 41 00 41, www.anderschristiansen.dk.

Anders Christiansen, the artistic director and choreographer of (Stilleben) (Still Life) has achieved cult status in the Copenhagen dance world with his deeply poetic, trance-like performances.

Uppercut Danseteater

35 82 11 71, www.uppercutdance.dk.

Uppercut Danseteater was one of Denmark's first professional dance theatre groups. In 1999 the company began a new project, Dance in the North-West, which aims to promote modern dance among young people in Copenhagen's multi-ethnic north-western neighbourhood.

X-Act

29 91 87 13, www.kittjohnson.dk.

With a background in martial arts, butoh and German expressive theatre, X-Act co-founder Kitt Johnson has made a name for herself as a dancer, teacher and choreographer, taking part in more than 20 site-specific performance projects all over Europe.

Sport & Fitness

From skateboarding to cycling to golf, Danes like to keep active.

Denmark is filled with sports nuts. The traditional cuisine may be somewhat on the solid side and the population may be beset by the same bad habits as the rest of the western world, but the statistics don't lie: half of all adults and three out of four children participate in sports. Every town has its own football, handball or gymnastics club, and it's all arranged with characteristic Danish efficiency.

The capital has plenty to offer too, from the groundbreaking DGI-Byen complex to shooting ranges, perfect conditions for yachting, a beautiful racecourse, a harbour for swimming in, a great indoor skatepark and a spectacular outdoor one in the pipeline – plus the nation's top two football sides and a great national stadium with 42,000 seats and a roof, right in the centre of town.

PARTICIPATION SPORTS

Athletics

In mid May, international runners mingle with visitors and locals in a carnival atmosphere as the Copenhagen Marathon signals the start of summer. Although not on the same scale as its counterparts in London or New York, this is a key date in the athletics calendar.

Badminton

Denmark has a proud badminton tradition and boasts several of the world's top players. Contact the **Danish Badminton Association** (43 26 21 44, www.badminton.dk) for more details.

Copenhagen Badminton Club
Krausesvej 12, Østerbro (35 38 72 92, www.kbknet.dk). Train to Nordhavn, then

**INSIDE TRACK
DANISH SPORTS COUNCIL**

Sport in Copenhagen is highly organised and expertly overseen by the **Danish Sports Council** (43 26 26 26, www.dif.dk). If you're interested in a sport that's not included here, the council should be able to help you out.

5min walk or bus 3 to Randersgade. **Open** 8am-11pm daily. **Prices** non-members 150kr/hr; courts can be booked online. **No credit cards**. **Map** p248 C14.

Cycling

Cycling is part of daily life in Copenhagen (*see pp40-42*). The city was chosen by the **UCI**, the International Cycling Union, to be the world's first 'Bike City', from 2008 to 2011. In 2011, various pro and amateur cycling events – including world championships in track, road and BMX supercross – will take place in the city. For more information, visit www.bikecitycopenhagen.dk.

Fitness centres

Fitness centres are popular, with prices generally ranging from 55kr to 150kr for a single session. The **SATS** chain (www.sats.com) runs a series of well-equipped clubs throughout the city and suburbs (day membership is 150kr). Its central Copenhagen branches include Købmagergade 48 (33 89 89 11), Vesterbrogade 2E, 5th floor (33 32 10 02), Vesterbrogade 97 (33 25 13 10), Bragesgade 8, Nørrebro (35 81 27 81) and Øster Allé 42E, Østerbro (35 55 00 78). For further venues, *see p202* **Sports centres**.

Sporting Health Club
2nd floor, Gothersgade 14 (33 13 16 12, www.sportinghealthclub.dk). Metro Kongens

Nytorv. **Open** 6.30am-9pm Mon-Thur; 6.30am-8.30pm Fri; 9am-6pm Sat; 10am-6pm Sun. **Prices** 99kr. **No credit cards. Map** p247 L13.

Football

Fælledparken, in the shadow of the national stadium (Parken) in Østerbro, holds amateur tournaments each Sunday (April-November). If you want to join, just show up around 10am.

Go-karting

Ballerup Event Center
Tempovej 35, Ballerup (44 66 60 04, www. ballerupeventcenter.dk). Train to Malmparken, then 10min walk. **Open** 10am-10pm daily. **Prices** 190kr/15mins. **Credit** AmEx, MC, V.

City Go Kart
Saltværksvej 6-12, Kastrup (70 20 53 11, www.citygokart.dk). Metro Kastrup or bus 2A, 12, 36, 250S. **Open** 10am-10pm Mon-Sat; 10am-6pm Sun. **Prices** from 300kr/30mins. **Credit** AmEx, MC, V.

Golf

Among Sjælland's main golfing draws is Europe's biggest indoor venue, the massive Copenhagen Indoor Golf Center, with space for 60 tees as well as two golf simulators and an indoor putting green. For alfresco golfers, courses tend to be busy (especially from March to October), and a round plus equipment hire doesn't come cheap (around 350kr on weekdays, 500kr at weekends – be sure to book in advance).

Golfing enthusiasts might also like to consider a trip to southern Sweden, which boasts some excellent courses, the best of which is Barsebäck, regular host of the Scandinavian Open. The **Danish Golf Union** can be reached on 43 26 27 00 (www.danksgolfunion.org). **Malmö Tourist Information** (+40 34 12 00, www.malmotown.com/en) can provide details of Swedish courses.

Hørsholm Golf Klub
Grønnegade 1, Hørsholm (45 76 51 50, www.hoersholm-golf.dk). Train to Rungsted Kyst/bus 381. **Open** phone for details. **Prices** Mon-Fri 450kr/round; Sat, Sun 550kr/round. **Credit** AmEx, MC, V.
▶ *Another club, the Rungsted Golf Klub, is a short distance away on Vestre Stationsvej 16 in Rungsted (45 86 34 44, booking 45 86 34 14, www.rungstedgolfklub.dk).*

Københavns Golf Klub
Dyrehaven 2, Klampenborg (39 63 04 83, www.kgkgolf.dk). Train to Klampenborg.

DGI-Byen. *See p202.*

Open phone for details. **Prices** 450kr/day.
Credit AmEx, MC, V.

Horse riding

Mattssons Rideklub
*Bellevuevej 10-12, Klampenborg (39 64 08 22,
www.mattsson.dk). Train to Klampenborg, then
5min walk.* **Open** 6am-9pm daily. **Prices** phone
for details. **No credit cards**.

Ice skating

Each winter, outdoor public ice skating rinks
spring up at locations across the city, with hot
chestnut stalls and romantic lights adding to
the chocolate-box atmosphere. The winter
skating rink on Kongens Nytorv was moved
to **Toftegårds Plads** in 2010, where skate
hire was available and a small fee charged;
the season runs from the start of December
to the end of February.

Temperatures dropped so low at the end of
2010 that skating was also permitted on some
of Copenhagen's lakes (with municipal signs
confirming that it was safe). Lakes with thick-
enough ice included Peblinge Sø, Sortedams
Sø, Østre Anlæg, HC Ørstedsparken
and Fælledparken.

Jogging

Copenhagen is relatively flat, making jogging
an attractive proposition. The city's numerous
parks are both safe and spacious, and joggers
can outnumber walkers in some areas. In the
city centre, try Ørstedsparken near Nørreport
Station, or the lakes area at Nørre Søgade.
Further out, Søndermarken by the zoo in
Frederiksberg and, for more serious runners,
Dyrehaven in Klampenborg are also popular.

For information on marathons and half-
marathons held in the city, *see p200*.

Rollerblading & skateboarding

With the opening of a new outdoor skatepark
in Fælledparken in June 2011 (*see right* **Skate
Copenhagen**), visiting skaters have even more
places to go. In the harsh winter months, the
fine **Copenhagen Skatepark** (Enghavevej
78, 33 21 28 28, train to Enghave, bus 3A), is
popular and has a selection of ramps and rails.
the park hosts skateboard competitions which
draw pro skaters from all over the world.

Rowing

Rowing clubs exist to the north and south of the
city centre. Beginners and experienced rowers
can contact **Københavns Roklub** (Copenhagen

Rowing Club, Tømmergravsgade 13, 33 12 30
75, www.koebenhavnsroklub.dk). The **Danish
Rowing Association** can be reached on 44
44 06 33 (www.roning.dk).

Rugby union

It often comes as a surprise to learn that rugby
union has a devoted following in Copenhagen.
The season runs from the end of March to the
end of June, and from August to October. The
local top team is **CSR-Nanok** who play on
grounds at Holmen (bus 66). For more info
call the **Danish Rugby Association** on
43 26 28 00 (www.rugby.dk).

Sports centres

For most of the many racket sports played in
Copenhagen, plus basketball, table tennis and
occasionally martial arts or swimming,
Copenhagen's many sports centres remain your
best bet. For sporting cool there's **DGI-Byen**,
while **Grøndal Centret**, though a little way out
of the centre, is northern Europe's largest sports
complex and features everything from aerobics
to bowling.

★ DGI-Byen
*Tietgensgade 65 (33 29 80 00, www.dgibyen.dk).
Train København H.* **Open** Phone for details;
bookings can be made online. **Admission**
phone for details. **Credit** AmEx, MC, V.
Map p250 Q11.
This sports complex features a yoga studio,
swimming pool, bowling lanes, fitness centre and
a climbing wall, among other facilities. *Photo p201*.

Grøndal Centret
*Hvidkildevej 64, Vanløse (38 34 11 09,
www.groendalcentret.dk). Train to Fuglebakken or
bus 21.* **Open** 7am-11pm Mon-Fri; 9am-6pm Sat,
Sun. **Prices** 50kr-100kr/hr. **No credit cards**.

Nørrebrohallen
*Bragesgade 5, Nørrebro (35 31 05 50,
www.kubik.kk.dk/noerrebrohallen). Train to
Nørrebro or bus 5A, 16.* **Open** 7.30am-11pm Mon-
Fri; 7.30am-9.30pm Sat; 8am-11pm Sun. **Opening
hours** may vary in June-Aug, phone to check.
Prices 35kr-325kr/hr. **No credit cards**.

Swimming pools & saunas

The most central place for a swim is **DGI-
Byen** sports centre (*see above*). This state-
of-the-art building is fine for a dip, and has
a great spa, but is pricey and tends to be full of
families. For a quieter swim, the pools stay open
until midnight on weekdays. If you don't mind
colder water, you should also check out the

Skate Copenhagen

The city has a new outdoor skatepark.

Despite being burdened with snow and ice for several months of the year, Copenhagen has an active, friendly skateboarding scene that gets plenty of international interest. In fact, its annual **Copenhagen Pro** event, held in the last week of June, has grown into being Europe's largest professional skateboarding contest in the four years it's been going, attracting some of the world's best skaters, including, of course, local legend Rune Gliffberg, who makes the pilgrimage from his home in sunny southern California.

For years the scene has centred around the city's indoor **Copenhagen Skatepark** in Vesterbro (Enghavevej 78, 33 21 28 28, www.copenhagenskatepark.dk), especially when snow and ice make skating outdoors difficult. But now, as part of the refurbishment of Østerbro's **Fælledparken** (*see venue index*; a council operation funded by the AP Muller–Mærsk shipping company) skaters can look forward to a new 4,000-square-metre outdoor skatepark, built by Grindline. The company is part of a new breed of skatepark designers and

have built parks all over the world that are the antithesis of run-down, underused local council skateparks. The space is due to open in late spring 2011.

The new Fælledparken skatepark, which will be free to use, will comprise three areas (*see projection below*): a plaza-style street section, which will contain steps, handrails, flatbars and ledges; a large half-pipe, and a third mixed-terrain space, with bowls, quarter-pipes and ledges, which will also be used for competitions.

Other skateparks in the city include Nørrebro's indoor X-hall, consisting of three bowls and currently being partially rebuilt, and Christiania's bowl. For the lowdown on the city's plethora of street spots, head to **Circus Circus** skateshop in Nørrebro (Guldsbergsgade 16, 26 79 62 84, www.circuscircus.dk), **Street Machine** in the centre (Kronprinsensgade 3, 33 33 95 11, www.streetmachine.com) or **Sidewalk Skateshop** in Vesterbro (Istedgade 138, 33 24 70 71, www.sidewalkshop.dk), where staff will be happy to let you know where's currently good to go.

ARTS & ENTERTAINMENT

Islands Brygge.

fantastic, open-air harbour bathing complex
Islands Brygge (*see p82* **Come On In, the
Water's Lovely**). It's free, but only open
during the summer.

★ Frederiksberg Svømmehal
*Helgesvej 29, Frederiksberg (38 14 04 00,
www.frederiksbergsvoemmehal.dk). Metro
Frederiksberg.* **Open** *7am-9pm Mon-Fri; 7am-4pm
Sat; 9am-4pm Sun.* **Admission** *36kr; 145kr incl
aromabath, massage chair, Turkish bath &
jacuzzi.* **Sauna** *47kr.* **Credit** AmEx, MC, V.
This local institution is one of Denmark's oldest
swimming pools, and a popular spot for socialising
and relaxing. It consists of a main pool area, the
walls of which are decorated with colourful paintings, a heated baby pool, a 'luxury' area with steam
baths, saunas and cold plunge pools, and a spa section with a large saltwater pool (Saltbassinet), electric massage chairs, a jacuzzi and a massage parlour.

Hillerødgade Swimming Pool
*Sandbjerggade 35, Nørrebro (35 85 19 55,
www.kubik.kk.dk/hillerodgadebad). Bus 66, 69.*
Open *Sept-May* 10am-3.30pm Mon; 7am-7.30pm
Tue; 7am-4.30pm Wed; 7am-9pm Thur; 7am-
3.30pm Fri; 8am-2pm Sat, Sun. *June-Aug* 10am-
3.30pm Mon; 7am-7.30pm Tue-Thur; 7am-3.30pm
Fri; 8am-2pm Sat, Sun. **Prices** 31kr; 14kr
concessions. **No credit cards.**

Øbro-Hallen
*Gunnar Nu Hansens Plads 3, Østerbro (35 25 70
60, www.kubik.kk.dk/obrohallenbad). Bus 1A, 14.*
Open *7am-8pm Mon, Tue, Thur, Fri; 10am-8pm
Wed; 9am-3pm Sat, Sun.* **Prices** *31kr; 14kr
concessions; ticket includes access to sauna.*
No credit cards.

Vesterbro Swimming Pool
*Angelgade 4, Vesterbro (33 22 05 00,
www.kubik.kk.dk/vesterbrobad). Train to Enghave
or bus 1A, 3A, 10.* **Open** *May-Aug* 10am-9pm
Mon; 7am-6pm Tue; 7am-7pm Wed; 7am-5.30pm
Thur; 7am-4.30pm Fri; 9am-2pm Sat, Sun.
Prices 31kr; 14kr concessions. **No credit
cards.** **Map** p245 T6.

Tennis

Tennis courts are in pretty short supply in
Copenhagen and many belong to private clubs,
so you will need to know a member in order to
gain access. An additional factor is the cost of
hiring a court: most central venues charge
between 100kr and 150kr per hour (sometimes
with an additional fee for non-members), so a
proper five-set marathon can prove expensive.
   Most central is the **Hotel Mercur**, which rents
out its own private, rather rundown rooftop courts
to non-residents. **KB Tennis Club** has indoor
and outdoor courts; reservations required. **B93
Sports Club** is another tennis-friendly venue.
More information is available from the **Danish
Tennis Association** on 43 26 26 60
(www.dtftennis.dk).

B93 Sports Club
*Ved Sporsløjfen 10 (39 27 18 90, www.b93.dk).
Train to Svanemøllen/bus 1A, 14.* **Open** *7am-
10pm daily.* **Prices** *Outdoor* 75kr/hr per person.
Indoor 150-200kr/hr per person. **No credit cards.**

Best Western Mercur Hotel
*Vester Farimagsgade 17 (33 12 57 11,
www.mercurhotel.dk). Bus 5A, 6A, 12, 14.* **Open**
8am-8pm daily. **Prices** 100kr/hr per person (incl
racket). **Credit** AmEx, MC, V. **Map** p250 N11.

KB Tennis Club
*Peter Bangsvej 147, Frederiksberg (38 71 41 50,
www.kb-boldklub.dk, www2.banebooking.dk/kbk).
Train to Peter Bangs Vej/bus 15.* **Open** *Sept-Apr*
7am-11pm Mon-Fri; 8am-5pm Sat, Sun. *May-Sept*
8am-dusk daily. **Prices** 120kr-180kr/hr per
person. **No credit cards.**
Other location Pile Allé 14 (36 30 23 00).

Ten-pin bowling

Ten-pin bowling, which is usually accompanied
by drinks and/or a meal, is a very popular night

out in Copenhagen. Remember to call and reserve a lane in advance, especially if you want to play at the weekend. Contact the **Danish Bowling Association** (43 26 29 11, www.spilbowling.dk) for details.

Bowlehuset
DGI-Byen, Tietgensgade 65 (33 29 80 20, www.dgi-byen.dk/bowling). Train København H. **Open** noon-11pm Mon, Tue; 3-11pm Wed, Thur; 2pm-1am Fri; 10am-1am Sat; 10am-5pm Sun. **Prices** 125kr-325kr/hr; 10kr shoe hire. **Credit** AmEx, MC, V. **Map** p250 Q11.

Windsurfing

There is certainly plenty of water as well as more wind than most Copenhageners know what to do with, the city's windsurfers are truly blessed by these geographic coincidences. There are several places to rent boards. **Nautic Surf & Ski** (35 82 07 77, www.nautic-surfogski.dk), near to Arken art gallery, is the closest.

Yoga

Yoga classes at the venues below work out cheaper if you buy a monthly pass, or pay for several classes at once. There is usually also a small charge for mat hire.

Astanga Yoga Skolen
Vesterbrogade 24B (33 31 32 83, www.astanga.dk). Train København H.

Open call or visit website for class times. **Prices** *Drop-in class* 100kr. **No credit cards**. **Map** p250 P10.

Yoga Mudra
Strandgade 36D, Christianshavn (32 96 95 91, www.yogamudra.dk). Metro Christianshavn or bus 2A, 19, 47, 66, 350S. **Prices** *Drop-in class* 120kr. **Credit** MC, V. **Map** p252 O17.

SPECTATOR SPORTS
Athletics

The biggest event is the annual marathon. Athletics meetings take place at the city's **Østerbro Stadion** (Gunnar Nu Hansens Plads 11, Østerbro, 35 26 45 36, bus 1A, 14), but Malmö in Sweden is the place to catch the more famous names. Call Malmö Tourist Information on +46 40 34 12 00 for details of events.

Boxing

Banned in Sweden and Norway, professional boxing is popular in Denmark. Bouts are regularly held in arenas such as **KB Hallen** (Peter Bangsvej 147). Try www.billetlugen.dk for tickets.

Football

You can't really call Copenhagen a football hotbed, so whenever local rivals **FC**

Best Western Mercur Hotel.

ARTS & ENTERTAINMENT

ARTS & ENTERTAINMENT

København or Brøndby IF (for both; *see below*) win another title – which they do, year after year – don't expect the streets to be bursting with Danes honking their car horns. This is, after all, a country where the top players were all amateurs less than 30 years ago. That said, the atmosphere at a league match at Brøndby or Parken certainly gets a lot more intense than anything the *Roligans*, the national fans, can come up with. However, that's not to say that you should dread going; Danish league matches (held on Saturday or Sunday afternoons) are among the most relaxed in Europe, and the biggest risk to your health is a dodgy hot dog (an essential part of any game; *see p59* **Profile Pølsevogne**.

FC København

Parken, Øster Allé 50, Østerbro (70 26 32 67, www.fck.dk). Train to Østerport or bus 1A, 14, 15. **Tickets** *Club matches* 190kr-295kr; 70kr-115kr concessions. *Internationals* 230kr-410kr; 185kr-215kr concessions. **No credit cards.** **Map** p248 D12.
FCK now enjoys the biggest crowds and boast a number of internationals in the squad. Their claim to succeeding Brøndby as the leading club was finally justified in 2010/2011 as they became the first Danish club in the UEFA Champions League to make it through to the last 16 of the competition.

Brøndby IF

Brøndby Stadion 30, Brøndby (43 63 08 10, www.brondby.com). Train to Brøndbyøster, then bus 135 or train to Glostrup, then bus 166. **Tickets** 130kr-250kr; 65kr-130kr concessions. **Credit** MC, V.
Brøndby IF were the first club to turn fully pro in a league that only allowed amateur football until 1978. Recent times, however, have seen rivals København overtake them. Michael Laudrup may have been a great player, but he was no good as a coach, and

---

INSIDE TRACK
WALKING ROUTES

All right, Denmark is flat. Maybe not as level as Holland, but still pretty horizontal. Nevertheless there are plenty of picturesque walking routes just a short bus or train ride from the city centre. **Amager Nature Reserve** is a real wilderness just five kilometres (three miles) from Central Station (Metro Islands Brygge, DR Byen or Sundby). Another alternative is the former royal hunting ground, **Dyrehaven** (*see p216*), a few minutes' walk from Klampenborg Station, 25 minutes north of the city.

---

since his departure in 2006 Brøndby have found themselves in a period of rebuilding, with the 2008 Danish Cup their only recent silverware of note.

Golf

There are a staggering 25 full-sized 18-hole courses in the Greater Copenhagen area alone. Hardly surprising, then, that the country has produced two of Europe's top golfers, Thomas Bjørn and Anders Hansen. Major events are regularly held on Zealand. For more information contact the **Danish Golf Union** (43 26 27 00, www.dgu.org). For a list of places to play gold, *see p201*.

Handball

The nation's favourite indoor sport, handball is unique in that the women's game is far more popular than the men's version. The rules are simple and games are easy to follow, fast-moving and exciting. Contact the **Danish Handball Association** (43 26 24 00, www.dhf.dk) for details of up-and-coming local games.

Horse racing

For chariot-style trotting racing, take a ride out to the **Travbane** course at Charlottenlund (Traverbanevej 10, 39 96 02 02, www.travbanen.dk). Nearby is Denmark's only flat racing course, **Klampenborg Galopbane** (39 96 02 13/www.galopbane.dk), home to the Scandinavian Open and the Danske Derby (held on the last Sunday in June).

Ice hockey

When the football season breaks for winter, ice hockey takes over. Denmark hosted the world 'B' Championships in 1999 and the national team has produced some impressive recent results. For details of forthcoming matches for local teams, contact the **Danish Ice Hockey Association** (43 26 54 64, www.ishockey.dk).

Tennis

Denmark's flagship event is now the Women's Tennis Association (WTA) run **e-Boks Danish Open** (http://e-bokssony ericssonopen.dk); the country's star player, Caroline Wozniacki, won the inaugural tournament, held at the Farum Arena (some 25 kilometres – 15 miles – north of Copenhagen) in August 2010. For details of the event, call the **Danish Tennis Association** on 43 26 26 60 or visit www.tennis.dk.

Escapes & Excursions

Malmö 209
 Twisted Logic 21:

The Danish Riviera 21(
 Profile Louisiana Museum
 For Modern Kunst 218

North Sjælland 220
 Art for a Laugh 22:

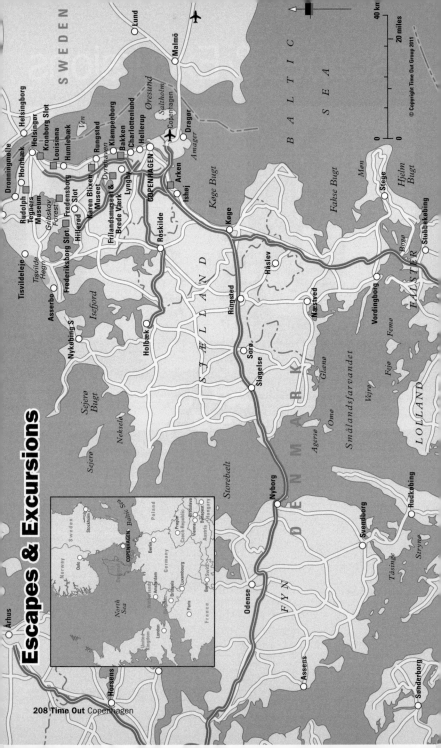

Escapes & Excursions

Malmö

It's just a short hop across the sea to one of Sweden's most vibrant cities.

Copenhagen ought to have more than enough to occupy you for at least a long weekend, but another city – smaller but equally scintillating – lies just 30 minutes away by train. It happens to be in another country and across a sea, but Malmö – Sweden's third largest city – is worth the short trip via the spectacular **Øresund Bridge**. Its unusually cosmopolitan population includes 15,000 university students, who give Malmö a youthful, vibrant energy, and it is also an eminently liveable place. There are some excellent art museums, an atmospheric castle, a sizeable sandy beach and some unique shops. At night most people head for the cobbled square of **Lilla Torg** with its lively bars and restaurants, but as a whole the city is awash with great nightlife venues.

INTRODUCING MALMÖ

Malmö is particularly hard to resist during summer when its long sandy beach, **Ribban** (a short walk west from the city centre), its beautiful parks and its peaceful, almost southern European atmosphere really come into their own. The city has some excellent cultural facilities, too, and a varied ethnic mix (around 40 per cent of its total population of 270,000 are originally from Eastern Europe, Latin America, the Middle East and Africa). The **Malmö Festival**, the oldest city festival in Sweden, takes place at venues throughout the city in August each year and attracts 1.5 million visitors with live music, theatre and a massive crayfish binge (www.malmo.se).

The most recent addition to the city has been in the Western Harbour area. This was once one of the most important dockyards in Europe but the decline of industry in the 1980s threatened the city's entire economy. In recent years, however, a radical housing project, **Bo01** ('bo' is the Swedish for 'to dwell' and '01' for the year it was founded as an international European housing expo), has sprung up beside the sea. This environmentally sustainable, expertly built and highly desirable housing has won architectural plaudits from around the globe for its 'organic' approach to planning, diverse use of materials and environmentally friendly touches (natural gas is extracted from waste and energy comes from wind turbines). The

restaurants, harbour, bathing deck, cafés, promenades, leisure facilities and shops here are now a major attraction, as is the Exhibition and Convention Centre which is housed in a former Saab factory nearby.

Some critics say Bo01 is a yuppie ghetto which is unrepresentative of the city's diverse population, but there are lower cost housing developments being built nearby. At the centre of it all is the astonishing **Turning Tower** by Santiago Calatrava (*see p211* **Twisted logic**).

Sightseeing

The historic heart of Malmö is a beguiling mix of timbered buildings, wide canals, beautiful parks and a sizeable pedestrian shopping area, Södergatan, which connects the **Stortorget** and **Gustav Adolfs Torg** squares before continuing down Södra Förstadsgatan to Triangeln, the triangular area in front of the Scandic Hotel. All are within easy reach of one another, with the railway station and beach also nearby.

While Södergatan is no Strøget, it does boast good international chain stores and independent shops, as well as plenty of restaurants and bars – the Davidhallstorg shopping area has recently undergone a major trendification. A little further south you come to **Möllevångstorget**, which has several Asian, African and Eastern European shops and restaurants. Delve a little deeper and you'll find a couple of decent bars

as well as a large produce market (8am-2pm Mon-Sat), while to the north-west sits the beach, **Ribban**.

The centre of Malmö is encircled by a canal, and a pleasant way to get your bearings is to take a canal tour. **Rundan Canal Tours'** boats (*see p214*) leave every hour from a berth opposite Central Station (available from May to September) and the tour takes 45 minutes. You can also hire pedalos from City Boats, which is based on Södertull and open between April and September. The latter option will allow you to do the tour under your own steam (although give yourself plenty of time if you intend to pedal the full circuit).

Malmö might not offer the rich cultural and historical tapestry of Copenhagen, but it does have one or two museums and galleries that are worth spending some time in. Conveniently for the day tripper, most of them are located on a single site within the walls of **Slottet Malmöhus** (Malmö Castle).

The Danish king Erik of Pomerania was the first to build a castle on the site (which at that time was right on the seafront) in 1434, and for a while afterwards it was the home of the Danish mint. In the 16th century the castle underwent a major rebuild under Christian III of Denmark, with the addition of ramparts, four red cannon towers (two of which still stand) and a moat. The castle's usefulness continued long after

the Swedes liberated this part of the country from the Danes in 1658, so much so that, Christian V tried unsuccessfully to take it back again. Up until 1937 the castle served as a prison, and only then was it converted to house the museums.

Today a rather stern, functionalist extension within the walls of the old castle contains the city's most important museums. **Naturmuseet** (Natural History Museum) boasts an enjoyably chaotic collection of stuffed animals (including one gargantuan moose), a small aquarium, various live insects and reptiles and a fascinating nocturnal room.

Upstairs on the left, you'll find the **Malmö Konstmuseum** (Malmö Art Museum; *see p213* Malmö Museums), which gives visitors a bite-size tour of Scandinavian art and design. The museum has an important collection of modern art, featuring a range of ceramics, paintings, sculpture, furniture, silverware and glassware.

The **Stadsmuseet** (City Museum; *see p213* Malmö Museums), which is to the right and up the stairs, covers the history of Malmö from the flint miners and reindeer hunters of 1000 BC onwards. This leads into the castle itself and its collection of tapestries, weaponry, art, furniture and other pieces from the 16th and 17th centuries (English information is available).

On the opposite side of the road, a short walk along Malmöhusvägen in the direction of Ribban (Malmö's beach) is **Teknikens och Sjöfartens Hus** (Technology and Maritime Museum) which opened in 1978. The highlight of the exhibits is a 1943 U3 submarine – a claustrophobe's idea of hell.

Just before you reach the museum, if you turn right into Banérskajen you will come to **Fiskehoddorna**. This row of pretty, coloured wooden fishermen's huts looks like a relic from the town's herring fishing past, but the local fishermen still sell their fresh catches from stalls in front of the houses every morning (except Sunday and Monday).

Ribersborgs Stranden (Ribersborgs Beach, otherwise known as **Ribban**), Malmö's fine, two-kilometre (one-mile) long sandy beach, further west, is the town's unique selling point, but this wasn't always the case. The beach is actually a fake, constructed on a festering swamp in the 1920s. These days, however, it has given the city a very attractive seafront, the water is crystal clear and the sand slopes gently out into the sea – perfect for children. The first stretch of beach as you walk from the town centre is an unmarked nudist (and sometimes gay cruising) area, but from then on there is a more family-oriented mix of sand, picnic areas, cafés and ice-cream vendors.

For an authentically Swedish experience, a visit to the **Ribersborgs Kallbadhus**

(Ribersborgs Cold Bath House; see p214) is worth a gamble depending on the weather. This charming green wooden bathhouse, dating from 1898, is at the end of a short pier located on the eastern end of the beach. Walk through the café at the front, pay the entrance fee and you enter the segregated open-air deck areas (men to the left, women to the right), with their bracing sea water plunge baths and saunas. It goes without saying that nudity is the norm here. A masseur is on hand to pummel weary bodies and there is also a solarium.

In the south-east corner of Kungsparken, in one of Malmö's grander quarters, is the town's answer to Copenhagen's Black Diamond, the **Stadsbibliotek** (Town Library). As with the

Black Diamond, Malmö's 19th-century redbrick library received an uncompromising, modern glass extension in 1999, designed by Danish architect Henning Larsen and nicknamed the 'Cathedral of Light'.

Lovers of contemporary Scandinavian and European interior design should head for the **Form/Design Center**, housed in a converted warehouse. The first floor contains a changing programme of design-related exhibitions. On the second floor is an excellent design shop selling everything from garden furniture to jewellery, kitchenware and clothes.

The Center – one of numerous excellent design shops to be found throughout the city centre – is located in a courtyard adjacent to

Twisted Logic

Unmissable: Malmö's tallest landmark.

Drive over the Øresund Bridge from Denmark to Sweden and one building dominates the horizon on the Swedish coast. The **Turning Tower** is Scandinavia's most impressive construction project since the Øresund Bridge itself, and a real challenge to the supposed architectural dominance of neighbouring Denmark. Like a lightning conductor, it marks the location of the city's radical new housing development in the Western Harbour, built over the last five years on a former industrial site just outside the city centre.

The tower was designed by the Spanish architect Santiago Calatrava after the MD of developers HSB saw a two-metre white marble sculpture of a human torso by the architect. 'That would look great in aluminium and glass, 190 metres high,' thought the developer, and he commissioned Calatrava. The result was completed in November 2005. It's the tallest building in Sweden, and boasts an extraordinary external 'spine' of steel framework that twists through 90 degrees as it lifts nine stacks of white aluminium cubes – in all 54 storeys of, mostly, apartments. With its bombastic scale and show-stopping theatricality it could hardly be less Swedish. And some have criticised the high cost of the apartments while residents complain of living in a 'goldfish bowl'. However, most have embraced their new city symbol and are immensely proud of it.

The apartments themselves – which are rental only – dispense with the conventions of rectangular, regular rooms, in favour of all manner of curves and angles. The views,

needless to say, are breathtaking. And Calatrava's next project? Like many, he is involved in the rebuilding of New York's Ground Zero, after an astounding, but sadly aborted, project in Chicago to build America's tallest building. Watch this space.

ESCAPES & EXCURSIONS

Malmö's prettiest square, **Lilla Torg**. By night Lilla Torg is the hub of Malmö's mainstream nightlife scene. As well as its many pubs, the city also claims to have more restaurants per square kilometre than any other city in Sweden, and this is where you'll find some of the best. Lilla Torg dates from 1591 when it developed as an overflow for Stortorget. In 1903 the square was given its own roof, but that was demolished in 1967 and the area was recobbled. These days it is packed with busy bars and restaurants and has a convivial, party atmosphere in the spring and summer.

Just west of Lilla Torg is **Gamla Väster**, the pretty historic heart of the city with its rows of small, pastel-coloured 18th- and 19th-century houses interspersed with the odd designer shop and restaurant.

During the 16th century nearby Stortorget was one of the largest market squares in Scandinavia. At its centre is a statue of the comically rotund King Carl X Gustav (who

Sankt Petri Kyrka.

was responsible for the chain of events that climaxed with the Treaty of Roskilde), astride his horse, Hannibal. Surrounding the statue stand some grand old buildings which include: on the east side, Malmö's **Rådhuset** (Town Hall) dating from 1546 but rebuilt in 1812 in the neo-classical style; on the western side, the 16th-century home of the former Danish mayor and controller of the Mint, Jörgen Kock; on the north side the splendid **Scandic Hotel Kramer** (*see p215*), said to be modelled on Copenhagen's Hotel d'Angleterre; and also on the north side **Residenset** (Governor's Residence), dating from the early 18th century but rebuilt most recently in 1851. It was on the balcony here that the kings of Norway, Sweden and Denmark met in 1914 to confirm their joint statement of neutrality. Shortly after the summit the balcony was found to be on the brink of collapse (it was, in fact, held on by a couple of rusty screws), which could have had serious repercussions, not only for Scandinavia but the whole of Europe. Around the corner is the wonderful art nouveau Hotel Savoy where Lenin dined en route to Russia in 1917.

An unsuccessful attempt at a coup by Danish sympathisers in the 1650s resulted in a number of grisly retaliatory executions in Stortorget. In 1678 the Danish nobleman Jörgen Krabbe, who lived in the castle at Krageholm in Sweden, was beheaded here after being (probably wrongly) accused of plotting against Sweden. Much later, in 1811, executions and floggings took place here following an uprising by farmers and peasants opposed to conscription to fight Napoleon in Europe. During the August festival, Stortorget hosts another, slightly more palatable massacre: the world's largest crayfish party.

Behind Stortorget and to the east is **Sankt Petri Kyrka** (St Peter's Church), Malmö's main place of worship, built at the beginning of the 14th century. It has many similarities with other Hanseatic churches of the period, particularly Marienkirche in Lübeck. Like most other Catholic churches at that time, Sankt Petri Kyrka suffered during the Reformation and in 1555, in an act of artistic vandalism, its medieval frescoes were whitewashed over (some have been restored and can be seen in the nearby Krämer Chapel).

As well as the Konstmuseum, Malmö has a couple of other highly regarded art spaces. **Malmö Konsthall** (*see right*), built in neo-brutalist style in 1975, holds around ten temporary exhibitions of contemporary art a year in its capacious rooms (at 2,000 square metres, 21,500 square feet this is one of the largest contemporary art sites in northern Europe). It also has a fine bookshop as well as a courtyard café that hosts the occasional jazz concert. **Modern Meseet** has, since late 2009,

inhabited the former gasworks plant that was once home to another contemporary art space, Rooseum. An outpost and extension of the original Stockholm modern and contemporary art museum, exhibitions range from classic early modernism to up-to-the-minute contemporary installations.

Malmö's striking **Stadsteatern** (Town Theatre) was built on the corner of Fersens Väg and Östra Rönne in 1944 and, with three separate stages, is one of the largest theatres in Europe. Ingmar Bergman was dramatic director there in the 1950s and these days it is often visited by foreign ballet, opera and theatre groups. In 1985 Malmö gained **Konserthuset** (Concert House), situated on the corner of Föreningsgatan and Amiralsgatan, now home to the respected Malmö Symfoni Orkester (Malmö Symphony Orchestra).

A little south of the city centre is the newest arrival on Malmö's thriving cultural and nightlife scene, **Kulturhuset Mazetti** (Mazetti Culture Centre; *see below*). Housed in a former Fazer chocolate factory, this is now home to several organisations with a cultural bent, as well as a hotel, nightclub and, nearby, a rather more exclusive *chocolatier*.

★ Form/Design Center
Lilla Torg (040 664 51 50/www.formdesign center.com). Train Centralstation. **Open** 11am-5pm Tue, Wed, Fri; 11am-6pm Thur; 11am-4pm Sat; noon-4pm Sun. **Admission** free. **Credit** AmEx, DC, MC, V.

Kulturhuset Mazetti
Bergsgatan 29 (040 34 48 00, www.malmo.se/ mazetti). Bus 2, 5, 7, 8 to Triangeln. **Open** *phone enquiries* 8am-8.30pm Mon-Thur; 8am-7pm Fri. **Credit** varies.
This new centre inside a former chocolate factory houses a wide variety of cultural organisations as well as a nightclub and hotel.

Malmö Konsthall
St Johannesgatan 7 (040 34 12 86 , www.konsthall. malmo.se). Bus 2, 5, 7, 8 to Triangeln. **Open** 11am-5pm Mon, Tue, Thur-Sun; 11am-9pm Wed. **Admission** free; charges applicable for some exhibitions. **Credit** MC, V.

Malmö Museums & Art Museum
Malmöhusvägen, Slottet Malmöhus (040 34 44 37, www.malmo.se/museer). Bus 32. **Open** *Sept-May* 10am-4pm Mon-Fri; noon-4pm Sat, Sun. *June-Aug* 10am-4pm daily. **Admission** 40Skr; 10Skr-12Skr concessions; free under-6s. **Credit** MC, V.
The listings above cover Malmö Konstmuseum, Stadsmuseet, Naturmuseet and also Teknik och Sjöfartsmuseet.

Moderna Museet
Gasverksgatan 22 (040 685 79 37, www. modernamuseet.se). Train Centralstation/ Bus to Gustav Adolfs Torg. **Open** Tue, Thu-Sun 11am-6pm; Wed 11am-9pm. **Admission** 50Skr; 40Skr concessions; free under-18s. **Credit** MC, V.

★ Ribersborgs Kallbadhus

Ribersborgs Stranden (040 26 03 66, www.ribban. com). Bus 32. **Open** *Baths and sauna* 10am-7pm Mon, Tue, Thu, Fri; 10am-10pm Wed; 9am-4pm Sat, Sun. *Café* 10am-10pm Mon-Fri; 9am-10pm Sat, Sun. **Admission** 65Skr; free under-7s; 40Skr towel hire (80Skr deposit). **Credit** MC, V.

Rundan Canal Tours

Norra Vallgatan, opposite Central Station (040 611 74 88, www.rundan.se). Train Centralstation. **Open** Apr-Oct 11am-6pm. Tours depart on the hour every hour. **Admission** *120Skr; 60Skr concessions.* **Credit** MC, V.

Stadsbibliotek

Kung Oscars väg 11 (040 660 85 00, www. malmo.stadsbibliotek.org). Train Centralstation. **Open** 10am-8pm Mon-Thur; 10am-6pm Fri; 11am-4pm Sat, Sun. **Admission** free.

Where to eat & drink

Brogatan

Brogatan 12 (040 30 77 17, www.brogatan. com). **Open** 11.30am-1am Mon-Tue; Wed-Thur 11.30am-2am; 11.30am-3am Sat; noon-1am Sun. **Main Courses** 85Skr-179Skr. **Credit** AmEx, DC, MC, V.

Brogatan combines a locally sourced, largely organic menu – steak tartare, herring and wild boar meatballs, say – with a good selection of drinks, including beer from local microbreweries. The wooden bistro decor is more Marais than Malmö, which makes it as good a place for a coffee as a long lunch. Later on, it has more of a buzz as it switches into bar mode.

Centiliter & Gram

Stortorget 17 (040 12 18 12, www.etage gruppen.se). Train Centralstation. **Open** *9pm-3am Tue, Wed; 8pm-3am Thur-Sat; 10pm-3am Sun.* **Main courses** 65Skr-179Skr. **Credit** AmEx, DC, MC, V.

Just around the corner from Lilla Torg on the city's main square is this large, open-plan bar and club whose dressy, mature clientele usually spill outside if the weather allows.

★ Koi

Lilla Torg 5 (040 757 00, www.koi.se). Train Centralstation. **Open** 11.30am-midnight Mon-Thur; 11.30am-3am Fri, Sat. **Main courses** 99Skr-599Skr. **Credit** AmEx, DC, MC, V.

This Lilla Torg stalwart is still going strong, noted for its inventive, quality 'New Japanese' cuisine and excellent cocktails.

Lemon Grass

Grynbodgatan 9 (040 30 69 79, www.lemon grass.se). Bus to Gustav Adolfs Torg. **Open** 6pm-midnight Mon-Thur; 5.30pm-1am Fri, Sat. **Main courses** 158Skr-258Skr. **Credit** AmEx, DC, MC, V.

More Asian-influenced fusion magic is on offer in this stylish, minimalist eaterie.

Mellow Yello

Lilla Torg 1 (040 30 45 25, www.melloyello. se).Train Centralstation. **Open** 5pm-midnight Mon, Tue; 5pm-1am Wed, Thur; 4pm-1am Fri; noon-1am Sat; 3pm-midnight Sun. **Main courses** 159Skr-259Skr. **Credit** AmEx, DC, MC, V.

One of the prime bars in Lilla Torg with a great atmosphere and a young-ish clientele. All of the venues on Lilla Torg come equipped with outdoor rain covers and parasol heaters.

Metro

*Ängelholmsgatan 14 (040 23 00 63, www.metropamollan.se)***Open** 6pm-1am Mon-Thur; 5pm-1am Fri; noon-1am Fri; noon-5pm Sun. **Main Courses** 69Skr-215Skr. **Credit** MC, V.

The menu at this bar-restaurant ranges from ambitious fusion that reflects the area's multicultural feel, to hearty, wintry fare: choose between fish soup or roast lamb with roast potatoes and garlic butter, and noodles with marinated vegetables, fried Haloumi and wasabi. Local DJs play from Thursday to Saturday, with occasional one-off events on Mondays. In summer, its outdoor tables come into their own.

Moosehead Bar & Restaurant

Lilla Torg 1 (040 12 04 23, www.moosehead.se). Train Centralstation. **Open** 6pm-midnight Mon, Tue; 4pm-1am Wed-Fri; midday-1am Sat, Sun. **Main courses** 130Skr-245Skr. **Credit** AmEx, MC, V.

Another recommended Lilla Torg eaterie, this time serving hearty steaks and burgers but with a local twist (moose meat burgers, for one). Great atmosphere, especially outside on a summer evening.

Restaurang Smak

Scaniaplatsen 2A (040 50 50 35, www. restaurangsmak.se). Bus to Triangeln. **Open** *Kitchen* 11.30am-3.30pm Mon-Sun; open for coffee until 5pm daily. **Brunch** Skr85-145Skr; weekend buffet 155Skr. **Credit** AmEx, MC, V.

This contemporary seafood brunch restaurant is one of the newest places in the hot Western Harbour area.

★ Salt & Brygga

Sundspromenaden 7, Västra Hamnen (040 611 5940, www.saltobrygga.se). Bus 2, 3. **Open** 11.30am-3pm, 5-9pm Mon-Fri; 12.30-9pm Sat. **Main courses** 129Skr-295Skr. **Credit** AmEx, DC, MC, V.

If you are visiting the fabulous new Western Harbour residential area, this is a great summer restaurant

serving modern Scandinavian-Italian cuisine in a light, trendy venue beside the water.

★ Spot

Stora Nygatan 33 (040 12 02 03). Bus to Gustav Adolfs Torg. **Open** 11.30am-9pm Mon-Thur; 11am-10pm Fri, Sat; 11am-6pm Sun. **Main courses** 75Skr-165Skr.**Credit** AmEx, MC, V.
Desirable and refreshingly modern Italian cooking in a stylish setting close to the centre of town. As with most of Sweden's restaurants, chic design does not equal stuffy or exclusive and children are very welcome here. An in-house delicatessen is an bonus.

Victors

Lilla Torg 1 (040 12 76 70, www.victors.se). Train Centralstation. **Open** 11.30am-10.30pm Mon-Sat, kitchen closed 3-5pm. **Main courses** 169Skr-225Skr. **Credit** AmEx, DC, MC, V.
Experience modern Scandinavian cooking in this quintessential Swedish bar/restaurant which, come night-time, transforms into a club space. The food offers good value and Victors boasts its own bartending academy, so, as you would expect, the selection of cocktails is excellent.

Where to stay

If you want to stay overnight and can't get into the places listed below, contact **Malmö Tourist Hotel Booking** (040 10 92 10, www.malmo town.com/en/accommodation).

Clarion Hotel Malmö

Engelbrektsgatan 16 (040 710 20, www.choice hotels.se). Bus to Gustav Adolfs Torg. **Rates** 1,090Skr-1,640Skr double. **Credit** AmEx, DC, MC, V.
One of Malmö's oldest hotels (dating from the turn of the 19th century) retains many of its period features and, although it is not the finest hotel in town (that accolade goes to the pricier Hotel Kramer), it is centrally located and is good value.

Hilton Malmö City

Triangeln 2 (040 693 47 00, www.hilton.com). Bus to Triangeln. **Rates** 1,250Skr-1,400Skr double. **Credit** AmEx, DC, MC, V.
Modern high-rise international hotel chain with a decent restaurant, the Lean Grill & Bar. The hotel is located at the southern end of Malmö's pedestrian shopping area.

Scandic Hotel Kramer

Stortorget 7 (040 693 54 00, www.scandic-hotels.com). Train Centralstation. **Rates** 940Skr-1,670Skr double. **Credit** AmEx, DC, MC, V.
Malmö's poshest hotel is a smaller replica of Copenhagen's swanky French chateau-style Hotel d'Angleterre, but without the overbearing snobbery of its Danish counterpart. It was built at the end of the 19th century and thus, unlike later hotels, enjoys a prime location right in the centre of town.

RESOURCES

For speedy exploration, you can rent a bicycle at **Fridhems Cyklar** (Tessinsväg 13, 040 26 03 35) or **Rundan** (Norra Vallgatan, opposite Central Station, 040 611 74 88, 16 April to 2 Oct only).

Tourist information

Malmö Tourist Office, Börshuset, Skeppsbron 2 (040 34 12 00, www.malmotown.com). **Open** June-Aug 9am-7pm Mon-Fri; 9am-5pm Sat, Sun. Sept-May 9am-5pm Mon-Fri, 10am-2.30pm Sat, Sun. **Credit** AmEx, DC, MC, V.
The Malmö Card (1 day 170Skr, 2 days 200Skr) is valid for one adult and two children under 15 and is worth considering. It provides free transport on local buses, free parking and discounts on travel to Copenhagen. In addition, use it to gain free or discounted entrance to a number of Malmö's sights, including Malmöhus Castle. Should you decide to linger a while in town, the card also procures discounts on car, bike and pedalo hire.

The Danish Riviera

Crystal clear water, seaside fun and a world-class art gallery.

Known variously as the 'Danish Riviera', the 'whisky belt' or the 'Beverly Hills' of Copenhagen (this is where most of the showbiz and sports stars reside), the road that leads north along the coast from the capital is flanked by some of the most expensive housing in the country. As well as the architectural horrors and delights that wealthy Danes have constructed here, there are several interesting attractions for visitors.

Chief among them – and the main reason visitors leave Copenhagen and travel half an hour north in this direction – is the stunning modern art museum, **Louisiana Museum For Moderne Kunst**. As well as this, there is the beautiful home of Karen '*Out of Africa*' Blixen and, at the end of your journey north, Hamlet's home town, Helsingør, with its indomitable castle.

ESCAPES & EXCURSIONS

HEADING OUT

The Riviera begins at **Charlottenlund**, with its pleasant beach and camping area. Next is **Klampenborg** with another popular beach, **Bellevue**, **Bakken** amusement park (*see right*) and a large wild deer park.

Bakken is on the edge of a 1,000-hectare (2,470-acre) former royal hunting ground, now a rather more serene deer park, **Dyrehaven**. Dyrehaven, as it's better known, dates from 1231 and is to Copenhageners what Richmond Park is to Londoners. The park is closed to traffic; all the better for its large herds of free-roaming deer and the many walkers who come here from the city. Expensive horse-drawn carriage rides are also available. In its grounds is the enigmatic former hunting lodge, Eremitagen, which has wonderful views

INSIDE TRACK COASTAL ROAD

The coast road, Strandvejen, often comes within metres of the sea, and is frequently congested during the height of summer. Happily, the train service to Helsingør also runs parallel to the water, stopping at most of the towns and villages along the way. As is usual in Denmark, it is quick, efficient and reasonably priced, and there are stations roughly every ten minutes.

to the sea (but is not open to the public). Nearby is Klampenborg's **Galopbane** (*see index*), a racing and trotting course.

Dyrehaven, Bakken and Bellevue Beach are within easy walking distance of Klampenborg Station, 18 minutes by train from Copenhagen.

The next major point of interest along the coast is **Rungstedlund**, the former home of the Danish novelist Karen Blixen, now the site of **Karen Blixen Museet** (*see right*). The internationally acclaimed author spent much of her life (apart from 17 years in Kenya) in Rungstedlund. Blixen is buried in the gardens of Rungstedlund, at the foot of Ewald's hill, beneath a large beech tree.

The house was also once the residence of another eminent Danish writer, Johannes Ewald (1743-81). He lived here in 1773 and wrote several of his lyric poems and heroic tragedies in verse in the same room in which Blixen also chose to write. Rungstedlund is about ten minutes' walk from the nearest railway station, Rungsted Kyst. Alternatively, you can catch a train to Klampenborg and take bus number 388.

Between Rungstedlund and Helsingør are several more small harbours, but the main attraction is the **Louisiana Museum For Moderne Kunst** (Louisiana Modern Art Museum; *see right*). There may be larger modern art collections in the world, but none is located in more blissful surroundings than Louisiana. A more peaceful setting for this diverse collection of modern art amid leafy gardens that cascade down to the shore would be hard to imagine.

Bakken

Dyrehavesbakken, Dyrehavevej 62, Klampenborg (39 63 35 44, www.bakken.dk). Train Klampenborg. **Open** *Last Thur Mar-Last Sun Aug opening hours vary; call for details or the calendar on the website.* **Admission** free, rides extra (reduced prices Wed). **Credit** AmEx, MC, V.

Tivoli may be Denmark's most famous amusement park, but Dyrehavesbakken (known as Bakken for short) is equally popular with Danes. Bakken was founded in 1583 and claims to be the oldest amusement park in the world. It is, nevertheless, usually seen as Tivoli's downmarket cousin and does have more of a funfair/beer hall atmosphere but that doesn't mean less enjoyment. There are 100 or so rides (which tend to be cheaper than Tivoli's), as well as 35 cafés and restaurants. Admission to the park is free.

Karen Blixen Museet

Rungstedlund, Rungsted Strandvej 111, Rungsted (45 57 10 57, www.karen-blixen.dk). Train to Rungsted Kyst. **Open** *May-Sept* 10am-5pm Tue-Sun. *Oct-Apr* noon-4pm Wed-Fri; 11am-4pm Sat, Sun. **Admission** 60kr; 50kr concessions; free under-14s. **Credit** AmEx, MC, V.

This simple, early 19th-century house set in 16 hectares (40 acres) of gardens also acts as a bird sanctuary. Its north wing has been preserved as if Blixen had just left, with her furniture, paintings and even her distinctive flower arrangements as they were when she lived here. There's a gallery of Blixen's drawings and paintings, and a biographical exhibition, library and small cinema upstairs.

★ Louisiana Museum
For Moderne Kunst

Gammel Strandvej 13, Humlebæk (49 19 07 19, www.louisiana.dk). Train Humlebæk. **Open** 11am-10pm Tue-Fri; 11am-6pm Sat, Sun. **Admission** 95kr; 75kr-85kr concessions; free under-18s. **Credit** AmEx, MC, V. *See p218* **Profile.**

Where to eat

Close to Bellevue Beach and Klampenborg Station are two notable restaurants: **Den Gule Cottage** and **Restaurant Jacobsen** (for both, *see p127*). The latter is housed in a building designed by the legendary Danish architect and designer Arne Jacobsen and features many of his most famous furniture designs. It is part of the famous Bellevue housing and theatre complex, which was one of his earliest and most influential works.

Getting there

By train

There are trains at least every 20mins heading north along the coast from Copenhagen Central Station via Nørreport. It takes 18mins to get to Klampenborg, 30mins to reach Rungsted Kyst and 41mins to Humlebæk. Note that if you're visiting Louisiana, the cheapest option is to buy a combined train/museum ticket for 176kr.

Klampenborg.

Profile Louisiana Museum For Modern Kunst

A more beautiful setting for an art gallery is hard to imagine.

ESCAPES & EXCURSIONS

Louisiana (*see p217*) began life as a purely Scandinavian art collection. It was founded in 1954 by the industrialist and art collector Knud Jensen, but international works were added thanks to donations from the Ny Carlsberg Foundation. Architects Jørgen Bo and Vilhelm Wohlert added new galleries to the existing 19th-century villa (which already had the name Louisiana after the previous owner's three wives who, bizarrely, were all named Louise), and the

resulting, much enlarged, complex is characterised by a vaguely Japanese style.

The irregular-shaped, open-plan, whitewashed rooms with their large windows blur the divide between the galleries and the outside sculpture park, giving Louisiana its uniquely tranquil atmosphere. Somehow, the reassuring proximity of beech trees, lawn and (crystal-clear) sea (with the Swedish coast in the distance) creates a harmony between the buildings and their

UPCOMING EXHIBITIONS
Future exhibitions include 'The Frontiers of Architecture III-IV: Living' (May-Oct 2011); 'Paul Klee & Cobra' (Oct 2011-Jan 2012); and new works by Ai Weiwei (Dec 2011-Mar 2012).

environment that counterbalances the frequently confrontational, disturbing and/or impenetrable nature of the works on display. And the light here is unique.

The first pieces bought by the museum were by Danish artists like Richard Mortensen, Asger Jørn (one of the founders of the abstract COBRA Group; the name was formed from COpenhagen, BRussels and Amsterdam, the home cities of the artists involved) and the constructivist sculptor and graphic artist Robert Jacobsen. The collection soon grew to encompass works by many notable post-war French sculptors like Herbin, Albers, Gabo and Alexander Calder and, from the 1950s, Louisiana acquired paintings by Dubuffet, Bacon, Rothko and Reinhardt. Paintings from several of Picasso's periods are among the museum's highlights, while the Pop Art movement of the '60s is also well represented (in fact, the whole museum has something of a flower-power feel) with pieces by, among others, Warhol, Lichtenstein, Oldenburg and Rauschenberg. Louisiana's collection of '70s German art is strong. Bringing things right up to date are a few contemporary pieces, including a video installation by British artist Sam Taylor Wood.

The museum's south wing was added in 1982 and a corridor built connecting it to the old buildings. Along the corridor now hang the colourful geometric paintings of Richard Mortensen. In 1991 a subterranean wing exhibiting graphic art opened.

In the garden you'll find sculptures by Calder, Henry Moore, Joan Miró, Max Ernst and Giacometti, among others (Giacometti also features inside the gallery in a dedicated room that is one of the highlights of the museum). The gardens are very

popular with children, who also benefit from their own indoor area, Børnehuset (Children's House).

Louisiana holds regular lectures, film screenings and concerts and is famed for its superstar retrospectives (there are usually around six temporary exhibitions each year; 'Picasso: Peace and Freedom' was held in early 2011.

After you've had your fill of art, head to the superb retro café for a delicious choux pastry or sandwich, plus beautiful views overlooking the Øresund, a terrace graced by one of Calder's amusing sculptures, and a log fire in winter. The large shop, too, is a don't miss, selling some of Denmark's most covetable design items.

COMBO TICKET

You can buy a ticket for 176kr that combines a return train journey from Copenhagen Central Station with entrance to Louisiana.

North Sjælland

Take a dip with the Danes.

If you find yourself in Copenhagen for more than a few days and fancy a breath of old-fashioned, fresh seaside air, then a trip to the timewarp fishing villages and glorious beaches of the northern coast of Sjælland could be just the ticket. Many Copenhageners have summer houses in the region, and much of the city decamps to the beach from late June to the end of July so it can get crowded then, although there are plenty of campsites and holiday homes to rent.

On your way north to the coast – about an hour's drive from Copenhagen, a little longer if you take the train – you would do well to stop off at one of Denmark's most important castles. **Frederiksborg Slot** (not to be confused with Frederiksberg Slot in Copenhagen), is half an hour north of Copenhagen by train. This majestic early 17th century Dutch Renaissance red-brick castle, with its ornate copper spires and sandstone façade, stands on three small islands in Slotsø (Castle Lake), in the middle of the town of Hillerød. The castle is complemented by elegant baroque gardens and an English garden with a chateau.

The castle was gutted by fire in 1859 and for a while it looked as though it would remain a ruin. Fortunately, JC Jacobsen volunteered to use some of his considerable Carlsberg wealth to restore Frederiksborg and subsequently helped found **Det Nationalhistoriske Museum** (Museum of National History) within 70 or so of its rooms. The museum opened in 1882 and charts Denmark's history through paintings arranged in chronological order.

One of the decorative highlights of Frederiksborg is its chapel, which, between 1671 and 1840, was used for the coronations of Denmark's absolute monarchs. Since 1693 it has also been the chapel for Danish knights, whose shields hang on the walls; remarkably, it's also the local church. Its altar and pulpit are the work of the Hamburg goldsmith Jakob Mores, while the priceless Compenius organ, dating from 1610 and boasting 1,000 pipes, is played every Thursday between 1.30pm and 2pm. It is worth timing a visit to hear it.

From Frederiksborg Slot it is a short journey north to the fishing towns of Hornbæk, Gilleleje and Tisvildeleje, ranged along the northern coast of Sjælland. In between are expansive, natural stretches of sand, with shallow, clean water and all the facilities required for a day

at the beach (though they are usually kept well out of sight of the beach itself). The beaches are typically fronted by grassy dunes, rugged heathland and ancient forests.

Hornbæk became popular during the 19th century with artists such as PS Krøyer and Kristian Zahrtmann, who took a shine to the picturesque life of the local fishermen. Its beach is excellent for children as it shelves gently. There is wheelchair access. As with all the beaches mentioned, it is possible to walk from the nearest railway station.

Hornbæk has a wide range of accommodation and several restaurants, mainly located in the town centre, but for cheap, fresh snacks you are best off heading for the seafood kiosks in the harbour. For more information, contact the local tourist office (49 70 47 47, www.hornbaek.dk).

Dronningmølle (Queen's Mill), the next stop five kilometres (three miles) along the road west towards Gilleleje, also has a great beach. Alternatively, you could take the road south towards Villingerød and turn left at the church to reach **Rudolph Tegners Museum** (*see 222* **Art For A Laugh**).

Gilleleje (tourist office: 48 30 01 74, www.visitnordsjaelland.com) is the most northerly town in Sjælland, the island's largest fishing harbour and was one of the main escape routes for Danish Jews in 1943 (there is an exhibition on this in Gilleleje Museum). Many of the Jews hid in the roof of Gilleleje Kirke in Hovedgade, which dates from the 16th century. Gilleleje has a bustling fishing harbour and a 14-kilometre (nine-mile) long beach.

Tisvildeleje (tourist office: 48 70 74 51, www.visitnordsjaelland.com) is another attractive coastal village west of Gilleleje. Its long, broad, sandy beach is a short walk downhill from the railway station, past 18th century fishermen's cottages, most of which are now summer houses. Nearby is one of Denmark's largest forests, **Tisvilde Hegn**,

planted 200 years ago to stop coastal erosion, which offers bracing walks (the tourist office has maps).

Frederiksborg Slot
Hillerød (48 26 04 39, www.frederiksborg museet.dk). Train to Hillerød. **Open** *Apr-Oct* 10am-5pm daily. *Nov-Mar* 11am-3pm daily. **Admission** 60kr; 15kr-50kr concessions; free under-6s. **Credit** AmEx, MC, V.

Gilleleje Museum
Pyramiden, Vesterbrogade 56, Gilleleje (48 30 16 31, www.hhkc.dk). **Open** *June-Aug* 1-4pm Mon, Wed-Sun. *Sept-May* 1-4pm Wed-Fri; 10am-2pm Sat. **Admission** 25kr; free under-18s. **No credit cards**.

Frederiksborg Slot.

Where to eat

Restaurant Søstrene Olsen
*Øresundvej 10, Hornbæk (49 70 05 50, www.
sostreneolsen.dk).* **Open** *Mar-Oct* noon-9pm daily.
Main courses 298kr. 4-course set menu 428kr.
Credit AmEx, MC, V.
The location for this restaurant– a pretty thatched
cottage overlooking the beach – couldn't be better,
and the food is just as good. Seafood a speciality.

Where to stay

Gilleleje Badehotel
*Hulsøvej 15, Gilleleje (48 30 13 47, www.
gillelejebadehotel.dk).* **Train** Gilleleje. **Rates**
1,190kr-1,590kr double. **Rooms** 24. **Credit**
AmEx, MC, V.
This freshly renovated 'bathing hotel' makes an
excellent base for a visit to the north coast.

Hotel Villa Strand
*Kystvej 2, Hornbæk (49 70 00 88, www.villa
strand.dk).* **Train** to Hornbæk. **Rates** 995kr-
1,420kr double. **Rooms** 16. **Credit** AmEx, MC, V.

Peaceful and serene accommodation option close to
the centre of town and the beach.

Resources

Tourist information
Visit Nordsjælland *(49 21 13 33, www.visit
nordsjaelland.com).* **Open** 10am-4pm Mon-Fri.
Gilleleje *Gilleleje Hovedgade 6F (48 30 01 74,
www.visitnordsjaelland.com).* **Open** *Summer
only* 10am4pm Mon-Fri; 10am-noon Sat.
Hornbæk *Hornbæk Bibliotek, Vestre Stejlebakke
2A (49 70 47 47, www.hornbaek.dk).* **Open**
Summer only 1-7pm Mon; 10am-5pm Tue,
Wed, Fri; 1-5pm Thur; 10am-2pm Sat.

Getting there

By train
To get to Hornbæk and Dronningmølle, take trains
from Central Station and change at Helsingør (about
1hr 30mins in total, 1 train an hour). To reach
Gilleleje or Tisvildeleje, take the S-tog from Central
Station and change at Hillerød (1hr 20mins in total,
around 2 trains an hour).

Art for a Laugh

Some of Rudolph Tegner's sculptures are entertainingly bad.

A couple of kilometres inland from
Dronningmølle on the north coast of
Zealand lies one of Denmark's most
idiosyncratic museums. The **Rudolph
Tegners Museum** is dedicated to the
work of a Danish artist who was either
a crazy genius or the world's worst
sculptor, depending on who you ask.

Born in 1873, Rudolph Tegner
considered himself a great artist. But
the difference between Tegner and your
average arty megalomaniac was that,
thanks to his wife Elna's inherited fortune,
he had the financial wherewithal to realise
his vision. In 1916, Tegner bought a piece
of heath beside the coast and set about
preserving his life's work.

Tegner had had limited success
in persuading the rest of Denmark
to appreciate his symbolist/art
nouveau/Nietzschean-influenced
sculptures, and critics were rarely positive.
Berlingske Aften, the leading evening
paper, wrote of one of his pieces: 'The
most disheartening thing about Tegner's
plaster monstrosity is not... its purely
sculptural mediocrity, but the mentality it
expresses. If you have studied the statue
long enough and close your eyes, you can

hear boots tramping in time and bombastic
band music, and before your inner eye rise
the contours of Haus der Deutschen Kunst
in Munich.'

Today, Tegner's monumental, histrionic
works can be seen both dotted among the
heather in the 46-acre sculpture park and
inside the museum building. This sinister,
virtually windowless, raw concrete bunker,
built in 1937, squats among the grazing
sheep like the villain's lair from a Bond
movie. It's certainly in stark contrast to
the exceptionally beauty that surrounds it.

It is hard to pick out 'highlights', but
Sankt Peder med Nøglen (St Peter with
the Key) is notably dreadful – a monstrously
ugly figure with oversized thighs. To be fair,
Tegner did occasionally create something
with genuine grace and beauty; it's just that
his bad stuff is so much more entertaining.

Rudolph Tegners Museum
*Museumsvej 19, Dronningmølle (49 71
91 77, www.rudolphtegner.dk).* **Train** to
Kildekrog or Dronningmølle. **Open** *Mid Apr-
May, Sept, Oct* noon-5pm Tue-Sun. *June-
Aug* 9.30am-5pm Tue-Sun. *Nov-mid Apr*
closed. **Admission** 50kr; 30kr concessions;
free under-12s. **No credit cards**.

Directory

Christiansborg Slot. *See p65*.

Getting Around	224
Resources A-Z	**227**
Travel Advice	227
Weather Report	233
Vocabulary	**234**
Further Reference	**235**
Content Index	**236**
Venue Index	**238**

Getting Around

ARRIVING & LEAVING

By air

Copenhagen Airport (also known as Kastrup) is often voted best in the world by air passengers. It receives direct flights from 140 cities worldwide and 21.5 million passengers passed through in 2010.

Flight time from London is about one-and-a-half hours; direct flights from New York (Newark) take seven-and-a-half hours; while the fastest direct flight from the west coast is nine-and-a-half hours (from Seattle; coming from LA or San Francisco you'll have to change and journey time is approximately 14 hours). International flights arrive and depart from **Terminals 2** and **3**. (Terminal 1 is for domestic flights only.) The new low-cost airline terminal, CPH Go, opened in October 2010, and is currently used by easyJet. The airport is ten kilometres (six miles) south-east of Copenhagen on the island of Amager.

The Copenhagen Metro link has recently been extended as far as the airport. The station is located in Terminal 3 – just walk straight ahead out of the arrivals hall, and head up the escalator. Metro trains take roughly 14 minutes to reach Central Station (København H) and a single fare costs 34.59kr. You can buy tickets from the machines located just before the Metro platform. The Metro runs to and from the airport 24 hours a day, seven days a week. For additional information, call 70 15 16 15 or visit www.m.dk.

There are plentiful **taxis** at Terminals 1 and 3; the fare into the centre of the city should be around 300kr. Tips are not expected in Danish taxis.

Local **buses** (5A goes to both Rådhuspladsen and Copenhagen Central Station) run from Terminal 3 every ten to 20 minutes (the night bus is twice an hour), but most visitors take the Metro as the bus fare is only slightly cheaper and the journey longer.

For further information on bus services, contact **Movia** on 36 13 14 15, www.moviatrafik.dk.

A free transit bus runs every ten to 15 minutes between international and domestic terminals.

Airport facilities

The airport's facilities include shops and restaurants, banks (most open 6am-10pm daily) in the Transfer Hall and Terminals 2 and 3, as well as cash machines (ATMs) in Terminals 1, 2 and 3. There are lockers in Terminals 1 and 2 and left luggage facilities in Arkaden between Terminals 2 and 3 (see p229). Though Copenhagen is a pedestrian-friendly city, there are car hire desks in Arkaden, between Terminals 2 and 3 (see p225).

Copenhagen Airport
Central switchboard 32 31 32 31, flight info 32 47 47 47, www.cph.dk. The website gives details of live information on arrival and departure times. For more specific flight information, call the relevant handling agent: Novia (32 47 47 47); British Airways (70 12 80 22); Iberia (70 10 01 52); Turkish Airlines (33 14 40 55); SAS (70 10 20 00); KLM (70 10 07 47); Air France (82 33 27 01); Alitalia (70 14 24 21); Swiss (70 10 50 64); easyJet (70 12 43 21).

By rail

DSB (De Danske Statsbaner – Danish State Railways) connects Copenhagen with all of continental Europe's capitals. It also connects to the UK, though you have to change trains in the Netherlands. All international trains arrive and depart from **Central Station (Hovedbanegård)**.

By road

The Danish capital is 300 kilometres (186 miles) from the German border, and only a half-hour drive to Malmö.

Eurolines runs express coaches to Copenhagen.

Danish Road Directorate
Niels Juels Gade 13 (72 44 33 33, Traffic Information Centre 70 10 10 40, www.vejdirektoratet.dk). **Open** *Traffic Information Centre* 24hrs daily.
Route, roadworks and traffic info.

Eurolines
Halmtorvet 5 (33 88 70 00, www. eurolines.com). **Open** 8am-5pm daily. **Credit** MC, V. **Map** p250 P11.

The Eurolines station is located near Central Station.

By sea

There are direct ferries between Copenhagen and Oslo (16 hours) and Swinoujscie in Poland (ten hours). In addition, there's a ferry route from Helsingør (47 km/28 miles north of Copenhagen) to Sweden, from Esbjerg (200 km/124 miles west) to the UK, from Rødby (150km/93 miles south) to Germany, and from Frederikshavn or Hirtshals (450 km/280 miles north-west) to Sweden and Norway.

DFDS Seaways
Copenhagen–Oslo; Esbjerg–Harwich.
Dampfærgevej 30, Østerbro (33 42 30 00, www.dfdsseaways.dk). **Open** *Phone enquiries* 9am-5pm daily. **Credit** AmEx, MC, V.

Scandlines
Helsingør–Helsingborg.
Copenhagen Office: Dampfærgevej 10, Østerbro (33 15 15 15, www. scandlines.dk). Train to Helsingør. **Credit** AmEx, MC, V. Open *phone enquiries* 24hrs daily.

PUBLIC TRANSPORT

Trains, Metro & buses

Copenhagen is blessed with an efficient network of local buses (**Trafikselskabet Movia**), trains (**S-tog**), run by Danish State Railways (**DSB**; see p225), and, since 2003, the smart new **Metro** system (officially named the world's 'best metro' at an industry conference in 2010).

The Metro has two lines, M1 and M2, both of which run from Vanløse in the north-west to Vestamager and the airport respectively. Both lines run through Nørreport, Kongens Nytorv and Christianshavn. The driverless, automatic trains run roughly every six minutes (every 15-20 minutes at night), 24 hours, every day of the week. For ticket prices, see p225.

Another big extension of Copenhagen's Metro is currently being constructed. Called the 'City Ring', it will feature 17 stations and link the 'Bridge Quarters' of the city with the centre via an underground tunnel ring. The City Ring will be completed in 2018. For further information, call 33 11 17 00 or visit www.m.dk.

The S-tog local train system is made up of seven lines, six of which pass through Central Station.

Buses, S-tog trains and the Metro all use the same ticket system and zoned fare structure. There is a map of the S-tog system and Metro lines on p256 of this guide.

Trains and buses run from 5am Monday to Saturday (from 6am on Sundays) until around half past midnight, although some of these buses do run through the night.

Movia

Gammel Køge Landevej 3 *(36 13 14 15, www.moviatrafik.dk).* **Open** *Phone enquiries* 7am-9.30pm daily. **No credit cards**. **Map** p250 O12. The Movia office can supply journey plans, timetables, discount cards and lost property information.

Tickets & discount cards

The Copenhagen metropolitan area is split into seven zone rings, radiating out from the centre of the city. The **basic ticket** allows passengers to travel within two zones on a variety of transport: buses, trains and the Metro. It costs **24kr** (12kr for children 12-16). As the two central zones include almost every attraction, hotel, restaurant and bar covered in this guide, it's unlikely that visitors will need to buy anything more than this basic ticket. Such a ticket also allows transfers between buses and trains, providing that the transfer is made within an hour. All tickets are stamped with the date, time and departure zone. Two- and three-zone tickets are valid for a period of one hour from the stamped time; four- to six-zone tickets can be used for one-and-a-half hours; all-zone tickets are valid for two hours.

Tickets are on sale at all railway station ticket offices. They can also be purchased from machines at stations and from bus drivers. Coloured zone maps can be found at bus stops and in railway stations.

Children

Two children under 12 can travel for free when accompanied by an adult. Children aged 12 to 15 pay the child fare or can use a child's discount card. Two 12- to 15-year-olds can travel on one adult ticket or on one clip of an adult's discount card.

Discount Cards

Discount clip cards (*klippekort*) are available for ten journeys within two, three, four, five, six or all zones (two-zone cards cost **140kr**; 70kr children under 16). When you start your journey, you must punch your card in the yellow machine on the bus or in the station or your ticket will not be valid and you will be fined.

One clip covers you for travel within the zones printed on the card. If you want to travel beyond those zones, then several simultaneous clips are needed (for example, if you have a two-zone card, two clips allow you to travel within three or four zones, three clips allow five or six zones, and so on). Cards can be bought from stations, most ticket machines and HUR ticket offices.

24-hour ticket

This ticket allows unlimited travel within zones 1, 2, 3 and 4 for 24 hours on Copenhagen's buses and trains. It costs **70kr** (35kr children) and should be clipped in the yellow machines in buses and stations at the start of the journey. Two children under ten can travel free with an adult holding a 24-hour ticket. The ticket can be bought from manned rail stations. An all-zone 24-hour card costs 130kr (65kr children).

Copenhagen Card

As well as free admission to more than 60 museums, galleries and sights, the **Copenhagen Card** offers unlimited travel by bus and train within Greater Copenhagen. Cards are available in two formats: 24 or 72 hours. For prices, *see above*. The card can be bought from DSB ticket offices in Rådhuspladsen and Toftegårds Plads. It can also be purchased at main stations, most tourist offices and from many hotels.

National rail system

For mapping out journeys and itineraries, **DSB** (Danish State Railways) boasts an excellent integrated journey planner (for the English version; see www.dsb.dk/english) on its website for rail (and bus) journeys within Denmark.

DSB

Central Station (domestic & international journeys 70 13 14 15, S-tog 33 53 00 33, www.dsb.dk). **Open** *International* 9.30am-6pm daily. *S-tog/domestic* 6am-10.30pm daily. **Credit** AmEx, MC, V. **Map** p250 P11.

Waterbuses

During the summer DFDS runs three hop-on, hop-off waterbus routes around the harbour area. One-day tickets (valid on all routes) are **40kr** (30kr children). For more details, visit www.canaltours.dk.

DRIVING

When it comes to driving, we have one simple word of advice: don't. The Danes, or rather their government, detest private cars and do everything to discourage their use. If you can't do without wheels, here are some tips.

The Danes drive on the right. When turning right, drivers give way to cyclists coming up on the inside and to pedestrians crossing on a green light. You must drive with dipped headlights during the day.

In most places drivers have to pay for parking within the city centre from 8am to 8pm Monday to Friday, and from 8am to 2pm on Saturdays.

Car rental

The prices below are for basic rental of the cheapest car class.

Avis

Kampmannsgade 1 (70 24 77 07, www.avis.com). Train to Vesterport. **Open** 7am-5pm Mon-Thur; 7am-6pm Fri; 8am-2pm Sat, Sun. **Map** p250 N10. *Terminal 3, Copenhagen Airport (32 51 20 99).* **Open** 24hrs daily. **Rates** 678kr/day; 1,672kr/week. **Credit** AmEx, MC, V.

Budget Rent a Car

Vester Farimagsgade 7 (33 55 05 00, www.budget.com). Train to Vesterport. **Open** 8am-4pm Mon-Fri; 8am-1pm Sat, Sun. **Map** p250 P10. *Terminal 3, Copenhagen Airport (32 52 39 00).* **Open** 7am-10pm daily. **Rates** 636kr/day; 2,614kr/week. **Credit** AmEx, MC, V.

EuropCar/Pitztner Auto

Gammel Kongevej (33 55 99 00, www.europcar.dk). Bus 14, 15. **Open** 7.30am-6pm Mon-Fri; 8am-2pm Sat, Sun. **Map** p245 P8. *Terminal 3, Copenhagen Airport (32 50 30 90).* **Open** 7am-11pm daily. **Rates** 950kr/day; 2,284kr/week. **Credit** AmEx, MC, V.

Hertz

Ved Vesterport 3 (33 17 90 20, www.hertzdk.dk). **Open** 7am-6pm Mon-Thur; 7am-7pm Fri; 7am-5pm

DIRECTORY

Sat; 8am-5pm Sun. **Rates** 486kr/day; 1,646kr/week. **Credit** AmEx, MC, V. **Map** p250 O10.

Breakdown services

Falck Redningskorps
Emergency 70 10 20 30. **Open** 24hrs daily. **Rates** Non-members approx 700kr/hr Mon-Fri; 1,300kr/hr Sat, Sun. **Credit** MC, V.

TAXIS

Taxis can be flagged down just about anywhere in Copenhagen. If the yellow 'Taxa' light on the roof of the car is on, the taxi is available for hire. The basic fare is 24kr plus 11.50kr per kilometre (rising to 12.50kr at night and up to 15.80kr at weekends). Fares include a service charge, so there's no need to tip. Most cabs accept credit cards (though, take note: you are supposed to tell the driver at the start if you intend to pay with a card).

CYCLING

Cycling is hugely popular. During the summer you can borrow a City Bike from one of the many ranks throughout the city centre for a deposit of 20kr (*see p40* **Bike Copenhagen**).

Bike hire

Baisikeli
Turesensgade 10 (26 70 02 29, www.baisikeli.dk). 8am-6pm Mon-Fri; 10am-2pm Sat. *Apr-Oct* 10am-6pm daily. **Rates** 50kr-160kr/day. **Credit** MC, V. **Map** p250 M11.
This laid-back, ethical bike-hire place offers used bikes for hire at competitive rates. Profits go towards financing the collection and shipment of used bicycles to Africa (hence the name: 'baisikeli' means bicycle in Swahili).

Københavns Cyklebørs
Gothersgade 157 (33 14 07 17, www.cykelboersen.dk). Metro or train to Nørreport. **Open** 9am-5.30pm Mon-Fri; 10am-1.30pm Sat. **Rates** 75kr-150kr/day; 300kr-500kr deposit. **Credit** MC, V. **Map** p247 L14.

Københavns Cykler
Reventlowsgade 11, Central Station (33 33 86 13, www.copenhagen-bikes.dk). **Open** 8am-5.30pm Mon-Fri; 9am-1pm Sat. **Rates** 85kr-230kr/day; 500kr-1,000kr deposit. **No credit cards. Map** p250 P11.

Organisations

Dansk Cyklist Forbund
Rømersgade 5 (33 32 31 21, www.dcf.dk). Metro or train to Nørreport. **Open** 10am-noon, 1-3pm Mon-Fri. **Map** p246 L12.
The Dansk Cyklist Forbund has good cycling maps, an excellent website and runs cycling tours.

WALKING

Compact, flat Copenhagen is the ideal walking city. Even the main shopping street, Strøget, is pedestrianised. For organised walking tours, *see below*.

TOURS

By bike

Bike Copenhagen with Mike
26 39 56 88, www.bikecopenhagen withmike.dk. **Tours** *Mar-Oct* daily; call for times. *Nov-Feb* Tours available if booked in advance; call for details. **Duration** Call for details. **Price** 260kr (including bike rental). **No credit cards**.
These sociable bike tours leave from the bike-hire shop Baisikeli (*see above*). Tours take in all the sights, and also get off the beaten track. Booking isn't necessary; just turn up ten minutes before the tour starts. Personalised tours are also available.

Copenhagen X
32 57 19 30, www.cphx.dk. **Tours** June-Sept; call for dates. **Duration** 1-1.5hrs. **Price** 1,400kr + VAT per group (max 30 people). **Credit** MC, V.
Until 2012, the Danish Architecture Centre are offering guided tours by bike of Copenhagen's exciting new architecture and new urban areas, such as Ørestad, and along the new green routes. Tours must be booked two weeks in advance, and you need to bring your own bike.

Flying Tigers Rickshaw
Strandlodsvej 15E (27 31 38 33, www.flyingtiger-cykeltaxa.dk). **Tours** all-year; call to book. **Duration** 1-3hrs. **Price** from 375kr (per person). **Credit** MC, V.
Tour the city in a recling rickshaw; audio guides to Copenhagen are offered as part of the 'safari', in various different languages.

By boat

In summer, especially, boat tours are a great way of crossing the city and seeing the sights.

DFDS Canal Tours
33 96 30 00, www.canaltours.com. **Depart** from Nyhavn & Gammel Strand. **Tours** *Late Mar-late Oct* half-hourly daily (Gammel Strand). *Mid June-late Aug* half-hourly daily (Nyhavn). **Duration** 50mins. **Price** 70kr; 40kr concessions. **Credit** AmEx, MC, V.
DFDS runs guided tours around the harbour, including the Opera House, the Little Mermaid and Christianshavn. Dinner tours are available, and there's also a hop-on, hop-off option for those who prefer to tour independently.

Netto-Bådene
32 54 41 02, www.netto-baadene.dk. **Depart** from Holmens Kirke & Nyhavn. **Tours** all year; call for times. **Duration** 1hr. **Price** 50kr; 30kr concessions. **No credit cards**.
Harbour and canal tours on the blue Netto boats.

On foot

For details of personal guided tours, visit **www.guides.dk**.

Copenhagen Walking Tours
Skydebanegade 38 (40 81 12 17, www.copenhagenwalkingtours.dk). **Depart** from various points. **Tours** Sat, Sun; *June-Aug* Thur-Sun. **Duration** 1.5-2hrs. **Price** 1,300kr per group (1-13 people). **No credit cards**.
This well-known operator offers English-language private, pre-booked walking tours on a variety of specialised and general themes including, of course, Hans Christian Andersen and historic Copenhagen, as well as the city's Jewish heritage. Dressed in red, the guides are hard to lose and they walk all year, in sun or snow.

Ghost Tour
51 92 55 51, www.ghosttour.dk. **Departs** from Nyhavn 22, next to Café ship Liva. **Tours** 8pm Thur-Sat. **Duration** 90mins. **Price** 100kr; 70kr concessions. **No credit cards**.
With its old architecture and romantic atmosphere, Copenhagen is ideal for a ghost tour. This guided (English) walk explores some of the spookier sites.

Jazz Guides
33 45 43 19, www.jazzguides.dk. **No credit cards**.
A variety of tours of the city's many jazz venues. Every Thursday there's a tour costing 850kr per person, that includes club entrance fees, meal and drinks.

Resources A-Z

AGE RESTRICTIONS

In Denmark, you have to be 16 to drink in a bar. You also have to be 16 to buy cigarettes. You can drive at 18 and have sex at 15.

BUSINESS SERVICES

Couriers

Bring Express *Fuglebaekvej 5-7, Kastrup (70 10 31 03, www.bring. dk)*. **Open** 24hrs. **Prices** from 80kr in the city centre. **No credit cards**.

Photocopying/printing

Vester Kopi *Vesterbrogade 69, Vesterbro (33 27 88 33, www.vester kopi.dk)*. **Open** 9am-5pm Mon-Fri. **Map** p245 P9. *Nørregade 7 (33 14 58 33)*. **Open** 9am-5pm Mon-Fri. **Map** p250 M12. *Gothersgade 12 (33 32 58 33)*. **Open** 9am-5pm Mon-Fri. **Map** p251 M15. **Credit** MC, V.
Copying and printing services.

Secretarial

Manpower *Glydenløvesgade 11 (70 20 10 00, www.manpower.dk)*. **Open** 7.30am-4.30pm Mon-Thur; 7.30am-4pm Fri. **No credit cards**. **Map** p250 M10.
Manpower matches clients with secretaries who speak two or more languages. Rates vary.

Translation

Check also the *Yellow Pages* under *'Oversættelse'*.

Berlitz *Vimmelskaftet 42A, Jorck's Passage (70 21 50 10, www.berlitz. com)*. **Open** 8am-6pm Mon-Fri. **No credit cards**. **Map** p251 N13.

A global company that offers translators and interpreters in most languages. Prices vary according to requirements.

CUSTOMS

The following can be imported into Denmark without incurring customs duty by non-Danish residents arriving from an EU country with duty-paid goods purchased in an EU country:

• 10 litres of spirits
• 20 litres of fortified wine (under 22 per cent)
• 90 litres of table wine (no more than 60 litres sparkling)
• 800 cigarettes
• 400 cigarillos
• 200 cigars
• 1,000 grammes of tobacco
• 110 litres of beer.

Residents of non-EU countries entering from outside the EU with goods purchased in non-EU countries can bring in to Denmark:

• 1 litre of spirits over 22 per cent; or 2 litres of sparkling/fortified wine (maximum 22 per cent)
• 16 litres of beer
• 2 litres of table wine
• 200 cigarettes or 100 cigarillos or 50 cigars or 250 grammes of tobacco
• 500 grammes of coffee or 200 grammes of coffee extracts
• 100 grammes of tea or 40 grammes of tea extracts
• 50 grammes of perfume
• 250 millilitres of eau de toilette
• 10 litres of fuel
• other articles up to a value of 3,250kr if arriving from outside the EU by air; 2,250kr if arriving from outside the EU by car, bus or train.

Only those aged 16 or over can import alcohol and spirits from inside the EU, and you have to be aged 18 or over to import tobacco. From outside the EU you must be 17 or over to use the alcohol and tobacco allowance, including beer: 1,350kr.

It is forbidden to import fresh foods into Denmark unless they are vacuum packed.

Although duty-free goods within the EU were abolished in 1999 and there is now no legal limit on the quantities of alcohol and tobacco travellers may import into most EU countries (provided they are for personal use), Denmark, Finland and Sweden will continue to impose limits for the foreseeable future. For enquiries about customs regulations, phone 72 22 18 18 or check out the website www.skat.dk.

DISABLED VISITORS

Facilities for disabled people in Copenhagen are generally excellent relative to other European capitals. *Access in Denmark – A Travel Guide for the Disabled* is available from the Danish Tourist Board in London at 55 Sloane Street, SW1X 9SY (020 7259 5959).

In addition, much Danish tourist literature, including the Wonderful Copenhagen website (www.woco. dk), lists places that are wheelchair-accessible plus useful information on specific facilities for the disabled.

Two Danish organisations may be able to offer help:

Dansk Handicap Forbund
Hans Knudsens Plads 1A, 2100 Copenhagen Ø (39 29 35 55, www.danskhandicapforbund.dk).

DIRECTORY

Open *Phone enquiries* 10am-3pm Mon-Thur; 10am-1pm Fri. Staff members speak English and may be able to help tourists, but members have priority.
Videnscenter for Bevægelseshandicap *PP Ørumsgade 11, 8000 Århus (89 49 12 70, fax 89 49 12 76, www.vfb.dk).* **Open** 10am-3pm Mon-Thur; 10am-2pm Fri. The Danish Information Centre for Physical Disability can give information about a variety of subjects relating to physical disability in Denmark.

ELECTRICITY

Denmark, in common with most of Europe, has 220-volt AC, 50Hz current and uses two-pin continental plugs. Visitors from the UK will need to buy an adaptor for their appliances, while North Americans won't be able to use their 110/125V appliances without a transformer.

EMBASSIES & CONSULATES

American Embassy *Dag Hammarskjöld Allé 24 (35 41 71 00, http://denmark.usembassy.gov).* **Open** *Phone enquiries* 8.30-5pm daily. **Map** p247 G15.
British Embassy *Kastelsvej 36-40, off Classensgade (35 44 52 00, www.britishembassy.dk). Train to Østerport Station, then 10min walk.* **Open** 9am-12.30pm, 1.30-3pm Mon-Fri. *Visa dept* 9am-11am Mon-Fri (by appointment only). **Map** p248 F15.
Canadian Embassy *Kristen Bernikowsgade 1 (33 48 32 00, www.canada.dk). Metro Kongens Nytorv.* **Open** 8.30am-noon, 1-4.30pm Mon-Fri. **Map** p251 M14.
Irish Embassy *Østbanegade 21 (35 42 32 33). Train to Østerport Station, then 6min walk.* **Open** 10am-12.30pm, 2.30-4.30pm Mon-Fri. **Map** p249 G16.

EMERGENCIES

To contact the police, the ambulance service or the fire service in an emergency, phone **112** (free of charge). For central police stations, *see p230*.

HEALTH

All temporary foreign visitors to Denmark are entitled to free medical and hospital treatment if they are taken ill or have an accident.

Accident & emergency

The following (relatively centrally located) hospitals have 24-hour emergency departments. Note that the largest and most central hospital in the city, the Rigshospital, does not have an accident and emergency department.

Amager Hospital *Italiensvej 1, Amager (32 34 32 34, www.amagerhospital.dk). Bus 4A, 2A. Emergency department: Kastrupvej 63 (32 34 35 00). Bus 4A, 2A.*
Bispebjerg Hospital *Bispebjerg Bakke 23, Bispebjerg (35 31 35 31, www.bispebjerghospital.dk). Bus 6A, 21, 69.*
Frederiksberg Hospital *Nordre Fasanvej 57, Frederiksberg (38 16 38 16, www.frederiksberghospital.dk). Metro Fasanvej or Bus 29, 831.*

Contraception

Condoms are widely available and are sold in most supermarkets and pharmacies as well as from vending machines in bars and on the street. Birth control pills can be obtained from pharmacies but require a doctor's prescription.

Dentists

Tourist offices (*see p232*) can refer foreign visitors to local dentists.

Dental Emergency Service *Oslo Plads 14 (35 38 02 51, www.tandvagt.dk).* **Open** 8am-9.30pm Mon-Fri; 10am-noon, 8-9.30pm Sat, Sun. **No credit cards.** **Map** p247 H15. Personal enquiries only. Treatment must be paid for in cash.

Doctors

Lægevagten *70 13 00 41.* **Price** from 400kr per visit. EU citizens are not charged.

Insurance

Citizens of other EU countries are entitled to have free medical treatment and essential medication.
The UK has a reciprocal health agreement with Denmark, which means that, in addition to free emergency treatment, UK citizens can usually obtain free medical care from a doctor, and hospital treatment if referred by a doctor.
The European Health Insurance Card (EHIC) has replaced the defunct E111. The free card entitles

you to the same state-provided treatment as a resident in European Economic Area countries and is valid for three to five years. For more information visit www.fco.gov.uk/en/travel-and-living-abroad.
Citizens of non-EU countries should have adequate health insurance before travelling.

Pharmacies

Look for the '*apotek*' sign.

City Helse *Vendersgade 6 (33 14 08 92, www.cityhelse.dk). Metro or train to Nørreport.* **Open** 9.30am-5.30pm Mon-Thur; 9.30am-6pm Fri; 9.30am-2pm Sat. **Credit** AmEx, MC, V. **Map** p246 L12. City Helse stocks a good selection of health food and natural medicine.
Steno Apotek *Vesterbrogade 6, by Central Station (33 14 82 66).* **Open** 24hrs daily. **Credit** MC, V. **Map** p250 P11.

INTERNET

Public libraries are a good place for free internet, and there are numerous Wi-Fi hotspots throughout the city and in many cafés. In addition, most hotels provide internet access.

Nethouse 2000 *Sundholmsvej 67 (32 95 21 20, www.nethouse.dk). Metro Amagerbro.* **Open** 10am-midnight Mon, Tue; 10am-3am Wed, Thur; 24 hours Fri-Sun.
Sidewalk Express *Copenhagen Central Station (www.sidewalk express.com).* **Open** 24 hrs daily (automated internet kiosks).

LANGUAGE

See p234 **Vocabulary**. For language classes, *see p231*.

LEFT LUGGAGE

Airport

Copenhagen Airport's left luggage facility is located in **Terminal 2** and is open from 6am until 10pm daily, from 5am in the summer months (32 31 23 60). You can store your belongings there for a period of up to four weeks. Charges start from 50kr per piece, per day (odd sizes 70kr per day). Self-service baggage lockers are located in the Parking Garage, level P4. The charge for a locker is 30kr-60kr per 24 hours dependent on size. The maximum rental period for use of the lockers is 72 hours.

Rail station

There are left luggage lockers by the Reventlowsgade entrance of Central Station. Prices are 30kr or 40kr for 24 hours, depending on the size of the locker. Prices for personally supervised storage (available 5.30am-1am Mon-Sat; 6am-1am Sun) depend on the quantity and size of the items and vary from 30kr to 50kr per day.

LOST PROPERTY

The main lost property office is:

Copenhagen Police
Slotsherrensvej 113, Vanløse (38 74 88 22). Train to Islev. **Open** 9am-2pm Mon, Wed, Fri; 9am-5.30pm Tue, Thur. *Telephone enquiries* 10am-2pm Mon-Fri.

Airport

If you lose luggage or other possessions on a plane, contact the relevant airline. Any lost possessions at the airport will registered online at www.cph.dk and kept for 30 days before being moved to the Police lost property office, given above.

Buses/trains

If you lose something on a bus, call Movia general information (36 13 14 15; 7am-9.30pm daily); if you lose it on a train or Metro train, phone the relevant terminus or the central S-tog information line (33 53 00 33; 7am-10.30pm daily).

Taxis

Call the taxi company. After a couple of days items will be transferred to the central lost property office (*see p230* **Police headquarters**).

MEDIA
Newspapers & magazines

Most of the national newspapers in Denmark started out as pamphlets for political parties. Today they target a wider readership. But with their comparatively small readerships and minuscule pool of journalists (most from the same training course), Danish newspapers struggle to achieve a consistently high standard. Denmark also has its tabloid papers, which can be just as distasteful, sexist and enjoyable as those in the UK.

Berlingske A conservative, right of centre broadsheet with decent coverage of Copenhagen. *Berlingske Tidende* is well designed and tries hard but can be slow with international news.
Børsen *Børsen* keeps tabs on the latest stock market developments, economic predictions and the major players in the Danish financial world.
BT A tabloid paper that lags a little way behind *Ekstrabladet* in the sleaze and celebrity stakes and so in recompense places an emphasis on football and other sports.
Ekstrabladet The most controversial of the Danish tabloids, *Ekstrabladet* relies heavily on celebrity sleaze, opinionated editorials and endless reactionary campaigning. As well known in Denmark as *The Sun* in the UK.
Information *Information* was founded as 'the newspaper of the Danish Resistance' on the night of Denmark's liberation at the end of World War II. Today the paper has no significant political leaning, its objective being to give its readers important background information on current affairs. Weighty, dry but respected.
Jyllandsposten The most royalist and conservative of the national papers.
Kristeligt Dagblad A Christian publication that focuses on questions concerning ethics, belief and religion.
Politiken Once the paper of the Social-Liberal Party, *Politiken* now focuses on cultural issues. Strong on Copenhagen matters.

English-language press

Most of the major British and American newspapers are available from one or two outlets on Strøget, or the newsagents in Central Station, Illum and Magasin du Nord department stores.

Copenhagen Post *www.cphpost.dk*
This weekly paper features some Danish news and Copenhagen listings in English.

Radio

Copenhagen's biggest radio stations are all run by the state-owned Danmarks Radio (the Danish Broadcasting Corporation), which has a fine tradition of high quality programming. It's also possible to pick up a number of foreign radio stations from Sweden and Germany. News in English is

broadcast on their website at www.dr.dk/news.
P1 *90.8 Mhz*
Typical broadcasts include a good range of radio plays, current affairs magazines, documentaries and news. Broadcasts from 6am to midnight.
P2 *88.0 Mhz*
P2 is mainly a classical music station, but also plays jazz from time to time.
P3 *93.9 Mhz*
Targeted mainly at Danish youth, this station features young comedians and DJs who play pop and chart music during the day, with programmes offering more alternative content during the night. Broadcasts 24 hours a day.
P4/Københavns Radio *96.5 Mhz*
P4/ features pop music (including the Danish pop charts), listeners' requests, phone-ins, local news and traffic reports.
POPFM *100.0 Mhz*
Plays pop 24 hours a day.
The Voice *104.8 Mhz*
A 24-hour chart/dance music station, the Voice is the only commercial station with more than a million listeners a week. Some of the station's DJs also play at Copenhagen's nightclubs.

Television

Founded as a public service organisation and funded by individual licence fees, Danmarks Radio still dominates the television scene (it actually enjoyed a monopoly on radio and TV broadcasting until 1986). However, over recent years, the old stations (DR1 and DR2) have been steadily losing ground to younger, more challenging, commercial broadcasting companies that are not subject to any public service obligations.

DR1 The first television channel in Denmark, DR1's strengths include news and current affairs, documentaries, and children's and youth programming.
DR2 The little sister to DR1 and a slightly more alternative watch.
TV2 Despite introducing morning television and *Wheel of Fortune* to the Danes, TV2 pretty much resembles DR1, principally because TV2 is also a licence-financed station, with similar public service obligations.
TV3/TV3+ Targeting young people and families, TV3 is a commercial station that aims to provide quality light entertainment, with Danish

soap operas and docu-soaps among the most popular programmes. Its sister channel TV3+ is the leading station for sport.

Kanal 5 Most of the programmes on Kanal 5 (previously known as TVDanmark1) are American sitcoms and soap operas, though it occasionally broadcasts Danish docu-soaps.

MONEY

The Danish *krone* (crown) is divided into 100 *øre*. There are coins in denominations of 25 *øre*, 50 *øre* (both copper), one *krone*, two *kroner*, five *kroner* (all three silver in colour, the latter two with a hole), ten *kroner* and 20 *kroner* (brass). Notes come in 50, 100, 200, 500 and 1,000 *kroner* denominations. In this guide the abbreviation 'kr' is used, though you may also see 'DKK' or 'KR' before the figure in question.

At the time of writing, £1 = 8.76kr; €1 = 7.45kr; US$1 = 5.38kr, but this of course is likely to have changed.

There is no limit to the amount of foreign or Danish currency you can bring into the country, though you will be required to explain the source of amounts over €10,000 (roughly 75,000kr).

ATMs/cash machines

The majority of Danish banks have ATMs, which offer a convenient way of withdrawing Danish kroner on a credit or debit card. Most major cards are accepted.

Banks & bureaux de change

Banks in Denmark tend to open from 10am to 4pm on weekdays, with late opening until 5.30pm on Thursdays. Some in the centre of town have longer hours and open on Saturdays. Most will change foreign currency and travellers' cheques, as will bureaux de change. There are also a number of machines scattered that will exchange foreign currency for kroner.

Lost or stolen credit cards

Emergency numbers:
American Express
70 20 70 97.
Diners 36 73 73 73 (24hrs).
MasterCard/Eurocard
80 01 60 98 (24hrs).
Visa 80 01 02 77 (24hrs).
For other credit cards, call the 24-hour **Danish PBS Hotline** (44 89 29 29).

Money transfers

Usually, Den Danske Bank can make money transfers within 12 hours. Ask for a so-called 'swift address' and a registration number, which you pass on to the local bank in your home country. Then contact your local bank concerning the amount of money you wish to transfer. Transactions normally cost around 150kr. Den Danske Bank has a number of branches in Copenhagen, including:

Den Danske Bank *Holmens Kanal 2 (45 12 60 00). Metro Kongens Nytorv.* **Open** 10am-4pm Mon-Wed, Fri; 10am-5pm Thur. **Map** p250 O12.

OPENING HOURS

The majority of shops in Copenhagen open from 10am to 6pm or 7pm on weekdays and from 10am to 2pm or 5pm on Saturday, with only bakers, florists and souvenir shops open on Sunday. Office hours are usually 9am to 4pm from Monday to Friday.

POLICE & SECURITY

Crime is not really an issue as far as tourists are concerned, though from time to time there are stories of confidence tricksters pretending to be policemen and, of course, the very entertaining card sharps in Strøget. Otherwise Copenhagen is generally safe compared with other cities in Europe. There are places where you should exercise caution late at night, however. These include side streets in Vesterbro, and the area around Rådhuspladsen stretching part of the way up Strøget – drunken violence is fairly common here at night. The area behind Central Station stretching up much of Istedgade is a hangout for alcoholics and junkies, but they are peaceable in the main. In the unlikely event that you are a victim of crime, contact the Danish Police immediately. In emergencies, call **112** (free of charge), or dial 114 to be connected to your nearest local station. Open 24 hours, the Police HQ can direct you to your nearest station. These include Central Station (33 15 38 01; map p250 P11); Halmtorvet 20, Vesterbro (33 25 14 48; map p250 Q10) and Store Kongensgade 100 (33 93 14 48; map p249 L16). To connect with any local station or sub-station outside of an emergency

situation, dial the Police Headquarters switchboard (33 14 88 88) and they will connect you.

Police headquarters *Polititorvet (33 14 14 48).* **Open** 24hrs daily. **Map** p250 Q13.

POSTAL SERVICES

Most post offices open from 10am to 5.30pm Monday to Friday, and from 10am or 11am until noon or 2pm on Saturday. Larger branches have fax facilities. Copenhagen's largest post office is listed below.

Central Station Post Office *Central Station (80 20 70 30, www.postdanmark.dk).* **Open** 8am-9pm Mon-Fri; 10am-4pm Sat, Sun. **Map** p250 P11.

Postal rates

In addition to the rates below, express delivery services are also available. Contact any post office for details. Letters up to 50 grammes cost 5.50kr to Denmark, 7kr to Europe and 8.50kr to other countries; letters up to 100 grammes cost 16kr to Denmark, 23kr to the rest of Europe and 31kr to other countries.

Poste restante

Mail can be received care of 'Poste Restante' and collected from any post office in Denmark; it will normally not be kept for a period of longer than two weeks.

If Poste Restante mail isn't addressed to a specific post office, it will be sent to the main post office at Central Station (*see above*).

Express delivery services

Budstikken is a private courier company approved by the public mail services. Call 70 20 02 00 (24 hours) for information.

PUBLIC HOLIDAYS

The following are public holidays in Denmark:
New Year's Day (Nytårsdag; 1 Jan).
Maundy Thursday (Skærtorsdag; ; 21 Apr 2011; 5 Apr 2012).
Good Friday (Langfredag; 22 Apr 2011; 6 Apr 2012).
Easter Sunday (Påske; 24 Apr 2011; 9 Apr 2012).
Easter Monday (2.påskedag; 25 Apr 2011; 9 Apr 2012).

Common Prayer Day (Stor Bededag; 20 May 2011; 4 May 2012).
Ascension Day (Kristi Himmelfartsdag; 2 Jun 2011; 17 May 2012).
Whit Sunday (1.pinsedag; 12 Jun 2011; 27 May 2012).
Whit Monday (2.pinsedag; 13 Jun 2011; 28 May 2012).
Constitution Day (Grundlovsdag; 5 June; from noon).
Christmas (Jule; 24-26 Dec).

PUBLIC TOILETS

You're unlikely to be caught short in Copenhagen because there is no shortage of public toilets. Even better, most are clean and free to use.

RELIGION

There are close ties between Church and State in Denmark and the Constitution declares the Evangelical Lutheran Church to be the national church. The Danish Folkekirken (the People's Church) is funded by church members through 'Church Tax', but in spite of the fact that most Danes (82 per cent) are members, a minority of Copenhageners would call themselves religious. While churches are often empty on Sundays, and are mainly used at Christmas, Easter, or for private arrangements such as weddings, there appears to be something of a revival of interest in the Church in Denmark. The second largest religious community in Denmark is Muslim, the third Roman Catholic. The following churches hold services in English.

Great Synagogue *Krystalgade 12 (33 12 88 68). Metro or train to Nørreport.* **Services** 6.45am Mon, Thur; 7am Tue, Wed, Fri; 9am Sat; 8am Sun (8.30am in the summer). **Map** p251 M13. Orthodox Judaism.
St Alban's Church *Churchill Parken, Langelinie (www.st-albans.dk). Bus 1A, 15.* **Services** Holy Communion 10.30am Wed; 9am, 10.30am Sun. **Map** p249 J18. Anglican.
Sakrementskirken *Nørrebrogade 27, Nørrebro (35 35 68 25). Bus 5A.* **Services** 5pm Wed (English Mass); 9.30am (Danish); 6pm Sun (English). **Map** p246 J10. Roman Catholic.
Sankt Annæ Kirke *Dronning Elisabeths Allé 3 (32 58 41 02, www.saintanneschurch.dk). Bus 5A.* **Services** 5pm Sat, Sun. Roman Catholic.

SMOKING

Smoking is banned in all indoor public spaces in Denmark, including public transport, cinemas and (most) cafés and restaurants.

STUDYING

Danish institutions for higher education have a friendly and open-minded policy towards international students. Exchange programmes provide links between Danish universities and their international counterparts and in recent years exchanges have increasingly been developed through programmes such as Socrates/Erasmus, Lingua and Tempus which are all supported by the larges of the European Union and its unfortunate taxpayers. Some of the institutions also have summer schools and the largest universities and colleges have their own international offices.
For more information on courses, contact the individual institutions.

Universities/colleges

Copenhagen's universities and colleges offer a variety of qualifications over a broad spectrum of subjects. The **University of Copenhagen** (35 32 26 26, www.ku.dk) is the city's flagship establishment. Founded in 1479, it is Denmark's oldest educational institution, and, with 35,000 students, it can also lay claim to being the largest.
The city has two business schools, **Copenhagen Business School** (38 15 38 15, www.cbs.dk) and **Niels Brock College** (33 41 91 00, www.brock.dk), which combine expert tutoring with strong ties to the wider Danish business community.
Det Kongelige Danske Kunstakademi (33 74 46 00, www.kunstakademiet.dk), the Royal Academy of Fine Arts, offers a variety of fine art courses and tutoring, as well as incorporating the **School of Architecture** (32 68 60 00, www.karch.dk), the excellent **Danish Film School** (32 68 64 00, www.filmskolen.dk), the **National Drama School** (32 83 61 00, www.teaterskolen.dk) and the **Rhythmic Music Conservatory** (32 68 67 00, www.rmc.dk).
Det Kongelige Danske Musikkonservatorium (72 26 72 26, www.dkdm.dk), the Royal Danish Music Conservatory,

concentrates, as you might have guessed, on classical music training.

International offices

Copenhagen Business School *International Office, Porcelaenshaven 26, 2000 Frederiksberg (38 15 30 06, www.cbs.dk). Bus 29, 4A.* **Open** 9am-noon, 1-3.30pm Mon-Fri.
Roskilde Universitetscenter *International Office, Bygning 4, 1, Postbox 260, 4000 Roskilde (46 74 20 58, www.ruc.dk). Train to Trekroner.* **Open** 8.15am-4pm Mon-Fri.
The international office has the overall responsibility for international activities at Roskilde University. These include programmes like ERASMUS.
University of Copenhagen *International Office, Fiolstræde 1, Ground Floor (35 32 29 18, www.ku.dk/international). Metro or train to Nørreport.* **Open** 10am-3pm Mon-Wed, Fri; noon-5pm Thur. **Map** p251 M13.
Offers advice to exchange students at the University of Copenhagen on practical as well as academic matters, including admission, course registration, housing and contacts with other universities.

Other organisations

AFS Interkultur (American Field Service) *Nordre Fasanvej 111, 2000 Frederiksberg (38 34 33 00, www.afs.dk). Bus 2A, 4A.* **Open** 10am-3pm Mon-Fri.
AFS is an international, voluntary organisation that provides educational exchange programmes for people between 15 and 30 years.
STS High School & Au Pair *Langebrogade 5 (88 51 01 67, www.sts.dk). Train Copenhagen Central Station.* **Open** 9am-4.30pm Mon-Thur; 9am-3pm Fri. **Map** p251 N13.
STS provides personal and/or academic education at high schools, language schools or for au pairs. You have to be between ten and 26 years of age, depending on which programme you want to follow.

Language classes

Berlitz *Vimmelskaftet 42A, Strøget (70 21 50 10, www.berlitz.com).* **Open** 8am-6pm Mon-Fri. **No credit cards**. **Map** p251 N13. Courses are taught by native teachers; most are tailored to individual needs.

Libraries

Hovedbiblioteket *Krystalgade 15 (33 73 60 60, www.bibliotek.kk.dk). Metro or train to Nørreport.* **Open** *Apr-Sept* 10am-7pm Mon-Fri; 10am-2pm Sat. *Oct-Mar* 10am-7pm Mon-Fri; 10am-4pm Sat. **Map** p251 M13. The central library has international newspapers, magazines in English and colour photocopying.

Det Kongelige Bibliotek *Søren Kierkegaards Plads 1 (33 47 47 47, www.kb.dk). Metro Kongens Nytorv.* **Open** 8am-10pm Mon-Sat. *Study rooms* 9am-9pm Mon-Fri; 9am-5pm Sat. *Exhibitions* 10am-7pm Mon-Sat; all departments close at 7pm during July and Aug. **Admission** *Main building & library* free; *Exhibitions* free-40kr; free under-16s. *Concerts* prices vary. **Credit** MC, V. **Map** p251 P15.
The Royal Library on Slotsholmen is Denmark's national library, but the building also serves as a general research centre, a cultural centre and a meeting place.

TELEPHONES

Like most public services in Denmark, the phone system is efficient and simple to use. Danish phone numbers have eight digits and there are no area codes.

International codes

The international dialling code for Denmark is 45. So, to dial Copenhagen from outside Denmark, dial 00 45 and then the eight-digit number.
To call abroad from Denmark, dial 00 followed by the country access code, the area code (minus the initial 0, if there is one), and then the local number. The international code for the UK is 44; 1 for the US/Canada; 353 for Ireland; 61 for Australia.

Mobile phones

Denmark is part of the worldwide GSM network, so compatible mobile phones should work without any problems. If your phone is not GSM compatible, contact your service provider. Below are two central mobile phone shops linked to Denmark's main service providers:

Telenor *Store Kongensgade 45 (60 50 40 02/www.telenor.dk).*
TDC *Nygade 4 (33 11 24 14, www.tdc.dk).* **Map** p251 N13.

Operator services

For **directory enquiries**, call 118 (domestic) or 113 (international). You will be charged only if you are connected.

Public phones

You'll find both card- and coin-operated phones in Denmark. **Cards** (*telekort*) come in denominations of 30, 50 and 100kr and can be used for both local and international calls; they are available from kiosks and post offices.

Telegrams

You can no longer send telegrams from Danish post offices.

TIME & DATES

Denmark observes Central European Time, one hour ahead of Greenwich Mean Time, and six hours ahead of Eastern Standard Time. Danes use the 24-hour clock.
When writing dates, Danes follow the day with the month, so 7 January 2012 will be written 7/1/12.

TIPPING

Service is often included on hotel and restaurant bills, so any tips should only be given for unusually good service. It's not uncommon, however, to round up a bill.

TOURIST INFORMATION

In addition to the resources available at the tourist offices below, the website **www.aok.dk** is an indispensable source of information on festivals, arts and entertainment in Copenhagen as well as good places to eat and drink.

Danish Tourist Board *Islands Brygge 43 (32 88 99 00, www.visitdenmark.com).*
If you plan to travel beyond the capital, check out the DTB's state-of-the-art website – it's very useful for both practical advice and news about forthcoming attractions. The DTB doesn't encourage personal callers.
Wonderful Copenhagen Tourist Information Bureau *Vesterbrogade 4A (70 22 24 42, www.visitcopenhagen.dk).* **Open** *Oct-Apr* 9am-4pm Mon-Fri; 9am-2pm Sat. *May, June, Sept* 9am-6pm Mon-Sat. *July, Aug* 9am-8pm Mon-Sat; 10am-6pm Sun. **Map** p250 O11.

The official Copenhagen tourist office is located opposite the Radisson SAS Royal Hotel, across the road from Tivoli. It has a wealth of information on the city's attractions as well as a small souvenir shop, and offers a free accommodation booking service.

TAX REFUND

Tax on goods (MOMS) in Denmark is levied at 25 per cent. Non-EU residents are entitled to claim back up to 19 per cent of the total price of any item bought in the country (providing that the purchase exceeds 300kr and that Denmark is their final EU destination before returning home). Visitors should ask shops to issue a Blue Tax Free Cheque for each purchase. These can then be stamped and handed in at the Global Blue desk in the Arkaden, between Terminals 2 and 3 (6am-9pm daily). Alternatively they can be stamped by Customs (in Copenhagen Airport's Terminal 3) before you check in your luggage, and then handed in to Global Blue. For further information, contact Global Blue Danmark (32 52 55 66, www.global-blue.com).

VISAS/PASSPORTS

Citizens of EU countries (outside Scandinavia) require a national ID card or passport valid for the duration of their stay in order to enter Denmark for tourist visits of up to three months within a period of six months. Tourists (EU citizens) can stay in the country for another three months if they are working or applying for a job. For stays lasting more than six months you need a residency visa. US citizens require a passport valid only for the duration of their stay, but citizens of Canada, Australia and New Zealand require passports valid for three months beyond the last day of their visit. South African citizens need to apply for a tourist visa prior to leaving South Africa. For more information contact the Danish Immigration Service on 35 30 84 90, or visit www.nyidanmark.dk, their multi-language advisory website.

WEIGHTS & MEASURES

Denmark uses the metric system. Decimal points are indicated by commas, while thousands are defined by full stops. In this guide we have listed all measurements in both metric and imperial.

WEATHER REPORT

Average temperatures and monthly rainfall in Copenhagen.

	Average daily max temperature (°C/°F)	Average nightly temperature (°C/°F)	Daily hours of sunshine	Monthly rainfall (mm/inches)
Jan	2/36	-2/28	1	49/1.9
Feb	2/36	-3/27	2	39/1.5
Mar	5/41	-1/30	4	32/1.3
Apr	11/52	3/37	6	38/1.5
May	16/61	8/46	8	42/1.7
June	20/68	11/52	9	47/1.9
July	22/72	14/57	8	71/2.8
Aug	21/70	14/57	7	66/2.6
Sept	18/64	11/52	6	62/2.4
Oct	12/54	7/45	3	59/2.3
Nov	7/45	3/37	1	48/1.9
Dec	4/39	1/34	1	49/1.9

WHEN TO GO

Considering its northerly location, the climate in Denmark isn't particularly severe. In midsummer it hardly gets dark at all and the evening light can last well past 11pm. However, winter is cold, wet and dark and some tourist attractions are closed. Tivoli, for example, is closed for most of the winter aside from Halloween and its Christmas Market. Spring kicks off in late April, but can take a while to warm up. May and June are usually fresh and bright, with reasonable temperatures. Summer peak season is in July and August, when Copenhagen offers plenty of festivals and open-air events and the weather is probably as good as it ever gets in Scandinavia. Cruise ships bring in plenty of visitors but on the other hand July is when all of Copenhagen migrates to the seaside for its summer holidays, so the city can seem quieter and many top restaurants and some other businesses are closed.

WOMEN

Denmark is a country famously committed to equal opportunities for all citizens and a lot of effort has been made to achieve equal rights for women.

Women visitors to Denmark are very unlikely to encounter any harrassment problems. Copenhagen is one of the world's safest cities, even after dark, although, of course, remain vigilant.

Kvindehuset (Women's House)
Gothersgade 37 (33 14 28 04, www.kvindehus.dk). Metro Kongens
Nytorv. **Open** 1-6pm Mon-Fri.
Map p247 L14.
A cultural centre for women. Recycling of clothes, lesbian films, a choir, an artists' group, folk dances, social events and debates are held.
KVINFO *Christians Brygge 3 (33 13 50 88, www.kvinfo.dk). Metro Kongens Nytorv.* **Open** *Reception and Centre* 10am-4pm Mon-Thur; 10am-3pm Fri; *Library* Sept-June 10am-6pm Mon; 11am-5pm Tue-Thur. July, Aug 1-5pm Mon-Thur.
Map p251 P15.
The Danish Centre for Information on Women and Gender has many resources relating to women's issues, including a library and information centre for gender studies.

WORKING IN COPENHAGEN

Even though most people in Denmark speak English, and many companies use English as a working language, there is still a deeply ingrained prejudice in the workplace against those who are not fluent in Danish. However, the current unemployment rate is very low so there are always some vacancies open to foreigners, particularly in unskilled fields such as cleaning, catering and hotels.

EURES (www.ec.europa.eu/eures) is a database of job vacancies throughout the EU and contains useful information about working conditions throughout Europe.

Det Danske Kulturinstitut
Vartov, Farvergade 27L, 1463 Copenhagen K (35 30 84 90, www.dankultur.dk). Bus 2A, 5A. **Open** 9am-3pm Mon-Fri.
The Institute publishes a range of literature about the country and arranges job exchange programmes for a number of professions.

Work permits

All EU citizens can obtain a work permit in Denmark; non-EU citizens must apply for a work permit abroad and hand in the application to a Danish embassy or consular representation. The rules for obtaining work permits vary for different jobs; contact the Danish Immigration Service:

Udlændingestyrelsen *Ryesgade 53, 2100 Copenhagen Ø (35 36 66 00, fax 35 36 19 16, www.nyidan mark.dk).* **Open** 8am-3.30pm Mon-Thur; 9am-3pm Fri.

Useful addresses

The EU has a website (www. europa.eu) and helpline (00 800 6789 10 11) providing general information on your rights and useful telephone numbers and addresses in your home country. It also holds specific information on the rules for recognition of diplomas, your rights on access to employment and rights of residence and social security.

For general information about the **Danish tax system**, take a look at the Skatteministeriet (Danish Ministry of Taxation) website (www.skm.dk) or contact SKAT (Customs and tax administration; www.skat.dk) with more specific questions.

SKAT *Sluseholmen 8B, 2450 Copenhagen SV (72 22 18 18, www.skat.dk).* **Open** *Phone enquiries* 9am-4pm Mon-Wed; 9am-6pm Thur; 9am-2pm Fri.

Vocabulary

If you have a good knowledge of Swedish or Norwegian, you should be able to understand Danish well enough to get by. And if you are fluent in German, you may also recognise a fair percentage of words. For the rest of us, however, Danish is mostly impenetrable.

The problem comes not with the grammar, which is comparatively simple, but with the pronunciation, which is full of its own idiosyncrasies, particularly the seemingly endless glottal stops and swallowing of parts of words. And be warned, Copenhageners are the worst offenders in Denmark – they talk the fastest too. But do not fear, the majority of Danes have excellent English and it's tempting for visitors not to bother to try to learn any Danish at all. But an attempt to learn a few basics is always appreciated.

Here's a brief guide to pronunciation and some useful basic words and phrases.

VOWELS

a – as in 'rather' or as in 'pat'
å, u(n) – as in 'or'
e(g), e(j) – as in 'shy'
e, æ – as in 'set'
i – as in 'be'
ø – a short 'er' sound
o – as in 'rot' or as in 'do'
o(v) – a short 'ow', as in 'cow'
u – as in 'bull' or as in 'do'
y – a long, hybrid of 'ee' and 'oo'

CONSONANTS

sj – as in 'shot'
ch – as in 'shot'
c – as in 'send', but as in 'key' before a, o, u and consonants
(o)d – as the 'th' in 'those'
j – as the 'y' in 'year'
g – as in 'got', when before vowels
h – as in 'heart'
k – as in 'key'
b – as in 'bag'
r – a short guttural 'r' (less guttural after a vowel)
w – a 'v' sound

USEFUL WORDS/ PHRASES

yes *ja, jo* ('yer', 'yo')
no *nej* ('ny')

please *vær så god* ('verser-go'), *vær så venlig* ('verser venlee')
thank you *tak* ('tack')
hello (formal) *goddag* ('godday'); **hello** (informal) *hej* ('hi')
I understand *jeg forstår* ('yie for-stor')
I don't understand *jeg forstår ikke* ('yie for-stor icker')
do you speak English? *taler du engelsk* ('tarler doo engelsk')?
excuse me (sorry) *undskyld* ('unsgull')
go away! *forsvind!* ('for-svin')
entrance *indgang*
exit *udgang*
open *åben*
closed *lukket*
toilets *toiletter* (**men** *herrer*, **women** *damer*)

DAYS/MONTHS

today *i dag*
tonight *i aften/i nat*
tomorrow *i morgen*
yesterday *i går*

Monday *mandag*
Tuesday *tirsdag*
Wednesday *onsdag*
Thursday *torsdag*
Friday *fredag*
Saturday *lørdag*
Sunday *søndag*

January *januar*
February *februar*
March *marts*
April *april*
May *maj*
June *juni*
July *juli*
August *august*
September *september*
October *oktober*
November *november*
December *december*

NUMBERS

0 *nul;* 1 *en;* 2 *to;* 3 *tre;* 4 *fire;* 5 *fem;* 6 *seks;* 7 *syv;* 8 *otte;* 9 *ni;* 10 *ti;* 20 *tyve;* 30 *tredive;* 40 *fyrre;* 50 *halvtreds;* 60 *tres;* 70 *halvfjerds;* 80 *firs;* 90 *halvfems;* 100 *hundrede;* 1,000 *tusind;* 1,000,000 *million*

FOOD & DRINK

apple *æble*
egg *æg*
peas *ærter*
orange *appelsin*
banana *banan*
bread *brød*
beans *bønner*
mushroom *champignon*
chocolate *chokolade*
lemon *citron*
steamed *dampet*
vinegar *eddike*
draught beer *fadøl*
fish *fisk*
cream *fløde*
trout *forel*
fresh *frisk*
fruit *frugt*
grilled *grilleret*
stew *gryderet*
green bean *grøn bønne*
vegetables *grøntsager*
carrots *gulerødder*
tomatoes *tomater*
garlic *hvidløg*
ice-cream/ice *is*
strawberry *jordbær*
coffee *kaffe*
cake *kage*
cabbage *kål*
potato *kartoffel*
meat *kød*
boiled *kogt*
cold *kold*
chicken *kylling*
salmon *laks*
lamb *lamme*
onion *løg*
marinated *marineret*
milk *mælk*
nuts *nødder*
beef *oksekød*
beer *øl*
oil *olie*
cheese *ost*
roasted *ovnstegt*
pepper *peber*
poached *pocheret*
fries/chips *pommes frites*
hot dog *pølse*
rice *ris*
smoked *røget*
raw *rå*
mustard *sennep*
herring *sild*
ham *skinke*
butter *smør*
fried *stegt*
sugar *sukker*
soup *supper*
pork *svinekød*
tea *te*
cod *torsk*
water *vand*
warm, hot *varm*

Further Reference

BOOKS

Non-fiction

Christianson, JR *On Tycho's Island: Tycho Brahe and His Assistants, 1570-1601.*
Biography of the famous astronomer.
Dyrbe, Helen, Steven Harris & Thomas Golzen *Xenophobe's Guide to the Danes.*
Irreverent dissection of the Danes.
Jones, Gwyn *A History of the Vikings.*
A readable account of the not-so-vicious Vikings and their world.
Levine, Ellen *Darkness over Denmark: The Danish Resistance and the Rescue of the Jews.*
The remarkable story of the exodus of Danish Jews to Sweden during the war.
Monrad, Kasper, Philip Conisbee & Bjarne Jornaes *The Golden Age of Danish Painting.*
The works of 17 painters from the first half of the 19th century.
Poole, Roger & Henrik Stangerup *A Kierkegaard Reader.*
The leading resource on Denmark's leading philosopher.
Pundik, Herbert *In Denmark It Could Not Happen: The Flight of the Jews to Sweden in 1943.*
Another account of the wartime escape of the Jews in Denmark.
Sawyer, Peter (ed) *The Oxford Illustrated History of the Vikings.*
An enjoyable survey of the Vikings.
Spangenburg, Ray & Diane K Moser *Niels Bohr: Gentle Genius of Denmark (Makers of Modern Science).*
An accessible analysis of the great Danish nuclear physicist.
Thomas, Alastair H & Stewart P Oakley *Historical Dictionary of Denmark.*
An invaluable reference book charting Denmark's cultural history.
Thoren, Victor E *The Lord of Uraniborg.*
Detailed biography of 16th-century astronomer Tycho Brahe.
Thurman, Judith *Isak Dinesen The Life of Karen Blixen.*
Authoritative biog of one of Denmark's finest prose writers, and most famous daughter.
Wullschlager, Jackie *HC Andersen: The Life of a Storyteller.*
Comprehensive biography of Denmark's top tale-teller.

Fiction

Andersen, Hans Christian *The Complete Fairy Tales.*
More than 150 of the great Dane's best-loved fairytales.
Blixen, Karen *Seven Gothic Tales.*
Blixen's darkly powerful masterpiece.
Frayn, Michael *Copenhagen.*
Extraordinary play based on the visit of the great German physicist Werner Heisenberg to his erstwhile mentor and friend Niels Bohr.
Høeg, Peter *Miss Smilla's Feeling for Snow.*
Bestselling thriller set in Copenhagen and Greenland.
Simpson, Jacqueline (ed) *Danish Legends.*
This collection comprises over 160 Danish folktales and legends.
Shakespeare, William *Hamlet.*
The bard's Danish blockbuster – possibly the greatest play ever written.
Tremain, Rose *Music and Silence.*
Beautifully written fictional account of the latter years of Christian IV.

WEBSITES

AOK.dk
www.aok.dk/Copenhagen/Visiting_Copenhagen
Extensive details of the major museums, galleries and sights.
Bed and Breakfast Denmark
www.bbdk.dk
While not as commonplace as it Britain, B&Bs do exist in Denmark.
Copenhagen News
www.copenhagennews.com
Portal to news about Denmark appearing in the world's media.
Copenhagen Post
www.cphpost.dk
Weekly news in English from the Danish capital.
Copenhagen This Week
www.ctw.dk
This site somewhat misleadingly covers everything that's on in the city each month.
Danish Youth Hostels Association
www.danhostel.dk
Search for a hostel and book online.
Danish Metereological Information
www.dmi.dk
Daily and long-term weather reports.
Danish Tourist Board
www.visitdenmark.dk
This national tourist board website has has extensive information on the Denmark.
Denmark Hotels
www.danishhotels.dk
An online guide to all the star-rated hotels in Denmark.
DSB (Danish State Railways)
www.dsb.dk
Journey planner for train journeys within Denmark (in English).
Hamlet Sommer
www.hamletsommer.dk
The website for the annual theatrical festival.
HUR
www.hur.dk
Comprehensive site on Copenhagen's efficient and excellent public transport system.
Metro
www.m.dk
The official website of Copenhagen's shiny new Underground system.
Malmö Tourist Board
www.malmo.se
Information on the sights, attractions, restaurants, festivals and accommodation in this charming city.
Øresund
www.visitoresund.info
An online guide to the strait that divides Denmark and Sweden, and the land on either side.
Rejseplanen
www.rejseplanen.dk
Useful site for journey planning within the city and country.
Skåne
www.skanetur.se
The website of the Swedish province of Skåne (Scania), now easily accessible via the Øresund Bridge.
Ungdomsinformation
www.ui.dk
Copenhagen City Council's site is full of helpful information for those planning a longer stay.
Use It
www.useit.dk
This excellent government-funded organisation offers a wealth of free information for young and budget-conscious visitors to Copenhagen.
Wonderful Copenhagen
www.visitcopenhagen.dk
The regularly updated official website of the city's efficient tourist authority offers detailed information about the city's hotels, restaurants, cafés, bars, galleries, theatres, theme parks and museums, and many useful links.

Content Index

A

accessories 155-156
alfresco drinking 130
age restrictions 227
Amager 96
    galleries 180
Anderson, Hans Christian 63
antiques 145-146
apartments 110
art & design shops 146-147
Art Copenhagen 166
Assistens Kirkegård 91
architecture 38-39
athletics 200, 205
auctions 147

B

badminton 200
bars *see* Cafés & Bars
beauty shops 147
Bike Copenhagen 40-42
Bispebjerg 95
blues 190
books 235
bookshops 147-148
boxing 205
Brumleby Village 92
buses 224-225
business services 227

C

Cafés & Bars 128-142
By area:
    Christianshavn 135-136
    Frederiksstaden 134
    Nørrebro 139-142
    Nyhavn & Kongens Nytorv 134
    Østerbro 142
    Rosenborg & around 134-135
    Strøget & around 129-132
    Tivoli & Rådhuspladsen 128-129
    Vesterbro & Frederiksberg 136-139
Features:
    alfresco drinking 130
    Danish delicacies 133
    microbreweries 140
By type:
    gay & lesbian 182-184
canal district, the 80-82
Calendar 164-167
car hire 225-226
Carlsberg brewery 86
Central Strøget & Gammel Strand 58-60
ceramics shops 148

Charlottenlund *see* Hellerup & Charlottenlund
Children 168-173
    childrenswear 150
    Christianshavn 171
    Frederiksberg 171
    Østerbro & further north 172
    Rosenborg & around 171
    Strøget & around 169
    Tivoli & Rådhuspladsen 168-169
    toyshops 162
Features:
    Christiania Bike 170
    Lego Flagship 173
Christiania 82-84
Christiania Bike 170
Christiansborg Slot 65-67
Christianshavn 80-84
Areas::
    Canal District, the 80-82
    Christiania 82-84
    Cafés & Bars 135
    Children 171
    Galleries 180
    Map 252-253
    Restaurants 120
Features:
    harbour baths 83
Christmas 167
Christmas Fairs & Parade 167
cinemas 176-177
classical music 191-195
    festivals 194
clothes shops 148-154
clubs 188-190
contraception 228
Copenhagen Blues Festival 166
Copenhagen Jazz Festival 165
Copenhagen Marathon 164
Copenhagen Pride 166
Copenhagen Today 26-31
Copenhagen Whitsun Carnival 164
CPH:DOX 167
CPH:PIX 164
customs 227
cycling 40-42, 200, 226
    Christiania Bike 170
    shops 160

D

dance 198-199
Danish delicacies 133
Danish Derby 165

Danish Design 32-39
    fashion 149
Danish Riviera 216-219
Dannebrog 20
DCCD Images Festival 166
disabled visitors 227-228
dentists 228
department stores 143
design 32-39
doctors 228
driving 225-226
dry cleaning 160

E

Eastern Strøget & Købmagergade 54-57
electricity 228
embassies & consulates 228
emergencies 228

F

fashion shops 148-154
    designers 149
Fastelavn 167
festivals *see* Calendar
    art festivals & parties 181
Film 174-177
fitness centres 200
folk music 190
food & drink shops 155-156
football 201, 205-206
Frederiksberg
    children 161
    shops 161
    see also Vesterbro & Frederiksberg
Frederiksstaden 71-75
    Cafés & Bars 134
    Hotels 104
    Map 249
    Restaurants 118
Features:
    parks & palaces walk 72
    furniture shops 156-157
Further Afield 94-96
Areas:
    Amager 96
    Bispebjerg 95
    Hellerup & Charlottenlund 94-95
    Ishøj 95-96
    Lyngby 95

G

Galleries 178-181
Gammel Strand *see* Central Strøget & Gammel Strand
Gauguin, Paul 48

Gay & Lesbian 182-184
    bars & clubs 182-184
    events 184
    fitness & sauna 184
    hotels 184
    organisations 182
Getting Around 224-226
go-karting 201
golf 201, 206
gourmet burger bars 116

H

handball 206
harbour baths 83
health 228
Hellerup & Charlottenlund 94-95
History 16-25
    Tivoli 47
home entertainment shops 157
homewares 158
horse racing 206
horse riding 202
hostels 109-110
Hotels 98-110
By area:
    Further afield 108-109
    Nørreport & around 106-107
    Nyhavn, Kongens Nytorv & around 104-106
    Tivoli, Rådhuspladsen, Strøget & Around 98-104
    Vesterbro & Frederiksberg 107-108
By type:
    apartments 110
    gay 184
    hostels 109-110
Features:
    best design hotels 101
    chain hotels 106
    eco-friendly 105
    Radisson Blu (SAS) Royal Hotel 99

I

ice hockey 206
ice skating 202
insurance 228
internet 228
Ishøj 95-96

J

jewellery shops 159
jogging 202
Junge Hunde 167

K

Købmagergade *see*
Eastern Strøget
& Købmagergade
Koncerthuset 197
Kongens Nytorv 62-64
Kulturhavn 166
Kulturnat 166

L

language 228
Latin Quarter 57-58
left luggage 228
Lego Flagship 173
lesbian *see* Gay & Lesbian
lingerie 152
lost property 229
Louisiana Museum For
Modern Kunst 219-219
Lyngby 95

M

malls 145
Malmö 209-215
May Day 164
media 229
Metro 224-225
Metropolis 165
microbreweries 140
Mix Copenhagen 167
money 230
music
  shops 159
  venues 190
  see also Nightlife and
    Performing Arts

N

New Nordic cuisine 118
newsagents 148
New Year 167
Nightlife 185-190
  clubs 188-190
  live music venues 190
  lounge & music bars
    186-188
Noma 121
**Nørrebro & Østerbro
  90-93**
  Areas:
    Nørrebro 90-92
    shops 161
    Østerbro 92-93
  **Cafés & Bars
    139**
  Map 248
  Restaurants 125
  Features:
    Assistens Kirkegård 91
    Brumleby Village 92
    North Sjælland 220-222
**Nyhavn & Kongens
  Nytorv 61-64**
  Areas:
    Kongens Nytorv 62-64
    Nyhavn 61-62
  Cafés & Bars 134
  Hotels 104
  Map 252

Restaurants 115
Features:
  Hans Christian
    Anderson 63

O

Ølfestival 164
opening hours 230
opera 191
opticians 159
Østerbro 92-93
  Cafés & Bars 142
  Children 172
  Restaurants 126
  Shops 161

P

**Performing Arts
  191-199**
pharmacies 159-160, 228
photography shops 160
police 230
Pølsevogne 59
postal services 230
public holidays 230-231
public toilets 231
public transport 224-225

Q

Queen's Birthday 164

R

Radisson Blu (SAS)
  Royal Hotel 99
Rådhuspladsen 52-53
Redzepi, Rene 121
religion 231
Resources A-Z 227-233
Restaurants 111-127
  By area:
    Christianshavn
      & Christiania 120-123
    Frederiksstaden 118-120
    Further afield 127
    Nørrebro 125-126
    Nyhavn & Kongens
      Nytorv 115-118
    Østerbro 126-127
    Rosenborg & around 120
    Slotsholmen 118
    Strøget & around
      113-115
    Tivoli & Rådhuspladsen
      111-113
    Vesterbro &
      Frederiksberg 123-125
  Features:
    gourmet burger bars
      116
    New Nordic cuisine 118
    Noma and Rene Redzepi
      121
  By type:
    children 168
rock & pop music 190
rollerblading 202
Round Sjælland Yacht
  Race 165
Royal Copenhagen 54

Royal Danish Theatre
  192-193
**Rosenborg & Around
  76-79**
  **Cafés & Bars
    134**
  Children 171
  Map 246-247
  Restaurants 120
Roskilde Festival 165
rowing 202
Rudolph Tegners Museum
  222
rugby union 202

S

Sankt Hans Aften 164
saunas 202-204
Shakespeare at Kronborg
  165
shoe shops 156
**Shops & Services
  143-162**
skateboarding 202, 203
Slotsholmen 65-70
  Areas:
    Around Slotsholmen
      67-70
    Christiansborg Slot
      65-67
  Map 251
  Restaurants 118
  Features:
    Bertel Thorvaldsen
      69
smoking 231
**Sport & Fitness
  200-206**
centres 202
gay 184
participation sports
  200-205
shops 160
spectator sports 205-206
stationery shops 160
**Strøget & Around
  54-60**
  Areas:
    Central Strøget &
      Gammel Strand 58-60
    Eastern Strøget &
      Købmagergade 54-57
    Latin Quarter 57-58
    Western Strøget 60
  Cafés & Bars 129
  Children 169
  Hotels 98
  Map 251
  Restaurants 113
  Features:
    Pølsevogne 59
studying 231
supermarkets 160
swimming 83, 202-203

T

taxis 226
tax refunds 232
telephones 232

tennis 204, 206
ten-pin bowling 204-205
theatre 195-198
tickets 162
tipping 232
**Tivoli &
  Rådhuspladsen
  44-53**
  Areas:
    Around Tivoli 49-52
    Rådhuspladsen 52-53
    Tivoli 44-49
  Cafés & Bars 128
  Children 168-169
  Hotels 98
  Map 250
  Restaurants 111
  Features:
    best places to go
    Gauguin, Paul 48
    Jens Olsen's World
      Clock 52
Tivoli Christmas Season
  167
Tivoli Halloween Opening
  167
tourist information 232
tours 226
Tivoli 47-48
toyshops 162
trains 224-225
Turning Tower 211

V

**Vesterbro &
  Frederiksberg
  85-89**
  Areas:
    Frederiksberg 97-89
    Vesterbro 85-87
  Cafés & Bars 136
  Galleries 180
  Hotels 107
  Map 245
  Restaurants 123
  Shops 161
  Features:
    Carlsberg brewery 86
    vintage clothes 152-154
    visas 232
  Vocabulary 234

W

walking 72, 206, 226
waterfront 29
websites 235
weights & measures 232
Western Strøget 60
windsurfing 205
Winter Jazz Festival 167
women 233
Wondercool Copenhagen
  167
working in Copenhagen 233
world clock 52
world music 190

Y

yoga 205

INDEX

Venue Index

★ indicates a
critic's choice

(Stilleben) 199
1.th 115
42°Raw 129
71 Nyhavn 104

A

A Pair 155
Aamanns Etablissement
126★
Åben Dans Productions
199
Abigail's 156
AC Perchs Thehandel
155★
Accord 159
Acne Jeans 150★
Adidas Originals 148
Adina Apartments 110
AFS Interkultur (American
Field Service) 231
Agent Provocateur 152
Agnes Cupcakes 156
Alberto K 113
Alexander Nevsky Kirke
74
Amager Bio 190
Amager Hospital 228
Amager Museum 96
Amalienborg Museum 74
Amber Museum 64
American Embassy 228
Amigo Bar 182
Amigo Sauna 184
Andersen S Contemporary
180
Anemoneteatret 194
Antikhallen 145
Antique Toys 145★
AOC 118★
Apropos 136
Arbejdermuseet 77
Aristo 135
Arken Museum For
Moderne Kunst 96★
Arnold Busck 147
Asfalt 161
Assistens Kirkegård 92★
Astanga Yoga Skolen 205
Atelier Décor 153
Atlas Bar 129
Avenue Hotel 107
Avis 225

B

B.APS 161
B93 Sports Club 204
Baisikeli 226
Bakkehus Museet 88
Bakken 217

Bakken i Kødbyen 186★
Ballerup Event Center 201
Bang & Olufsen 157
Bang og Jensen 136
Bankeråt 134★
Bar Rouge 186
Barbar Bar 136
Barbarellah 186
Bastionen og Løven 135
Bellevue Teatret 198
Berlitz 227, 231
Best Western Mercur Hotel
204
Bibliotekshaven 68
Bike Copenhagen
with Mike 226
BilletNet 162
Bio Mio 123
Birger Christensen 150
Bispebjerg Hospital 228
Bjørgs 128
Black Diamond 194
Bloomsday Bar 129
BLUS at Studenterhuset
182
Bodega 139
Botanisk Have & Museum
77★
Boutique Chic 153
Boutique Lize 186
Bowlehuset 205
Bøf & Ost 113
Brede Vaerk 95
Bring Express 227
British Embassy 228
Brogatan 214
Brøndby IF 206
Bruno & Joel 155
Bruun Rasmussen
Kunstauktioner 147
Bruun's Indretning 161
Bruuns Bazaar 150
Bryggeriet Apollo 140
Budget Rent a Car 225
Build-a-Bear Workshop
162
Burger & Bun 116
Butcher's Lab 179
Butik for Borddækning 148
By Malene Birger 151

C

Café 22 139
Café à Porta 134
Café André Citroën 136
Café Bopa 142, 187
Café Elefanten136
Café Europa 129
Café Hovedtelegrafen 168
Café Intime 182★
Café Luna 135
Café Norden 130
Café Sommersko 130

Café Victor 130
Café Viggo 137
Café Wilder 136★
Café Zeze 130
Cafeen På 4 129
Canadian Embassy 228
Cantabile 2 196
Cap Horn 117
Carlsberg Visitors Centre
& Jacobsen Brewhouse
88
Carsten's Guest House 184
Casa Shop 156
Cascabel Madhus 118
Celcius 188
Centiliter & Gram 214
Central Station Post Office
230
Centralhjørnet 182★
Chapeaux Petitgas 154
Charlottenborg
Udstillingsbygning 178
Chit Chat Brasserie 113
Christiania Cykler 160
Christians Kirke 81
Christiansborg Slot 66
Christiansborg Slotskirke
68
Christianskirke 194
Cinematekets Bog og
Videohandel 148
CinemaxX 176
Circus Circus 203
Cisternerne – Museet For
Moderne Glaskunst 88
Citlet Apartments 110
City Go Kart 201
City Helse 228
Clarion Hotel Malmö
215
Clausens Kunsthandel
178
Club Christopher 183
Cocks and Cows 116
Cofoco 123
Comfort Hotel Esplanaden
106
Companys 151
Conditoriet La Glace
155
Copenhagen Admiral Hotel
104
Copenhagen Airport 224
Copenhagen Badminton
Club 200
Copenhagen Business
School 231
Copenhagen Gay Center
184
Copenhagen International
Theatre (KIT) 198
Copenhagen JazzHouse
130★, 190★

Copenhagen Marriott Hotel
98
Copenhagen Opera House
194★
Copenhagen Plaza 98
Copenhagen Skatepark
202
Copenhagen Theatre Circle
196
Copenhagen Walking
Tours 226
Copenhagen X 226
Cos 148
Cosy Bar 183
Crowne Plaza Copenhagen
Towers 109
Culture Box 188★
Cykelfabrikken 160★

D

Dag H 142
Dagmar Teatret 176
Dan Turèll 131
Danacord 159
DanHostel Copenhagen
Amager 109
DanHostel Copenhagen
City 110★
Danielsen's Successors
145
Danish Arts and Crafts
Association market 146
Danish Badminton
Association 200
Danish Bowling
Association 205
Danish Dance Theatre
199
Danish Film School 231
Danish Golf Union
201, 206
Danish Handball
Association 206
Danish Ice Hockey
Association 206
Danish International
Theatre Institute
& Theatre Union
(DITITU) 198
Danish Jewish Museum
68★
Danish Road Directorate
224
Danish Rowing
Association 202
Danish Rugby Association
202
Danish Sports Council 200
Danish Tennis Association
204, 206
Danish Tourist Board
232
Danmarks Akvarium 94

Dansescenen 198
Dansk Arkitekturcenter 81
Dansk Cyklist Forbund 226
Dansk Design Center 50★
Dansk Handicap Forbund 227
Dansk Håndværk 162
Danske Bank, Den 230
Danske Kulturinstitut, Det 233
Danske Revymuseum, Det 88
Davids Bistro127★
Davids Samling 77★
DAY Birger et Mikkelsen 151
Dental Emergency Service 228
Designer Zoo 146★
DFDS Canal Tours 226
DFDS Seaways 224
DGI-Byen 202★
DGI-Byens Hotel 103
Diamantboghandlen 148
Diesel 149
Donn Ya Doll 161
DR Koncerthuset 194★
Dragør Museum 96
Drop Inn 131
DSB 225
Dyrehaven 137★

E

e-Boks Danish Open 206
Egefeld 156
Elektriske Hjørne, Det 131
Els 117
Emmerys 155
Empire Bio 176
Era Ora 120
Eurolines 224
EuropCar/Pitztner Auto 225
Eventyr Sport 160
Experimentarium 94★

F

Færgekroen Bryghus 140
Fætter BR 162
Falck Redningskorps 226
Falernum 137
Falkoner Biografen 176★
Faraos Cigarer 162
FC København 206
Field's 145
Filippa K 151
Filmhuset/Den Danske Filminstitut Cinemateket 176★
Fiskebaren 124
Fisken 134
Fisketorvet 145
Flottenheimer 1331
Flying Tigers Rickshaw 226
Fogal 152

Folketeatret 195
Folketinget 67
Fona 157
Fontaine, La 190
Form/Design Center 213★
formel B 124
Fortunens Ponyudlejning 172
Fotografisk Center 178
Frederiks Bastion 180
Frederiksberg Have 89★
Frederiksberg Hospital 228
Frederiksberg Slot 89
Frederiksberg Svømmehal 204★
Frederiksborg Slot 221
Fridhems Cyklar 215
Frihedsmuseet 74
Friis & Company 154
Frilandsmuseet 95
Fru Heiberg 142

G

Galathea Kroen 131
Galleri Bo Bjerggaard 180★
Galleri Christina Wilson 180
Galerie Asbæk/Martin Asbæk Projects 178
Galerie Mikael Andersen 179★
Galerie Pi 179
Galerie Stamkunsten 146
Galleri Nicolai Wallner 180★
Galleri Specta 179
Galleri Susanne Ottesen 179
Galleri Tom Christoffersen 179
Gammel Strand stall 156
Garnisons Kirken 194
Gefährlich 187
Geologisk Museum 78
Georg Jensen 159★
Geranium 2 127
Ghost Tour 226
Gilleleje Badehotel 222
Gilleleje Museum 221
Glace, La 131
Global 190
Gloria 177
Gourmandiet 142★
Grand Teatret 177★
Granhøj Dans 199
Granola 137★
Great Synagogue 231
Green Square Copenhagen 146
Gregory Pepin's Danish Silver 146
Grøndal Centret 202
Grønnegårds Teatret 195
Grundtvigs Kirke 95
Guinness World Records Museum & Mystic Exploratorie 55
Gule Cottage, Den 127
Gule Hus, Det 137

H

H&M 148
Haché 116
Hælebaren 160
Halberstadt 159
Halifax 116
Harbo Bar 139
Harry's Place 59
Hay CPH 157
Hay4you 110
Helbak/Scherning 148
Helene Nyborg Contemporary 179
Helligåndskirken 58
Henrik Vibskov 151
Herman 111
Hertz 225
Hillerødgade Swimming Pool 204
Hilton Malmö City 215
Hirschsprungske Samling, Den 78
Holland House 196
Holmens Kirke 70, 195
Hotel Alexandra 101★
Hotel d'Angleterre 104★
Hotel Fox 108
Hotel Guldsmeden Bertrams 108★
Hotel Jørgensen 107
Hotel Nora 106
Hotel Opera 106
Hotel Pro Forma 196
Hotel Sct Thomas 108
Hotel Selandia 103
Hotel Skt Petri 106★
Hotel Tiffany 108
Hotel Twentyseven 103
Hotel Villa Strand 222
Hovedbiblioteket 232
Hørsholm Golf Klub 201
Husbryggeriet Jacobsen 140
Huset Med Det Grønne Træ 113
Husets Biograf 177

I

Ibsens 107
Ideal Bar 187
Illum 143★
Illums Bolighus 157
Imperial 177★
Imperial Hotel 103
Invasion 152
InWear/Matinique 152
Irish Embassy 228
Irma 160
Isola Bar 187

J

J Lindeberg 151
Jailhouse Copenhagen 183
Jazz Guides 226
Jolene 189★

K

K-Bar 132
Kafe Kys 132
Kaffe & Vinyl 138★
Kaffesalonen 141
Kaiku 158
Kajak-Ole 169
Karen Blixen Museet 217
Karriere 138
Kastellet 75
Kastelskirken 195
KB Hallen 205
KB Tennis Club 204
Kiin Kiin 125
Kim Anton 146
Kitsch Bitch 153
Kjær og Sommerfeldt 156
Klampenborg Galopbane 206
Klint, Le 158
Koi 214★
Kokkeriet Spisehus & Catering 120
Kong Arthur 106★
Kong Frederik 103
Kong Hans Kælder 113
Kongelige Afstøbningssamli, ng, Den 75
Kongelige Bibliotek, Det 68★, 232
Kongelige Danske Haveselskabs Have, Det 89
Kongelige Danske Kunstakademi, Det 231
Kongelige Danske Musikkonservatorium, Det 231
Kongelige Stalde og Kareter 67
Kongelige Teater, Det, Gamle Scene 199★
Konservatoriets Koncertsal 194
Kontant Foto 160
Københavns Cyklebørs 226
Københavns Cykler 226
Københavns Farvehandel 146
Københavns Golf Klub 201
Københavns Roklub 202
Københavns Musikteater 195
Kreutzberg Café & Bar 132
Kulturhuset Mazetti 213
Kunstforeningen 179
Kunstindustrimuseet 75
Kvindehuset (Women's House) 233

L

Lægevagten 228
Lagkagehuset Bageri og Konditori 155
Landbohøjskolens Have 89
Langelinie Pier 159
Laundromat Café 141★
Lego Flagship 162★, 173

INDEX

Lemon Grass 214
Lê Lê 124
LGBT Danmark –
  Landsforeningen
  for Bøsser, Lesbiske,
  Biseksuelle og
  Transpersoner (LGBT)
  182
Library Bar 128
Lille Fede, Den 114
Lille Havfrue, Den 73
Lille Mølle 81
Lille Teater, Det 194
LLLP 161
London Toast Theatre 196
Loppen 190★
Louisiana Museum For
  Moderne Kunst 217★
Løgismose 156
Lust 152

M

Madklubben 118★
Mads Nørgaard 151
Magasin 143
Malmö Konsthall 213
Malmö Museums &
  Art Museum 213
Malmö Tourist
  Information 201
Manpower 227
Marionet Teater
  i Kongens Have 194
Marmorkirken 75★
MASH 117★
Masken 183
Mattssons Rideklub 201
Meet Gay Copenhagen 183
Mêlée 125★
Mellow Yello 214
Men's Bar 183
Meridiano Teater 196
Metro 214
Meyers Deli 138★
MJ Coffee 135
Moderna Museet 213
Mojo 190
Monies 159
Moosehead Bar &
  Restaurant 214
Morgenstedet 120
Moshi Moshi 151
Mother 125★
Movia 225
Mungo Park 195
Munthe plus Simonsen 151
Museum of Copenhagen 86
Musikhistorisk Museum
  og Carl Claudius'
  Samling 76
Musikteatret
  Undergrunden 195

N

NASA 189
National Drama School 231
Nationalmuseet 51
Nautic Surf & Ski 205
Nethouse 2000 228

Netto-Bådene 226
Never Mind 184
Neye 154
Niels Brock College 231
Nikolaj – Copenhagen
  Contemporary Art
  Center 179
Nimb Hotel 101★
Noma 122★
Nordatlantens Brygge 146
Nordisk Korthandel 148
Normann Copenhagen 158
Norse Store 149★
Nørrebro Bryghus 126★
Nørrebrohallen 202
nué 161
Ny Carlsberg Glyptotek
  51★
Nyboders Mindestuer 78
Ny Teater, Det 195

O

Oak Room 141, 187
Øbro-Hallen 204
Odin Teatret 196
Øksnehallen 180
Ølbaren 140
Ølbutikken 156★
Operaen 194★
Ordning & Reda 160
Ordrupgaard 94★
Orlogsmuseet 81
Oscar Bar & Café 134,
  184★
Østerbro Stadion 205
Østerlandsk Thehus 156
Østre Gasværk Teater 195
Overgaden 180

P

Palace Hotel 101★
Palads 177
Palæ Bar 134
Panzón 142★
Park Bio 177
Park Café 189
Parterre 151★
PatéPaté 125
Paustian 157★
Peder Oxe 114
Peder Oxe Vinbar 132
Peter Beier 155
Peter Grosell 147
Peter Lav Photo Gallery
  180
Peter Schaufuss Ballet 199
Phoenix Copenhagen 104
Photografica 160★
Plan-B Teater 196
Pluto Børne Sko 150
Police headquarters 230
Politihistorisk Museum 92
Politikens Boghallen 148
Post & Tele Museum 57
Posthus Teatret 177
Poul Stig Briller 159
Pure Shop 147★
Pussy Galore's Flying
  Circus 141

Q

Quote 134

R

Rådhuset 53
Radisson Blu (SAS)
  Royal Hotel 99, 101★
Radisson Blu Scandinavia
  Hotel 108
Rasmus Oubæk 119★
Relæ 126★
REMA 1000 160
Republique 196
Restaurang Smak 214
Restaurant d'Angleterre
  117
Restaurant Ida Davidsen
  119
Restaurant Jacobsen
  127
Restaurant Kanalen 122
Restaurant L'Alsace 114
Restaurant Søstrene Olsen
  222
Rhythmic Music
  Conservatory 231
Ribersborgs Kallbadhus
  214★
Ricco's Coffee Bar 138
Rice Market 115
Ripley's Believe It
  Or Not Museum 53
Riz Raz 115
Rocca, La 168
Rosenborg Slot 78★
Roskilde
  Universitetscenter
  231
Royal Café 132★
Royal Copenhagen 143★
Royal Copenhagen Factory
  Outlet 159
Royal Danish Academy
  of Music 194
Royal Danish Ballet
  199
Royal Danish Playhouse
  196
Royal Danish Theatre,
  Old Stage 199★
Rudolph Tegners Museum
  222
Ruinerne under
  Christiansborg 66
Rundan 215
Rundan Canal Tours
  214
Rundetårn 57★
Rust 189★

S

Sabine Poupinel & Co
  151
Saint-Jacques, Le 127
Sakrementskirken
  231
Salt & Brygga 214★
Salt 117
Samarkand 154

Sand 152
Sankt Annæ Kirke 231
Sankt Ansgar Kirke 75
Savoy Hotel 103
Scandic Front 104
Scandic Hotel Kramer
  215
Scandlines 224
Schleisner Rens 160
School of Architecture
  231
Sebastopol Café 142
Sex Beat Records 159
Sidewalk Express 228
Sidewalk Skateshop
  203
Signa 196
Skovshoved Hotel 109
Skuespilhuset 196
Slagteren ved Kultorvet
  155
Slotskælderen Hos Gitte
  115
Soelberg Kunst &
  Antikvitetshandel 146
Sögreni of Copenhagen
  160★
Solspejlet 162
Sommelier, Le 119
Sølvkælderen 146
Sømandshjemmet Bethel
  106
Sømods Bolcher 155
Søpavillonen 190
Søren K 118
Søstrene Gren 158
Spicey Kitchen 123
Spiseloppen 123
Sporting Health Club
  200
Sporvejen 134
Spot 215★
Square, The 103
St Alban's Church
  75, 231
Stadsbibliotek 214
Statens Museum
  For Kunst 79★
Steno Apotek 228
Sticks 'n' Sushi 120
Stig P 152, 161
Stop Aids 182
Storm 152★
Storm P Museet 89
Street Machine 203
STS High School &
  Au Pair 231
Studenterhuset 132
Sult 120
Susanne Juul 155
Sushitarian 115
Sushitreat Fox 128

T

Teatermuseet 67
That Theatre Company
  196
Thé à la Menthe 132
Thorvaldsens Museum
  69, 70★

Time's Up Vintage
154★
Tivoli 49★, 199
Tivolis Koncertsal
194
Tom Rossau Showroom
158
Tøjhusmuseet 70
Travbane 206
Trinitatiskirke 57
Trois Cochons, Les 125
Tycho Brahe Planetarium
87
Tycho Brahe Planetarium
Omnimax 177

U

Udlændingestyrelsen
233
Uldstedet 147
Ultimo 129
Umami 120★
Underwood Ink 142★
University of Copenhagen
231
Uppercut Danseteater 199
Urban Outfitters 148
US Import 150

V

V1 Gallery 181★
Vega 190★
Velour 161
Vero Moda 152
Vester Kopi 227
Vester Vov Vov 177
Vesterbro Bryghus
140
Vesterbro Swimming Pool
204
Vi Ses 158
Victors 215
Videnscenter for
Bevægelseshandicap
227
Vincaféen Bibendum
135
Vinstue 90 138
Viva 123
Vor Frelsers Kirke 81★
Vor Frue Kirke 57

W

Wagamama 113, 168
Weber Furniture 161
Wettergren & Wettergren
152
Whyred 152★
Wokshop Cantina 118
Wonderful Copenhagen
Tourist Information
Bureau 232
Wood Wood 150★

X

X-Act 199

Y

Yoga Mudra 205

Z

Zirup 132★
Zone 1 152
Zoo Bar 132, 188
Zoologisk Have 89★
Zoologisk Museum 93

Advertisers' Index

Please refer to the relevant pages for contact details.

The Copenhagen Metro   **IFC**

Introduction

MoneyGram International	**4**
Statens Museum for Kunst	**6**
Visit Carlsberg	**14**
The Copenhagen Post	**14**

Sightseeing

Copenhagen Card	**44**
BrewPub	**56**

Consume

Hotels	
Best Western Hotel	**100**
Generator Hostel	**102**
Hay4U	**144**

House of Amber   **IBC**

INDEX

Maps

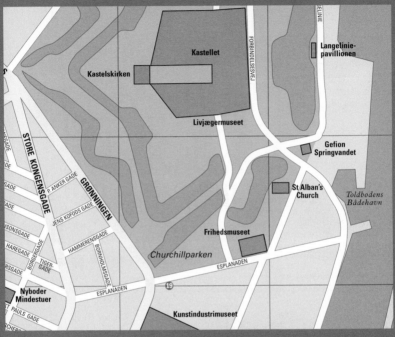

Major sight or landmark	
Hospital or college	
Railway station	
Parks	
River	
Motorway	
Main road	
Main road tunnel	
Pedestrian road	
Steps	
Airport . . . . ✈
Church . . . . ✠
Metro station . . . . M
Area name . . . . VESTERBRO

Copenhagen Overview	**244**
Street Maps	**245**
Street Index	**254**
Local Trains & Metro	**256**

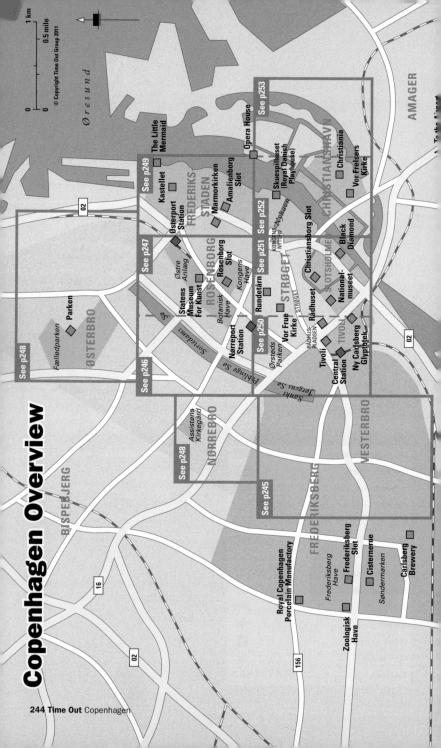

Copenhagen Overview

Øresund

AMAGER

See p253

Opera House

The Little Mermaid

Kastellet

See p249

Marmorkirken

Amalienborg Slot

FREDERIKSSTADEN

Skuespilhuset (Royal Danish Playhouse)

CHRISTIANSHAVN

Christiania

Vor Frelsers Kirke

Østerport Station

See p247

ROSENBORG

Rosenborg Slot

See p252

See p251

Christiansborg Slot

Black Diamond

Østre Anlæg

Kongens Have

KONGENS NYTORV

Statens Museum For Kunst

Botanisk Have

Rundetårn

SLOTSHOLMEN

Nationalmuseet

STRØGET

Vor Frue Kirke

Rådhuset

STRØGET

Norreport Station

See p250

RÅDHUSPLADSEN

TIVOLI

Ørsteds Parken

Ny Carlsberg Glyptotek

Tivoli

Sankt Jørgens Sø

See p246

Central Station

VESTERBRO

Peblinge Sø

See p248

Assistens Kirkegård

NØRREBRO

See p248

See p245

FREDERIKSBERG

Frederiksberg Have

Frederiksberg Slot

Cisternerne

Carlsberg Brewery

Royal Copenhagen Porcelain Manufactory

Søndermarken

Zoologisk Have

BISPEBJERG

ØSTERBRO

Fælledparken

Parken

Sortedams Sø

02

16

02

156

02

Rigshospitalet

Amorparken

① Hotels pp98-110
① Restaurants pp111-127
① Cafés & Bars pp128-142

G

HELGESENSGADE

RYESSA

BLEGDAMSVEJ

TAGENSVEJ

TREPKASGADE

Fredens
Kirke

Penum
Institutet

FREDENSGADE

RYESGADE

LUNDINGSGADE

SØPASSAGEN

SORTEDAM DOSSERING

NØRRE ALLÉ

66

H

BLEGDAMSVEJ

Nørre
Hospital

FREDENS BRO

MØLLEGADE

POPPELGADE

AHORNS GADE

Mosaik
Kirkegård

GULDBERGSGADE

LÆSSØESGADE

RYESGADE

NØRREBRO

SANKT
HANS TORV

SORTEDAM DOSSERING

EGEGADE

SANKT HANS GADE

47

RYESGADE

LÆSSØESGADE

RØRHOLMSGADE

ELME. GADE

FÆLLEDVEJ

SCHLEPPEGRELLS-
GADE

Sø

OLE SUHRS GADE

J

GAMMELTOFTSGADE

RAVNSBORGGADE

RAVNSBORG
TVÆRGADE

Sortedams

ØSTER SØGADE

NØRREBROGADE

Kommune
Hospital

ØSTER

SORTEDAM DOSSERING

BLÅGÅRDSGADE

See
p248

BAGGESENSGADE

BARTHOLINSGADE

K

WESSELSGADE

PEBLINGE DOSSERING

DRONNING
LOUISES BRO

SØTORVET

GOTHERSGADE

Botanisk
Institut

FREDERIKSBORGGADE

Arbejdermuseet

RØMERSGADE

LINNÉSGADE

KORSGADE

THORUPSGADE

PEBLINGE DOSSERING

Peblinge Sø

NØRRE SØGADE

24

25

NANSENSGADE

VENDERSGADE

26

RØMERSGADE

L

VALDS-
GADE

31
38

36

See
p250

NØRRE FARIMAGSGADE

KJELD LANGESGADE

AHLEFELDTSGADE

ISRAELS
PLADS

LINNÉSGADE

Nørreport
Station

Nørreport

NØR

M

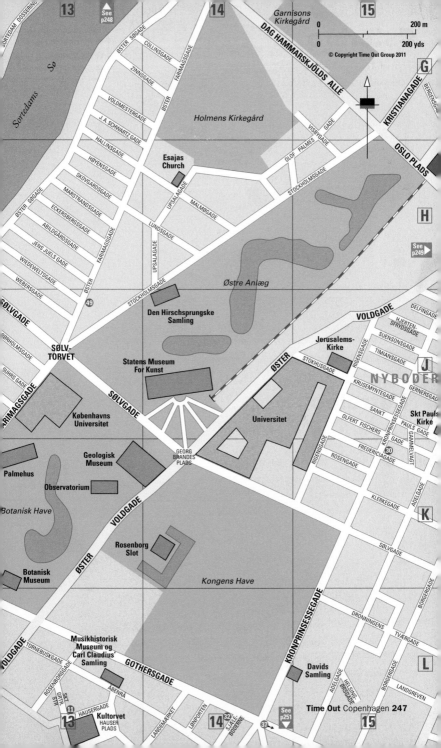

Jürtedam Dossering

See
p248

14

15

Garnisons
Kirkegård

DAG HAMMARSKJÖLDS ALLÈ

0   200 m
0   200 yds
© Copyright Time Out Group 2011

G

ØSTER SØGADE

COLLINSGADE

KRISTIANAGADE

BIRGENSGADE

ZINNSGADE

FARIMASSGADE

OSLO PLADS

VOLDMESTERGADE

ØSTER

VISBYGADE

GADE

J. A. SCHWARTZ GADE

Holmens Kirkegård

OLOF PALMES GADE

H

HALLINSGADE

HØYENSGADE

Esajas
Church

SKOVGÅRDSGADE

MARSTRANDSGADE

UPSALAGADE

MALMØGADE

STOCKHOLMSGADE

ØSTER SØGADE

ECKERSBERGSGADE

LUNDSGADE

See
p249

ABILDGÅRDSGADE

FARIMAGSGADE

JENS JUELS GADE

UPSALAGADE

WIEDEWELTSGADE

Østre Anlæg

VOLDGADE

DELFINGADE

WEBERSGADE

ØSTER

49

STOCKHOLMSGADE

HJERTEN-
SFRYDSGADE

SØLVGADE

Den Hirschsprungske
Samling

SUENSONSGADE

RØRHOLMSGADE

Jerúsalems-
Kirke

RIGENSGADE

TIMIANSGADE

J

SØLV-
TORVET

SUHRS GADE

ØSTER

STOKHUSGADE

NYBODER

GERNERSGADE

Statens Museum
For Kunst

KRUSEMYNTEGADE

FARIMAGSGADE

Skt Pauls
Kirke

SANKT

SØLVGADE

København
Universitet

Universitet

OLFERT FISCHERS

KRONPRINSESSEGADE

PAULS GADE

GAMMELVAGT

Geologisk
Museum

GEORG
BRANDES
PLADS

RIGENSGADE

FREDERICIAGADE

30

Palmehus

ROSENGADE

ADELGADE

Observatorium

KLERKEGADE

K

Botanisk Have

VOLDGADE

SØLVGADE

ØSTER

Rosenborg
Slot

BORGERGADE

Botanisk
Museum

Kongens Have

DRONNINGENS

KRONPRINSESSEGADE

TVÆRGADE

VOLDGADE

Musikhistorisk
Museum og
Carl Claudius
Samling

ADELGADE

HELSING
ØRSGADE

L

Davids
Samling

BORGERGADE

LANDGREVEN

TORNEBUSKGADE

GOTHERSGADE

ÅBENRÅ

ROSENBORGGADE

SKT.
GRTR.
STTR.

11

See
p251

HAUSERGADE

LANDEMÆRKET

LØNPORTEN

SJÆLE.
BODERNE

13

Kultorvet
HAUSER
PLADS

14

32

37

15

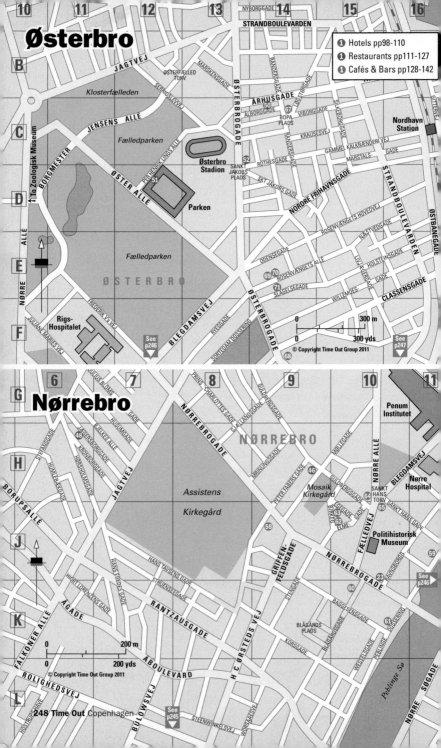

Østerbro

Østerbro

Østerfælled Torv
Marskensgade
Serridslevvej
Jagtvej
Jensens Allé
Klosterfælleden
Fælledparken
Borgmester
Øster Allé
Per Henrik Lings Allé
Østerbro Stadion
Parken
Fælledparken

ØSTERBRO

Ålborggade
Randersgade
Åbenrågade
Århusgade
Viborggade
Bopa Plads
Krausesvej
Gammel Kalkrænderi Vej
Rothesgade
Sankt Jakobs Plads
Marstals Gade
Sankt Jakobs Gade
Nordre Frihavnsgade
Rosenvængets Hovedvej
Næstvedgade
Odensegade
Rosenvængets Allé
Livjægergade
Holsteinsgade
Slagelsegade
Willemoesgade
Classensgade
Strandboulevarden
Østbanegade

Øster Søgade
Frederik V's Vej
Blegdamsvej
Ryesgade
Sortedam Dossering

Rigs-Hospitalet
Juliane Maries Vej
Nørre Allé

Nyborggade
Strandboulevarden
Randersgade
Gittervej
Nordhavn Station

Hotels pp98-110
Restaurants pp111-127
Cafés & Bars pp128-142

0   300 m
0   300 yds
© Copyright Time Out Group 2011

See p246
See p247

57
52
51
69 70
71
68

Nørrebro

Nørrebro

Julius Blooms Gade
Prins Charlottes Gade
Guldbergsgade
Sjællandsgade
Nørrebrogade
Penum Institutet

Stengade
Husumgade
Fælleds Allé
Jægersborggade
Kronborggade
Horsorsnsgade
Humlebæk Gade
Jagtvej
Møllegade
Nørre Allé
Blegdamsvej
Nørre Hospital

Borups Allé

Assistens Kirkegård

Mjølnersgade
Møinichsgade
Peter Fabers Gade
Mosaik Kirkegård
Guldbergsgade
Sankt Hans Torv
Sankt Hans Gade

Birkegade
Egegade
Elmegade
Fælledvej
Politihistorisk Museum

Hans Tavsens Gade
Struensgade
Griffenfeldsgade
Nørrebrogade
Ravnsborggade

Falkoner Allé
Hjort Lorenzens Gade
Hans Egedes Gade
Rantzausgade
Stengade
Baggesensgade

H C Ørsteds Vej
Blågårds Plads
Korsgade
Blågårdsgade
Wesselsgade
Peblinge Dossering
Ahlefeldtsgade
Søgade

Ågade
Aboulevard
Rolighedsvej
Bülowsvej
Steenwinkelsvej
Worsaaesvej

Peblinge Sø

Nørre Søgade

49
46
64
63 62
65
58
59
60
61
23

0   200 m
0   200 yds
© Copyright Time Out Group 2011

See p245
See p246

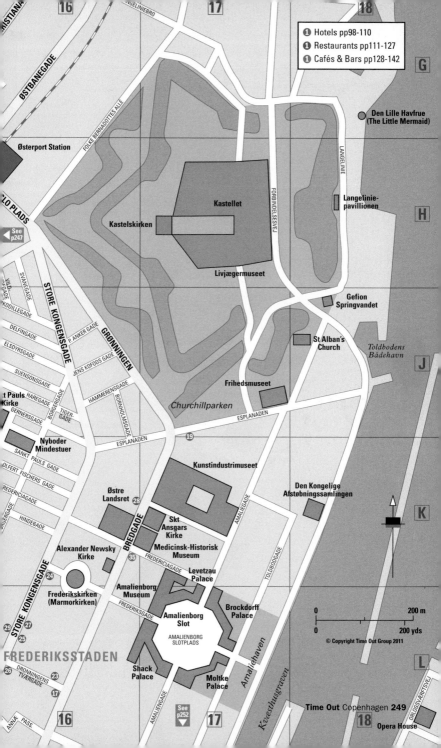

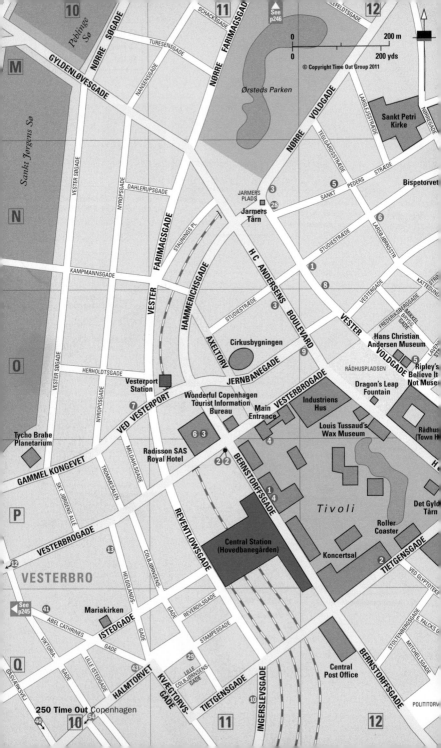

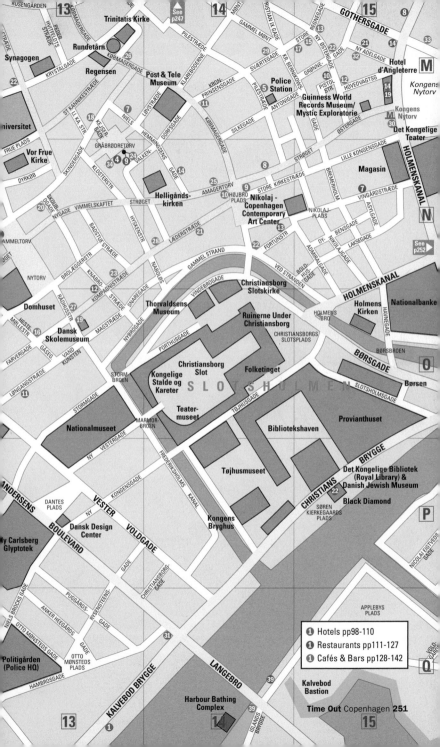

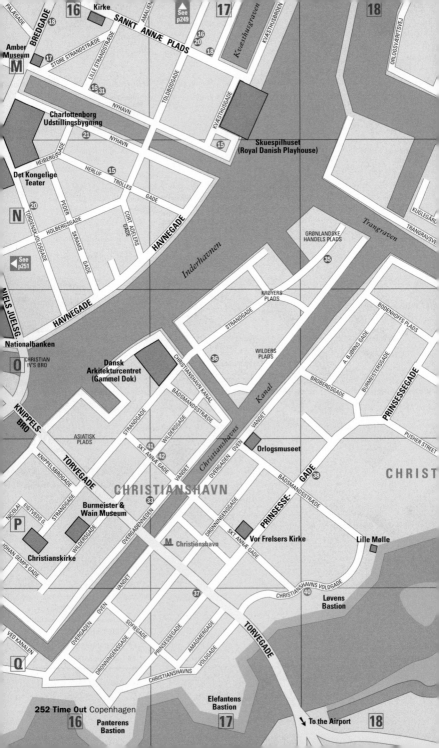

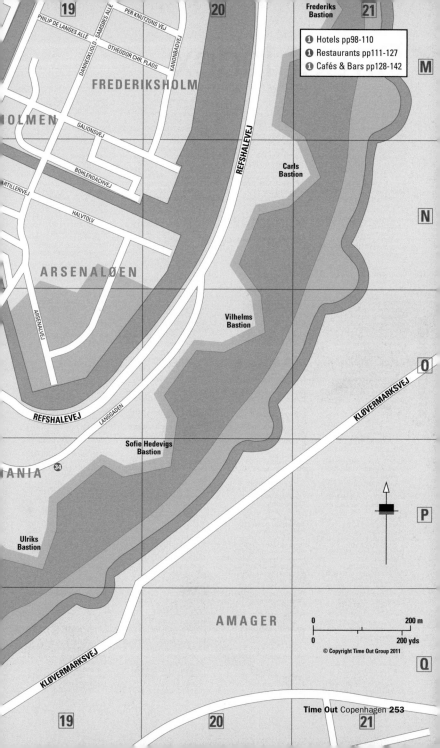

Frederiks
Bastion

19   **20**   **21**

M

❶ Hotels pp98-110
❶ Restaurants pp111-127
❶ Cafés & Bars pp128-142

FREDERIKSHOLM

PHILIP DE LANGES ALLÉ
SAMSØES ALLÉ
PER KNUTZONS VEJ
OTHEODOR CHR. PLADS
DANNESKJOLD
KANONBADVEJ

HOLMEN

GALIONSVEJ

BOHLENDACHVEJ

ARTILLERIVEJ

HALVTOLV

Carls
Bastion

N

ARSENALØEN

ARSENALVEJ

Vilhelms
Bastion

REFSHALEVEJ

O

KLØVERMARKSVEJ

REFSHALEVEJ

LANGGADEN

Sofie Hedevigs
Bastion

ANIA   ㉞

P

Ulriks
Bastion

AMAGER

0 _____ 200 m
0 _____ 200 yds

© Copyright Time Out Group 2011

Q

KLØVERMARKSVEJ

Street Index

A Bjørns Gade - p252 O18
Abel Cathrines Gade - p250 Q10
Åbenrå - p247 L13
Abildgårdsgade - p247 H13
Åboulevard - p248 L7-8
Absalonsgade - p245 Q9
Adelgade - p247 K15/L15
Admiralgade - p251 N15
Ågade - p248 K6-7
Ahlefeldtsgade - p246 L11-12, p250 M12
Ahorns Gade - p246 H10
Ålborggade - p248 C14
Alhambravej - p245 P7
Alsgade - p245 S6
Amagertorv - p251 N14
Amagmergade - p252 Q17
Amaliegade - p249 K17
Amalienborg Slotplads - p249 L17
Amaliengade - p249 L17
Amaliengade - p252 M16-17
Amalievej - p245 N7
Amerikavej - p245 Q6/R6
Amicisvej - p245 O6/P5
Angelgade - p245 T6
Anker Heegårds Gade - p251 Q13
Antoniagade - p251 M14
Applebys Plads - p251 Q15
Århusgade - p248 B14-15
Arkonagade - p245 S9
Arsenalvej - p253 O19
Asagårdsvej - p245 P5
Asger Ryss Gade - p245 S8-9
Asiatisk Plads - p252 O16/P16
Asylgade - p251 N15
Axeltorv - p250 O11
Bådsmandsstræde - p252 O17/P17-18
Badstuestræde - p251 N13
Baggesensgade - p246 K10, p248 K9-10
Bartholinsgade - p246 K11-12
Bergensgade - p247 G15
Bernstorffsgade - p250 P11/Q12
Birkegade - p248 J10, p246 J10
Bjelkes Allé - p248 G6/H7
Blågårdsgade - p246 K10, p248 K9-10
Blågårdsplads - p248 K9
Blegdamsvej - p246 H10-11/G11-12, p248 H10, p248 E13/F12-13
Bodenhoffs Plads - p252 O18
Bohlendachvej - p253 N19
Boldhusgade - p251 N15
Bopaplads - p248 C14
Borgergade - p247 K15/L15, p249 J16/K16
Borgmester Jensens Allé - p248 C11-12/D10-11/E10-11
Bornholmsgade - p249 J16
Børsbroen - p251 O15
Børsgade - p251 O15
Borupsallé - p248 J6
Bredgade - p249 K16-17/L16, p252 M16
Bremerholm - p251 N15
Brobergsgade - p252 O18
Brolæggerstr - p251 N13
Bülowsvej - p245 N6-7, p248 L7
Burmeistersgade - p252 O18
Carit Etlars Vej - p245 P6/Q6
Carl Bernhards Vej - p245 Q6-7
Carlsberg Vej - p245 S6-7
Carstensgade - p245 R5-6

Ceresvej - p245 N5
Christian IV's Bro - p252 O16
Christian IX Gade - p251 M14
Christians Brygge - p251 P14-15
Christiansborggade - p251 P14
Christiansborgs Slotsplads - p251 O14/15
Christianshavn Kanal - p252 O17
Christianshavns Voldgade - p252 P18/Q16-17
Classensgade - p248 E16/F14-15
Colbjørnsensgade - p250 P10-11/Q11
Collinsgade - p247 G13-14
Cort Adelers Gade - p252 N16
Dag Hammarskjölds Allé - p247 G14-15
Dahlerupsgade - p250 N10/11
Danasvej - p245 N8-9
Dannebrogsgade - p245 Q9/R9
Dannekliold - Samsøes Allé - p253 M19
Dannevirkegade - p245 S6/T6
Dantes Plads - p251 P13
Delfingade - p247 J15, p249 J16
Dr Abildgaards Allé - p248 L6/M6
Dronning Louises Bro - p246 K11
Dronningens Tværgade - p247 L15, p249 L16
Dronningensgade - p252 P17/Q16
Dybbøls Gade - p245 S8-9
Dybensgade - p251 N15
Dyrkøb - p251 N13
Eckersbergsgade - p247 H13
Edisonsvej - p245 O5
Edvard Falcks Gade - p250 Q12
Egegade - p246 J10, p248 J10
Ejderstedvej - p245 R6/S6
Elmegade - p246 J10, p248 J10
Elsdyrsgade - p249 J16
Enghavevej - p245 R7/S7/T7
Eskildsgade - p245 Q9
Esplanaden - p249 J17
Estlandsgade - p245 R8-9
Ewalds Gade - p246 L10
Fælledvej - p246 J10
Fælledvej Nørre Allé - p248 G10/H10/J10
Falkoner Allé - p248 K6
Farvergade - p251 O13
Fensmarkgade - p248 G8-9
Fiolstræde - p251 M13
Flensborggade - p245 S8
Folke Bernadottes Allé - p249 G16-17/H16
Forbindelsesvej - p249 H17
Forchhammersvej - p245 N8-9
Forhåbningsholms Allé - p245 O8
Fortunstr - p251 N14
Fredens Bro - p246 H12
Fredensgade - p246 G11/H12
Fredericiagade - p247 K15
Fredericiagade - p249 K16-17
Frederik V's Vej - p248 E11/F11-12
Frederiksberg Allé - p245 N5-8

Frederiksberggade - p250 O12
Frederiksborggade - p246 K11/L12
Frederiksgade - p249 L16-17
Frederiksholms Kanal - p251 P14
Frederiksstadsgade - p245 R7-8
Frue Plads - p251 N13
Fuglevangsvej - p248 M7-8
Galionsvej - p253 M19/N19
Gammel Kalkrænderi Vej - p248 C15-16
Gammel Kongevej - p245 O5-7/P8-9
Gammel Kongevet - p250 P10
Gammel Mønt - p251 M14
Gammel Strand - p251 N14
Gammeltoftsgade - p246 J12
Gammeltorv - p251 N13
Gammelvagt - p247 J15/K15
Gåsegade - p251 O13
Gasværksvej - p245 Q9, p250 Q10
Georg Brandes Plads - p247 K14
Gernersgade - p247 J15, p249 J16
Gittervej - p248 B16/C16/D16
Godsbanegade - p245 S9
Gothersgade - p246 K11-12, p247 L13-14, p251 M15
Gråbrødertorv - p251 N13
Griffen-Feldsgade - p248 J9
Grønlandske Handels Plads - p252 N18
Grønnegade - p251 M15
Grønningen - p249 H16/J16-17
Grundtvigsvej - p245 N5-6
Guldbergsgade - p246 H10, p248 G9/H9-10
Gyldenløvesgade - p248 M10, p250 M10
HC Andersens Boulevard - p250 N11/O11-12, p251 P13
HC Ørsteds Vej - p245 N7-8/O7, p248 K8-9/L8
Haderslevgade - p245 R7/S7
Hallinsgade - p247 G13/H13
Halmtorvet - p250 Q10
Halvtolv - p253 N19
Hambrosgade - p251 Q13
Hammerensgade - p249 J16
Hammerichsgade - p250 N11/O11
Hans Egedes Gade - p248 J7/K7
Hans Tavsens Gade - p248 J7-8/K8
Haregade - p249 J16
Hauchsvej - p245 P7
Hauser Plads - p247 L13
Hausergade - p247 L13
Havnegade - p251 O15, p252 N16-17/O16
Hedebygade - p245 R7
Heibergsgade - p252 N16
Helgesensgade - p246 G12
Helgolandsgade - p250 P10/Q10
Helsingørgade - p247 L15
Henrik Ibsens Vej - p245 P6/Q6
Herholdtsgade - p250 O10
Herluf Trolles Gade - p252 N16-17
Hestemøllestr - p251 O13
Hindegade - p249 K16
Hiort Lorenzens Gade - p248 K6-7
Hjertenfrydsgade - p247 J15

Højbro Plads - p251 N14
Holbergsgade - p252 N16
Holmens Bro - p251 O15
Holmenskanal - p251 N15
Holsteinsgade - p248 E15-16
Hørsholmsgade - p248 H6
Hostrups Have - p248 L6
Hovedvagtsg - p251 M15
Høyensgade - p247 H13
Humlebækgade - p248 H6/J6
Husumgade - p248 G6-7/H7
Hyskenstr - p251 N13
Ingerslevsgade - p245 S9/T7-8, p250 Q11
Islands Brygge - p251 Q14
Israels Plads - p246 L12
Istedgade - p245 Q9/R8-9, p250 Q10-11
JA Schwartz Gade - p247 G13
JM Thieles Vej - p245 N7
Jægersborggade - p248 G6/H6-7
Jagtvej - p248 G7/H7/J7, p248 B11-13
Jarmers Plads - p250 N11
Jens Juels Gade - p247 H13
Jens Kofods Gade - p249 J16
Jernbanegade - p250 O11
Johan Semps Gade - p252 P16
Jul Thomsens Gade - p248 L9/M9
Juliane Maries Vej - p248 F10-11
Julius Bloms Gade - p248 G7
Kalvebod Brygge - p251 Q13-14
Kammannsgade - p250 N10
Kanonbadvej - p253 M20
Kastanievej - p245 N7
Kattesundet - p250 N12/O12
Kejsergade - p251 M13
Kingosgade - p245 P7/Q7
Kjeld Langesgade - p246 L11
Klareboderne - p251 M14
Klerkegade - p247 K15
Klosterstræde - p251 N13
Kløvermarksvej - p253 O21/P20/Q19
Knabrostræde - p251 O13
Knippelsbro - p252 O16
Knippelsbrogade - p252 P16
Købmagergade - p251 M13-14/N14
Kochsvej - p245 P5-6/Q5
Kompagnistræde - p251 N13/O13
Korsgade - p246 L10, p248 K9/L9-10
Krausesvej - p248 C14-15
Kristianagade - p247 G15, p249 G16
Krokodillegade - p249 J16
Kronborggade - p248 H6-7
Kronprinsensgade - p251 M14
Kronprinsessegade - p247 J15/K15/L14-15
Krøyers Plads - p252 O17
Krristen Bernikows Gade - p251 M15
Krusågade - p245 S9
Krusemyntegade - p247 J15
Krystalgade - p251 M13
Küchlersgade - p245 R5-6
Kuglegårdsvej - p252 N18
Kvægtorvsgade - p250 Q11
Kvæsthusbroen - p252 M17
Kvæsthusgade - p252 M17
LI Brandes Allé - p248 L6/M6
Læderstræde - p251 N14
Læssøesgade - p246 H11/J11

Laksegade - p251 N15
Landemærket - p247 L14
Landgreven - p247 L15
Langebro - p251 Q14
Langebrogade - p251 Q15
Langelinie - p249 G18\H18
Langeliniebro - p249 G16-17
Langgaden -
  p253 O19-20/P19
Larsbjørnsstræde - p250 N12
Larslejsstræde -
  p250 M12/N12
Lavendelstræde - p250 O12
Lille Colbjørnsensgade -
  p250 Q11
Lille Istedgade - p250 Q10
Lille Kannikestræde -
  p251 M13
Lille Kongensgade -
  p251 N15
Lille Strandstræde -
  p252 M16
Lindevej - p245 O7
Linnesgade - p246 L12
Livjægergade -
  p248 E15/F16
Løgstørgade -
  p248 B14-15/C14
Løngangstræde - p251 O13
Lønporten - p247 L14
Løvstræde - p251 M14
Lundingsgade - p246 G12
Lundsgade - p247 H14
Lykkesholms Allé -
  p245 N8/O7-8
Lyrskovgade - p245 R6-7
Madvigs Allé - p245 O6/P6
Magstræde Snaregade -
  p251 O13
Malmøgade - p247 H14
Marmorbroen - p251 O13
Marskensgade - p248 B13
Marstalsgade - p248 C15-16
Marstrandsgade - p247 H13
Martensens Allé -
  p245 O6/P6
Meldahlsgade - p250 P10
Mikkel Bryggers Gade -
  p250 O12
Mitchellsgade - p250 Q12
Møllegade - p246 G10/H10,
  p248 H9-10
Møntergade - p251 M14
Mrinungsgade - p248 H9
Murergade - p246 L10
Mynstersvej - p245 O7/P7
NJ Fjords Allé - p248 L6/M6
Naboløs - p251 N14
Næstvedgade -
  p248 D15-16/E15
Nansensgade - p246 L11,
  p248 M10-11,
  p250 M10-11
Nicolai Eigtveds Gade -
  p251 P15, p252 P16
Niels Brocks Gade -
  p251 P13/Q13
Niels Ebbesens Vej -
  p245 N8-9
Niels Hemmingsens Gade -
  p251 M13-14/N14
Niels Juelsgade - p252 O16
Nikolajgade - p251 N15
Nordre Frihavnsgade -
  p248 D14-15
Nørre Allé - p246 G10/H10,
  p248 C10-F10
Nørre Farimagsgade -
  p246 L11-12, p250 M11
Nørre Søgade - p246 L10-11,
  p248 L10/M10,
  p250 M10
Nørre Voldgade - p246/7
  L12-13, p250 M12/N11
Nørrebrogade - p246
  J10/K10, p248 G6-7/
  H8-9/J9-10
Nørregade - p250 M12/N12
Ny Adelgade - p251 M15
Ny Carlsberg Vej - p245 S5-6
Ny Kongensgade - p251 P13
Ny Østergade - p251 M15
Ny Vestergade -
  p251 O13/P13

Nyborggade - p248 A14
Nybrogade - p251 O13-14
Nygade Vimmelskaftet -
  p251 N13
Nyhavn - p252 M16-17
Nyroposgade - p250
  N10/O10
Nytorv - p251 N13
Nyvej - p245 O6/P6
Odensegade - p248 E14
Oehlenschlægersgade -
  p245 Q8-S8
Ole Suhrs Gade -
  p246/7 J12-13
Olfert Fischers Gade -
  p247 J15/K15, p249 K16
Olof Palmes Gade -
  p247 G15/H14-15
Orlogsværftsvej -
  p249 L18, p252 M18
Oslo Plads - p247 H15,
  p249 H16
Østbanegade - p248 B16-
  F16, p249 G16
Øster Allé - p248 C11/
  D11-12/E13
Øster Farimagsgade - p246/7
  K12-13, p247 G14/H13
Øster Søgade - p246
  J12/K11, p247 G13-
  14/H13
Øster Voldgade -
  p247 J14-15/ K13-14
Østerbrogade -
  p248 A13-E13-14/F14
Østerfælled Torv -
  p248 B12-13
Østergade - p251 M15
Otheodor Chr. Plads -
  p253 M19-20
Otto Mønsteds Gade -
  p251 Q13
Otto Mønsteds Plads -
  p251 Q13
Overgaden Oven Vandet -
  p252 O17/P16-17/Q16
Overgadenneden Vandet -
  p252 P16-17
Palægade - p252 M16
Peblinge Dossering - p246
  K10/L10, p248 K10/L10
Peder Hvitfeldts Stræde -
  p251 M13
Peder Skrams Gade -
  p252 N16
Per Henrik Lings Alle -
  p248 C12/D12
Per Knutzons Vej -
  p253 M19-20
Peter Fabers Gade - p248 H9
Philip de Langes Allé -
  p253 M19
Pilestræde - p251 M14
Pistolstræde - p251 M15
Plantevej - p245 P6/Q6
Polititorvet - p250 Q12
Poppelgade - p246h10
Porthusgade - p251 O14
Poul Anker Gade - p249 J16
Prins Charlottes Gade -
  p248 G8/H8
Prinsessegade - p252
  O18/P17-18/Q17
Puggårdsgade -
  p251 P13/Q13
Pusher Street -
  p252 O18/P18
Pustervig - p251 M13
Rådhuspladsen - p250 O12
Rådhusstræde - p251 O13
Randersgade - p248 B14
Rantzausgade - p248 K7-8
Ravnsborg Tværgade -
  p246 J11
Ravnsborggade - p246 J10-
  11, p248 J10
Refshalevej - p253
  M20/N20/ O19-20
Reventlowsgade -
  p250 P11/Q11
Reverdilsgade - p250 Q11
Rigensgade - p247 J15/K15
Rolighedsvej - p248 L6-7
Rømersgade - p246 L12

Rørholmsgade -
  p246/7 J12-13
Rosenborggade - p247 L13
Rosengade - p247 K15
Rosengården - p251 M13
Rosenørns Allé -
  p248 L7-8/M8-9
Rosenvængets Allé -
  p248 E14-15
Rosenvængets Hovedvej -
  p248 D15
Rothesgade - p248 C14
Ryesgade - p246
  G12/H11/J11, p248 F13
Rysensteensgade -
  p251 P13/Q13
**Sankt Annæ Gade -
  p252 P17**
Sankt Annæ Passage -
  p249 L16
Sankt Annæ Plads -
  p252 M16-17
Sankt Gjertruds Stræde -
  p247 L13
Sankt Hans Gade -
  p246 J10-11, p248 J10-11
Sankt Hans Torv - p246 H10,
  p248 H10/J10
Skt Jakobs Gade - p248 D14
Sankt Jakobs Plads -
  p248 D13
Sankt Jørgens Allé -
  p250 P10
Skt Knuds Vej - p245 N8/O8
Sankt Pauls Gade - p247
  J15, p249 K16
Sankt Peders Stræde -
  p250 N11-12
Skt Thomas Allé - p245 P7-8
Saxogade - p245 Q8
Schacksgade - p250 M11
Schleppegrellsgade -
  p246 J11
Schønbergsgade -
  p245 O8/P8
Serridslevvej - p248
  B12/C12-13
Silkeborggade - p248 C15
Silkegade - p251 M14
Sjæleboderne - p247 L14
Sjællandsgade - p248 G9
Skindergade - p251 N13
Skoubogade - p251 N13
Skovgardsgade - p247 H13
Skydebanegade - p245 R9
Slagelsegade - p248 E14
Slesvigsgade - p245 S6/T6
Slotsholmsgade - p251 O15
Søartillerivej - p253 N19
Sofiegade - p252 Q16
Sølvgade -
  p247 J13/ K13-15
Sølvtorvet - p247 J13
Sommerstedgade -
  p245 R9/S9
Sønder Boulevard -
  p245 R9/S8-9/T7
Søpassagen - p246 H12
Søren Kierkegaards Plads -
  p251 P15
Sortedam Dossering - p246
  G12-13/H12/J11, p248
  F13-14, p247 G13
Søtorvet - p246 K11
Stampesgade - p250 Q11
Staunings Plads - p250 N11
Steenwinkelsvej - p248 L8
Stefansgade - p248 G6/H6
Stengade - p248 J9/K9
Stockholmsgade -
  p247 H14-15/J13
Stokhusgade - p247 J15
Stoltenbergsgade - p250 Q12
Store Kannikestræde -
  p251 M13
Store Kirkestræde -
  p251 N14-15
Store Kongensgade -
  p249 K16/L16
Store Regnegade - p251 M15
Store Strandstræde -
  p252 M16
Stormbroen - p251 O13
Stormgade - p251 O13

Strandboulevarden -
  p248 A14-15/B15/C15/
  D16/E16/F16
Strandgade - p252
  O16/P16/O17
Strøget - p250 N11/O11,
  p251 N13-15
Struenseegade - p248
  Studiestræde - p250
  N12/O11
Suensonsgade - p247 J15,
  p249 J16
Suhmsgade - p251 M13
Sundeveds-Matthæusgade -
  p245 Q7-8/R7-8
Sværtegade - p251 M14
Svanegade - p249 H16/J16
**Tagensvej - p246 G10-11,
  p248 G10-11**
Tårnborgvej - p245 O7
Teglgårdsstræde -
  p250 M12/N12
Thorupsgade - p246 L10,
  p248 L9-10
Tietgensgade - p250
  P12/Q11-12
Tigergade - p249 J16
Timiansgade - p247 J15
Tøjhusgade - p251 O14
Toldbodgade - p249 K17,
  p252 M17
Tøndergade - p245 Q7
Tordenskjoldsgade -
  p252 N16
Torvebuskgade - p247 L13
Torvegade -
  p252 P16-17/Q17
Trangravsvej - p252 N18
Trepkasgade - p246 G12
Trommesalen - p250 P10
Turesensgade - p248
  M10/11, p250 M10-11
Upsalagade - p247 H14
Uraniavej - p245 O7
Værnedamsvej - p245 P8
Valdemarsgade -
  p245 Q8/R8/S8
Valkendorfsgade -
  p251 M14/N13
Ved Kunsten - p251 O13
Ved Glyptoteket -
  p250 P12/Q12
Ved Kanalen - p252 Q16
Ved Stranden - p251 N14-15
Ved Vesterport -
  p250 O10-11
Vendersgade - p246 L11-12
Vester Farimagsgade -
  p250 N11/O10
Vester Søgade -
  p250 N10/O10
Vester Voldgade -
  p251 P13-14/O12
Vesterbrogade - p245 P8-9/
  Q5-8, p250 O11-12/ P10
Vesterbrotorv - p245 P9
Vesterfælledvej - p245
  R6/S6/T6
Vestergade - p250 N12/O12
Viborggade - p248 C14-15
Viktoriagade - p250 O10
Vildandegade - p249 H16/J16
Vindebrogade - p251
  N14/O14/15
Vingårdstræde - p251 N15
Visbygade - p247 G15
Vodroffsvej - p245 N9/O9
Vognmagergade - p251 M14
Voldgården - p251 Q15
Voldmestergade - p247 G13
Vordingborggade -
  p248 B14-15
**Webersgade -
  p247 H13/J13**
Wesselsgade - p246
  K10/L10, p248 K10-L10
Westend - p245 Q8
Wiedeweltsgade - p247 H13
Wilders Plads - p252 O17
Willemoesgade -
  p248 E15-16/F14
Worsaaesvej - p248 L8-9
Zinnsgade - p247 G13-14

STREET INDEX

Local Trains & Metro

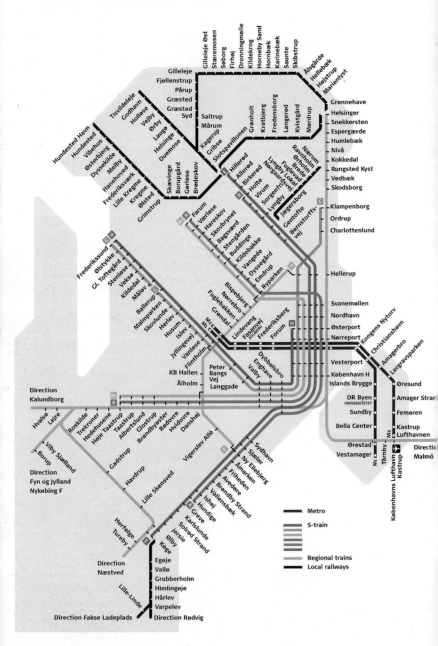

| Metro |
| S-train |
| Regional trains |
| Local railways |

PENGUIN BOOKS

EATING NAKED

Stephen Dobyns is the author of many novels, the best-selling Saratoga Mystery series, and several collections of poetry, *Pallbearers Envying the One Who Rides* being his latest collection. *The Church of Dead Girls* and *Boy in the Water* are also published in Penguin.

He lives in Boston with his wife and three children.